NIMROD

Courts, Claims, and Killing on the Oregon Frontier

NIMROD

Courts, Claims, and Killing on the Oregon Frontier

Ronald B. Lansing

Washington State University Press
Pullman, Washington

Washington State University Press
PO Box 645910
Pullman, Washington 99164-5910
Phone: 800-354-7360
Fax: 509-335-8568
E-mail: wsupress@wsu.edu
Web site: wsupress.wsu.edu

Library of Congress Cataloging-in-Publication Data

Lansing, Ronald B.
    Nimrod : courts, claims, and killing on the Oregon frontier / Ronald B. Lansing.
      p. cm.
    ISBN 0-87422-280-X
    1. O'Kelly, Nimrod, d. 1864. 2. Frontier and pioneer life—Oregon—Willamette River
Valley. 3. Willamette River Valley (Or.)—History. 4. Land tenure—Oregon—Willamette River
River Valley—History—19th century. 5. Murder—Oregon—Willamette River Valley—
History—19th century. I. Title.

F882.W6L36 2005
979.5'3—dc22   2005001335

Fine Quality Books from the Pacific Northwest

For Jewel

who abided Nimrod
in our home as guest
for many years

Table of Contents

Illustrations

Acknowledgments

W hile it goes without saying that the author needed help, the author's deep gratitude for that help needs saying. Among the many helpers were those who read and responded to drafts of the manuscript: Cary Collins, Paul Dodds, Jack Landau, Jewel Lansing, Mark Lansing, Donald Large, Terence O'Donnell, Martha Spence, and Bill Williamson. I particularly want to single out my son Mark whose critique and encouragement came at a time when the pages and the author needed a boost.

Others gave direction or insight into particular events: Janice Barclay, Malcolm Clark, V. June Collins, Pat Horning, Connie Janes, D.R. Jones, Scott McArthur, J. Kenneth Munford, David O'Longaigh, Carol Coe Ransom, Mary Jane Sorber, and Diane Masters Wagner.

Books cannot be crafted without the packagers: Lisa Frenz, Kim Gillette, Shirley Johansen, Andy Marion, Valerie McCourt, Lenair Mulford, and Duane Wheeler, with added thanks to Shirley and Lenair.

Then too, there were the staff members of many libraries, museums, archives, and research centers:

A.R. Bowman Museum (Prineville, Oregon)
Barry County Genealogical Society (Cassville, Missouri)
Boley Law Library, Northwestern School of Law of Lewis and Clark College (Portland, Oregon)
Benton County Historical Society (Philomath, Oregon)
Benton County Land Records Office (Corvallis, Oregon)
Catholic Archdiocese Archives (Portland, Oregon)
Genealogical Forum of Oregon (Portland, Oregon)
Linn County Historical Museum (Brownsville, Oregon)
Missouri State Archives (Jefferson City, Missouri)
Mount Angel Abbey Archives (Mt. Angel, Oregon)
Multnomah County Library (Portland, Oregon)
National Archives, Pacific Northwest Region (Seattle, Washington)
National Archives and Records Center (Washington, D.C.)
Oregon City Historical Society (Oregon City, Oregon)
Oregon Historical Society (Portland, Oregon)
Oregon State Archives (Salem, Oregon)
Oregon Supreme Court Library (Salem, Oregon)
State Historical Society of Missouri (Columbia, Missouri)

U.S. Bureau of Land Management (Portland, Oregon)
Watzek Library, Lewis and Clark College (Portland, Oregon)

Finally, dreamers cannot forget to acknowledge the dreammakers: Glen Lindeman and the staff of the Washington State University Press, whose editorial and publishing efforts have brought all of this work and help to fruition.

There is always the sinking feeling that I may have omitted some. To them I offer my forgetfulness for their forgiveness—hardly fair barter.

Preface

The Nimrod O'Kelly yarn has been spun at many campfires, but the full story has never been woven. I first heard the tale from the late historian Malcolm Clark about a century after Nimrod lived. But it was not until the 1990s that I took to the trail of the mysterious Oregon pioneer. Along the way, I found the spoors of those who had hunted him before.

The freshest tell was a 1987 series of newspaper articles by Kenneth Mumford. Farther down the path came the tracks of a 1940 newspaper feature by L.M. Lowell. Both of these accounts trailed back to a prominent and somewhat seminal article by Lawrence McNary in a 1935 *Oregon Historical Quarterly*. Beyond that, the signs began to fade. But there in 1886, off to the wayside and hidden by the oversight of microfilmers was an extensive newspaper article by Samuel A. Clarke—the first author to put the story to ink. Clarke took his account from an interview with T.B. Odeneal. Both men were contemporaries of Nimrod O'Kelly. All along the hunt were the traces of those who merely glimpsed the O'Kelly saga—David D. Fagan, Lancaster Pollard, Harriet Munnick, Preston Onstead, A.L. Strand, Terence O'Donnell, Fred Leeson, and John Terry. They were lured up the course, but turned back in pursuit of other missions.

An old maxim of law is that judges "will not stoop to pick up pins." The reports of history exhibit the same airs. The story here told, however, condescends for pins. This is not the story of beauty, wealth, grandeur, or mileposts of glory. Momentous forces impacting the nation are not the focus, albeit they are the setting. Nimrod was by no means a saint, certainly not a hero, and nothing of a celebrity or role model. He did not shape events, but was buoyed along by them. His life was made to play out at high levels of government—a jackstraw caught up in the winds of the law and the land. He was not great, but he was touched by greatness as his wayfaring seemed always to be either in the way of, or in the wake of, power. He did not make history; he lived it. His story is a testament to the wisdom of Thomas Gray, who reminds us of the final equalizer—"the annals of the poor" and the "paths of glory lead but to the grave."

In reading history, events and attitudes should be judged in their own times. For instance, Nimrod's contemporaries might have described him as "ornery." Today that might mean his temperament was mischievous and cantankerous. But in his time, *ornery* was a corruption of *ordinary*. An ornery man was not a contrary man, but rather just a plain, simple man. Nonetheless, Nimrod was both—a simple man with a mulish spirit. Oregon pioneers, like early Oregon itself, were down hard roads and at far corners. At this edge of new beginning and old ending, life was a time of seizing—the private taking of public land and the sovereign taking of tribal land. And it was a place of massacre and hanging; of slavery and chaining; of racial, gender, and religious persecution. That context must be understood when appraising, yet not confused with condoning.

Nimrod is not the only sojourner in this narrative; the journey of land and law is also chronicled. Land may be seen as either property or environment—the difference between title and place, between belongings and belonging. On the Oregon frontier in the mid-1800s, title to land was gained by searching, staking, surveying, notifying, inhabiting, cultivating, certifying, patenting, and, most of all, lasting. In the beginning, land could not readily be bought. Title did not come so easy. Land had to be earned; and that endurance bred a respect, not just for title, but for the land itself—a lesson that American Indians had always understood and a hallmark that has become an Oregon heritage. When it comes to land and the bounties that it gives, what matters is not what we *own*, but rather what we *owe*.

The scribes of mid-nineteenth century documents were notorious spellers, punctuators, and composers of words. The absence or lack of access to lexicons and grammar books or other standard guides made discord inevitable. Proper names were a particular source for different orthography—e.g., "Wright" or "Right," "Loose" or "Luce," "McLoughlin" or "MacLaughlin." Nimrod's family name was no exception; it received various treatment even within his immediate family—"O'Kelly," "O'Kelley," "O,Kelly," "Okelly," "Kelly." Nimrod himself sometimes spelled it "O.Kelly." All of the spellings stemmed from the Gaelic ancestral "O'Ceallaigh."

Throughout this book, the mistakes and variety in quoted materials are so prevalent that I have discarded the use of the Latin *sic*—the reader is left to trust in my assurance that the discrepancies originated there, not here. When penmanship or the age of a document make the text unclear, brackets are used to enclose what this author believes was probable or omitted.

The Willamette Valley on the distant Oregon frontier was for many a place of dreams. Therefore, it is no wonder that it also became a kind of fairyland of names—something out of a midsummer night's dreams, a Dickensian novel, or Mother Goose fantasy. Where else might one find places like Jennyopolis, Starrs Point, Bellfountain, Winkles Butte, and the Long Tom River, or people with storybook names like Greenberry Smith, Aunt Polly, Fooks Dixon, Uncle Sib, Wiley Winkle, Mister Loose, Charity Lamb, Abiather, Obediah and, of course, Nimrod.

Where else might the "boister" and babble of lawyers be captured by two trial adversaries named Boise and Babb? Where else might there be proper dignitaries with names like Prigg, Prim, and Pratt, and sheriffs whose names were as telling as their badges—Starr, Stout, Right, and Fargo?

And sprinkled throughout that faraway valley were other kinds of names covered by ancient earth and dust. Names that had passed from mouth to ear until their phonics were eventually—yet feebly—set to pen by intruders. Names still used today, but reaching back long before the inscriptions that preserve them. Names like Willamette, Kalapuya, Clackamas, Klickitat, Tualatin, Multnomah, Mollala, Chemeketa, Chemawa.

Finally, a word must be said about the balance struck between hard fact and imagination—a balance that has always troubled the search for, and report of, history. I have given the *absolute* truth as taken from primary authorities. I have given the *probable* truth as taken from secondary authorities. I have given the *truth as I saw it* in those gaps where the benefit of direct authority was lacking, but where my study of the verifiable whole might be a helpful perspective on the probable parts. Most of all, I have tried to make clear when I was doing which. Then too, every researcher must be humbled and every reader cautioned by the mystery in the gap, no matter how slender, between knowledge and truth.

> *One came forward for a closer look.*
> *Another stepped away to get a broader look.*
> *One saw paint.*
> *The other saw portrait.*
> *So, is it any wonder,*
> *When it comes to knowledge,*
> *How we glean truth at all?*
> —R.B.L.

1

The Inquest

May 22, 1852

East are the Cascade foothills. The west horizon is the Coast Range. In between "is the valley of the Willamette River." Back then it was just called "the Valley." And the Valley was tucked within a vast country called "Oregon," bordered by the Rockies, California, the Pacific, and what is now Canada.[1] The fences and fields of the Valley were not always so—not back then—not in the time of the tale here told. That tale began at this spot. What is now the smell of fresh plowed dirt, was then the smell of prairie grass. What is now the sound of motors on the highway and a harvester in the next field, was then the sound of the wind coming off the buttes and down the rivers and sloughs, making whispers on the sward. It was all an ocean of prairie with floating meadows of wildflower, pocked with islands of scrub oak, rimmed by cottonwood groves and stands of fir, pine, ash, and cedar. But mostly it was grass—grass shoulder high for cattle to feed on and get lost in.

Indians of the Valley called the grass *kalapuya*. They were the tenders. They burned the fields to keep back the forest and to make the gardens—then, but not any more. Pioneer settlers from the east saw it as good farm and pasture land—enough fir and pine for siding, ash for stakes, cedar for posts and paling, oak and alder for fire, grass for livestock, creek and rain water for crops, spring water for drink, and fish and deer plenty for belly. Through the center of the Valley ran the Willamette River, as it does now—fed here by nearby streams like Mouse River, Muddy Creek, and, closer still, the Long Tom. All of that runoff was laced by gullies and sloughs that gave shed and drink to the earth. Any farmer could see the *kalapuya* was prime growing country.

The whole Willamette watershed was 180 miles long and in some places 60 miles wide. And right here was the heart of it. Close by and a bit to the west there used to be a wagon trail weaving south to the top of the Valley. The trail was on a lie with where the highway is now. Back then, of course, the trail was just dirt, first carved by the hooves of deer and elk and the moccasins of the Indians of the *kalapuya*, then by the engagés of the Hudson's Bay Company, then by the wagons of the forty-niners who went south five hundred miles when gold was struck—some called it "the Gold Miners' Road." Eleven miles north, the trail cut through the village of Marysville. A few days farther north at Oregon City, the route connected to the Overland Trail which headed back to the States—two thousand, unfriendly miles away.

That large hill two miles north is Winkle's Butte, called such because settler Isaac Winkle was the first to lay claim to it. At the foot of the butte and to the west was Winkle's neighbor, Richard Irwin. Irwin had a store at trailside. They called it Jennyopolis. Headed south, the trail came upon the Starrs Point store four miles away. Farther south, the trail passed *Ya-po-ah* Butte and Skinner's post office. Still farther, maybe ten days ride, beyond the Valley and beyond the Umpqua and Rogue country was the top of the Siskiyou divide—the end of the Oregon Territory and the start of a newly made state in the Union called "California."

That was the lay of these surrounds on Saturday afternoon, May 22, 1852. A number of men gathered here in what was then a dried up slough—a backwater bed for the Long Tom River in winter rains. Just southeast about 130 steps there was a small, one-room, log settler's cabin with some pelts, racks, and other signs of the hunter pegged to the walls. The day was sunny and cheery, but no cheer was in these men's faces. Their jaws were long and squared by duty. Some stood; some were in saddles. Some were silent, some had heads together in whisper. All were fixed in vigil on a single purpose.

Their purpose lay dead at their feet in the dry, cracked crust of the slough. It was once a human soul. Flies buzzed around a giant wound in the carcass— a huge hole running from the nipple and across the chest and neck to the chin. Crows and other scavengers had been the first to smell out death. The body, a young man, was bent stiff into a clutch over the wound. Its "rigor'd" bones would have to be made straight to fit into the fresh lumbered box on the back of a buckboard nearby. An undertaker measured the dead man's arms and legs with a tailor's tape. But this assembly was more than a burial. Other offices came first. There were no women or widow at this vigil. The business of this afternoon was left to menfolk.

The sun was getting hotter now, kindling patience and bringing to boil the need to finish up and get the ripening corpse into dark and cool ground. One of the men—R.B. Hinton—came forward over the body and broke into the still of the moment with his best official voice. He proclaimed that he was the justice of the peace and that he was appointing Richard Irwin to be the coroner for this inquest "over the dead body of Jeremiah Mahoney two miles south of Jennyopolis in the County of Benton, Territory of Oregon on Saturday, May 22nd 1852 about one hundred and thirty steps from the dwelling house of one Nimrod O'Kelly."

Irwin stepped out of the crowd and put a hand to heaven so Hinton could give him this oath: "You do solemnly swear to act as Coroner to the best of your ability, over the Dead Body of Jeremiah Mahoney now present laying Dead. So help your God!" The oath giver, Hinton, signed the oath, not Irwin, the oath taker. No answer was taken. It was not a question. It was a command: *You will be coroner, do your best, and help your God.*

Irwin, the Jennyopolis store owner, took over the proceedings. In a voice rich with the accents and rhythms of his Irish birth, Coroner Irwin called on the sheriff to muster a coroner's jury. Sheriff Sam Starr was ready. He called out twelve names, and twelve men moved away from the crowd into a separate group. The jurors were all settlers in the nearby countryside. William Barclay was the neighbor most nigh—as far as a mile off. The land claims of John Loose, Davey Williams, and John Lloyd were three miles away. Bill Coyle and Lewis Dennis came from as far as four miles. Juryman Isaac Winkle lived two miles off at Winkle's Butte. Some of the jurors were kin. John and Abner Lloyd were father and son, and Tom Reeves had married into their family. Bill and John Porter were also blood. The jurymen's ages ranged from twenty-four to fifty-six. John Lloyd was the oldest; but Tom Reeves, at age thirty-nine, had the oldest claim, six years running. Juryman Dave Hawley had not yet laid his claim. Juryman Davey Williams lost his claim to prior settlers.

Twelve were called, although six was the minimum required by the "Coroners" chapter of the territorial statutes. If Coroner Irwin, Justice of the Peace Hinton, and Sheriff Starr were not aware of that law, it was understandable. This was all brand new business for Benton County. White civilization had come to this part of the Valley just seven years before. Now came the county's first murder. The laws that reckoned with murder were leather fresh and would take some breaking-in.

Coroner Irwin, in his best Irish, told the jurymen to raise a hand.

You as jurors do solemnly swear that you will proceed and examine and investigate the now Dead Body of Jeremiah Mahoney and report to me how the said Jeremiah Mahoney came to his death to the best of your knowledge… So help your God.

Once again the oath was framed as a mandate to be followed, not an offer to be accepted. The task was twofold: Did this soul likely die by homicide; and if so, by whose likely hand? The first would be easy. That hole in the breast was a shotgun blast. Shot and slugs had penetrated six inches and most surely made death come. Because no shotgun was found in sight, it was not likely accident or suicide. The second task was a bit more puzzling but not unsolvable. Strange and telling was the absence of one man from the inquest. After all, he had the shortest distance to come. His bed was just 130 steps away. Where was Nimrod O'Kelly? The slough bed, the cabin, the gatherers, and the corpse were all on the land O'Kelly claimed. All knew of O'Kelly's crust—a jackstraw, lone wolf, and poor neighbor with a sour attitude and no kin. That taint and his absence gave focus and headstart to the job at hand.

Jeremiah Criss, James Barclay, and Tom Richardson came forward as witnesses. Jim Barclay, age twenty-five, was the younger brother of juryman Bill Barclay. Criss, age forty-nine, owned a claim just south of O'Kelly's line. Tom Richardson, age sixteen, was the son of Aaron "Doc" Richardson. Barclay could not read or write. They called him "Sib" because his middle name was Eusibius. All three witnesses testified that on that very morning about seven or eight o'clock, Missus Mahoney had reported to them that her husband had been missing all night. She asked them to search for him. Their search took them, they said, in the direction of a shotgun blast that Criss had heard yesterday, between noon and two o'clock. That direction was through the *kalapuya* toward O'Kelly's cabin. As their track came within sight of the cabin, they went across this dry slough and found the body of Mahoney "where it is as it now layeth," so said all three.

From that discovery, rounding up the sheriff, a magistrate, and others to serve as coroner, jurors, and deputies was done in a matter of hours and on a lot of horseback. Folks had to put aside farm chores and tend to civic duty. But the call was not just born of duty. On a frontier parched by dry routines, slaking thirst with the excitement of murder and inquest took no great wheedling.

Coroner Irwin then asked the witnesses, "Do you know of any person threatening to take the life of the Deceased?" Criss answered first. He testified that the deceased Mahoney told him some time back that "O'Kelly had frequently forbid him from passing on his [O'Kelly's] Premises to his [Mahoney's] work in the timber" and in the future Mahoney "would do it at his own Risk." Mahoney had settled in the area just two months prior; so, it was true that he would have been busy building a cabin for his wife and himself and their four-month-old baby. Fetching timber would have taken him across O'Kelly's claim toward the wooded banks of the Long Tom. From the slough, the new roof of the Mahoney cabin could be seen just a half mile to the north and west. Young Tom Richardson testified that O'Kelly some weeks ago had asked Tom to tell Missus Mahoney that, "if she wished to live in Peace and happiness hereafter" that she had best "advise her Husband to move a way." Sib Barclay, on the other hand, would not say that he ever heard O'Kelly make any threats.

Coroner Irwin told the jurymen to go off and come to a verdict. They went over and examined the dead carcass of Mahoney and counted thirty-seven buck shot wounds and three or four slug wounds—all from a single blast. They probed some of the wounds and found six inches of penetration. Nods and words passed between them. Tails, hats, and hands swished at flies on the cracked, dry slough bed. In short order, *jurymen* came together as *jury*. The verdict was written out and signed by each:

> We, as Jurors, Report, as our Verdict, that the Deceased Jeremiah Mahoney came to his Death by Wounds inflicted in his neck and Breast by Shot and lead slugs! Shot out of a Shot Gun or Musket, By one Nimrod O'Kelly from Evidence before us! the wounds of which being sufficient to take life.

The verdict in an inquest is no more than a temporary bidding to set the wheels of law in motion. It was a long way from the moral certainty that was necessary to convict in a full-fledge trial that would some day follow.

The inquest was not yet over. Coroner Irwin took the advice given him by his jury. He put pen to paper, made out a coroner's arrest warrant, and handed it to Sheriff Starr.

> Sir you will proceed and take the Body of Nimrod O'Kelly If found in your County or Territory and bring the same to the nearest Majestrate in your County to answer the charge of the murder of one Jeremiah Mahoney.

The justice of the peace had previously given the task to the coroner. The coroner had passed it on to the jury. The jury handed it back to the coroner. And now the coroner was sending it along to the sheriff. Sheriff Starr was not to be outdone. He too knew how to delegate. He took the coroner's warrant and wrote on the back of it that he "hereby intrusted" the arrest to certain deputies. He thereupon deputized four men. Juryman Isaac Winkle, age fifty, was picked to lead—probably on account of his senior years and perhaps because he put himself forward and seemed warm to the task. The other deputies were Silas Belknap, age thirty-five; Juryman Bill Porter, age thirty-two; and Juryman Tom Reeves, age thirty-nine. There were younger men the sheriff could have roped in, but the sheriff probably figured that bringing in this wily killer would need a cautious hand, not a daring one. The corpse at their feet had been a young buck who took no regard of threat.

After checking with Justice of the Peace Hinton, Coroner Irwin said *done to the doings*. Mahoney's body could now be lifted up and taken to his widow where undertaker Irwin White would suit him up and box him. The whole inquest would cost the county $30.90, including $2.00 for each of the jurors, $5.00 for the coroner's presidence, and $1.40 for the coroner's written record. The undertaker also put in a claim with the county for $3.75 for grave clothes. Likely it would be the first time that Mahoney was in a suit since his wedding day. Likewise, Isaac Winkle would charge the county $2.00 for the coffin lumber. The county commissioners paid both claims, albeit it was customary for the dead man's estate to pay for the burial. Perhaps the pay of the county was just a kindness—a farewell to the deceased and a welfare to the widow—her chance to see the last of her mate in the same tucker as she had seen the first of her groom. It is one thing to pester government about its empty head, but quite another thing to carp on its full heart.

The gathering broke up. Most rode back to their chores and fields. But for some, the new business was just beginning. The deceased Mahoney had to be buried. The coroner had to write out a report of the inquest doings.[2] The sheriff and juryman Lewis Dennis had to ride twelve miles north to Marysville, the county seat, to report murder and the coroner's findings. The four deputies had to find and arrest the fugitive. If O'Kelly stayed to the road, he would be easy to track and easy to overtake. He was known to be a walker and did not suffer the saddle for too long a stretch. On the other hand, he did have a full day's jump on the pursuit—as much as thirty miles. Chances were he was headed north toward French Prairie and the settlements. He would not have had enough provender for an escape south into the mountains. Nevertheless, the deputies would have had to split their search north and south.

The inquest had steered a predictable course. There were no surprises, but it had to be played out. The routine was a step toward law and order. The difference between that gathering and a mob was the difference between cool heads with a procedure and hot heads with a rope. To be sure, naked process was not enough, but without it, fairness had nowhere to root.

Nimrod O'Kelly was a marked man. His life would never again be the same. *Nimrod* means hunter. But from that moment forward, this hunter would be the hunted. Indeed, some would say he was prey and looked in sympathy upon him. Others would say he was a predator and called him a "menace."

He was seventy-two years old.

Notes

1. In May 1852, the British political entities that bordered Oregon Territory at the 49th parallel included the "Crown Colony of Vancouver Island" (established 1849, with the Queen Charlotte Islands soon to be annexed, July 1852), and "New Caledonia," which essentially

encompassed today's British Columbia mainland. New Caledonia was exclusively chartered to the Hudson's Bay Company and solely governed by its fur trade administration until 1858, when the "Colony of British Columbia" was created during the 1858 Fraser River gold rush. In 1871, the "Province of British Columbia" joined a new confederation known as "Canada" (established 1867).

2. On the day following the inquest, Sunday, May 23, Coroner Irwin penned a "correct transcript" of what occurred. What is here reported is based upon his detailed record.

2

The Migration

1845

The inquest was at the middle of this story. The beginning was seven years before. In 1845, Nimrod O'Kelly was among the herds of pioneers waiting to jump off for the Oregon Country from the Missouri River. Corralled by winter's gate slowly opening by spring's thaw, Nimrod may have taken his spare time to survey the western horizon. Tomorrow he would be out there somewhere in that faraway. And that was barely the start. The trail went on and on past hundreds of horizons more. It would take two months to cross those plains, and that would still not be the all of it. Then began the climb to the top of the Stoney Mountains divide at South Pass. At the top, the United States of America ended.

From there he would ride down into the vast Oregon Country, where he would have to cross two huge walls, the Blue Mountains and the Cascade Range; two mighty torrents, the Snake and Columbia rivers; and two huge expanses, the Snake River plains and the Columbia plateau. And all of it was stretched out in six months of dreams and tomorrows. At the end of it all was said to be an Eden—a lush land with soil so rich that even a broom stuck into it might bud. It was the Willamette Valley, and it made the dread, the dull, and the endurance all worthwhile.

Whether Nimrod felt such stirrings on the eve of his migration cannot be known. But this much is clear: in 1845 he was sixty-five years of age, and he was alone. There was more past than future in him, more memories than dreams. Yet, old and alone, he struggled to start life anew. He would travel between that mix of nightfall and daybreak for many years to come.

Migrations on the Overland Trail to Oregon by pioneer families went on for more than forty years. The migration of 1845 was near the beginning. Prior to 1841, the path overland beyond the Stoney divide was not fit for wagon travel. Without wagons, the trail was not fit for families. Without families, the Oregon Country could not be settled. Before 1841, only Indians, fur traders, missionaries, and pathfinders were in Oregon, and their callings would not abide a tether to land ownership. When word came that mountain men Doc Newell and Joe Meek had bullwhacked their wagons over the last piece of untested trail to Oregon, it uncorked a swelling, and settlement began its pour. At first it was a trickle—virtually one small wagon company in each of the years 1841 and 1842. Then in 1843 and 1844 there were two large migrations. In those first four years, less than twenty-five hundred men, women, and children had pioneered their way to the Willamette Valley to stake land claims. Those claims did not have the benefit of any government's backing. Before settlers could make their claims good, a nation had to make its claim good. Private ownership goes only as far as public recognition. As of 1845, the Oregon Country was not part of the United States. Both Great Britain and the States had a yen for Oregon. To keep peace, they promised each other in 1818 and in 1827 to let Oregon be "free and open," but the treaty really meant Joint Occupancy. The fact that Indians had been native to the Pacific Coast long before white folks had sails to cross oceans or wagons to cross mountains was of *no-never-mind*.

Without a reigning order, a settler's claim to land was about as tight a hold as a fist on butter. And so, the early settlers in the Valley decided to make their own authority—an Oregon self-government. They passed the Organic Act of 1843 and promised to each of those who came and settled in Oregon 640 acres of land—one square mile *free* for the taking! That was an expanse of land far greater than normally allotted to those who staked a claim. Oregon pioneers declared themselves a public sovereign and then gave themselves huge private ownerships. And so there was a time when Oregon was, by its own proclamation, a temporary and very generous nation.

While all of this was going on out west, back east in Washington City things were coming to a reckoning between Britain and the States as to just who was going to be the rightful sovereign in Oregon. In 1845, James Polk, the new President of the Union, was for expanding the Union northwest to the Pacific Ocean and up to the Russian Alaska border at parallel 54° 40' north latitude. He promised it would be that or fight. The fight for Oregon was a call to journey, not arms. Rather than war, the fight could be won by that nation with the most citizens settled in the Oregon Country. To secure a land claim, settlers needed sovereignty, and so too, sovereignty needed settlers. The boundaries of the nation were moved, not just by conquest or purchase, but also by pioneering. In a democracy, public and private were not enemies. They were but different sides of the same coin. As Frederic Paxson would put it: "The landless man and the landless state…held the tottering Union upright while it was learning how to walk."

The new government in Oregon was provisional—a temporary solution that awaited Polk's plan. The opening paragraph of the Oregon pioneers' 1843 Organic Act said: "if the United States extends its jurisdiction over this country within the next four years, it will not be expedient to form an independent government." Word of the 1843 Oregon Provisional Government's loyalty to the States and its generous allotment provision reached back east in 1844. So now, there dangled at trail's end a carrot of free land with a patriotic sovereign to back it up. It was all that Nimrod and the pioneers of 1845 needed. Upwards of three thousand men, women, and children started for Oregon in that fifth year of white migration. They spread out in more than five hundred wagons with seven thousand animals in some twenty different companies. More headed for Oregon in that one year than all who had gone before. The Oregon government pulled, the United States government pushed, and the pioneer wagons rolled. "Ho to the West!" "Root, Hog, or Die!" "Oregon or Bust!" They strained at the yoke to "see the elephant!"

Why did they go? Patriotism? Escape from poverty, disaster, disease, pursuit? Obedience? Adventure? Or was it just westering? Nimrod was typical of an endless current westward. Many years before he decided to go to Oregon, he had moved west into the Ozark Mountains of Missouri. Before that, he had come west from the Cumberland Mountains of Tennessee. Before that, he had been farther east in the Great Smoky Mountains of Tennessee. Before that, he was born and raised still farther east over the Blue Ridge Mountains. His ancestors had come west from Ireland. For Americans of that day, westering was a heritage—a flow as certain as the travels of the sun itself. In Nimrod's day, editor Horace Greeley championed that notion, and Henry Thoreau wrote:

> Eastward I go only by force; but westward I go free…[S]omething like this is the prevailing tendency of my country men. I must walk toward Oregon, and not toward Europe.

But whatever the fuel, the spark was land. So what did Nimrod want with it? At sixty-five, he was in his winter years. Land for labor, for market, and for commerce were younger men's visions. He would not stretch his neck with the flock to soar two thousand miles just to turn the land for profit. An old gander would want to nest. Native Americans would have understood. They held the land with great reverence. Land gave place. It gave belonging, not belongings. Land was not a place to take from; it was a place to come from and return to. The land was the parent, not a child. Perhaps then, for Nimrod, that 1845 caravan snaking its way across plains and up mountains toward Oregon was a life cord seeking loins—heading home.

On the other hand, maybe Nimrod was not after land at all. Maybe he just enjoyed a good walk. There is much to suggest that Nimrod was a bird of passage, a wayfarer, a land loper. Whatever the motive, let it not cloud the deed: This old man in 1845 was about to undertake the longest hike in America.

Nimrod was on his own in that 1845 journey. He knew some of the families—Benjamin and Elizabeth Nichols, Peyton and Anna Wilkes, and Benjamin and Elizabeth Cornelius. But he did not wind up in the same wagon train with any of them. Going alone was in keeping with his ways.

He probably had just a horse and a pack animal. They would be loaded with *possibles* and provender, and that would put Nimrod on foot most of the time. All of the pioneers spent more time walking than riding; and Nimrod, more than most, seems to have enjoyed the freedom of shanks' mare—his courser through life.

Unlike the previous emigrant bands, the 1845 migration did not travel in one caravan. Led by captains, they teamed up in different companies that jumped off at several towns along the Missouri—places like Fort Leavenworth, Saint Joseph, Westport, Liberty, and Council Bluffs. There was even a town called Oregon. Nimrod started at Independence. All of these souls and companies from all of these starts with all of their wagons and cow columns, funneled down to one trail, where camps and companies mixed and realigned. By the time they reached South Pass at the top of the Stoney divide, the companies became about twenty in number.

To a maverick traveler with no family or wagon to hold him back, the staggered companies became stepping stones and an open invitation to hurry. Nimrod probably fell in and out of companies before eventually settling in with travelers of his pace and liking. In speaking of that mass pilgrimage, Peyton Wilkes wrote that he and Nimrod were "often times…in the same company." It may not have suited Nimrod to be in any group at all; but, surrounded by mysterious country, he knew the safety in union. He may have been crusty, but not crack-brained.

Of course, any group that Nimrod accepted would have to accept him as well, and there were disturbing things about Nimrod that might have denied him welcome. He was rumored to have killed a man in Missouri and another while crossing the plains. It may have been gossip born of his private ways. A rogue will either be maligned by the malicious or mystified by the merciful. His stature was called "menacing." T.B. Odeneal, who met and talked with Nimrod, described him as tall, with a long gray beard, "patriarchal," "venerable," and "commanding." Those in whose graces he fell found him to be a "pleasant talker" and an educated man. Odeneal probably exaggerated when he said that Nimrod spoke several languages; but even excess tells something of a man. No doubt he was "well informed" because in his vocabulary were words like "sophistry," "equivocation," "nefarious," "duplicity," "pernicious," "sanctimonious," "assiduous," and "propitious." His penmanship was a bold hand with a clarity that would have shamed the best scribes.

Born during the War for Independence, Nimrod was three years old when the colonies won their freedom. He was twenty-three when the States purchased the Louisiana country up to the Stoney divide. He was twenty-six when pathfinders Lewis and Clark returned from over the divide with their tales of the far Pacific Northwest. He was thirty-two when the War of 1812 began. He claimed to be a veteran of that war. He lived in the Cumberland Mountains when fellow Tennessean Andrew Jackson was raising volunteers for an army. At times, Nimrod told of "the laws that I faithfully fought to defend," of offering "his blood upon the altar of liberty," of baring "his bosom to danger," of rushing "at the mouth of cannons," and of withstanding "the iron hail." Indeed, if his boasts were true, he could have been in Jackson's Army of the Cumberland that won the Battle of New Orleans in January 1815. Now here, thirty years later, pioneers weary of the trail would have enjoyed this graybeard's spinning of tales at day's end campfire, while skeptics would have resented his yarns of conceit about hallowed battles. He either preened or ruffled feathers with his war memories, his big words, his maverick ways, and his use of wagon companies as stepping stones across a dangerous two-thousand-mile journey. Trouble followed a man who would neither lead nor follow, control nor be controlled. Odeneal observed that Nimrod was "of a past generation of mankind." But although his times were gone, momentous times were yet in store for him—times wherein he would be torn between the mercy of some and the malice of others.

Nimrod eventually found a niche in the wagon train of John and Mary Stewart. John was the captain of that company. As small as thirteen wagons, it was a faster moving caravan. Two of the men Nimrod met in that company would become valuable allies in the years to come—Joseph Avery and William Fooks Dixon. Avery, Dixon, and the Stewarts stayed together and were destined to settle in the heart of the Willamette Valley where they founded their own town. Others in the 1845 trek would cross Nimrod's path on more unfriendly terms in the years to come. John and Abner Lloyd were on the coroner's jury. Tom Read and Bill Knotts would also sit in judgement on Nimrod. Still others on the 1845 migration would have a better word to say about Nimrod: Greenberry Smith, John Daniel Boon, Alfred Rinehart,

Johnson Mulkey, and Prier Scott. But no matter how spread apart in companies or in regard, all three thousand migrants that year shared the company of
misery. In decades ahead, they drank from the common cup of memories and
were called the "Old Oregonians."[1]

The stories of that two-thousand-mile migration have been told many
times. The real enemies were not menacing; they were niggling. Boredom,
loneliness, hard work, and just plain distance weighed down upon the spirit
far more than the imagined dread of beasts, weather, or savage attacks. Each
day greeted them with the rigors of fires to build, boots to mend, wheels to
grease, teams to hitch up, defiles to descend, streams to ford, and passes to
cross. And along with all of the tasks came the swarms of dust and critters that
chewed, sucked, and stabbed.

By mid-August, the forward wagon companies had crossed the Rocky
Mountains and the Snake River plains. Ahead of them lay the trail northwest
to the Columbia River and then a float around Mount Hood through the
Cascade divide. At Fort Boise, a mountain man, Stephen Meek, convinced
many of the pioneers to follow him on a cross-cut through deserts that he
promised would shorten their travels by two weeks. Then at Mount Hood,
Sam Barlow figured he could blaze a mountain road through the Cascades
south of Mount Hood. Those two cut-offs proved to be disasters. Many died
on the Meek trek, and most who followed Barlow spent the winter trapped
in the mountains.

Nimrod did not follow Meek or Barlow. He was a no-nonsense graybeard
whose age taught that, for him, time was better cut by tested ways than by
testing ways. He stayed on route and arrived in the Willamette Valley in
September 1845 in advance of most of the migration and well ahead of the
impetuous. Presumably, he made the trip in the short time of four-and-one-
half months. He could rest up now and turn to look at what was left behind.
Perhaps he thought of family. Family was another of his tales. He said he had
a wife, children, and grandchildren back in Missouri. He left them there,
he said, until he settled on a claim. For the next seven years he continued to
claim both family and land. Proving each was the heart of his trouble ahead.

Note

1. Being called an "Old Oregonian" was a label of respect that at first attached to settlers
who came in 1845 or before, when the vast Oregon Country yet remained ungoverned
and open to joint occupancy by British and American citizens. The "Old Oregonians
particularly" were those in the Willamette and south Puget Sound regions who staked out
the lower half of the Oregon Country (south of the 49th parallel) for the United States by

1846. Later on, the term "Old Oregonians" was expanded to include those who came in years prior to Oregon officially becoming a U.S territory (1848–49). Still later it might apply to those arriving before Oregon statehood (1859), and so forth. The moving bounds of what was "old" was a matter of passing time, the blurring of what was momentous, and the need to be remembered.

3

The Arrival and the Search

1845–46

The Willamette Valley must have been a wonder for weary eyes. Through the doorway of the Columbia Gorge, the landscape turned from dry, sage, canyon country into green forests, foaming streams, crystal springs, and lush prairie. The Valley was huge—11,000 square miles cut down the middle by the Willamette River, and stretching north-south between the Columbia River and the Siskiyou headwaters, and east-west between the Cascades and the Coast Range. It was a stark contrast to where the pioneers had been and a full measure of what they had dreamed.

Just as fires go the way of smoke, companies parted and wagons went in separate search. Some would stop at Fort Vancouver, the Hudson's Bay Company trading post on the north side of the Columbia. Others would go south up the Willamette River to Linnton, a jumping off place to the Tuality Plains. Yet others might go farther upriver to what had been called "The Clearing," "Middletown," or "Stumptown"—henceforth, to be known as Portland, on account of a recent coin toss. But for most, the Overland Trail led to Oregon City on the east bank of the Willamette—a town founded by John McLoughlin of the Hudson's Bay Company. Oregon City was the gateway to French Prairie, center of Oregon's Provisional Government, and home for two hundred souls. Its mud and early beginnings had shops, offices, and two saloons. Most important to those fresh from the trail were two blacksmiths, one physician, and an inn where for a few dollars a traveler could get a bed and a meal of salmon, potatoes, coffee, bread, and molasses.

Somewhere in this tangle of trail endings, Nimrod's track vanishes. He had a head start in the search for a land claim, but did not file a claim until fourteen months later. Where had he been for over one year? Likely, both his purse and his bones needed mending. Often the incoming pioneers would winter over by sharing the roof and table of earlier settlers in exchange for a promise to help in the season's planting and harvest. There is evidence to show that Nimrod upon his arrival went to French Prairie south of Oregon City and worked his bed and board for Joseph Gervais, a retired French-Canadian trapper.

Gervais had been in the Oregon country for half of his life, having arrived just six years after Lewis and Clark's explorations. He and most French-Canadian engagés were Catholic, and they chose to retire where arose the St. Paul Catholic mission on French Prairie. In 1852, twenty-eight persons, mostly French-Canadians and Catholic priests, would report that "the Mission of St. Paul's and vicinity" was the "neighborhood in which O.Kelly formerly resided." In spite of religious differences, a fellowship developed between sixty-eight year old Gervais and sixty-five year old Nimrod. That fellowship, as shall be seen, was destined to become more of a "fatherhood."

St. Paul's Catholicism was in contrast to the Protestantism of most of the rest of the Valley. Nimrod too was in contrast; he was a Bible-belt Methodist. By the time of his arrival, the Methodists had moved their original mission out of French Prairie and farther upstream toward Chemeketa—a settlement now calling itself "Salem." The two missions were but a day's ride apart. Their parishes, like the joint occupancy treaty of the American and British governments, co-existed because of a preoccupation with surviving the elements in a valley big enough for separate trails.

Back in 1841 to 1843, Protestant and Catholic pioneers alike were brought together by three emergencies on this lawless frontier—rewards were needed to encourage the killing of wild predators that were ravaging livestock and poultry, dispersal rules were required for parceling out a dead pioneer's belongings, and a structure was needed for the orderly staking of claims. Thus, pioneers gathered in a series of meetings held at the Gervais farm and a nearby abandoned Indian village called "Champoeg." Bounty, probate, and land claim systems were created out of these so-called "Wolf Meetings." From such systems came the need for money and administrators; and those in turn meant taxes, courts, and enforcement; which then grew into the need for organization—a thing called "government."

While Gervais and most of the French-Canadians had accepted the need for some rules, they resisted any overseeing authority. They wanted laws without government. But that was like striking flint without steel. Though rugged and self-reliant, individuals needed the support of community, and nowhere was the wisdom of this marriage between private and public more clear than to those who had rolled their wagons to the brink of a separation of the two. While freedom for the few could survive upon wealth or power, freedom for all required unity. And so, out of a need to protect—not just liberty, but life and property as well—the Oregon Provisional Government emerged. One day, Nimrod's fate would be to face accusers who set out within this new structure to deny him all three values—his life, his liberty, and his property.

In 1846, at a cost of $20,000, the Catholics at St. Paul built a large, brick church with a belfry eighty-four feet high. On that early frontier, the cost and the undertaking were enormous. High wages were paid in order to attract mechanics and laborers from a countryside that had, according to an 1845 census, no more than nine hundred adult males. Nimrod could have been one of many drawn to the dual reward of top wages and lofty towers. His trade as a blacksmith would be needed. The site was not far from the Gervais farm. Construction commenced after spring planting on May 24, 1846, and was completed in five months. On November 1, 1846, the edifice was consecrated; and shortly thereafter, Nimrod's hidden whereabouts ended.

Nimrod climbed out of wherever he was on French Prairie and stirred once again to the call of the land. His choices ran in all directions. He could go north to the settlements on the Tuality Plains, west into the Coast Range, or east into the Cascade foothills. He might head back into Oregon City and the necklace of towns developing along the lower Willamette River. But Nimrod had no taste for neighbors and was belly-full of hill country. His nose was to the south—upriver to bottomland where the Valley had not yet been searched. His friends on French Prairie had trapped there and told of the rich and untapped lands far beyond the Methodists at Chemeketa. The Canadians called those distant fields the *coeur d' vallee* because it was the heart of the Valley. Joel Palmer, like Nimrod, had come to Oregon in the 1845 migration, but had spent his winter in search of good farm country. Palmer was on his way back from the south valley, when Nimrod may have heard him tell of the lands along the Mouse and Long Tom rivers: "beautiful valleys…good land…fine grounds for pasturage…timber close at hand…good mill sites…[streams] well filled with trout…luxuriant soil."

So, Nimrod headed south in 1846 to find his place. His hunt would not turn serious until the skies were empty of *blue-gray towers*—columns rolling up and out of the trees—plumes rooted to hearths and shaped by flues—signs of settlers huddled there. His search took him along an old Indian and engagé trail toward California, through the hunting grounds of the Santiam and Chemeketa bands of the Calapooya Indian nation. After passing the Methodist mission and ferrying to the west side of the Willamette River into Luckiamute country, Nimrod found no more communities. Road dwindled to path as double ruts narrowed to one. The blue-gray towers grew fewer and the land lonelier. After two or more days travel, he reached the Mouse River where it emptied into the Willamette. At that confluence, he may have been surprised and pleased to find familiar wagons from the 1845 migration. John and Mary Stewart, Joseph C. Avery, and William Fooks Dixon were

Joseph Conant Avery, close ally and fellow traveler with Nimrod during the 1845 Oregon Trail migration, and the co-founder of Corvallis, Oregon. *Portrait and Biographical Record of the Willamette Valley, Oregon (1903)*

staked and camped there. These were friends who shared the search for fresh country.

Avery chose to call Mouse River "Marys River." Some say it was after Mary Stewart. But others say it was after Mary Ann Lloyd, another 1845 immigrant. Still others say Adam Wimple named it for his sister. Then too, Avery's mother's name was also Mary. Archbishop Blanchet said the river was given the name *La Riviere de Marie* by the French Canadian voyagers. In a Christian world, the source of a name as plentiful as "Mary" would be difficult to trace. Indeed, Dixon and Avery had even bigger plans for the name. They dreamed of a town there to be called "Marysville." But for now, the fork of Marys River was no more than a few campfires and conceptions.

For Nimrod it was too many plans for far too many people. He was ready to move on. Seeing no blue towers on the south horizon, he knew that was where he wanted to be. So, he forded Marys River and went deeper into the hunt. After ten miles, he saw no signs of the advance of civilization other than the trail at his feet. Fifteen miles from Marys River, a large butte, rising from the prairie floor, may have triggered his fancy and put bead to his hunt. But atop the butte, he would have found Indian burial grounds and a vision quest site—sacred places that were not to be disturbed. Below the butte, he could see the flatlands filled with swards and swales. White-tail deer grazed in meadows. To the west were dark green curves of brush and scrub trees that marked the meander of Muddy Creek. To the east was the Long Tom River, snaking a lazy course north and emptying into the larger Willamette. The countryside was laced by run-offs and shallow sloughs, which were large enough in the

Figure No. One. Much of the original map (especially the southern portions) was taken from "verbal information" without benefit of survey instruments and was called "an approximation." Accordingly, the careful reader will observe that it is wrong in its appointments here and there. Nonetheless, it gives the look and feel of distance, direction, and location as early pioneers discovered it with naked eye and boot leather. The actual distance between Oregon City and

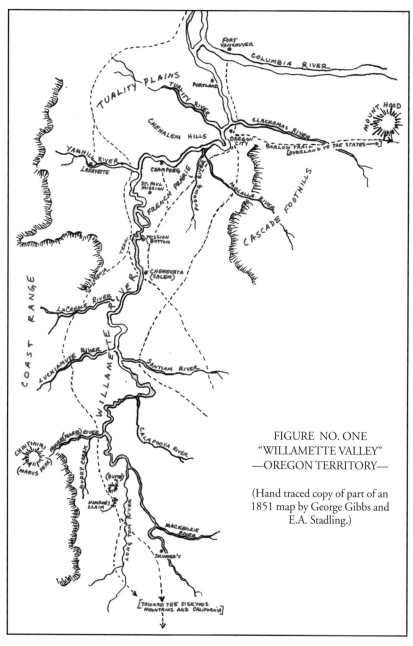

FIGURE NO. ONE
"WILLAMETTE VALLEY"
—OREGON TERRITORY—

(Hand traced copy of part of an
1851 map by George Gibbs and
E.A. Stadling.)

Nimrod's claim is about seventy-five air miles—much longer, of course, by the trails of that day. Some of the Gibbs-Stadling designations and spellings have been altered and some names have been added to fit 1846—the year of Nimrod's hunt up the valley.

spring to be called "lakes." The whole of this prairie land was the *kalapuya*. Beyond the *kalapuya* on the western horizon were the peaks and ridges of the Coast Range. The Calapooya Indians called the tallest peak *Chintimini* after a legendary Indian maiden who became a cunning warrior and savior of her people. White settlers, however, chose to call it "Marys Peak" in keeping with a Christian name descended from a maiden who was mother of a different savior.

In the foreground, two miles south of Nimrod's perch on the butte, a small ravine sliced across the trail. Shadows formed by the north-south trail and east-west ravine made a large cross on the prairie below him. Whether omen or blind chance, the "X" marked the spot he had come for. Water for thirst. Trees for fire and cabin. Open clearing for a field. Game and fish for gut. There he would try his hand as a flatlander.

He came down from the butte, made his way along the trail to the ravine, then traced the ravine east to high ground and spring water. There he made camp. After biscuits, or whatever morsel he may have carried, he would have settled into his blankets and listened to the sounds—tall grasses swishing gently around him in the moon winds, the music of crickets, the gurgle of the nearby spring, and faraway a chorus of wolves beckoning the moon. Against a sky peppered with stars, *Chintimini*, far to the northwest, may have peeked out above the *kalapuya* horizons.

With a pillow of earth against his cheek, Nimrod hugged the ground and smelled yesterday's rain. He would have fallen asleep knowing that this was trail's end, that here would be his claim—his land—his.

4

Staking

Fall 1846

The next morning Nimrod scouted the area in order to make precise his *druthers*. Out of the vast tray of land surrounding him, he was entitled to help himself to a very large piece—one square mile—640 acres. He found it; now he had to stake it. The Oregon Provisional Government land law required that claimants designate their claims "by natural boundaries, or by marks at the corners and upon the lines…in a square or oblong form," and "conform, as near as may be, to the cardinal points."

What was easy enough in saying, offered two major problems in doing—one concerned measuring, the other concerned marking. Markers in a wooded area were slash marks cut into bark on the claimed side of a boundary tree. "Tomahawk claims" they were called. But this land was not forested. Another way of "marking" was simply to take advantage of a neighbor's previously marked boundaries and buildings, as was true of a county boundary description in 1861:

> the middle of Hinton's Ford on Long Tom…; running through Luther Hashbrouck's field…; passed about four feet north of John Williamson's house…and Cooper' old house…; over north part of Long Ridge, south of Kizer's…; through north part of Mahew's pasture…; south to D. Hawley's saw-mill.

But Nimrod was at the edge of the frontier. No borders had gone before him. There were no hitching posts. Then too, markers could be "natural boundaries"—an escarpment, hedgerow, defile, divide, or pond. David Pease's Clatsop County claim read in part:

> commensing…on a large spruce tree three feet or more through there is another tree close to the spruse with the name of David E. Pease cut in the bark…then west 1 mile to the bank of the river then down the bank of the river following all of the meanderings.

Nimrod's choice was in open prairie with none of nature's rhythm to note its close. His markers would have to be artificial. Fencing four miles of border was far beyond a sensible undertaking. Rocks piled into cairns might help, as would digging trenches here and there. But for the most part, staking his claim on open prairie would have to be, as it says, "a staking."

Nimrod found an ash grove and with his hatchet fashioned some sturdy stakes. He then drove one of the stakes deep into the soft rich loam until it stood firm. It was the most important stake of all—the ever-critical *place of beginning.* There began Nimrod's second problem—accuracy in the measurement of distance and direction. If he was to get the full benefit of a square mile, with the least amount of staked boundary, the markers would have to be in four straight lines, and each of those lines had to be exactly one mile long. His corners needed to be ninety-degree angles. A mistake of one foot or one degree might affect acres. And further, his measurements, as a matter of law, had to conform to the cardinal points—north, east, south, and west. These squares or oblongs of private land could not be tilted and askew. Full use of all the land—the utmost desire of government—meant that borders had to be orderly patches. A *quilt* was tolerated, but not a *crazy quilt.*

How could Nimrod know with precision which way was north? How would he know the distance of exactly one mile? How could his corners be measured at ninety degrees? Pioneers traveling toward far horizons were often called upon to eyeball distance and direction in approximation. But laying a claim to no more than 640 acres demanded a focus that no mere inner sense of direction could box and package. Precision required the right tools—sextants, magnifiers, compasses, plumb lines, measuring chains, mapped points of reference, benchmarks, and more. But skilled surveying and its tools were not at hand in a countryside invaded by headstrong squatters. Makeshift, gerry rigging, and savvy born of generations of frontiering were the tools.

Nimrod had put down and pulled up stakes on his westering through the Blue Ridge, Great Smoky, Cumberland, and Ozark mountains. He knew the squatters' tricks in posting a claim—ways that would produce a fair estimate until government surveyors with proper tools could set keener perimeters. Accordingly, if Nimrod did not have a pocket compass, he could have determined a northerly direction by observing the Pole Star in the evening sky. In 1846 Oregon, the deviation between the two—compass north and the north star—was as great as twenty degrees. Those who relied upon their compasses—carried from the east where the deviation from true north was more negligible—would have followed a magnetic line that took them twenty degrees to the east of polar north. Without adjustment, this laid their claims on tilt, and not on a grid pattern keyed to the "cardinal points."[1]

Official surveys in later years show Nimrod's claim was anchored true north, and therefore, he probably had his eye on the night sky and not a needle. Using that north-south line, he could have found an east-west line by devising a *try-square*—four knots tied in a cord, with the three spaces between them separated by carefully measured units of three, four, and five. The cord, drawn taut, could now be shaped into a right triangle. Placing the knot opposite the five-unit side at the corner stake and another knot at a stake along the predetermined north-south line, the ninety degree angle thus formed would point the third knot east-west.

From his corner stake, Nimrod chose to lay his claim toward the north and the west. He could now look down a true westerly line and know that he had to trace it out for one mile. The distance could be stepped off, knowing his pace (a double-step) to be, perhaps, six feet in length. While such a reckoning might serve for short distances, it would never do across an uneven surface for 5,280 feet or 880 paces. More likely, Nimrod's cord measured a specified length—say sixty-six feet—four *rods* in length. Laying the cord

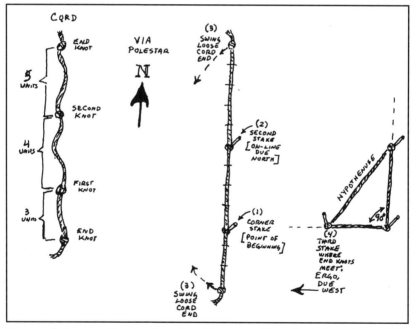

Home made "try-square" used to determine with some precision what is ninety degrees (90°), i.e. E-W, from a N-S line, based upon the Pythagorean Theorem. When the separate lengths of two side of a triangle (e.g., "3" and "4") are each squared (e.g., 3 X 3 = 9; 4 X 4 = 16) and their sum (e.g., 9 + 16 = 25) then equals the square of the longest side (e.g., 5 X 5 = 25), a right triangle is formed. The longest side is then called "the hypothenuse," and the angle opposite the hypothenuse becomes a ninety degree (90°) angle.

end-to-end eighty times would measure one mile. The risk of stretching a cord was why trained surveyors chose to use chain links—rig not yet available on the frontier. Surveyors worked in teams that included the surveyor, two chainmen, and an axeman. But Nimrod was undoubtedly alone in his effort. In later years, no one ever came forward to testify to helping lay the claim or to confirm having witnessed Nimrod's effort. Working alone with the cord could have made his trudging threefold. In order to keep the cord reasonably taut, he would have had to tie or stake one end down, which then would have required a trip back down the cord to free it. Thus, he would have had to walk three miles to measure one mile of distance.

Furthermore, in extending his cord end to end, Nimrod had the problem of keeping a straight line. The lay of the land did not yield kindly to straight lines. It was one thing to map with a straight edge on an even surface of paper, but it was quite another to make a beeline across the rough surface of reality. The *kalapuya* grasses obscured vision. Grove, brush, scrub, and tangle had to be bushwhacked. Slough, swash, and swale had to be crossed. A ravine had to be descended. Keeping a line straight for eighty swings of a sixty-six foot cord would call for a horizon marker upon which to anchor vision. Nimrod apparently chose a tall tree in the distance, which, in squatter parlance, was called a *sight tree*. Six years later, J.C. Alexander retraced Nimrod's steps in an unofficial search for the lines: "We found the SE corner & the Sight tree on the S line as Mr. O'Kelly had described them." The ninety-degree corner at the point of beginning, the one-mile reach of the south border, and the true westerly course of that baseline, were all critical. Angle, distance, and direction were the three footholds that had to be firm. The rest could slip and slide a bit.

Nimrod would have set off on his best westerly course with stakes, axe, cord, and provender for a day's work. He proceeded along the brink of the ravine and across the California Trail with his end-to-end measurements. And when he came to a distance of what he deemed to be one mile, he drove down a second stake at the southwest corner. Then, with the aid of his try-square cord, he turned north to repeat the tedious process, knowing all too well it would have to be done a third time to the east, along the north side of his claim. His fourth and final leg would be the test of his measures. If the beginning stake back at his camp proved to be *nigh onto* one mile due south of his final northeast corner stake, that proof would vouch for the accuracy of his labors—unless, of course, none of it was ever done. With no other settlers for miles and miles, with a seemingly uncaring Indian population, and with such bountiful takings, the need for precision might not have been a high priority. Accordingly, Nimrod's work that day may have yielded to educated guesswork with just a bit of ciphering.

If Nimrod gave his borders more muzzle-sight than proper bead with try square, cord, and other squatter rigs, then he might have staked more than his entitlement. This was of no immediate concern, but it became a crucial issue in future years. Some argued that Nimrod had claimed 1½ square miles, and others said as much as six square miles. Arguably, his sixty-seven years betokened against a full day of hard labor and mental reckonings deduced there. On the other hand, a day's honest labor in helping oneself to a generous portion of free land may not have been so far-fetched for an old man who just 1½ years before had shown his mettle on a two thousand mile quest for that very land.

If the Calapooya and Klickitat Indians had watched Nimrod's effort that day, it must have seemed to them an amusing ritual. Curiously, white men seemed driven to make lines. They would bring a line around in full circle so as to rope in the land by their unseen thing called "boundary." Indeed, it was a ceremony for head scratching. White men with their hairy faces were like wolves staking their dens with urine. Little did the first dwellers suspect that this seemingly harmless ritual was the beginning of a displacement of their way of life.

Near sunset on his day of staking, Nimrod may have drug his saddle closer to the campfire and sat with pipe and parched-pea coffee in the fading light to turn his thoughts inward upon the day. Any doubts about his choice were now buried by his labor. His heart, like his sweat and the stakes, was soaked and driven into the soil.

Note

1. Evidence for the use of these two different "north" locators yet remains on the land today. Downtown Portland is a clear example. About the same time that Nimrod was laying his claim lines, surveyor Thomas Brown platted streets in the newly envisioned town of Portland, over one hundred trail miles north. Brown chose to aim his streets on a bead with the compass and the flow of the Willamette River at that point. Later, additional Portland streets were platted by John H. Couch. A sea captain, Couch was accustomed to navigating by the stars. Accordingly, he platted the new streets abutting the core area in alignment with the North Pole and true longitudes. As a result, today's Portland streets bend at a twenty-degree angle (of declination) in the core of the city. The home-made surveys of the 1840s, like the paths of goats in the Old World, have left their mark on the present day.

5

Filing and Converting

Late 1846

Nimrod had roped and knotted his claim upon the earth, but that was not enough. While rock cairns, trenches, stakes, and other postings may have given fair warning to future land-combers, notice to government required something more formal. The 1845 Organic Act of the Oregon Provisional Government required land claimants to file their claims "in the office of the territorial recorder, in a book to be kept by him for that purpose, within twenty days from the time of making said claim."

Claimants had to carve their claims twice—first, upon the land, then within a book. The book was back in Oregon City, one hundred trail miles away. Such is the respect paid to land. Nimrod's shotgun, horse, smithy tools, were all chattel—legally recognized belongings without the need for written record; possession itself was proof. Not so with land. One did not *prove up* land by mere possession. Land was immovable. If it was carried off, it ceased to be land. Land could not be placed because land *was* place. This land mystique drove laws toward a separation of *real* and *personal* property. Real property was a spot on the earth and all things affixed to it—growing trees and crops, cabins, fences, a vein of gold. But lumber, flour, and a gold watch were all personal property, albeit products of land and its resources. In democratic nations, the public sovereign shares with its citizens in a claim to real property. Whereas private citizens call their interests in land "property," the public citizenry calls its interest in the same land "domain." World history has been shaped by the yearning of both nations and individuals to claim dominion or property in real estate. Small wonder, then, that law has always been vigilant in keeping careful track of place. And so, Nimrod's *private* claim had to be recorded in the *public's* book.

As long as the creeks and rivers were not too swollen, Nimrod could get to the book within a week—well within the twenty-day deadline allotted by law. Still, there was not a lot of time for tarry. It was nearing winter. He faced a two hundred mile round trip.[1] On a lot of foot, some hoof, and a bit of mosey at Marys River and French Prairie, Nimrod re-traced his way back to the capital town of the Provisional Government.

On December 8, 1846, Nimrod arrived at the office of Frederic Prigg in Oregon City. Doctor Prigg was Oregon City's only known medical practitioner. He was a "man of fine education, excellent mind, and a good physician." And, he was the Secretary of the Provisional Government—the second highest officer in that organization—and as such was the duly designated *land recorder*. He was also the occasional town drunk.

Nimrod was not the only pioneer seeking to record his claim that day. He found a dozen men at Prigg's place waiting to file. Nimrod was next to last in line. By the time Nimrod's turn came, an exhausted Prigg may have been in need of "medicine." Whereas Nimrod was said to be a man of temperance, Prigg pulled a cork. Three years later, Prigg either fell, jumped, or was thrown from the bluffs at Oregon City into the Willamette River. His body was never found. The *Oregon Spectator* of November 1, 1849, speculated that Prigg's death was

> another admonition to those who visit the groceries…[the] destructive influence of Alcohol. As he had been known to be much intoxicated for sometime…, there is no doubt but that rum was instrumental in hastening on the fate from which temperance would have saved him.[2]

Thus on that late afternoon, Nimrod and Prigg met upon what may have been the uneven surface of abstinence and indulgence to describe the indescribable—distant borders in an uncharted countryside. What they were to put down that day would have its effect in far years to come.

Their business together would have to follow the dictates of the Provisional Government land law:

> [C]laimant shall state in his record the size, shape, and locality of said claim, and give the name of adjoining claimants, and the recorder may require the applicant for such record, to be made to answer, on his oath, touching the facts.

Based upon the final description recorded, the conversation between the public official and the private citizen, concerning "size, shape, and locality," must have gone something like this:

Prigg: *Name?*
Nimrod: *Nimrod O'Kelly.*
Prigg: *Where is your claim, O'Kelly?*
Nimrod: *South. Upriver.*
Prigg: *How far?*
Nimrod: *Four or five days' ride.*
Prigg: *I make that a hundred miles or so. What county would that be?*

Nimrod:	*Didn't know there were counties.*
Prigg:	*What side of the Willamette?*
Nimrod:	*West.*
Prigg:	*Well then, west of the Willamette, hundred miles south, that'd be the new Polk County. Used to be Yamhill, but last year about now we cut up Yamhill and made the south part Polk. Are you above Salem—the old Methodist Mission area?*
Nimrod:	*Farther still.*
Prigg:	*At Mouse River? By Avery?*
Nimrod:	*Folks up there call it Marys River now.³ My stakes are a half day yonder.*
Prigg:	*Well then, you're in Polk County for certain. What's the size of your claim?*
Nimrod:	*The all of it—six hundred forty acres. A full mile.*
Prigg:	*What's the shape of your claim?*
Nimrod:	*Rich bottom soil. Open prairie. Some ash. Swales. Sloughs. A drainage problem I can fix....*
Prigg:	*No, I mean shape. Is it oblong, square, what?*
Nimrod:	*Staked it myself—at the corners—pure square and plumb straight—cardinal lines.*
Prigg:	*What do your borders measure?*
Nimrod:	*Three hundred twenty poles on a side.*
Prigg:	*All right then. I can put it down as one square mile—three twenty by three twenty rods. Do you share those borders with any adjoining claimants?*
Nimrod:	*No neighbors. No cabins or fields anywhere up that far. Made sure of that.*

Prigg, the city dweller, may have glanced up from his notes at that point to take a closer look at this pioneer who chose a life alone in nowhere, without neighbors, without towns, without saloon.

Prigg:	*Now we need to take aim. We need to narrow things down to a specific locality—just like the law says, a precise point on the countryside. Where exactly did you begin?*
Nimrod:	*I drove an ash stake.*
Prigg:	*Yes, yes. But where exactly. I know it's Polk County and square, but that won't do. Where is this stake? How does your stake relate to the lay of the land? We gotta be able to find it.*

"Size" and "shape" of land were an easy swallow, but "locality" was gristle. In mind's eye, Nimrod could see the ash stake there, near the spring and within the *kalapuya* grasses. He could take Prigg there without trouble and show him the stake. But how could he turn that mind's eye into words for paper? It was like telling someone how to knot a girth hitch without benefit of rope. The problem could have been solved had there been a prior government survey of the whole valley. The two men could have simply located Nimrod's claim on a survey map and pinned it down by precise coordinates, using the survey lines and benchmark as points of reference.

Back in Washington City, political debate had ensued for decades over how government should allot its land to its citizens. Should government first parcel the land by survey before allowing claims? Or should citizens be allowed to stake the land before survey? Who goes first in laying boundaries—government surveyors or citizen squatters? Many in Congress, mostly northerners, were opposed to squatters and the idea of allowing citizens to dictate the place and extent of public generosity. Others, mostly southerners, felt it was the customary right of citizens to take up land without having to wait upon slow-moving government survey and paperwork. Beneath that surface was the deeper issue of which rights were preeminent: private or public. Ultimately, the choice between the two was not made by debate. Rather, it was made by yen and daring. Nothing would deny pioneers. They wandered far in advance of lawmaking and surveys. Indeed, it was what "pioneering" originally meant; the first "pioneers" were those who went into no-man's land between armies to make the ground ready for battle. Frontiering was not orderly, and any bans would have been like trying to keep critters from the root cellar.

Squatter custom made the problem now confronting Nimrod and Prigg. Without survey or maps of any kind, how could the location of Nimrod's claim be defined so as to prevent conflict? As best he could, Nimrod told Prigg where he had driven his starting stake—somewhere near a lake that bedded somewhere between the mouth of the Long Tom and another lake by two buttes on the trail to California.[4] Prigg could not press for more. He had long ago surrendered to muddy descriptions—dirt tracks across the carpet of his neatly kept record books. The first entry ever recorded back in 1845 located the beginning of George Neal's claim at a point as vague as "about five miles above the Rickreall." Joe Avery's claim read: "commencing at a tree marked on the bank of the Willamette and south of Marys River." Greenberry Smith's claim started at a "stake in a swamp." The problem of recording locality was not solved; it was merely stored.

Laying open on Doctor Prigg's table was a volume of the Provisional Government Land Claim Records. Approximately one thousand prior claims had been written in the sixteen months since the beginning—Volume I, page 1. Prigg dipped his pen and on page 107 of Volume IV, wrote:

> Nimrod O'Kelly claims 640 acres of land in Polk County, situate as follows: to wit: Commencing at the head of the lake, between at the mouth of the Long Tom Bath and the lake at the two butes on the California trail, at an Ash stake, thence running due W. along the brink of the ravine and across the California trail, 320 rods to an Ash stake, thence due N. 320 rods to an Ash stake, thence due E. 320 rods to an Ash stake, thence due S. 320 rods to the place of beginning, all lying W. of the middle lake, which he holds by personal occupancy. Recorded, Dec. 8th 1846—Attest, Fred Prigg Recorder.

And so, the book was closed. If there was any sense of completion in that closing, it was fleeting. Making a claim was a far cry from perfecting it. Savoring that moment was no more than a temporary rest stop on the long road to "proving up." Furthermore, the description on that page was just like the stakes that marked the land itself; it would decompose. It was, after all, the record of a temporary government. Until recognition was given by a more durable nation, the best evidence of borders was neither descriptions nor land markers. Rather, neighborly witness was the firmer hold. It was called "boundary reputation" in the law books. Once a community of settlers developed, mutuality would shore up each other's borders by cooperation and consideration. At those "stakes," Nimrod was destined to prove poorly.

Near the time that Nimrod and Prigg concluded their business, news reached Oregon that Great Britain and the United States had signed a boundary agreement on July 15, 1846. The treaty called for British withdrawal from Oregon south of the forty-ninth parallel—the new United States-Canadian border west of the continental divide. The divide did not, however, make Oregon a U.S. territory. It simply opened the door for that to happen.

The Provisional Government, while continuing to rule, was prepared nevertheless to yield to the States and to cancel all of its laws, offices, and records, including the land claim just inked and entered. Oregon land claimants were also ready for a new land law, but that submission did not come without the misery of wonder: Would the United States recognize the Provisional Government's book of claims? Would a claim as large as 640 acres be allowed? Would it be land *freely* given? Some assurance was given by the previous actions of both the Provisional Government at Champoeg and the U.S. Senate in Washington City. In 1843, both had officially approved the idea of 640 acres of free land for the two-thousand-mile migration. Although the Senate approval never reached passage in the House, the push and pull from each end of the continent gave pioneers hope. But that hope was countered by two ominous facts. First, the United States, with minor exception, had never before given free soil to squatters; and second, the sale of public lands was a principal source of income for the national government, there being no federal income tax in the nineteenth century. Congress put the future of Oregon public land on the shelf of debate, where pins and needles of wait would stick at Nimrod for the next two years.

Nimrod would not have returned to his Long Tom claim that December 1846. Winter was coming, and on the frontier that was a caution. This was the same winter the Donner Party, on their way overland to California through the Sierras, learned tragic lessons in trying to outrace winter's fury. Nimrod probably wintered over with friends on French Prairie. While there, Nimrod would have learned that John McLoughlin had retired from the HBC and Fort Vancouver and now was a storekeeper in Oregon City—the town he had founded. Like Gervais, now age sixty-nine, McLoughlin, age sixty-two, was also a kindred spirit for Nimrod, age sixty-six.[5] Sometime during that period, Nimrod may have gone to McLoughlin to lay in supplies for the beginning of a new home in the Long Tom country. Like so many immigrants, he had little money for store. But McLoughlin graciously took promises in exchange. In later years, his store books would show that "N. O'Kelley" was among the beholden at times.

In spite of his charity, or perhaps because of it, McLoughlin was not an easy man to like in the minds of some. U.S. Naval Lieutenant Neil Howison, in the summer of 1846, reported that McLoughlin was "not very popular" and had an "overbearing temper." But more than temper festered at the bottom of public mood. For one, taking charity was like taking castor oil—quick to swallow, but not easy to stomach. For another, McLoughlin had an Indian wife and half-breed children. For another, he was a foreigner. And further, his Oregon City claim took up the richest and most commercially promising land in the whole Willamette Valley. He claimed an island at the foot of the dynamic Willamette Falls—a coveted source of waterpower for saw and grist mills.

McLoughlin had done still another thing to bring stares and whispers. On November 18, 1842, he had embraced the Catholic faith, a conversion that rubbed the sores of Catholic-Protestant differences. A Methodist missionary called the French Prairie settlers "Papists of the most ignorant and bigoted type." On the other hand, Father Modeste Demers called Methodist ministers, "men without learning." These were among the mildest of the rebukes that passed between Oregon's religious rivals.

For those who fed on hate, McLoughlin the alien, the squaw lover, the Papist, the land baron, the creditor, was a man to be pre-judged. But not all settlers needed prejudice to feel secure. Most saw McLoughlin as a decent man to be respected. Nimrod was among the supporters. McLoughlin was likely the one who had sent Nimrod to Gervais and the Catholics on French Prairie in the previous winter. That winter Nimrod chose to follow McLoughlin's footsteps—on February 28, 1847, at the St. Paul mission on French Prairie while holed up by winter, Nimrod renounced Protestantism and professed Catholicism. He was baptized by Father Demers. Joseph Gervais and Catherine Pepin were named godparents. Why he converted is simply unknown. Whatever his reasons, they took shape during the preceding year wherein his associations with McLoughlin, Gervais, and the settlers on French Prairie began. Like McLoughlin, Nimrod's professing of the Catholic faith would polarize the people around him.

Notes

1. Nimrod's pilgrimage to the Oregon City land office was long, but by no means the longest; e.g., Californians made a fifteen hundred-mile roundtrip to Oregon City in the 1840s in order to file a plat map for their proposed city—San Francisco.
2. The office of territorial recorder seemed to be unlucky. Prigg's two predecessors in that office also met violent death—J.E. Long was drowned; George LeBreton murdered.
3. Four days after the O'Kelly-Prigg interview, the Provisional Government legislators recognized the name "Marys River" in enactment.
4. See Figure No. Four, "Southern Benton County Topography," 1852–53, in Chapter 20.
5. In the 1840s, about one out of every hundred Americans was age sixty years or more; and on the far frontier, sixty-year olds were even rarer. For the determination of Nimrod's age, see Appendix A.

6

Improving and Subsisting

1847–48

As soon as winter gave way, Nimrod left French Prairie to return to his claim. Between Salem and Marys River, he passed a growing number of blue towers. The influx of new claims put an added step to Nimrod's gait. The 1846 migration had added one thousand souls to the Oregon frontier. Now in 1847, three times as many emigrants were already lining the banks of the Missouri with hungry eyes on Oregon's free land. Nimrod would have been anxious to get settled in before that starved lot made feast upon the Valley.

At Marys River, Nimrod found that the claims of Avery, Dixon, and the Stewarts had been joined by those of Johnson Mulkey and Edmund Marsh. But for the time being, these newcomers' fires were cold, because they had gone back to the States to bring their families, including Avery's, to Oregon. This spring, they would be starting out on their return trip to Oregon. Nimrod had no such plan. He claimed that his alleged wife and sons, and their children, were coming to Oregon on their own. Those that did go back on such errand were younger men. A sixty-seven year old body would not take kindly to that two thousand-mile ordeal for a second and then a third time. On the other hand, being landlocked by age and the faraway was not an easy ending for a rover to accept. Backtracking the Overland Trail was a prospect that would one day come again.

Nimrod's fording of Marys River for a third time was more dangerous than in the last autumn. Crossing in the spring meant deeper waters. As he moved up through the *kalapuya*, he saw the Long Tom River and sloughs were made considerable. Having grown up in hill country, Nimrod was not mindful of flood signs. In staking his claim, he had taken no clue from the driftwood there. Now, as he looked upon his watery land for the first time in spring season, it must have given him pause. Furrows and ditching for drainage would be hard work, but small sacrifice for the lush soil the waters supplied.

Nimrod found his sight tree and ash stake, and made camp. Camping out, however, would not do. A bivouac was not an improvement or occupancy. Section 22 of Article III of the 1845 Provisional Organic Act stated:

All claimants shall, within six months from the time of recording...make permanent improvements...by building or enclosing, and also become an occupant...within one year.

That act, however, was provisional and now lame duck law; but the U.S. government had yet to put anything in its place. Surely, the forthcoming land law out of Washington City would agree that, in dispensing public lands, citizens must not simply *take* land, they must *use* it. It did not do a nation any good to have its claimants sit and speculate on market value. Land had to be lived on, logged, harvested, mined, irrigated, or converted for buildings, fields, factories, towns, roads. Use, not mere possession, was demanded in the trade for title. Undeveloped resources had no value to a nation seeking to improve itself by production.

To satisfy the law's insistence upon improvement and occupancy, a claimant's temporary proof thereof was usually an on-site, fixed lodging called "a claim cabin"—a roof, four walls, and door. The design was not new to Nimrod. His westering hops from Virginia through Tennessee and Missouri were valuable practice. He was probably alone for most, if not all, of the work. The first task would be cutting and hauling timber to the site. Then came hewing, shaping, and notching those logs with a broadax and saw. The dovetail wedging at the corners called for exact fit. Using his try-square cord, Nimrod would lay the ground poles at right angles. The cord could also serve as a plumb line to keep the corners *downright*. With a foundation "downright square," the hard labor could continue. The lifting and stacking of logs horizontally could be made easier by roping and sliding them up skids—debarked, green poles. Hoisting the logs could be aided by a "gin pole"—a temporary center post. Horse muscle served for tugging and towing.

Once the walls were in place, a clapboard roof was fashioned and held down by heavy poles, never by nails. Puncheon may or may not have been used for a floor; more often than not, floors stayed dirt. A chimney and hearth of baked clay and sticks were essential for heat and cooking. Next, chinks and cracks had to be pasted up with a mixture of mud and moss. The door may have been a bear hide or a piece of tent canvas. Later, such a door would have to be replaced with hewn planks and a latch, if wild and weather were to be denied. A latchstring also served as a lock against the world when the string was pulled inside. The string told something about the dweller behind the door. Was he social or alone? Was his heart open or shut? Where was his latchstring?

Built to satisfy the law and not comfort, the temporary structure was more shack than cabin. A frame house would follow as soon as there was a sawmill and spare time. But Nimrod's hut was destined to serve beyond the next six years. An 1853 visitor called it "a most miserable hovel." Just as trees flourish or wither in what they are rooted, so too a soul is nourished or infected by its mansion or shack. Over the years, an old man alone in wretched surroundings might be given to taking his latchstring inside.

Nimrod's next task was to clear a field for spring planting. To live on the land was to live off of it. Ground had to be plowed, furrowed, and ditched for drainage. A gnarly chunk of oak root could serve as a plow, and a log with snag branches could be a harrow for dragging out brush. Then too, no crop would last without fencing out the grazers. A snake or worm fence was easiest—split rails stacked, staggered, and laced. Nimrod could have cleared as much as ten to twenty acres that spring. He could have, but he probably did not. Sodbusting took a strong back and a stronger passion. He was at best a mere subsistence grower with a home garden.[1] Without family to feed and sons or farmhands to help, Nimrod had little need and less wish to market crops. He probably raised only enough wheat for his table and for exchange. Coin was scarce on the Oregon frontier in the 1840s, and wheat was a common currency.

Nimrod did not call himself a farmer. He was listed as a blacksmith by census-takers in later years. Of all of the strange work done by the fur-faced men from the east, none quite fascinated the Valley Indians like the work of the iron men in their hammer houses—with firebox, billows, and anvil—turning earth into points, blades, and edges. But the Valley Indians were not customers, and Nimrod chose to be far from towns and purchase. Apparently, he made no living as a smithy.

Some of Nimrod's livelihood seems to have been a dalliance at livestock. On the *kalapuya*, the work of the grazier was more relaxed. Rich grasses were plentiful on an open range. The animals were simply turned loose to graze or root with the deer and elk. Animals could walk themselves to market; crops had to be hauled. But at ranching, Nimrod was just a dabbler. By 1850, after three or four years of working his claim, he had only one horse, four cows, five hogs, and four sheep. The following year he added three more cows, eight hogs, and one sheep. Farther north in the Valley, there were horse ranchers with herds as large as thirty head, and hog ranchers with over a hundred swine.

Residing in the back-country, he may have made his way in venery—just as his parents had prophesied when they named him after the Biblical hunter, Nimrod. On any frontier, the market for venison was abundant. Then too, the Provisional Government had placed a fair bounty on predators. Scalp and ears of a coyote or prairie wolf brought 50¢, a wolf $3, a bear $2, and a panther as much as $5. A good tracker and marksman could have made a tolerable living.

Aside from livestock, predators, and game, there were other kinds of animals. Safe storage against the invasion of critters was a constant pursuit. There was no place that rats and mice could not or would not go. No food or documents were safe without a jar or a tin. The best safeguard against pests was pets. Nimrod wrote that he had "plenty of cats."

Surrounded by his own and nature's animals, by his own crops and nature's bounties, and by a land shared by few, Nimrod found living on the prairie *fat-pickings*—a pastoral life most welcome to an aging pioneer who had no more mountains to cross. Other Valley settlers embraced that way of life as well—so much so that the more industrious called them "vagabond farmers," "thriftless," "loungers," and a "misfortune to the State." In 1877, Wallis Nash described an old bachelor living on his hermitage in another part of Oregon. The description fit the so-called "subsistence settler," coming close to Nimrod and his quarters as well:

> A grey, weather-worn, one-storied cabin, [looked] as if neglect and slovenliness, not age, were bringing it to decay…A bit of rusty bacon and a hacked loaf of bread were on the shelf…He was tall and sallow…A long-stemmed pipe hung from his mouth, and the dark brown of the well-smoked meerschaum was the only bit of pleasant colour about him. His clothes, down to his boots, were of one uniform grey, and he looked as if he had always been too lazy to wash…[H]e found he had enough to live on, with the help of a pig or two, and a small band of cattle on the hill. He sold his oats and hay to passers by, and bought flour and bacon…and tobacco. He did not work now, why should he? He was very comfortable, and he slept a lot. If he got tired of bacon, he could go and shoot a deer most any day: but he didn't often go after them, why should he? No; he didn't think he should clear any more land; he had got enough…Yes, he went off to the town a time or two…but it was maybe three or four months since he had gone there, and he didn't know as he should go again.

Whether this fully agreed with Nimrod is hard to know. Certainly it did fit the definition of many settlers coming to roost in the bountiful Willamette Valley of the mid-1800s. In one important respect, Nimrod did not fit Nash's bachelor "sluggard." True, Nimrod may have chosen to put down his hammer and plow, but it seems he did not substitute sloth for his new-found abundance. Whatever energy he saved, he used in passage up and down the Valley and in wandering the countryside. Freed by nature's riches, he gathered no moss. He was a voyager. Like the Valley Indians and the mountain men, he was swallowed by and wallowed in the garden he had struggled to find.

Not all was Eden. There were still chores. Clothes had to be made and mended. Fabric was fashioned from tents, wagon covers, and hides, with flour sacks for patches. Buckskin britches were sturdy, but had the disadvantage of being quite stiff and bent at the knees on account of sitting. So, when a buck-skinned pioneer stood, he appeared "not yet up."

A cake of tallow could be taken in trade in order to make candles. Soap could be improvised by leaching water through burnt ashes and draining off the lye. Without salt for preservation, meat was jerked in the sun or at the hearth. For biscuits and cakes, the bulb of the camas plant grew wild and everywhere. It was a mainstay of the Indians. Its blue flower in vast fields gave the look of a lake upon the meadows of the *kalapuya*.

Fleas and bedbugs had to be dealt with. One's scalp could become "a festering mass of dandruff, blood, and matter alive with lice." The cure might be as easy as more soap and water, or as drastic as a shaved head. For poison oak—the best cure was to give it wide berth. George E. Cole got a case of "oak" so bad that the swelling blinded him for days.

In spite of nature's plenty, chores would include occasional trips to lay in supplies. In the early years, the markets were far to the north below the falls at Oregon City. Travel down river could be made by canoe. There was no riverboat transport up the Willamette to Marys River until 1853. Floating the Willamette down river as far as Oregon City in an empty canoe on high water could be done in one long sun up, more likely two. But each day downstream meant six days of aching shoulders when coming back upstream with a canoe full of supplies. Nimrod would never swap horse and hike for that ordeal.

Greater than all of the chores, however, was coping with the *lorn lost.* His nights were alone and so too his weeks, then his months, and eventually his years. On some evenings, before retiring, he might have put his reading down, pinched out the candle, and taken his pipe outdoors. Nights on the prairie were ink black. No campfires among wagons. No street lamps. No buggy lanterns. No saloons all lit up. No town lighting the horizon's clouds. On moonless nights, not even the shadow of *Chintimini* could be seen. The darkness made the stars torches.

On such a night in April 1848, Nimrod may have remembered that it was his birthday. Born in April 1780, he was entering his sixty-ninth year alone. He had been gone from Missouri for three years. Birthdays were a time for family. He should write, but letters were another chore. To write a letter, he had to gather what it took—a candle, inkpot, paper, pen, thought, and thoughtfulness. Writing was dip and scratch, and his hand was aging. The biggest rub was mailing. The "mailbox" was one hundred miles away in

Oregon City. That meant at least a week-long trip away and back. Mail runs, of course, could be shared among friends. Such favors involved neighborliness—a cooperation that Nimrod found hard to curry. And there were snags in the postal flow. Missing, dead, or delayed letters were common on the frontier. The urge to touch those distant had to be strong enough to overcome the prospect of having written on the wind. Years later, Nimrod would have important reasons for insisting that he had family and had written to them. They had not received his letters, he said, and he had not heard from them either. From such excuses, doubt festered. Did this old man have a family or not?

But for now, on that April evening in 1848, when the evening candle was snuffed, there was only a birthday in silent darkness and in the quiet madness it brings.

Note

1. The first official, government survey map of this locality, completed some years later, does not show any field on Nimrod's acreage. Written statements, however, mention a field on his land. Likewise, J.C. Alexander's 1852 makeshift map indicates a field; see Figure No. Three, "J.C. Alexander's Survey," in Chapter 17. Likely, it was no more than a *homefield*—a garden large enough for domestic harvest, but too small for traders or mapmakers.

7

The Neighbors

1847–48

Wintering-in whetted the appetite for news and reading. Back on February 5, 1846, the *Oregon Spectator* had begun publication at Oregon City. It was the first newspaper west of the Stoney divide and the fourth west of the Mississippi River. At the height of its existence, the four-page, fortnightly *Spectator* had a circulation of about 150 copies. Pioneers, marooned and forsaken, had heart for news of home. From the *Spectator*, they learned that the States had neighbor troubles—war with Mexico and border disputes with Canada. Nimrod was about to discover that, like nations, he too could be troubled by neighbors.

At one time, Nimrod may have believed he was the farthest pioneer to settle upriver in the Valley. But while building his cabin in 1847, he must have seen three towers of smoke far upriver and to the west. He may have hoped these were Indian camp-fires, but the columns went straight up—chimney fires—and were too far apart for a single encampment. In the still of dawn and dusk, he might have heard from that direction the faint *chonkings* of an axe.

Those sights and sounds, three to four miles away, marked the families of John Lloyd, Andrew Foster, and Thomas D. Reeves. Foster and Lloyd came to Oregon in the same migration as Nimrod.[1] Lloyd had a number of daughters. Reeves courted one: Nancy Jane. One of Foster's sons, John, took a fancy to another: Mary Ann. So, in June 1846, there was a double wedding, and the Reeves-Lloyd-Foster fires came together. Then, in late 1847, four other families clustered just south of the Reeves-Lloyd-Foster group. They were the families of Samuel F. Starr, Lorenzo Gilbert, and Ranson and Oren Belknap. Starr would later become sheriff. They took their square mile sections together, around what would come to be known as the Bellfountain Settlement.[2]

The horse trail through Nimrod's property became a wagon road. Not all migrants on that road came from the north. Wagons from the south also increased. The Applegate Cutoff gave overlanders a choice of approaching the Valley from across the Humboldt plateau and the Siskiyou Mountains. Settlers going to and fro through Nimrod's land, and seeking what others left behind, made him even more aware that he no longer was at the edge of the frontier.

Among others who rolled into the *kalapuya* were R.B. Hinton and his family. Hinton would later become a justice of the peace. He built alongside the road, just a little over four miles south of Nimrod. It is said that Hinton bought his land from the Indians for a bushel of potatoes. If Hinton rode off from the parlay with a smile, the Indians had a smile as well, for they had made *huy-huy* (barter) of a thing that was nobody's to give. It was like trading tomorrow's rain. Solomon K. Brown gave the Calapooyas an ox for the land he staked, but, unlike Hinton, he wrote in his ledger that he gave the ox in exchange for good will, not for title. Apparently, he understood that making a home was not so much a taking of possession, as it was a gaining of respect. A wise man like Brown would have made a good neighbor, but he abandoned his claim and moved on.

Then came two families who set claims on the trail disturbingly close to Nimrod—Isaac Winkle's family to the north and Aaron "Doc" Richardson's family to the south. Although they built their cabins more than two miles off, their stakes were stitches that began a hemming in. Winkle's claim took the butte from which Nimrod had surveyed the countryside in search of claim land. In later years, Nimrod labeled these two as "his adversaries." Unlike Nimrod, both of his new neighbors were industrious farmers. In his 1848 diary, Methodist minister George H. Atkinson gave an insight into Doc Richardson's work efforts.

> I dined at Mr. R.'s on the Long Tom Bath…I promised Mr. R. that I would come up and preach at his new house next year…He had in more than 20 acres of wheat, and has as much fenced. He has corn, potatoes, tobacco and vegetables. He has broken up ten acres more. Besides he has built a small cabin and has got out the timber mostly for a large and good one. This has all been accomplished within a year. His farm has the appearance of years of labor.

Although Richardson was kind to a man of the cloth, that was not his usual treatment of strangers. In 1850, Bushrod "Bush" Wilson and George E. Cole, two traveling newcomers low on supply, sought Richardson's hospitality. But Richardson met them at the doorstep with rifle at ready. To what was intended as a compliment, Richardson quickly took offense, lost temper, and gave hard words. Missus Richardson interrupted and was kind enough to give them bread and milk, but Cole and Wilson did not dawdle at that doorstep.[3]

The 1848 migration included a wagon company from Iowa that had more Belknap and Starr relatives, together with several Hawley families. They were all connected either by marriages or by their Iowa roots, and all were wed to their Methodist faith. Abiather Newton, later a justice of the peace, was also in the group. Their mission was to join with their relatives and friends who had preceded them at the Bellfountain Settlement. They made a solid Methodist core called a "class" by that Protestant denomination.

In 1849, Oregon's Methodist mission superintendent reported to his superiors in the east that somewhere in the "extreme upper part of the [Marys River] circuit," a place he had not been able to visit, "there was a class near Long Tom second to none in the territory for genuine Methodism." Preacher John McKinney, a Methodist circuit rider in Salem, rode out in search of the wayward class. When he arrived at the claims of Doc Richardson and R.B. Hinton, he inquired as to where these Methodists could be found. He was told that "them fellers left the road;…keep their wagon tracks and you will find them for nobody ever turned out there before." Preacher McKinney finally came upon them and was met by an enthusiastic fold that had been many months without a shepherd. The new flock dutifully gave McKinney their *letters*—statements from their former pastor officially certifying their Methodist membership. Devout adherence to orderly methodology was how and why they were so called.

Just as surely as unity drew close inwardly, it also grew distant outwardly. Shortly after "Bush" Wilson and George Cole left Doc Richardson's door, they came upon a quilting party at a farm in the Bellfountain area. The quilters patched more than fabric. They also fitted and stitched the countryside. Bush wanted to know "if there were any claims to be had?"

When the women found out the two men were not married, they said, "Well then we don't want you…; got plenty of bachelors already…Are you a school teacher?"

"No, ma'am," said Bush, "but my friend here is well qualified."

"Then he can stay and take up a claim; we have got three hundred and twenty acres here, we have been saving up for a school teacher; but as for you, young man, you can just go right on up the Valley."[4] The subject was closed. The land was closed. The government's free land had come to be proctored and parceled out by the needs of the community. As claim land became more scarce, the neighbors would play more and more a part in qualifying the residents. Claims might have to be recorded in Oregon City, but they had to pass muster in the community first. This was not law. This was the way of things. It was, indeed, a quilting party. Coming and going was all in keep with the stitching of settlement—finding a patch and fitting it into space, pattern, and color.

Nimrod always knew when it was Sunday morning. The first sign was a circuit rider coming up through his land from the north. A circuit rider was easy to spot. His saddlebags were loaded with books and literature. A Bible and hymnal were tucked under arm. His head bobbed in rhythm to the pace of a horse that knew where to go. Methodist circuit riders were respected for hardiness. An expression of bad weather became, "nothing out today but crows and Methodist preachers."[5]

For the second sign that the morning was a Sunday, Nimrod might have heard the faint sounds of church singing. My, how the Methodists loved to sing. They were as devoted to song as were the Baptists to the river and the Catholics to kneeling. Sunday morning was not the only time for Methodists. They had evening meetings throughout the week. Gatherings were often called at twilight on the frontier because daylight was best left for working in the fields and because sundown was a precise setting for the call to assembly in the absence of synchronized timepieces or church bells.

Perhaps the enthusiasm of Methodists brought them to Nimrod's cabin door to give away a Bible and to talk of God. If so, their mission would not have been received cordially, and they would have learned of the grievous error in his ways. He had forsaken his family's Protestantism and became, of all things, a Catholic. Nimrod, the maverick, went one way, and the neighboring herd went the other. The two shared only one thing in common: both kept inward. Their differences and resemblances were pocks that would turn cankerous.

Nimrod began to feel what the Indians of the *kalapuya* had felt. Like the drying of wet moccasins on swelling feet, gossip and borders squeezed at poor fit.

Notes

1. See Figure No. Four, "Southern Benton County Topography," 1852–53, in Chapter 20.
2. The record is confusing as to who could make the claim of being the first or farthest settler south of Marys River as of 1846. Historian David Fagan said it was Reeves and a man named McKissick. Author Lewis A. McArthur stated it was Lloyd. Pioneer Tolbert Carter said he sighted a cabin in 1846 on Grand Prairie near a butte called by the Indians *Yapoah*. This was probably Eugene Skinner's place, twenty-five miles south of Nimrod on the California Trail. Today, the butte is named after Skinner. Making claims about the first arriving settlers in the southern Valley, in the face of a yearly surge of ungoverned squatters left entirely to their own finds, is supported by little evidence and a whole lot of imagination.
3. This story was first published in 1880 in the *Corvallis Gazette*, and Wallis Nash republished it verbatim two years later without citing the *Gazette*. David D. Fagan repeated the story again five years later, but at least quoted and cited the *Gazette*. George Cole's

reminiscences suggest a different version of the encounter. It seems that copyright and plagiarism were at the low end of the many legal problems to be addressed in creating an orderly society. Doc Richardson's hostility extended to a ferry across the Willamette that he operated; story has it that he denied use to persons of Irish descent. Despite Richardson's attitude, many Irish in later decades settled in the vicinity—so much so that a crook of land in the nearby Willamette came to be known as "Irish Bend." See Figure No. Two, "Long Tom Area," May 1852, in Chapter 11.

4. Bush Wilson went to Marys River, where he became the county clerk many years later. George Cole did not take the school teaching job, but went north seven or eight miles, becoming a teacher there and also a territorial legislator.

5. The missionary circuit rider on the Oregon frontier has been immortalized by an equestrian statue of Reverend Robert A. Booth, located on the Capitol Mall in Salem.

8

Change

1847–49

The Valley Indians were foragers and hunters in the wild. From vision quests above and hideaways down-wind, they watched and listened just as they had for many snows as these strange, fur-faced men roped and speared and chewed the earth. Settlers were not like their white brothers—the mountain men and explorers—who had come before them and took to the wild. Instead, settlers were tethered to their takings and were set upon closing the wild. Eventually, it was bound to happen; coexistence reached an impasse. On November 29, 1847, a couple of hundred miles east of the Valley beyond the Cascades, Cayuse Indians of the Waiilatpu band killed missionaries Marcus and Narcissa Whitman and eleven pioneers and held sixty others hostage. All over the Valley, men volunteered for a civilian militia hastily organized to rescue the Whitman survivors. At his age, Nimrod felt neither duty nor conscience nor shame. His name does not appear on the muster rolls of the Oregon Volunteer Militia.

Oregon's first Indian uprising renewed pioneer frustration with their mother nation's failure to extend its government and protection to the frontier. It had been over eighteen months since Britain had pulled out to make way for American take-over below the forty-ninth parallel. The massacre made that delay a shame. In a petition to Congress hastily circulated, pioneer leaders Peter Burnett and George Curry wrote:

> [W]e have a right to claim…protection and care [from the United States]. Our forefathers complained that they were oppressed by the mother country…We do not complain of oppression, but of neglect. Even the tyrant has his moments of relaxation and kindness, but neglect never wears a smile.

When Sheriff Joe Meek brought news of the massacre to Washington City, Congress got off of its haunches. In August 1848, Oregon was finally made a United States territory. President James Polk immediately dispatched a military force, governor, secretary, prosecutor, marshal, and territorial judges to the Oregon frontier. Pioneers in the Valley had reason to rejoice. They were now protected by, and once again within, the folds of the American flag. Not all was good, however. Tucked away in the verbiage of the congressional act was this decree:

> All laws heretofore passed in said territory making grants of land…shall be… declared to be null and void.

The federal government now took away the 640-acre land claims that the Provisional Government had given. The record made by Nimrod and Prigg two years earlier in the provisional land book was laid waste. Nonetheless, for the next year, the wishful continued to limp into the provisional land office to have their claims recorded. The last entry was made on September 22, 1849. The eight volumes containing some 3,600 land descriptions were stored away—relics of a time when it might be said that the white man's Oregon was its own nation. With the books in storage, Nimrod and the rest of the settlers in Oregon had to pause for the next two years, holding fast to claims that had no sovereign support, and waiting to see what kind of land law would come out of Washington City.

The Whitman incident also rubbed at another sore—religious prejudice. Many, like Henry Harmon Spalding, blamed Catholic missionaries for the killings. Reverend Spalding, a Protestant missionary who had served with the Whitmans in eastern Oregon, escaped the Cayuse rage and moved just fifteen miles due east across the Willamette River from Nimrod. Spalding brought into the heart of the Valley more tinder for anti-Catholic fires. Gossip had it that Catholic priests had fanned the flames of Cayuse discontent against the Whitmans and supplied them with arms and ammunition. It was not the full truth, but the lifeblood of hatred has never been in need of truth.[1]

In December 1848, a petition to the Oregon legislature called for the removal of all Catholic clergy from Oregon. It did not pass. Then in September 1849, the territorial legislature entertained another resolution urging in part that Congress prohibit all Catholic missionaries from living among the Indians in Eastern Oregon. It too did not pass. While warm hearts and cool minds prevailed, nevertheless times were not the best for Nimrod and Catholics on the Oregon frontier.

Other events helped change the Oregon frontier in the final years of that decade. In the winter of 1848–49, movement along the trail through Nimrod's claim turned from a sprinkle to a steady trickle. Once winter passed, the trickle became a rush. The new travelers were men with no wagons or families. Their pack animals were strapped with picks, pans, and shovels. Gold had been discovered in central California. Over the next few years, an estimated two-thirds of the able-bodied men in Oregon made the rush for the gold fields. Joseph Avery went to the gold fields twice—once in 1848 and then again in 1849. The trail through Nimrod's land came to be called the "Gold Mine Road."

Nimrod would have eyed the flow of men crossing his land with a mix of good riddance and envy as they thinned the countryside and headed for new horizons. The record is unclear as to where Nimrod was in the years 1848 to 1850. Did he watch the parade or join it? Indeed, Nimrod's claim may not have been continuously occupied throughout those years. Later on when Nimrod tried to *prove up,* the affidavits of witnesses were conflicting as to when his *continued residency* began. The alleged starting dates ranged from as early as May 1, 1847, to as late as May 6, 1849.

In August or September of 1850, a United States census taker combed southern Oregon and took count of the "white and free colored population." It was the Seventh Census of the United States and the first for the new Oregon Territory. In the Long Tom countryside at "Dwelling House No. 34" (about where Nimrod's cabin ought to have been), the census listed "John Kelly of North Carolina" with no family. There can be little doubt that the census taker had incorrectly described the occupancy of an absent Nimrod O'Kelly of Missouri.[2] The misnomer had to be the product of second-hand information from neighbors not well acquainted with the old recluse, who had let run his fields and animals and whose dwelling had not advanced beyond a rundown claims cabin. It did not seem likely that a sixty-nine year old could have taken the long trail as a "forty-niner"; but then, where had he gone?

The demand for meat by hungry California miners gave Oregon suppliers "mines" of their own. Beginning in the 1850s, money began to flow into Oregon in trade for livestock and in the pokes of returning prospectors. That, in turn, drove market prices up. Wheat went from one dollar per bushel to six dollars per bushel. Thus, the currents of commerce began to flow into the quiet eddies of the frontier. Anyone in the backwaters away from that economic stream would not share in Oregon's good times. Nimrod was left behind with one saving grace: although without supply of his own, neither did he have demands.

As settlement kept moving farther and farther south, the districting of government into local units moved with it. Shortly after the so-called "Whitman massacre" and prior to the federal takeover, provisional lawmakers carved Benton County out of the southern part of Polk County, just as Polk County had been carved out of Yamhill County two years before. So, without moving, Nimrod's land had taken a journey of its own. It started out in Yamhill

County; then it shifted to Polk County; now it was in Benton County. Lawmakers created new counties whenever a county got too big for its keepers. Land record books were for keeping track of the land. But keeping track of the people on that land was another matter. The advent of government meant keeping book on people for purposes of voting, of locating schools, of legislative representation, of jury service, and, of course, of collecting taxes. Like hens, counties counted their chicks using more appropriate names like *census, voter tabulation*, and *property assessment rolls.*[3]

Once a county was created, then county commissioners, justices-of-the-peace, sheriffs, constables, clerks, and coroners had to be elected. In the early years, political offices were not yet coveted; rather they were meted out.[4] Responsibility, not ambition, was the greater pull. Nevertheless, in the early years of Benton County's roster of elected officials, one may trace the beginnings of a partisan break between north and south Benton County. Joe Avery, John Stewart, Joe Alexander, and Fooks Dixon were north Benton County officials. George Belknap, John Lloyd, Doc Richardson, R.B. Hinton, and Sam Starr were south county. The fracture would widen into a gap that threatened to swallow Nimrod's future.

In the 1840s, no official towns had ever been chartered within Benton County borders. When the territorial government took over in 1849, Governor Joseph P. Lane proclaimed Avery's home at the mouth of Marys River as the courthouse for Benton County judicial business. Unlike mining towns, settlement towns did not spring up overnight. To start a gold town, all that was needed was "several hundred assorted prospectors, a saloon, and a burying preacher." A settlement town in Benton County took more planning and commitment. First, Avery and Dixon donated forty acres from each of their claims for a city, from which grew two blacksmiths, a saloon, grocery, schoolhouse, and assorted offices. Avery named the town "Marysville." Territorial legislators provided the final touch, recognizing it as the county seat in 1851.

The name was logical inasmuch as it was located on Marys River, and also not far from Marys Peak. But Mary Stewart insisted that Avery gave the town her name. That too would have been logical. Mary Stewart was a matriarchal frontier woman, affectionately called "Aunt Polly." Nimrod and Avery had been among her friends since the days of the 1845 wagon train captained by her husband, John Stewart. In the future, Nimrod was destined once again to be under Aunt Polly's roof and order, but this time without choice. There is another possibility for why Avery chose the name Marysville—he had been successful in prospecting for gold near the city of Marysville, California. Two

Marysvilles in the west would confuse postal authorities one day and make the name in Oregon short-lived.

And so it was that prospectors, commerce, sovereigns, towns, counties, and names came and went across Nimrod's mile-wide claim. Surrounded by a whirlpool of uprising, fever, takeover, and shifting divisions, Nimrod and his land stayed put in the vortex.

Notes

1. One story was that certain Cayuses were concerned that Whitman, a doctor, was poisoning sick Cayuses with his medicines. A priest suggested a test—allow Whitman to treat one of the diseased with white man's medicines while the tribal shaman treated another with tribal medicine. Apparently, as chance would have it, Whitman's patient died, the shaman's patient lived. Another incident also fed the fires—a September 1848 *Spectator* news story reported that priests attempted to take into Cayuse country 700 to 800 pounds of gun powder, 1,500 pounds of lead, and three boxes of guns.
2. At "Dwelling House No. 33" (Nimrod's closest neighbor to the north), the census correctly listed "Isaac Winkle of Tennessee" and four others. At "Dwelling House No. 35" (Nimrod's closest neighbor to the south), the census correctly listed "Aaron Richardson of Kentucky" and eight others. Nimrod's cabin was the only dwelling in between.
3. In aid of the work to be done by official counters and tenders and for the convenience of citizens, county borders were often placed one day's round trip horseback ride from a centrally located county seat. Hence, on maps, the uniform size of early rural counties may be seen.
4. In an 1849 election for two Benton County representatives to the territorial legislature, Greenberry Smith and James Mulkey won. About forty votes were cast. One vote went to a "Timothy O'Kelly." Nimrod was the only "O'Kelly" at that time in Benton County. The name *Nim-ro-d* could have been misspelled, or misread as *Tim-o-thy*. Nimrod would not likely have voted for himself. If *Timo* was *Nimro*, it might have been the vote of some wag funning with an election system that was not taken too seriously.

9

The Land Law

1850

The turn into the decade of the 1850s was marked by two critical happenings. The first was the trial of five Cayuse Indians for the 1847 Whitman massacre. Territorial Governor Joe Lane and the Mounted Rifle Regiment brought the suspects from east of the Cascades to be put to white man's justice at Oregon City in the third week of May 1850. Judge Orville C. Pratt made certain that the jury found guilt and then ordered the hanging of all five prisoners. In Judge Pratt's court, justice was swift and rock hard—a callous rigidity Nimrod would have to face one day.

Between the trial and the hangings, Archbishop Francis Norbert Blanchet had baptized the prisoners. Before a crowd of one to two thousand spectators, two Catholic priests accompanied the prisoners to the gallows. And when the trap door rope was cut and the Cayuse fell, a priest called out, "Onward, onward to heaven, children." Before the eyes of avengers, it did Catholics no good to see benevolence given to those convicted of killing Protestant missionaries. It kept alive the suspicion of Catholic involvement in the massacre itself.

Just as bigots are given to excess, so too their foes may over react. From a distance, the eastern press saw Oregon City as "an accursed" and "nasty town," called the settlers "sunk in oblivion" and "born without souls," reported that "nine...including two Catholic Priests...have been convicted and put to death," and observed that the prisoners "were hanged, greatly to the satisfaction of the ladies." If it was not a good time to be a Catholic in Oregon, neither was it a good time to be an Oregonian in the rest of the nation. The rumble from the trial and hangings would have rolled across the *kalapuya* countryside in a matter of days. With it came new kindling for the embers of Catholic-Protestant difference along the Long Tom.

As dramatic as the hangings were, they were not the most exciting news of 1850. Late that year, word reached the Willamette Valley that Congress had finally enacted a land law for the Oregon frontier. It was a fulfillment long in coming—nine years since the first migrant families squatted on Oregon lands, four years since British withdrawal had cleared the way, and two years since the United States had embraced Oregon as a territory.

The delays were wrought by differences over sovereign-versus-citizen entitlements to land—a distinction made difficult, if not feeble, in a democracy where citizens are the sovereign. Throughout the early 1800s, public lands were the nation's purse; the federal government had to resort to the sale of its lands as a chief source of revenue. Somewhere in the second quarter of the 1800s, a land reform movement emerged arguing that it was the natural right of citizens to have the land. By the beginning of the 1840s, the new land reform attitude had gained an upper hand. Marching under that new policy and carrying the banner of manifest destiny, pioneering was encouraged because it served the interests of both citizens and their nation—even though it out-raced orderly land development.

But when the dust of pioneering had settled, the debate was renewed as to what should be done with those who had seized initiative and gone ahead of government takeover, surveying, and auctions. At one extreme were those who urged military ouster of all Oregon claimants and the seizing of all Oregon lands by government force until surveys and sales could be conducted. Oregon's delegate to Congress, Samuel Royal Thurston, reported that this was the position taken by Secretary of War Jefferson Davis and certain military officers in Oregon. Thurston took the lead in urging a more generous and appreciative attitude toward Oregon pioneers. It took no triumph of rhetoric to convince Congress that something special ought to be conferred upon those who had pushed the frontier westward as far as it could go. The real issues then became: Should Oregon pioneers be sold their land claims at a small price, or should those lands be given free of any charge? How much land should Oregon pioneers be allowed to claim? Should a substantial period of use be required as proof of permanent intentions? What personal qualifications should an allowable claimant have? Should the filing and perfecting of private claims be made to wait until completion of a general survey of all public lands in Oregon Territory?

On September 27, 1850, Congress answered those questions in the Oregon Donation Land Claim Act. As soon as copies were available on the frontier, settlers began at once to dissect its words and measure its meanings.

Personal Qualifications of Claimants

Unlike the Oregon Provisional Government land law, the Donation Act placed restrictions on who could be claimants. They had to be eighteen years of age or older if residing in Oregon prior to December 1, 1850; thereafter, age twenty-one was the minimum. That point in time was a key date for many different legal effects throughout the Donation Act. December 1, 1850, distinguished *Old Oregonians* from future Oregonians.[1] The act ushered in a new order while protecting the older reliance and advancement of existing settlers, as well as overlanders currently on the trail in the 1850 migration.

Biases of race, gender, and nationality were set forth in sections four and five of the Donation Act. Claimants had to be, or had to declare intent to become, a United States citizen. This would profoundly affect Nimrod's godfather, Gervais, and many other Canadians claiming at French Prairie and Fort Vancouver. The limitation was one of Oregon delegate Thurston's preferred provisions. He bore no love for the Hudson's Bay Company, Canadians, or anything foreign.

Claimants could be either men or women if they were Old Oregonians. If future Oregonians, only men were allowed to lay claim, but they could lay added claim for their wives, who could hold land in their own right. That wives were allowed to be awarded land titles in that day and age was remarkable. Thurston could take credit for that lobbying; it marked him as forward in some matters, as he was backward in others.

Under section four, Old Oregonian claimants could be either white or half-breed Indians. Under section five, future Oregonians had to be white. The deference allowed to those of mixed racial parents in residence prior to December 1850 was recognition of the many children born to mountain men and their Indian wives. The new law rewarded the contribution of mountain trappers in settling the west, while nonetheless disapproving of their marital acts. It humored their past practice, yet frowned upon any future unions. The white restriction did not go without considerable debate in Congress. Northern senators argued vigorously that black claimants should be authorized. Southern senators argued against. The debate expanded into slavery and racial-mixing oratories that foreshadowed the violence laying just a little over a decade away. But for now, the only compromise reached was the allowance of land claims to French-Indian métis and the offspring of mountain men and traders who made Oregon home before December 1850.

None of the limits on allowable claimants disqualified Nimrod. He was a seventy-year old, white, American male who enjoyed all of the privileges of popular sufferance except one—religion, which Congress by virtue of the First Amendment to the Constitution of the United States could not impose as a qualification. In the Donation Act, age, race, nationality, and gender were limitations—but not religion—not ever—not openly.

While Nimrod's claim so far seemed to be secure under a reading of the new law, his fellow Catholic, John McLoughlin, did not fare as well. Section eleven of the Donation Act expressly targeted McLoughlin's "Oregon City claim" and "Abernathy Island claim"—two highly coveted treasures. In the decade prior to the Donation Act, members of the Methodist mission, Provisional Governor George Abernethy, territorial Chief Justice William Bryant, and territorial Governor Joe Lane were all involved in a systematic encroachment of McLoughlin's earlier claims. Section eleven ended the conflict. In a few strokes of the congressional pen, the city that McLoughlin founded and his valuable island at the foot of Willamette Falls were taken from him. No doubt, Thurston was at the bottom of the usurpation.[2] Successful claim jumping in Oregon had its beginning in the very law enacted to make claim rights secure. Just as Nimrod had followed McLoughlin into religious conversion, so too one day would Nimrod be followed, like McLoughlin, by coveters.

Continuous Occupancy

Provisional Government land law had made no mention of a specific waiting-period requirement. But section four of Congress's Donation Act was more particular; a claimant "shall have resided upon and cultivated...for four successive years" before a land *patent* could be issued.[3] Furthermore, each claimant had to reside in person or by family. Section four of the original act voided all land sales between settlers until the seller had acquired a patent. Thus, the new land law operated to curtail the parceling out of smaller claims from old timers with too much to newcomers with nothing at all. Scarce acres and desperate seekers were not a good situation for the prevention of encroachment.[4]

The required four-year continuous residency was of no bother to Nimrod. Whether he had to wait one year or four years for title made no difference. At life, he may have been a short-timer; but at patience, he was long-suffering. He had nowhere else to go. Little did he suspect that the "four successive years" of expanse would be interrupted with narrows—as shall be seen.

General Survey and Claim Recording

Sections one and two of the act created the office of surveyor general for Oregon. Settlers were not permitted to record their claims until a general survey of the countryside had been mapped. To create the necessary precision for locating borders, section three provided that all of Oregon between the Cascades and the Pacific Ocean would have to be imprinted with a grid system—lines dividing the land into six mile squares called "townships," with each township divided into thirty-six, one-square mile "sections." It was called the "geodetic method" or "rectangular survey system." Its usefulness persists to this day.[5]

It would take the Oregon surveyor general considerable time to walk and mark the section and township grid lines over thousands of square miles in the Willamette Valley. Working south from the mouth of the Willamette River, the surveying teams were destined to take more than two years to reach Nimrod and the Long Tom area. Then and only then, could Nimrod make the trek to Oregon City to record his claim for the second time—this time with the United States government. But, meanwhile, the borders of Nimrod's claim would not be supported by any government record. Prigg's written description in the provisional land claim book had been voided and was now merely a spoor of an earlier Oregon. Until surveying was done, the only borders of Nimrod's claim would be those he had marked and those his neighbors honored. The problem, however, was this. Just as abundance had bred consideration, so too would scarcity breed disrespect.

Land for Free

A most debated issue in the 1850 Congress involved the price for allowable claims. Should public land be given free of charge or should Oregonians be required to pay a customary $1.25 per acre? Only once before, on a small scale, had Congress made any grant of free land. Led by Senator Henry Clay, opponents of free land argued that it promoted land speculation, not land cultivation. Moreover, they saw no reason why Oregonians should be given land free when citizens in other parts of the nation had to pay. Land freely given would add nothing to the public treasury. The federal government could not afford to simply give away its land, especially to speculators who would turn around and sell it at a profit that the government should have reaped in the first place.

Proponents of free land included the Free Soil Party, labor leaders, Horace Greeley of the *New York Tribune*, and, of course, Oregon settlers led by their non-voting congressional delegate, Samuel R. Thurston. They argued fairness. Ten thousand pioneers were already in place on the Oregon frontier. Lured by the promise of free land, they had journeyed two thousand miles over rugged terrain and settled on claims given by their own Provisional Government—a makeshift regime that yielded gladly to the United States. Moreover, unlike the recent winning of Texas, Oregon had been taken without a single saber drawn. Besides, as naval Lieutenant Neil Howison reported, to require payment for the land was senseless because Oregon patriots had no money to pay, and, even if they did, they would not buy what was already paid for with sacrifice.

As is the legislative way, a compromise was reached. The act provided that the land given in Oregon would be free, but only for a short while. Free land would extend to all Old Oregonians, and to those who came in the next three annual migrations: 1851, 1852, and 1853. An 1853 amendment would dangle the carrot for another two migrations: 1854 and 1855. After 1855, there would be no more free land for squatters. Nimrod was unaffected by these deadlines. He had already bit into the carrot. One trouble remained: How much of the carrot was he allowed to swallow? On that issue, Nimrod was about to receive a harsh awakening.

Size of the Claim

The final, heavily debated question for Congress was: What should be the maximum size of an Oregon land claim? Under the 1841 Preemption Act, squatters in the rest of the nation could claim 160 acres—one-quarter of a square mile. Under the Provisional Government land law, an Oregon settler, whether married or single, could claim 640 acres—one full square mile. The debate swung between those margins. Proponents of 640 acres keyed their arguments to need and use. They urged that farming and grazing were the work to which Oregon land would be put. Large acreage was needed for pasture and livable yield.

Although Horace Greeley was a land reformist who favored free soil, he adamantly opposed grants larger than 160 acres. He argued that 640 acres were simply too much for tending. Worse, large grants would spread the population too broadly, making schooling and other community services too difficult and expensive. Unlike Thomas Jefferson, who had envisioned the frontier as fields and barns, Greeley saw it as streets and shops. Others, who joined Greeley, further argued that large holdings were a greed that fostered sloth and inefficiency. Further still, grants of one square mile would quickly devour the best lands. Generosity might fill the bellies of those settled in, but would starve the immigrants.

Once again the congressional answer was to yield to both sides. Congress decided to keep faith with past practice in Oregon by giving one square mile to Old Oregonian couples. But to all couples arriving after December 1, 1850, only one-half of a square mile would be allowed.

Nimrod had a problem. To be sure, he was an Old Oregonian, but by all appearances he was also a single man. Under the provisional land law, Nimrod had been entitled to 640 acres whether single or wed. Under the new Donation Act only a married couple was entitled to 640 acres–320 acres to each spouse—whereas a bachelor or widower was entitled only 320 acres. Nimrod's claim was in jeopardy. The rules had changed. Only half of the claim he had staked back in 1846 was his. The other half belonged to a wife, if he truly had one. If he did not have a wife, then the 1850 congressional pen took 320 acres from him.

Notes

1. See note 1 in Chapter 2.
2. Section eleven was the special handiwork of delegate Thurston. He drafted the provision without formal instruction to do so from Oregon authorities. Thurston had been elected to the congressional delegate position with the help of Abernethy and certain Methodist political leaders. The financial interests of Abernethy, Bryant, and Lane in the island contest were clear. Thurston's interests ran deeper and were more insidious; his strong hostility toward McLoughlin was a well-known bias.
3. Land title transfers between people were embodied on a document called an "indenture"—modernly called a "deed." When government transfers title to land, the document is called a "patent." Land may be what settlers wanted, but, in law, a title paper was what they had to have.
4. The ban on claim sales proved unworkable and was repealed by an 1853 amendment to the Donation Act—but not in time to stop a rush of envy and overstepping.
5. See Figure No. Four, "Southern Benton County Topography," 1852–53, in Chapter 20.

10

Letters to Washington City

1851–52

Faced with what he called "calamity," Nimrod scratched a letter of petition to the men of Congress. It was in his usual clear and bold hand, and dated August 30, 1851. Calling himself a "memorialist," Nimrod began with a cargo of toady courtesies typical of the day:

> Hon sirs will this honorable body condescend to take my humble request in to consideration and do for me in this calamity what will seem to be Justice and equity to the eyes of a candid world.[1]

He then proceeded to explain that he had arrived in Oregon in late 1845, had come "with the intention of exploring," had "surveyed and recorded" a claim in 1846, and had "occupied the same all that time until the present time." He informed Congress of the family he "left…in the states…a large family a wife and 9 children." This brought him to his concerns about the Donation Act.

> The land law for oregon is so abstruse that the most sapient men in oregon have conflicting opinions among them wether I can hold my full section of land or not as my family cannot get to oregon before the time specified in the law for single men to be married in order to be able to hold a full section of land.

The problem was this: Section four of the Donation Act allowed a married settler "now residing" to claim "six hundred and forty acres, one half to himself and the other half to his wife." Nowhere did it say whether the wife also had to be residing in Oregon. Could Nimrod hold 320 acres on behalf of his non-resident and mysterious wife? Would her claim, if she existed and came to Oregon, be limited to 160 acres because her residency would commence after December 1, 1850? Not even "the most sapient" could agree on an answer. The letter concluded with a plea to grant a 640-acre section of land. J.C. Avery and Alfred Rinehart signed as verifiers.

One thing was certain: In order for Nimrod to eventually perfect a claim to 640 acres, he would have to have a wife in Oregon. Under the provisional land law, no one cared whether he was married or not. But now, a spouse was crucial. With open land becoming scarcer in the Valley, many began to take seriously the question of Nimrod's marital status. Sensing that Congress might have the same concern, Nimrod's letter to Congress reported that he had written

> to my family to come to me and I wrote every possible chance but they recived no letters from me until february 1850 and the letter had been writen very near 4 years before they got it. I recived no letters from them until november 1850. Since that time I have recived several letters. They write to me that they cannot get ready to come to this country before 1852.

A four-year delay in mail service between the Oregon Long Tom and the Missouri Ozarks was but one sign of the many troubles in frontier mail service. On July 7, 1850, the *Spectator* had reported difficulties in getting riders to run mail on postal routes. In that same issue, the newspaper published a list of dead letters lying unclaimed in the Oregon City post office. One of them was addressed to "Nimrod O. Kelly." Without a general survey and designated townships, Nimrod was a needle in a vast territorial haystack. The post office threatened to return the letter to the sender if it was not picked up in the next three months.

Was this the same letter that Nimrod told Congress he had received in November 1850? Or had it been returned to the east? Whoever was writing did not know Nimrod's whereabouts. If the dead letter to Nimrod had specified "Benton County" or "the Long Tom" or "Marys River" or "Marysville," it could have been forwarded to either Joe Avery or John Lloyd, whose homes in 1850 had been designated as the first postal stations in Benton County—one in north county and one in south county. But new postal stations would do no good if senders did not know those new addresses.

In what would later become a crucial letter, dated March 28, 1852, the address was "To Mr. Nimrod O. Kelley, Origan Sitty Origan teritory via New orleanes san fransisco." It contained a plea to Nimrod:

> I want you to Direct me where to send my Letters whether to marysville or to…origan sity you maile your Letters marysville Benton County, I shall write to origan sity & till you Direct me other wise.

Three months after Nimrod wrote Congress, he made a second plea, this time to Joe Lane in Washington City. Lane had resigned as Oregon Territory's first governor and had replaced the late Samuel Royal Thurston as Oregon's delegate to Congress. On December 5, 1851, Nimrod wrote Lane about a different kind of land claim—a pension bounty claim for his alleged military service in the War of 1812. He claimed to have been "drafted" in Tennessee in "the first days of september 1814 and mustered out 3d or 23d of May 1815."

He argued that his nation's call to arms had proved to be an extreme, personal hardship.

> I was a newcomer in tennessee a total stranger. I had to leave my wife & one child with strangers. I was gon from them about 9 months. When I returned home what little property I had was all destroyed. I lost a horse that give $150 dollars for & many other things & it was very near 3 years after I was mustered out of service before I drew my monthley pay…This has caused me to be poor & behind-hand now & for many years past.

Accordingly, he urged Lane to get the nation to give him a veteran's pension in the form of a half section, or 160 acres, or 80 acres, or "whatever they giv me will be thankfully received." These acres were in addition to the one square mile he already staked and would "join my donation claim on my south line." It was audacious, to be sure, to beseech for trust in a represented service that allegedly happened in a war whose records were obscured by four decades. Nimrod attempted to justify the delay in his request: "I never asked the government to remunerate me but now I am geting aged & and not able to labor"

Before closing his letter to Lane, Nimrod took aim at a couple of his neighbors—encroachers masked in smiles.

> My adversaries old Dr. richerdson & winkel has com to my hous & offerd me their hands for friendship with a promise to not envy me any more…It is only pretense for I understand that the old Dr. has been coaxing several persons to build a small house on the land that I have designated for my pension & he has offered to give them an undamnified bond & says that they will write on to you not to do anything for me in geting land for my pension…There is 8 or 10 much better places in 2 miles of the same place. It appears to pain them to the heart when they think I will draw a pension of land.

Congressional delegate Lane's response followed procedure. He sent forms to be filled out. Nimrod called them "the blanks…sent to me to fill up and send back." On June 4, 1852, Nimrod wrote back to Lane and thanked him for "your kindness & generosity," for "the papers you sent to me respecting my pension land," and for "the great pains to fix my land papers for me."

But, alas, Nimrod had to report that he no longer had the papers. He had kept the papers in his cabin "upon some boards a considerable hight from the ground" and "had a large bunch of hay on them." He did not have them in a jar because he was not worried about critters. "Ther was no mice or rats about the house," because "I had plenty of cats." His care in putting the papers high and under hay was on account of a concern for bigger intruders. He was not really storing the papers; he was hiding them.

As soon as it was known that I was to get pension land the ferocity and ambition of the hold neighborhood was set in motion against me…my hous was brok open and my papers taken out of or destroyed.

Nimrod's attempt at a war veteran's bounty claim had been sidetracked. Whether he would ever be able to get back on its path was a plan made dubious by events near to come. His troubles were not with a government at the far side of the continent any more. Now his troubles were with what was right outside of his door.

Note

1. This is the earliest known record of Nimrod's penmanship. His grammar, punctuation, spelling, and diction belie extensive formal training and suggest that he was largely self-taught. He simply did not use capital letters. Proper names were always lower case. The only exceptions to that were "God" and the pronoun "I." Lower case included his own name, "o kelly." His signature was also an exception; there he used capitals, "Nimrod O. Kelly." His signature was the only place that he used a period. He did not punctuate the end of sentences nor the end of abbreviations. In fact, he used no punctuation of any kind anywhere—no commas, no question marks, no colons, no apostrophes, no periods. Only the content of what he had to say marked the end of a thought and the beginning of another. Likewise, paragraphing was an unused tool. Throughout this book in his quoted writings, the breaks between perceived sentences have been supplied with periods and capital letters. It is the only punctuation added, and the reader should be aware that Nimrod's original words show no breathing space for exhaling an old thought and inhaling a new one.

11

Crowding and Killing
1850–52

In the summer of 1850, the United States canvassed the nation with its seventh census—the first for Oregon. It showed the population in Oregon Territory to be about 11,500 pioneer settlers. These were the Old Oregonians.[1] The migrations of 1851 through 1855 were destined to expand the population to 40,000. Thus, by the mid-1850s, for every one Old Oregonian, there would be three newcomers who were entitled to only half as much land.

The new land law and the Forty-niner gold rush poured people and gold into the Oregon economy. Bolstered by an influx of demand and supply, Old Oregonians went forward with more permanent building. Logs and poles gave way to frames with lumbered siding. Crops, herds, and market places grew. The new migrants had it different. Ragged, bedraggled, and short on meat, flour, beans, thread, leather, powder, money, and patience, they stood out like flour-sack patches on a gingham dress.

Old Oregonians had faced that struggle, but the end had been awarded with vast abundance. The new immigrants faced scarcity. Pettiness grew where hospitality had been. Keepers held fast to what seekers envied—an old standoff in a new land. The new families were frustrated, not only by the lack of vacant land, but also by the waste of it. Inefficient staking produced a patchwork that did not mesh. Claims that did not abut left zigzags, gaps, and slivers of vacant soil too long, too narrow, or too bent for cultivation. Furthermore, the absence of a government survey made claim borders indistinct. Extravagant and inexact boundaries, coupled with desperation and scarcity, was a situation ripe for claim jumping. To counter that potential, Old Oregonians organized informal associations against land grabbers.

Nimrod was hard to fit into either faction. To be sure, he was an Old Oregonian. But in purse, roof, and borders, he was beggared. His temporary cabin and field showed no improvement—perhaps because, like his neighbors, he was beginning to suspect that his family would never join him and because permanent-versus-temporary was a difference of little measure to a man waiting alone in final years.

Most of the new immigrants moved up through the Valley to find their homes in southern Oregon. By January 1851, that influx south caused Lane and Umpqua counties to be carved out of Benton County. Nimrod's cabin remained in Benton County, but the new Lane County border lay just seven miles south.[2] To aid the expansion into southern Oregon, a second road took shape on the east side of the Willamette River and joined the Gold Mine Road just twenty-five miles south of Nimrod's claim. An even bigger door to the south was opened in the autumn of 1851 when steamboat travel finally extended up the Willamette River as far as Marysville. Further atraction to Benton County came when, on June 20, 1851, the Bellfountain Methodists held a large camp meeting that brought Methodists and other Protestants from all over the territory to Nimrod's backyard. Methodist camp meetings could bring as many as five hundred or more in attendance. The advance of society magnified Nimrod's retreat. He was still the only Catholic in south Benton County, and the Catholic Church had yet to extend its mission into those outlands.

The surest sign that a civilization was growing on the *kalapuya* was another culture waning. Neither the term *Old Oregonian,* the federal census, nor the Donation Land Act included Indians. To ignore them was also to ignore the United States' own laws. The Northwest Ordinance of 1787 affirmed the absolute rights of Indians in their own lands.

> The utmost good faith shall be observed toward the Indians; their lands and properties shall never be taken from them without their consent; and in their property, rights and liberty, they shall never be invaded or disturbed, unless in just and lawful wars authorized by Congress.

That language was repeated verbatim in the Organic Law of Oregon's Provisional Government and in the 1848 Act creating Oregon Territory. Moreover, Chief Justice John Marshall of the U.S. Supreme Court, in *Johnson v. McIntosh* (1823), had ruled that citizens were not entitled to enter and stake Indian lands, unless there was a Senate ratification of purchase or a congressional declaration of war.

Nevertheless, against this background of respect for prior rights, the Oregon Donation Land Claim Act dangled the carrot of trespass. Congress and the president saw the inconsistency and appointed commissioners to negotiate purchases of tribal lands in Oregon. In the spring of 1851, agents set up bargaining tables at Champoeg on French Prairie. One by one, various bands of the Calapooya and Molalla nations rode to those fields to make *huyhuy wawa*—trade and talk.

The concept of parceling lands was as traditional to the one culture as it was foreign to the other. Chief Joseph (*Hinmaton-yalatkit*), a great Nez Perce leader of the eastern Columbia plateau in the 1870s, is said to have put it this way:

> The earth was created by the assistance of the sun, and it should be left as it was…[T]he country was made without lines of demarcation, and it is no man's business to divide it…I never said the land was mine to do with it as I choose. The one who has the right to dispose of it is the one who has created it. I claim a right to live on my land, and accord you the privilege to live on yours.[3]

Eventually, U.S. agents struck six bargains with the tribal bands represented. The tribes agreed to cede a vast portion of the Valley to white settlement and to limit their hunts to six areas reserved for them. An 1851 map sketched by George Gibbs and E.A. Stadling, done without benefit of any official survey, attempted to show prospective settlers the "purchases" for settlement and the "reservations" for the tribes.[4] But, having smoked the pipe of accord, it came to nothing. Not one bit of it was put to law. Bargaining took place on Indian ground where the Indian commitment came first and without strings attached, but United States commitment was conditioned upon ratification by the Senate back east. Having the privilege of the serpent's tongue, government headmen chose to disagree with their own agents. The deal was off. The Indian nations received nothing; and white migration, lured by the bait of government donation, continued to steal Valley lands in spite of vows that those lands "shall never be taken," and "shall never be invaded or disturbed."

Nimrod and the Indians shared a common trouble—white settlers came as does the bear, having no respect for camp, scent, or stakes.

Like a mule in mire, Nimrod stayed put, as he and his claim sank deeper into settlement. Back in 1847 and 1848, he had seen the Doc Richardson and the Isaac Winkle families stake down along the trail just miles to the north and south of him. Those pressures were but a small beginning. In the spring of 1850, the smoke of another new cabin rose off to the northwest. The southeast corner stake of that claim was just one mile from Nimrod's line. The new neighbors were John and Cynthia Fiechter.

Without a general land survey or fencing, only the neighbors could point out the difference between claimed and vacant land:

Yes sir, Lloyd's corner is set close to that large maple on the butte yonder.

No sir, that bottomland would be on the Belknap spread.

What's untook in these parts is what meanders along the banks of Muddy Creek—most all poison oak and takes to flood come spring.

That nigh is saved up for our schoolmaster.

On up the road yonder, another half day's ride, is the new County of Lane—tolerable pickings in there.

Immigrants searched not only for good soil, water, and trees—they also needed welcome. Just as they would not stake where they did not want, they would not stake where they were not wanted. The Fiechters were welcome. Cynthia was the daughter of Justice of the Peace Abiather Newton, a Methodist leader. They became Bellfountain Methodists.

In the spring of 1851, a new staking was laid between the claims of Nimrod and Isaac Winkle. Its cabin came the closest yet to Nimrod and belonged to Isaac's son, Wiley Winkle. At the young age of twenty-three, Wiley was nonetheless an *Old Oregonian*. To claim a full 640-acre section, Wiley married. Under the new land law, the purchase price for an extra 320 acres was simply a spouse. Abiather Newton made the same arrangement when he gave the hand of his sixteen-year old daughter, Cynthia, in marriage to John Fiechter.[5] Land owner wives were not limited by any minimum age, whereas the husbands had to be eighteen or twenty-one years of age. It was not unusual to see wives of twelve years, who, consequently, became grandmothers in their late twenties. In one case, it is said, a wife was four years old. The nuptials were holy—and good business.

Next to come were two single men—the Barclay brothers. William was forty-six and James twenty-four. William's wife died on the Overland Trail leaving him with seven young children to attend. James was a bachelor, with the middle name Eusibius, so he was "Uncle Sib." The Barclay brothers had arrived in the 1850 migration, and, therefore, were entitled to 320 acres each, even though they were unmarried and did not stake until the summer of 1851. They staked alongside of one another just one-half mile south of Nimrod's cabin door.

Richard Irwin also came that same summer and staked a claim just west of Isaac Winkle. The Irwins and Winkles joined in more than a boundary; they joined in company as well. Their doors were right across the road from one another. Irwin was born in Ireland. He soon erected a store on his claim, and by the spring of 1852 the store became a post office, called *Jennyopolis*. It formed a cracker-barreled, pot-belly-stoved, stoop-sitting center for news and talk about rain, crops, Indians, and, of course, one another. Likely, the jawing would sooner or later drift toward that ornery, menacing, old Papist living all alone up the road a few miles on land poorly tended and with borders far beyond what he could use and what he could rightfully claim.

If the Fiechter, Winkle, Barclay, and Irwin stakings disturbed Nimrod, then what came next would have surely put fat to his fires. Robert D. Grimsley was only a nineteen-year-old snippersnapper. Had he been a new immigrant, he would not have been allowed to make a claim at that age. But he had arrived in Oregon in 1847 with his parents; thus he was allowed to claim when he reached age eighteen. He married Isaac Winkle's daughter, Gilla Ann, in March 1851, and staked his claim four months later right at Nimrod's north border. The Isaac Winkle clan was spreading south. Much later on, Montgomery Winkle, Isaac's youngest son, would also file a claim at Nimrod's border. But, for now, the furrow in Nimrod's brow deepened when he saw where Grimsley built his cabin. According to Nimrod, the cabin overlapped his northeast corner, and his stakes had been removed. Without benefit of a survey, neither Grimsley nor Nimrod could be sure of precise borders. Was Grimsley a claim jumper, or was Nimrod a claim hog? Apparently, they decided to let the matter simmer until the general survey came along to sort everything out.

It would be a long wait. Surveyor General John B. Preston started the Valley survey on June 4, 1851. About one month before Grimsley staked his claim, Preston drove in a different stake near Portland. That cedar stake was the central reference point to which all surveys had to relate—the starting point for blanketing the Valley and beyond. Later on, the stake was made a monument called the "Willamette Stone," which stands today as the cynosure for all land descriptions in the entire Pacific Northwest.

Eight months later, on February 18, 1852, Joseph M. Blackerby of Marion County was the first in line to file a donation land claim at the Oregon City surveyor general's office. This meant the survey work had progressed about forty survey miles up the Valley in those eight months. The survey teams were halfway to the Long Tom area. It would take another eight or nine months to reach the disputed Grimsley-O'Kelly boundary. And so, in the interim, claim seekers and claim holders were separated by fences, fields, cabins, stakes, blazes, cairns, ditches, and paper descriptions tacked to trees. Everyone struggled to be accurate. No one wanted to have come two thousand miles and spend years cultivating a plot of land only to have it taken away by lagging surveyors. In that need to be right, neighborly respect—boundary reputation—was almost as valuable as a deed.

But talk on the Jennyopolis store stoop about Nimrod was not neighborly. The feelings were mutual. His early pioneering and veneration might give him some respect, but it would never give him extra land. If he was not married, why was he taking so many acres? If he was married, why was his wife not at his side? If he had deserted his family, why did he not pull back to a half-section? He had been on this prairie for six years without building a cabin fit for a family and without having cultivated his acres to full use. And to top it off, he was now claiming an added number of acres for what he called a pension bounty for alleged troopering in the War of 1812—a war fought forty years ago.

Such talk fed upon itself and outgrew the facts. At first, Irwin said that the old man claimed one and one-half sections—one square mile under the Donation Act plus one-half square mile as a soldier's pension. That gossip may have been triggered by Nimrod's flaunting the bounty pension forms sent to him by Joe Lane. Swagger would have put saddle to quarrel and spurs to rumor. Mites turned to monsters. Irwin got carried away and, later on, wrote that Nimrod's land was a "six mile claim." Others said Nimrod "claimed eight miles one way." The *Statesman* reported that Nimrod claimed "six sections"—one-sixth of an entire township—3,840 acres.

The *Oregon Spectator* at Oregon City was in its fifth year when, in 1850–51, it was joined by three Willamette Valley competitors. The first was the *Western Star*, later to become the *Oregon Weekly Times*. Then in December 1850 came the *Oregonian* out of Portland, and, four months later, the *Oregon Statesman* out of Oregon City. Partisan politics soon ripened on the Oregon frontier; and the *Oregonian* and *Statesman* took the lead as political rivals. Joe Avery at Marysville became the local sales outlet for the early quartet of journalism. Nimrod may have drawn upon his friendship with Avery in order to become a regular reader of back issues. Little did Nimrod know that he soon would be in the news himself.

Early in 1852 after winter's thaw, two more families came up the road from Oregon City. The first was Jeremiah and Elizabeth Criss, followed two months later by Asa and Deborah Stark. The Starks had been married thirty-five years; the Crisses, twenty-eight years. They were the stuff of which upright neighbors were made. When they reached Irwin's store at Jennyopolis, those on the stoop might have encouraged them with directions telling of free land just two miles up the road, between the Barclay claims and the shanty of an old, bachelor hermit. They may have advised that the old loner *don't mark up too clear and ain't too friendly about it, but don't fret over him none.*

Of course, there is no way to know exactly what the newcomers were told; but whatever may have been said, Criss and Stark squeezed their claims into that spot. They each staked 320 acres, and the north of their acreages cut deep into the southwest corner of Nimrod's square mile.[6] Nimrod's corner stake was either decayed or ignored. More certain was the fact that his boundary reputation was both decayed and ignored. In his June 4, 1852, letter to delegate Joe Lane, Nimrod reported:

> I dare not leave home only of a night when no one did know it. I knew they would burn my house and swear that I had no residence…I keep myself close at home for fear of getting into a fray…I knew that my house has been rifled each day…I saw so much ploting and schemes laid against me.

Nimrod now had three intruders making hay of his claim from the north and south, and that stacked the rick for a final straw.

Not much is known about Jeremiah and Mary Jane Mahoney. They came into the Long Tom and did not last long. They were a young couple with a baby. Nimrod called Jeremiah "the irishman" and "the oringman." Perhaps the Mahoneys knew Irwin, who was also Irish born. About April 1, 1852, the Mahoneys unhitched their wagon on the northwest portion of Nimrod's claim. It was the deepest cut of all. Their camp was within one-half mile of Nimrod's bed and almost dead center on his claim.

In his outcast state, Nimrod held to the belief that the Irishman had been deliberately brought to the Long Tom to challenge him. Nimrod wrote that Mahoney was "the bully for all of the rest and had been selected as the proper person to run me off my claim." Nimrod further described Mahoney's behavior to Lane:

> The party that has been formed against me for 2 or 3 years was joind by an raw irish man. He was very stern and resolut against me because he was abetted by the hold neighborhood. He came and settled on my land near the corner of my field and he would com about my house almost every day and vilifie me for holding a full claim…me an old no count man without a family. I saw design in him of some sort but could not tell what…This irish man came more frequent about my house. I told him that he must and should keep away from about my house. He told me that he would go where he pleased to go in defiance of all that I could do or say…I did not like the movements of the irishman. He was an oringman and he knew that I was a catholic.

An *orangeman* referred to the Loyal Orange Institution, formed in 1795 largely by Protestant Scottish immigrants in northern Ireland. Orangemen championed Protestant ascendancy over Ireland's native Catholic population, particularly in Ulster.[7] How Nimrod was aware of this is not certain. Nimrod was not born or raised in Ireland. Did Oregon Catholics school him on the

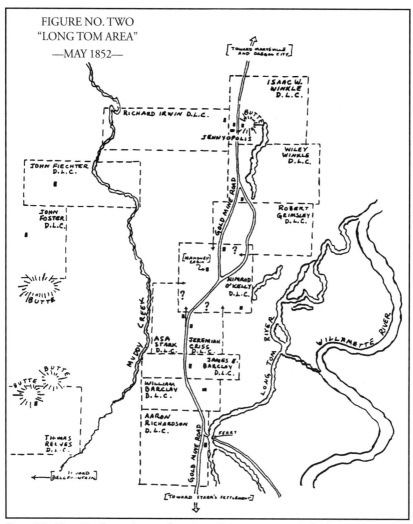

Figure No. Two. Hand-traced copy of portions of the surveyor general's claims maps (1861) and topographical maps (1852–53) of the Jennyopolis and Starrs Point townships. The borders of the donation land claims (D.L.C.) here depicted were not officially known in May 1852. They were straightened and made exact in 1861. They approximate, however, the more inexact, squatter-staked lines as of 1852.

subject? The internal conflicts of Ireland carried across the Atlantic with the mass migrations wrought by Ireland's potato famine of 1845–48.

On the other side of the ledger, Irwin, the Irish-born, Jennyopolis postmaster, gave Mahoney good marks, characterizing him as, "Not a quarrelsome man…but to the contra—a quiet Peaceable citizen. Guilty only of the crime of Poverty & Good Nature."

With Mahoney scouring the countryside for cabin poles and Nimrod out hunting crows and tending his home field, the two crossed paths frequently. Nimrod wrote, "This Irishman…would threaten me every time I would meet with him." But Irwin and neighbor Isaac Winkle wrote it was Mahoney who took "the constant abuse of Okelly dayly." According to Irwin and Winkle, when they warned Mahoney to be careful, Mahoney said, "the old man would not shoot," and that he "would talk him into good nature bye & bye."

Nimrod said that he simply told the Irishman "to keep off of my claim." But young Tom Richardson stated that Nimrod's command went beyond that. According to young Tom, Nimrod told Tom to pass along to Missus Mahoney an order to "move away" or else they would not "live in Peace & Happiness hereafter." Likewise, Jeremiah Criss claimed Nimrod's admonition was joined by threat.

From all of this, one curiosity surfaces: With land available farther up the Valley and with all of the tension at the present site, why would Mahoney risk his donation land claim rewards and the future of his wife and baby on a choice wrapped in doubt? As Samuel A. Clarke noted: "it is not easy to excuse a man setting up any doubtful claim over which he might waste years and lose the chance to secure a good donation." Who or what induced Mahoney to leave the road well taken?

Apparently, Mahoney was "breed up a Catholic," but had denied that faith. According to Nimrod, Mahoney had prodded Nimrod to denounce Catholicism, as he, Mahoney, had done. The situation could not have been worse—two devout converts headed in opposite directions, now face to face on rival claims. This ice crackled and gave way on Friday, May 21, 1852. Theodore Talbot described that spring season as "cold with incessant rains…May Day was dreary and stormy." It was weather fit to shadow minds.

The only firsthand account of what happened on that Friday is the declaration of Nimrod O'Kelly filed with the clerk of the court on June 3. According to that declaration, Nimrod was out hunting crows on his claim when he and Mahoney passed within a few steps of each other without speaking. Nimrod thereupon went home and got his horse in order to do some "ploughing" at his field. Later, they met again near Nimrod's house. Mahoney came toward the house and stopped about ten steps from Nimrod. "What are you always carrying that gun for?" Mahoney asked.

"None of your business," said Nimrod, "It's my own."

Mahoney continued coming toward Nimrod saying, "If you don't mind, you'll get that gun thrashed over your head."

Nimrod said, "Stand off" and stepped out of Mahoney's path. But then Mahoney got out of the path also and began "sidling up towards me in a stooped position." While Mahoney was still far enough off that he could not get hold of the shotgun, it went off while in Nimrod's hands. Nimrod had "no recollection of ever cocking the gun but held her down at arm's length."

Mahoney sat. Nimrod moved off. Then Mahoney "lay down." Life ended. Big trouble began.

Notes

1. See note 1 in Chapter 2.
2. See Figure No. Four, "Southern Benton County Topography," 1852–53, in Chapter 20.
3. The name *Hinmaton-yalatkit* in English means *Thunder rising in the mountains to loftier heights*. Missionaries gave him the name Joseph the Younger. We know him simply as *Chief Joseph*.
4. The borders of the Gibbs and Stadling map of 1851 (see Figure No. One in Chapter 3) were called "approximations." For a while, the map may have been helpful in keeping the tribes and settlers apart. Many Indians sought those sanctuaries, and many settlers gave berth. But the bounds were short lived, and soon were no more effective at keeping Indians *in* than they were at keeping settlers *out*. Land was becoming too scarce in the Valley, and forage and hunt was a way of life too old to be ended by a map of "approximations." Oregon Superintendent of Indian Affairs Anson Dart estimated that there were about 1,000 Indians in the Valley, of which 560 were Calapooyans and 123 Molallas. The rest would have been Klickitats. In the decade before white settlers arrived, the Klickitats of the eastern Cascades had come from north of the Columbia River down into the Valley. Their presence in the Valley, but yet absent from the bargains, raised serious questions about the negotiations. Not only were the Klickitats excluded, so too were other Calapooya bands, who may not have been represented by the headmen of the bands who came to Champoeg. Reportedly, there were Chemeketa, Ahantchuyuk, Yoncalla, and other unrepresented bands; in Nimrod's area—ceded by the Luckiamute band—there were a Chepenefa or Mary's River band, a Chemapho or Muddy Creek band, and a Chelmela or Long Tom band. The six treaties called for the transfer of more than one-half of the Willamette Valley in exchange for the usual blankets, clothes, tools, domestic animals, services, and small amounts of money and weapons. Some put the exchange at about two or three cents per acre.
5. To make amends to his young daughter, Abiather designed and built a large, two-story, frame house for her less than two miles from Nimrod's northwest corner. As a nationally registered historic place, located in the William L. Finley National Wildlife Refuge, the house still stands today—testament to the old business of child brides for land.
6. In addition to Figure No. Two, "Long Tom Area," May 1852, see also Figure No. Six, "L.A. Davis Survey," 1859, in Chapter 29.
7. The group named itself after William III, Prince of Orange, the Protestant ruler of England and Holland (1688–1702), who had ruthlessly subjugated Catholics in Ireland and Scotland.

Peace Justice Court

May 1852

Abiather Newton could have heard the distant plod of horse hooves approaching his home. From the window, he could see a stranger legging up the trail with his horse on a lead. The man was tall and imposing with a full gray beard. His long stride belied his weathered years. His clothes had not seen a needle in some time. As the man grew closer, Abiather recognized him to be that strange recluse from the new Jennyopolis area not far from the house he had built for his daughter, Cynthia Fiechter. Abiather may have skipped a heartbeat and his wife, Rachel, may have dropped a stitch when they saw that the old man was carrying a double-barreled shotgun. Pulse and needle steadied, however, when the old man politely set the gun against the fence before coming up to the porch.

At the door, the stranger would have stated his business short and to the point.

You the peace justice for these parts?

Yes. I'm Abiather Newton. Who might you be?

Nimrod O'Kelly. I shot and killed a man. Yesterday. On my claim. South of here fifteen miles. There's the gun. I'm turning myself over.

Abiather would have taken a few moments to collect himself. O'Kelly looked too menacing to be a joker. Abiather would have been at a loss for what to do. No one had been murdered in Benton County before. He was not an enforcer of the law. He was a proclaimer of the law—a justice of the peace. He did not make arrests. He wore no star. He had been in office for only nine months, and this would be his first homicide case. So, apparently, he told Nimrod to go back into Marysville and wait there at some designated place.

After Nimrod departed, Abiather took the gun from the fence where Nimrod had left it; one barrel had been fired and was still empty. The other barrel was loaded with shot and slugs. He had a confessed killer and the weapon. But he also needed a corpse. Now what? He went to his well-used copy of the Twenty Acts—a compilation of Oregon laws. It was Saturday, May 22, 1852.

Some hours after Nimrod left, Abiather was visited by Lewis Dennis and Sheriff Samuel F. Starr. They too had a murder to report. Jeremiah Mahoney had been shot and killed. Two killings to deal with! For this second one, he had a corpse, but no killer. The two came together quickly, however, when his visitors reported that a coroner's jury earlier that same day had found Nimrod O'Kelly to be the prime suspect.

The exact sequence of events that unfolded at Abiather's home on that Saturday is uncertain. More than likely, Nimrod arrived long before the sheriff. Nimrod had a twenty-four hour head start. In his written declaration of events, Nimrod stated that following the shooting, "I come down to town directly…and give myself up to the proper officer." He had to come a mere twelve miles to Marysville. Abiather's place was another three or four miles west of Marysville. In 1852, there were no government buildings in Benton County. Abiather's office was his home. So Nimrod would have been delayed somewhat by a search for the proper official to take his surrender.[1]

Nevertheless, if he would have come "directly," why did it take twenty-four hours to travel fifteen miles, even allowing extra time for ferreting out the peace justice? Where had Nimrod spent the night? Subsequent reports told the story. On Friday, immediately after the killing, Nimrod's flight north took him to a friendly face—Greenberry Smith. Greenberry's place was ten miles north of Marysville. Greenberry advised Nimrod to "go back and turn yourself in." Nimrod returned to Marysville, and sometime on Saturday had a talk with William Fooks Dixon about the killing. It is not known whether that visit with Dixon was before or after Nimrod reported to the peace justice. It is possible that Dixon or Greenberry had joined Nimrod on his trip to Abiather Newton's home.

When Lewis Dennis and Sheriff Starr told Abiather that a coroner's inquest had already been held, and that the coroner had issued a warrant to arrest Nimrod,[2] Abiather would have been puzzled, if not downright annoyed. *Under what legal authority had this inquest taken place? Who was the coroner? How did this so-called "coroner" get power to issue an arrest warrant? Where was this arrest warrant and the "coroner's" written report as required by law?* The sheriff and Dennis would have told Abiather that the coroner was Richard Irwin, who owned the Jennyopolis store; that Irwin had not yet written any report; and that the sheriff did not have an arrest warrant because it had been entrusted to deputy Isaac Winkle.

How did Irwin get to be coroner? Perhaps, the answer ventured was that it was fitting that victim, suspect, and coroner ought all be fellow country-men. Irwin and the deceased Mahoney were both born in Ireland, and it was thought, erroneously, that O'Kelly was also a native of that isle. Besides, Irwin was the storekeeper and postmaster at nearby Jennyopolis.

Who made Irwin a coroner? Answer: R.B. Hinton had appointed Irwin and had given him the coroner's oath.

But why in the world was Hinton taking it on himself to go around appointing coroners? Who gave him that power? Answer: Hinton had the authority because he was a justice of the peace.

But he was not! Since last September, Hinton ceased to be the justice of the peace for that precinct. Abiather knew this because Abiather was the replacement. Hinton must have known this. Sheriff Starr must have known this. Why else would the sheriff have come to Abiather to make this report? Then too, even if Hinton were a peace justice, he had no power to appoint coroners. There being no previous killings, the fledgling county had not yet got around to electing a county coroner. When a coroner was not available, a magistrate was to do the coroner's job. The Twenty Acts made that clear in Section 16 of the "Coroners" chapter. The folks in south county seemed to be making their own laws. Most irregular; but then too, all quite new. Along with homicide, the technicalities of homicide law had now come to Benton County. The murderous act, the inquiry into it, the trial of it, and the pun-ishment for it were all serious business. Careful step by step following of the Twenty Acts was called for.

The Twenty Acts was the Oregon frontier's law book. Abiather's copy would have been a lop-eared handful of loose pages stuck in a folder and wrapped by ribbon. Its 180 pages were unbound sheets because there were no bookbinders in Oregon. Two hundred copies had been printed in the summer of 1850. Every government officer should have had a copy of this compilation of laws.

In mid-1852, Oregon's enacted laws and the publication of them were in a mess. Legislators had been cooking in law's kitchen for almost a decade, but the servers were falling way behind. The Oregon frontier had four distinct statutory sources. Two of them—the so-called Bluebooks—had been adopt-ed, but never published and disseminated in Oregon. A third—the Hamilton Code—was somewhere in the process of either publication or distribution, and was simply too new to have been assimilated. In between these sources had come a temporary fourth compilation—the Twenty Acts—meant for intermediate use until a thorough codification could be made. And so, the laws to be digested in Nimrod's case were those that made it to the table, not those in the oven or the trash. The loose sheets of the Twenty Acts were most likely the only law pages in service.[3]

In the presence of Sheriff Starr and Lewis Dennis, Abiather concluded that the inquest had to be scrapped. The new peace justice, Abiather Newton, started anew. Most pressing was the need to take the culprit into custody. Section one of the chapter on "Preliminary Proceedings" for justices of the peace allowed Abiather to issue an arrest warrant merely upon "an affidavit," showing reason to believe that Nimrod had committed an indictable offense. The debunked coroner's inquest was not authority for that arrest—nor was Nimrod's voluntary surrender at Abiather's door. An affidavit was required by law. To make matters proper, Abiather had Lewis Dennis sign and swear to the following:

> on or about the 21st day of May [1852] in the county of Benton, Nimrod O. Kelley…did commit murder by shooting one J. Mahoney.

Based upon that simple, sworn statement, and not upon the inquest nor Nimrod's surrender, Abiather felt proper in writing out the following warrant to Sheriff Starr:

> It having been shown to me…by the affidavit of Lewis Dennis that Nimrod O'Kelley is guilty of murder…by killing J. Mahoney, [I]…command you that you arrest the said Nimrod O'Kelley…and bring him forthwith before me…or before some other justice of the peace in the county…to answer the charges against him.

Formal procedures were now correct. A new civilization with newer laws and its newest servant were teetering on first steps. The business of making a record was as essential to propriety as it was to posterity.

Undoubtedly, Abiather told the sheriff exactly where to find Nimrod. Apparently, Nimrod had gone to Fooks Dixon's place in Marysville. It was still Saturday, May 22, when the sheriff served Abiather's warrant on Nimrod and put him under arrest.

But here appears a confused state of events: Isaac Winkle and three others had been deputized at the inquest and given the coroner arrest warrant. The "return of service" on that coroner warrant claimed that Winkle made the arrest of "the within Body of Nimrod Kelly." The purported signature of "Isaac Winkle, Deputy Sheriff" appeared on the warrant, even though Winkle was illiterate and could only make a mark. Winkle charged the county and was paid $2.30 for "arresting Nimrod O'Kelly." Sheriff Starr also charged the county $1.60 for the arrest under Abiather's warrant. So, not only were there two separate warrants for the same man, there were apparently two separate arrests of that same man, two separate fees charged, and two separate fees paid—and all to bring in a seventy-two year old man who had, in effect, arrested himself.

Having put Nimrod under arrest, the question became: What to do with him until Abiather's preliminary court could convene? Benton County had no jail. The only thing to do was to secure him on someone's premises. Nimrod's house of detention for his first five days and nights was apparently the home of Fooks Dixon where Sheriff Starr probably had found him. Dixon was paid $15.00 by the county for five days of "keeping and providing for" the prisoner. The costs to the county of a homicide were at a beginning and far from an end.

Abiather went to bed Saturday evening with the county's first murder case on his mind. He and his wife Rachel had been Bellfountain Methodists. When he became a county officer, he and Rachel moved north to Marys River and helped start their own Methodist class. On Sunday, May 23, 1852, Abiather may have skipped church. That sabbath would not have been a day of rest for him. Court duties were in order. He had to prepare for another hearing. The "Justices of the Peace" chapter in the Twenty Acts called for a preliminary proceeding in murder cases. Accordingly, he wrote out three separate subpoenas for the sheriff to serve. The subpoenas commanded the attendance of seven witnesses: "Green B. Smith, Jeremiah Cris, Thomas B. Richardson, James Barclay, William Barclay, Lewis Dennis, and Isaac Winkle." Each subpoena was careful to require that the witnesses "appear before me…to give testimony concerning…Nimrod O'Kelley," but failed to state *when* the witnesses were to appear.

Sheriff Starr was also a Bellfountain Methodist. If the sheriff did attend church that Sunday, it would have made a long day for him. His service of the three subpoenas took him the length of the county, north and south, to reach the homes of all seven witnesses. He served all of the witnesses except Isaac Winkle. Winkle was never served, wrote the sheriff, "for want of time." Time was given as a problem even though Winkle lived closer to Abiather than all the other witnesses and even though Winkle had purportedly arrested Nimrod just the day before.

On a date not recorded, Justice of the Peace Abiather Newton held the hearing. Present were Nimrod, the sheriff, and six witnesses. After hearing the testimony, Abiather concluded that Nimrod should "stand committed and appear at the next term of the District Court." This written order, the subpoenas, and Dennis's affidavit were all filed with the county clerk on June 3, almost two weeks after Nimrod showed up at Abiather's door.

Included in the justice court file was "The Declaration of Nimrod O'Kelly." In keeping with the "Justices of the Peace" chapter of the Twenty Acts, the prisoner was entitled to make an unsworn statement in writing:

The Declaration of Nimrod O'Kelly.

this irishman has been an intruder on my land or claim for two or three months. I was not afraid of his holding claim but he would threaten me every time I would meet with him on my own claim. On the twenty first of this inst I started out around my field where I was expecting to find some crows intruding on my farm when I met this Irishman or come within a few steps of him but neither of us spoke as I had told him to keep off my claim he did not speak to me. I went home & got my horse & went to the field to plowing & continued to work until dinner time of day, after which I started he met me again near my house coming towards my house. When about ten steps apart he asked me what I was always carrying my gun for. I remarked to him it was none of his business it was my own. He continued coming towards me saying if I did not mind I would get it threshed out over my head. I made no reply for a short [time] but told him to stand off and got out of the path & he got out of the path also, rather sidling up towards me in a stooped position before however before getting near enough to me to get hold of the gun the gun went off in my hands hiting him I knew not where I have no recollection of ever cocking the gun but held her down at arms length. I saw him set down I left immediately after traveling some distance I saw him lay down I come down to town directly to town & give myself up to the proper officer, where I make this declaration

> Written by A.J. Babb
> [signed] Nimrod O. Kelly

Nimrod's declaration, like Abiather's final order, was not dated, but it was filed on June 3, 1852. How the lawyer A.J. Babb became the scrivener or what part he played in the justice court proceedings is not known. But he did represent Nimrod in future proceedings.

The day after that filing, Nimrod wrote his June 4, 1852, letter to congressional delegate Joe Lane. This was the letter in which Nimrod thanked Lane for having sent veteran land pension forms, but reported that those papers had been stolen. In this letter, Nimrod gave some further account of the killing day:

The irishman came in contact with me near to my house. All of a sudden I saw in a moment that my life was in jeopardy in two respects. I had no time to reflect or to deliberate for if he had goten my gun out of my hands I would have had but poor hopes of living one moment of time as there was no person about to say or do anything. I knew that if the irishman had of killed me he would have come clear without a struggle. He would never have had to wear chains and shackles. He would have had great applause.

The letter to Lane also reported Nimrod's current sorry state:

I am loaded with shackles and chains and charged with murder in the first degree…I have no chance to get counceal…The law dos not require that an old man that a child could outrun should wear chains & shackles. This is don in order to destroy my mind so that I will not be able to defend my selfe.

In his final words, he reflected upon an irony:

The papers that you sent me…is the cause of all this calamity…You wrote to me that you had taken great pains to fix my land papers for me. But sir you did not know that they was to cause me to lose my life. I am with much respect your humble servant.

Aside from ordering that Nimrod had to be kept in custody and appear before a full-fledged district court judge, Abiather Newton also entered judgment against Nimrod "for the cost of the suit." The proceeding before Peace Justice Newton cost $13.35, including fees for Abiather, Sheriff Starr, and a dollar apiece for each of the six witnesses. Although the coroner inquest was of dubious validity, the county nevertheless paid $30.90 for it and then billed Nimrod for payback. It was one thing to charge a man with murder, but quite another thing to bill him for his own judgment. If that was not enough, the county also charged Nimrod $5.75 for burial costs.

Murder was not a bailable offense. Nimrod's "jailing" without a jail would have to continue. As of June 3, he had been in custody for almost two weeks. Abiather's so-called "judgment" continued Nimrod's custody until a territorial judge would reach Benton County on circuit. After his first five days at the Dixon home, Nimrod was moved to the home of John and Mary Stewart at Marysville. The Stewart place had a backyard shelter that had to be made more secure for the long wait. Accordingly, the county paid $2.00 for "repairs on jail," $2.00 for "one door lock," and $13.25 for "chain, handcuffs, and hobbles." There would also have to be at least one guard at all times to keep watch. That would mean hiring at least two guards to spell one another. The fee for each guard was $3.00 per day. Aside from providing shelter and guard, the Stewarts also provided meals, not only for Nimrod, but also for the guards. Boarding costs for the guards were $5.00 per week. Board and keep for Nimrod were $8.00 per week. J.C. Avery had to be reimbursed $4.13 for "sundries"—perhaps including tobacco, a candle for reading, a change of stockings, soap, a basin, and some sweetmeat. Makeshift jailing would prove to be a mounting and monumental expense.

John and Mary Stewart, Nimrod's former wagon train captains, had always been kind to him, but now he was cuffed, hobbled, and chained behind a locked door in their backyard. Under different circumstances, he would have been a guest sharing their table. Mary Stewart was a founder of the Marysville class of Methodists, who used the Stewart house as their Sunday place of worship. Whether they continued to do so with a Catholic jailed in her backyard is dubious. It was not in the nature of "Aunt Polly," as friends called her, to keep another human in chains, especially not this man of the trail with whom she had walked and been pulled by wagons. She knew his fondness for the countryside. And so, from time to time she took the irons from her prisoner to let him wander. Nimrod returned the trust by making no effort to escape. In 1942, the *Camp Adair Sentry* (a military newspaper) reported the reminiscences of settler E.A. Blake, who remembered it this way:

> There wasn't any jail at the time, so the first murderer around here was put in her keeping. He killed a man for jumping his claim. The murderer was chained up in her backyard. But he wanted exercise, so Aunt Polly would unchain him and when he had enough he would come back and she would chain him up again. Aunt Polly wasn't afraid.

But in 1852, Oregon's four newspapers did not report Aunt Polly's kindness or Nimrod's honor. The real news was "Foul Murder." That was in the headline on Asahel Bush's June 1 *Statesman*. Immediately following the coroner's inquest, in a letter dated May 23, 1852, Coroner Richard Irwin sought swift publicity and sent the story to the papers. The *Oregonian* printed Irwin's story verbatim under the headline "Horrible Murder." The *Statesman* reworked the letter, but conveyed essentially the same message. They reported that Nimrod claimed 1½ sections of land—and sometimes as much as six sections—and an additional half-section or 320 acres as a war veteran's entitlement. The articles also reported that "he always refused to point out his corners or designate his claim," and, while Nimrod purportedly had family in the states, "the neighbors never believed his family would come…and therefore did not justify him…to hold more than a half section."

The newspapers went on to report that, even though the victim "had settled about two miles from O'Kelley," nonetheless the old man "warned him to move off," and then eventually "shot him with a musket loaded with shot and slugs." Finally, the *Statesman* article told the public that Nimrod was "reported to have killed a man in Missouri, and to have left there to escape the penalty."

The Mahoney shooting was big news on the frontier. The killer was now exposed and at the forefront of public scrutiny. Being chained and alone in a backyard was a grief to which an introvert could adjust. But being on parade was grief of quite a different order.

Notes

1. For the location of the Abiather Newton house and its distance from Marysville, see Figure No. Four in Chapter 20. The record is not entirely clear if Newton was the "proper officer" to whom Nimrod surrendered. But Newton later testified that Nimrod came to his house, "and pointing to a gun sitting against the fence stated that is the gun I killed Mahoney with."
2. See Chapter 1, The Inquest.
3. The Little Bluebook was the 1839 Iowa Territory code. The Oregon Provisional Government adopted that code in 1843. Iowa's code was copied from Michigan statutes, which, in turn, had been copied from Indiana's laws. Like cooking recipes and baby clothes, laws were frequently borrowed and handed down. The Big Bluebook was the 1843 Iowa Territory revised code. The Oregon Territory legislature adopted that code in one sweeping enactment in 1849. Some argued, however, that it was an illegal enactment and, therefore, the Little Bluebook remained the controlling law. In any case, neither Bluebook was ever published as an Oregon code and, consequently, was never made available to the growing body of Oregon officials. In all of Oregon Territory, it is said that there were only four copies of the Little Bluebook and two copies of the Big Bluebook.

   This was the situation in 1850 when the territorial legislators ordered the printing of no more than twenty selected enactments that "may be of immediate and pressing importance to the people." Thus, not all of the prior laws were contained in the Twenty Acts, but chapters on Justices of the Peace, Coroners, Crimes, and Jurors were printed. Strangely, the Criminal Procedure Act was not selected and compiled, and, therefore, resort to the Iowa Bluebooks was still necessary, albeit improbable in view of their rarity on the frontier.

   Due to this ungainly and incomplete state of law, the territorial legislature in its 1850–51 assembly authorized Secretary of the Territory Edward Hamilton to compile still another publication of Oregon's "statutes of a general nature." This Hamilton Code was certified as completed in April 1851. Asahel Bush of Oregon City, designated as the printer, had to send the compilation all the way to New York City for printing and binding. Based upon the delays experienced for similar printing arrangements done in the east, the Hamilton Code would probably not yet have been distributed to Abiather Newton and the justices of the peace in Oregon by May 1852. On the other hand, a November 11, 1851, article in Bush's own newspaper, the *Statesman*, reported that the Hamilton Code had just arrived from the east. Spreading the copies, especially to the lowest officials, would still account for delays. Then too, there would be sluggishness in assimilating the new laws and putting them to work. In short, while Abiather's copy of the Twenty Acts may have been dog-eared and dated, it was nonetheless tamed and handy.

13

Pre-trial

June 1852

On June 18, 1852, the wheels of the trial court system began to turn. Clerk A.G. Hovey issued written orders to Sheriff Starr to summon twenty-four undesignated grand jurors, and twenty-four undesignated petit jurors. That Starr was given the sole power to select who those potential jurors were to be would become a bone upon which lawyers and judges would later chew. The "Jurors" chapter in the code of Twenty Acts expressly stated that the county commissioners were to make the selection and the sheriff was simply to serve the summons.[1]

Both the grand and petit jurors were summoned to appear in court on June 29, 1852.[2] Benton County was within the second judicial district, meaning Judge Orville C. Pratt would preside at Nimrod's trial.[3] Pratt's designated circuit scheduled him to convene court in Benton County for a regular term in September, three months off. But contrary to the official schedule, Pratt decided to call a special session in Marysville in June just for Nimrod's trial. A speedy trial and ending an expensive incarceration appealed to both Nimrod and the county. More importantly, it appealed to Judge Pratt, who was anxious to leave Oregon for the rest of the year and sail back east for business, politics, and a visit with his wife. A special term of court was everyone's *druthers*. But did Pratt have the power to convene his court whenever he wanted? This would become another bone of contention for lawyers.

Law required that a defendant had to be given at least ten days advance notice of trial. While the Hovey orders to the sheriff were dated ten days beyond the trial date, there was nothing in the written record to show that Nimrod was formally notified of the advanced trial date. But, on June 19 Nimrod had Clerk Hovey issue subpoenas of defense witnesses for a June 29 trial. Logically, therefore, Nimrod must have known of the trial date ten days in advance. Nonetheless, he had not been given *formal* notice. Could an informal *notice-in-fact* override the absence of a required written notice? This too was to be a bone for gnawing, as the new system of law struggled to understand how much insistence on *process* should be allowed before it stifled *substance*.

One of Nimrod's three subpoenas was directed to the Polk County sheriff for service of summons on two defense witnesses in that county. Another subpoena went to the Clackamas County sheriff for service on four defense witnesses. The third subpoena was to Sheriff Starr of Benton County for fourteen defense witnesses. On the same day, June 19, the prosecution issued subpoenas to seven witnesses. Two days later, the prosecution subpoenaed two more. Three days prior to trial, Nimrod had the clerk and sheriff summon seven more witnesses, and the prosecution had one more witness subpoenaed. The day before the trial still another prosecution witness was served. While the trial was in session, subpoenas on nine more witnesses were issued—five by the prosecution and four by the defense.

Some of the witnesses could not be found and were never served. Then too, some of the subpoenas were repetitious of the same witness. Both the prosecution and the defense summoned Greenberry Smith, R.B. Hinton, and S.M. Stout. Taking into account these duplications and witnesses not found, the total number of bodies duly summoned to trial was thirty-four—twelve prosecution witnesses, nineteen defense witnesses, and three called by both sides.

Sheriff Starr and his deputy, S.M. Stout, rode at least 325 miles to serve thirty witnesses and charged at least $41.65 for doing so. Those subpoenas, coupled with the summonses of forty-eight grand and petit jurors, meant that the sheriff and his deputy had almost eighty homes to visit and proclaim aloud the call to court. The countryside had already been set afire for one month with news of "Foul" and "Horrible Murder." Now the sheriff and his deputy performed as town criers announcing the trial date. Based upon the federal census taken two years prior, the witnesses and jurors would be almost ten percent of all white settlers (women and children included) in Benton County.

Although the case of the *Territory of Oregon v. Nimrod O'Kelly* was the first murder trial in Benton County, by no means was it the first murder trial in the territory. The Whitman Massacre trial of 1850 has been previously mentioned, and in 1851 at least three other murders were tried. Two ended in hangings. The third defendant was sentenced to six years in a penitentiary that Oregon did not have; so the murderer was pardoned. Those three killings resulted from quarrels over gambling, a woman, and an accusation of theft. It did not seem to make much difference what motivated quarrel; whether gaming, women, slander, or land, it was hot blood that triggered most frontier murder. On the other hand, murder sometimes could be born of opposite passions. A religious man named Burris had no quarrel with his wife and three children. He killed them because he loved them. He wanted them to die while they were still good so they could reach heaven.

Sometimes murder was no more than vindictive barter—raw retribution, murder for murder. So it was when Robert Maynard killed J.C. Platt in the Rogue River country in southern Oregon and was promptly executed by a mob. Sometimes, vengeance by the vigilant calmed down just enough to parade under the false banner of makeshift justice. The hanging that swiftly followed was only a shade taller than a lynching. In Jackson County in 1853, when a man named Brown shot and killed, the gathering picked W.W. Fowler to act as judge. Likely, Fowler would have been hanged right alongside of Brown had he adjudged innocence instead of guilt. The lines separating an unruly mob, orderly lynchers, and civilized trial were lines that tracked the growing pains of justice and chronicled the evolution from *seizing* the law to *serving* it.

In Benton County in June 1852, serving the law was everyone's good intentions. But the task of serving the law was necessarily given to people— judges, jurors, witnesses, sheriffs, and more. While people were not *above* the law, they were everywhere *in* the law. Law could not operate without their service and could be no better than their service. Indeed, in such a partnership, quarrel and passion and vengeance lurked just beneath the surface of newborn law, just as they had led at the forefront of lawlessness.

On the eve of his trial, Nimrod had been confined almost forty days and nights. Under guard and iron, deprived of his hikes, hunts, and hermitage, and hung upon the hooks of doubt, Nimrod looked into emptiness. And so, he did what others do to make peace with despair. He wrote a will. On Monday, June 28, 1852, he scratched his final testament and called upon his friendly captors—John Stewart, William F. Dixon, and David Stump—to sign as witnesses. The will read in part:

> This is to certify to a candid world through all generations to come during time. That I…assign and entail my donation land claim, six hundred and forty acres… to my three children that are in their minority at this time, their names and ages are as follows, my Son John OKelly now in his eleventh year, Sarah OKelly now in thirteen years going into fourteen years. My son Nimrod O Kelly eighteen years of age.

No mention was made of wife. The three children designated as beneficiaries would have been four, six, and eleven when he left Missouri seven years before. He made no mention of any adult offspring. Surely, there must have been older children, just as there must have been a mother—if there was any family at all. A seventy-two year old mind could be fuzzy on a seven-year-old

memory. It was many miles ago. Were his enemies correct? Did his family
still exist? Did they ever exist? Was it all phantoms of the forsaken? Just weeks
before, on June 4, while jailed, Nimrod had described himself as "an old no-
count man without a family."

The will named only one property—his land claim. He did not list his
horse, livestock, gun, or other possessions. It mattered not that the land claim
was not yet his to pass along. The land was all he cared for and all he saw
worthy of passage from death to life. As a final testament, he saw the land as
his will. It signified him.

Notes

1. Clerk A.G. Hovey, like Justice of the Peace Abiather Newton, was probably operating from
   law embodied in the older Twenty Acts. Nevertheless, the "Juries" chapter of the more
   recent Hamilton Code was in accord with that procedure. See note 3, Chapter 12.
2. That the business of the two juries was scheduled to commence on the same day was irregular. Ordinarily, the grand jury finishes its work well in advance of the full trial, where
   the petit jury begins its job. If the grand jurymen did not authorize a prosecution, there
   would be no need for petit jurymen to decide guilt or innocence. Grand jury proceedings
   were designed to protect citizens from the burden and stigma of baseless prosecutions.
   But a special term of court, with only one item of business on the court docket, called for
   expediency as well as protection. Having a panel of petit jurymen in immediate readiness
   made horse sense whenever the grand jury would most certainly favor prosecution.
3. Oregon Territory was divided into three judicial districts with one judge assigned to
   each district, appointed by the President of the United States. They also served as the
   Supreme Court of Oregon Territory to hear appeals from their individual decisions as
   trial judges. The *third judicial district* was essentially all of Oregon Territory north of the
   Columbia River and the 46th parallel—what is today Washington, the Idaho panhandle,
   and Montana west of the Continental Divide—plus Clatsop County, Oregon. In 1852,
   William Strong was the judge for that district. The *first judicial district* was essentially all
   of the territory south of the Columbia River and 46th parallel and east of the Willamette
   River—what is today eastern Oregon, the pan of Idaho, and parts of Wyoming west of
   the Continental Divide. Thomas Nelson was the judge of that district. The *second judicial
   district* was essentially all of the territory south of the Columbia and west of the Willamette
   River, except for Clatsop County in the northwest. This was Orville C. Pratt's circuit, and
   it included Benton County.

14

Trial—First Day

June 29, 1852

The time had come—Tuesday, June 29, 1852. Settlers came to Marysville from every corner of Benton County and beyond. Accounts of the day do not say how many spectators were at the trial, but it seems fair to assume that on a frontier starved for occasion, no one would miss the *doings*. For certain, there would be eighty to ninety attending out of duty—witnesses, jurors, lawyers, clerks, jailors, and judge. One person would come neither to perform nor to be entertained; that one would be led to court in irons.

There was no courthouse or government building in Marysville. So the trial was held at territorial legislator Joseph C. Avery's house—located just *a holler* away from the town center at the corners of Avery's and Dixon's land claims. In 1849, Governor Lane had officially designated Avery's house as the place for Benton County business. The heart of the Willamette Valley was Marysville, and Avery's place in 1852 was the heart of that heart. Indeed, the district court had convened there on its regular circuit three times before—the last time being less than three months prior to this specially called session. Summer had just begun; thus the trial was likely conducted in Avery's yard under shade trees. No indoors was large enough to house all of the trial's participants, let alone the spectators. Then too, an outdoor courtroom was more suited to tobacco and whittling.

The first murder trial in Benton County put many in their best bib and tucker. In farm country, *go-to-meeting* clothes would have been different from the dress in the bigger towns to the north. Under the refined tastes of the new territorial governor, John P. Gaines, and with an increase in ocean ship passage to Oregon by those who could afford it, fashion had arrived in Oregon City society. But menfolk in Benton County did not "go much on broadcloth and biled shirts." Farmers preferred "stout flannel shirts, brown overalls, with knee-high trousers tucked inside knee-high boots."

Womenfolk turned out in a wider array of garments. Recent immigrants would have only their threadbare trail clothes or maybe a wrinkled bonnet and dress from the bottom of a trunk. *Old Oregonians* had the time and wherewithal for a needle and a bolt of cloth. But Benton County women—old or new—would not yet have adopted city fashions from the east. Certainly pioneer women would not be wearing the newest craze—bloomers, designed to permit women to "perch their feet up and sprawl about…masculinely," putting "bachelors…on the *qui vive…*, smitten." The skirts worn by the new immigrant women of the trail, however, may have done some smiting of their own, because petticoats had been sacrificed as patches, bandages, and rags to the rigors of the trail and of settling in. A sailor near that time observed that skirts without petticoats were "sails" that "lie close to the mast" and showed "bare poles" in the wind.

The outdoor courtroom itself had to be appropriately attired. Rough-hewn planks braced on saw horses may have served as tables for the court clerk and lawyers. Perhaps Avery's best kitchen table and rocking chair were brought out and elevated for the judge's bench and catbird seat. Two rows of puncheon laid on nail kegs may have formed the jury box. Avery's house would serve as judge's chambers and place of retirement and deliberation for the grand and petit juries. A rope between two trees may have formed *the bar*—a rail that separated spectators from the court. Only bailiffs, witnesses, litigants, clerks, judges, jurors, and lawyers could go inside the bar. It was more than a separation; it was a symbol. To go beyond the bar one had to be called—either by summons, subpoena, indictment, or license. Permission to enter the bar was a goal of all law apprentices. *Passing the bar* became the adage and the badge.

Reuben Patrick Boise served as the chief prosecutor in Nimrod's trial and at the appellate levels. He eventually was pitted against defense lawyer James K. Kelly, even while joining with Kelly as a political ally in Oregon's territorial legislature, and as a joint codifier with Kelly of Oregon's statutory laws. Later, Boise served as Chief Justice of the Oregon State Supreme Court. *Oregon Historical Society #9177*

Clerk A.G. Hovey and Sheriff Starr were *at bar*, waiting for the judge to convene court. Hovey was paid $100 per year for his services as court clerk, and Starr $150 per year for bailiff work. These court salaries were in addition to payment for their other record-keeping and law-enforcement work. Hovey's court clerk work supplemented his service as the schoolteacher in Marysville's log schoolhouse.

At the prosecutor's table sat Reuben Patrick Boise, the attorney for the district. He was assisted by Alexander Campbell. The *Oregon Weekly Times* reported Campbell as the prosecutor, but the official record listed Boise as prosecutor and never mentioned Campbell's presence. Both probably shared the task, just as they collaborated on other cases at the time.[1]

The chairs at the accused's table were empty. Neither Nimrod nor any defense counsel were present. They were not yet allowed to enter this backyard court—not until after the grand jury had decided to indict. The defense was permitted no voice in grand jury proceedings—a one-sidedness that is still law today.

In 1848, Democratic President James K. Polk appointed Orville C. Pratt as Associate Justice of the Oregon Territory Supreme Court. As trial judge, he sentenced Nimrod to be hanged. Seen here in later years, he had relocated to California and New York, where he was divorced for adultery. He also refused to testify on grounds of self-incrimination in a criminal gambling probe. *Oregon Historical Society #9176*

Judge Orville C. Pratt was there making last minute instructions and arranging his outdoor courtroom for protocol and decorum. Though only thirty-two, he had been presiding over cases in Oregon since September 1849—longer than any sitting judge. He was the judge who sentenced five Cayuse Indians to hang for the Whitman massacre. Youth was a useful attribute for frontier judges, who had to endure the rigors of riding the circuit. Pratt's rounds took him from Lafayette, the county seat of Yamhill County, to Cynthian in Polk County; then from Cynthian to Marysville; from there to Eugene City, Yoncalla, and Scottsburg; and then to the head of the Valley at Deer Creek and beyond to Jackson Creek—a four hundred mile circuit bordered by the Pacific Ocean, California, and the Columbia and Willamette rivers. In January 1852, the territorial legislature had added Marion and Linn counties to Pratt's jurisdiction, which then took him across the Willamette and put the cities of Salem and Takenah on his appointed rounds.[2]

An evening place to stay was still another problem for circuit riders. There were few roadhouses or inns along the way. Most of the time, judges boarded at hospitable cabins, where typically, one room served as bedroom, kitchen, and living quarters. Judge George H. Williams described the awkwardness of such occasions:

> I acquired a dexterity in undressing and dressing in the presence of the family that would fill a circus rider with envy. It was easy going to bed because the family sat with their faces turned away, but [not so] to get up in the morning while the women were around getting breakfast.

Unlike Williams, Pratt would not take lightly an affront to dignity. Pratt was a man large in stature and airs, and not an outdoorsman given to rugged traveling and frontier living. He came by ship to Oregon, made a number of voyages back to his home in New York, and would have been in a hurry to finish the Nimrod trial in order to make yet another scheduled sailing east. But in his court, his hand was strong. He was quick to hold many in contempt including his own bailiff, U.S. Marshal Joe Meek. When lawyer W.W. Chapman had sought a change of venue from Pratt's court on the grounds that the judge was prejudiced, Pratt jailed him for twenty days and defrocked him as a lawyer. Chapman was one of the founders of the *Oregonian*. So, it is no wonder that the newspaper carried on a constant feud with Pratt.

The three Oregon district judges were each paid an annual salary of $2,000. In addition, judges were entitled an extra fee for presiding at a specially called term. For sitting as judge on Nimrod's case, Pratt was paid $96.00 by the Benton County taxpayers. Pratt had other ways of supplementing his annual salary. He became a highly successful businessman; indeed, he ended his life a millionaire. His honesty in trading was sometimes questioned. Around the same time as Nimrod's trial, Pratt allegedly sold a buyer some cattle representing them to be "Durham cows." *Durham* was a name for prize-winning English stock. Pratt had bought the cows from a man whose name happened to be Durham, so Pratt felt justified in calling them "Durham cows." From that escapade, the *Oregonian* and other detractors gave Pratt and his clique of political allies the name *Durhamites*.

The Durhamite clique was a group of Democrats often led by Pratt and Asahel Bush, editor of the *Statesman*.[3] Lawyer Matthew Deady, ex-Governor Joe Lane, and Joseph Avery were others in that circle at this early time. Many thought it improper for a judge to take such an active part in politics, but Pratt was unperturbed. Depending on who was commenting on his activities, he was clever at either combining or separating his judicial, commercial, and political lives. If Nimrod was aware of Pratt's politics and business affairs, he would have reason to worry, because prosecutor Boise was also a member of the Durhamite clique, and assistant prosecutor Campbell was destined to become Pratt's law partner in the not too distant future. While Nimrod was not political, his trial was pulling him toward the political vortex.

All of the court officers at Nimrod's trial were young men. Sheriff Starr, Deputy Sheriff Silas Stout, District Attorney Boise, and Judge Pratt were either thirty-two or thirty-three years of age. Clerk Hovey was only twenty-two. This junior cadre was about to sit in reckoning upon a senior in his seventh decade—and the hour had now come. The sheriff called the court to order. Everyone stood as Pratt went to the bench. Above the hush of that ceremony, came the slush of Missus Avery churning butter inside the cabin—a reminder that, while deaths were at stake in the court's crucible, daily chores proceeded apace in the world beyond. How Pratt was attired is not known, but George E. Cole, Avery's co-legislator from Benton County, described Pratt on other such occasions. He was "arrayed in a faultless suit," and wore a "stove-pipe hat and a biled shirt with a stake-and-rider collar." He had "long curly hair, black and glossy."

The sheriff then called the grand jury to assemble. The record is not clear as to when these grand jurors were chosen. Recall that eleven days before trial, Clerk Hovey had instructed the sheriff, instead of the county commissioners, to pick the grand jurors. How did the sheriff do this? Did he, in advance of the trial date, ride out to twenty-two homes to summon jurymen randomly chosen, or did he pick the grand jurors from the spectators gathered at the trial? There is reason to suspect he may have done the latter. Nowhere in the Court Fee Journal or in the County Commissioners' Journal for Benton County does it show the sheriff made claim for fees or travel expense in summoning grand jurymen, whereas he did not hesitate to claim $58.80 for travel in serving subpoenas on the witnesses. Furthermore, the sheriff's official return of service on the *petit* jurors, showed he served them on June 18, 22, 24, 25, and 26, but his return of service on the *grand* jurors was dated June 29—the first day of trial. If, indeed, he served the grand jurors on June 29, then he could only have done so by seizing those who came to watch. Those who came to *see* a trial would want for there to *be* a trial. Because of that danger, both the Twenty Acts and the Hamilton Code chapters on "Juries" required service of summons on grand jurors to be made at least five days prior to sitting. Nimrod was not yet present nor represented in order to object to the sheriff's jury selection method, and nothing was ever made of this dubious process.

The law also required that twenty-four grand jurors be called for a special term, but for some unknown reason only twenty-two were selected.[4] Furthermore, the law also required that each grand juror be "examined as to his qualifications to serve." Nowhere in the judge's trial court minutes did it state that such examinations took place. The minutes did record, however, that the jurors were "good and lawful men of the county." Did that recitation mean that they had been examined? Failure to examine for qualifications would later become an objection, but not during the trial.

Before the grand jurors retired, Judge Pratt swore them to "diligently inquire," to "keep secret," to "present things truly…according to the laws of this territory," and to reject "envy, hatred, malice, fear, favor, affection, or hopes of reward." Pratt then appointed O.C. Motley to be the grand jury foreman. This put Motley in charge of the grand jury proceedings, which would be closed to public view and out of the presence of the judge and the accused. Only prosecutor Boise and witnesses would be allowed within the grand jury's domain. They retired to a secret place—probably Avery's house.

While the grand jury was off hearing the prosecution's case against Nimrod, Judge Pratt in open court called the roll of petit jurors summoned to trial. This was getting the wagon ahead of the team. A petit jury would not be necessary if the grand jury did not decide to prosecute. But, for this special term of court, the panel or pool of prospective petit jurors had to be ready to go into an immediate trial. Pratt had been a judge and a lawyer long enough to know that the grand jury deliberations on this case would be swift and predictable. After all, the accused admitted the killing. The grand jury's business was a shallow wade. The deeper ford was the business of the petit jury. The sooner the petit jurymen reached shore, the sooner everyone could get back to their fields or hearths or scheduled sailing for New York.

Twenty-three "good and lawful men of the county" responded to Pratt's roll call of petit jurymen. Good and lawful women, Indians, or slaves were not permitted to serve on grand or petit juries. Jurors had to be "qualified electors." Voters were limited to white or "free colored" males. Certain folks were entitled to be exempt from, albeit qualified for, jury duty—court personnel, attorneys at law, "ministers of the gospel,"[5] certain schoolteachers, doctors, and all people over sixty years of age. One man, now deliberating on Nimrod's grand jury, could have chosen exemption. John Fortson was a lawyer, who opted to serve. He turned out to be a vigorous opponent of Nimrod.

After a short while, Fortson, Motley, and the rest of the grand jury returned to court with a *true bill*, saying the prosecutor's Bill of Indictment was backed by a sufficient amount of evidence.[6] They were paid an average of $3.00 each for their services. Some may have gone home, but most, if not all, undoubtedly stayed on as spectators—after all, it was why they came. Now they would be more curious to know the defense evidence—the other side of the story that they were not permitted to hear in their deliberations.

Pratt then issued a bench warrant to the sheriff to bring the defendant into court. This was the third warrant issued on Nimrod. It was all protocol, but Nimrod must have been weary of the litany: Twelve coroner jurors, a justice of the peace, twenty-two grand jurors, and a district attorney had proclaimed in tandem: *Try him. Try him. Try him. Try him.* Finally, they were ready to do so. The sheriff did not take long to fetch Nimrod, kept in waiting nearby. Nimrod faced Pratt for the first time. The silence of that confrontation would have been accented by the whispers in the crowd, the murmurs of leaves overhead, and the occasional clank of Nimrod's chains. The two men had one thing in common—both were without family in Oregon. Just as the Long Tom neighbors had debased Nimrod, so too the *Oregonian* rebuked Pratt:

> This vaunted lover of the dear people of Oregon has neither wife nor child here, nor has he ever had, having left them in Atlantic states and came here as an adventurer.

Aside from that one point of commonality and the scorn that went with it, the two men were ends asunder. Nimrod was lean; Pratt ample. Nimrod had a full, untrimmed beard; Pratt was one of the few men on the frontier who stayed clean-shaven. Nimrod had long, gray hair; Pratt's hair was curly, black and glossy, and according to a miner, "the puttiest ha'r he ever seed." Nimrod was seventy-two; Pratt forty years younger. Nimrod took to old age with regret, yet resignation; Pratt, on the other hand, in his later years used shoe blackener to darken his grey hairs. Where Pratt would have worn refinement befitting the dignity of a judge, Nimrod's garb would have been duck cloth and hide. Perhaps Aunt Polly Stewart had washed, patched, and wrinkled out Nimrod's britches. Avery or Dixon might have given him a store-bought shirt. His long hair and beard may have been wet down and combed out for the trial. But however else he may have been rigged, he was harnessed in iron.

District Attorney Boise stood and moved for the court to arraign the accused. The first step in that arraignment process was to secure the defendant's right to a lawyer. Here, the minutes of the court proceedings say merely that Pratt appointed counsel for Nimrod. But unquestionably, the proceedings at that point required more exploration. Judge Pratt would have had to first find out if Nimrod had the opportunity and wherewithal to get his own lawyer.[7]

One of Oregon's "greatest jury trial lawyers of his time" was said to be David Logan from Portland. His father was an Illinois lawyer in partnership with a young attorney named Abraham Lincoln. Nine days before the trial on June 20, 1852, lawyer Logan wrote his sister the following letter:

I have as extensive and as profitable a practice as any lawyer in the territory and very nearly a monopoly of the criminal practice during the circuit just past. I have defended three men charged with murder and prosecuted one—and I leave here tomorrow to defend O. Kelley charged with murder at Marysville, at the head of the valley, Judge Pratt having appointed a special term to try him.

Logan was sure in his own mind that he would be Nimrod's lawyer. His skill as a trial lawyer called for such self-assurance. But, in Nimrod's case, his confidence was in for an awakening. How Logan and Nimrod caught wind of one another is not clear. Perhaps the matchmaker was J.C. Avery, who always seemed to be at Nimrod's side. However it came about, Logan and Nimrod met in Marysville a few days prior to trial. As payment for his legal services, Logan wanted Nimrod's land claim. Those were not unusual terms in frontier lawyering. Just a few months after Nimrod's trial, Adam Wimple was also put on trial for murder of his wife in Polk County. Lawyer Matthew Deady represented Wimple. In payment, Wimple willed his land claim to Deady. But those terms were unspeakable for Nimrod. Under no circumstances would he ever give up his land in order to save his life when he had already taken a life to save his land. If that was twisted logic, it nevertheless made sense to an old recluse whose company for the last six years had been his land. The trial was an evil attempt to take his life; now Logan's offer was an evil attempt to take his land. Nimrod put it this way: "I would not hire Satan to cut out Satan."

The "greatest jury lawyer" in the territory was sent packing, and Nimrod had no legal assistance in preparing for trial. Although one month prior to trial, attorney Andrew Jackson Babb prepared Nimrod's written "Declaration" about the shooting, not many days later Nimrod wrote Joe Lane claiming he had "no chance to get counseal." Apparently, Nimrod did not have enough confidence in Babb to keep him as a lawyer. And so, as Nimrod stood in chains, Judge Pratt would need to know: "Have you or have you not procured counsel?" According to Nimrod in a letter published in the *Oregon Spectator*, he responded that he had "no counsel, and no opportunity to procure counsel, such as could be depended upon."

Pratt then replied that he "did not care; you had 8 or 10 days to procure counsel." And with that, the judge beckoned attorney Babb to come before the bar. Babb came forward and took a position alongside of Nimrod. Nimrod disapproved: "I object to Mr. Babb as counsel…He would do me more harm than good."

Nevertheless, Judge Pratt wrote in the minutes: "Defendant having been brought into court, and having signified that he had no counsel, the court thereupon appointed A.J. Babb, Esq., as counsel to defend said Prisoner."

As reported in his *Spectator* letter, Nimrod continued to object. "If the court please, I wish then to be my own counsel." According to Nimrod, he had reduced this request to a written petition to appear as his own lawyer, but Pratt refused the request. No written petition or court minutes concerning the request appear in the court file. Pratt then said, "Mr. Babb is your only chance now." Nimrod persisted, but Pratt cut off the protest with: "You need not say another word!"

This exchange was all according to Nimrod's written recollection. Verbatim transcripts by court reporters were not kept at frontier trials. If counsel for either side desired to have a written summary of witness testimony and court rulings, then it was up to the lawyers to keep that record. Such a summary was called a "bill of exceptions." No bill of exceptions was filed in *Territory of Oregon v. Nimrod O'Kelly*. Without a bill of exceptions, appellate judges would not be able to know exactly what happened in the trial. As far as the written record was concerned, Nimrod raised no objection that he had no time to prepare, no objection that he had no opportunity to obtain counsel, no objection that he did not want Babb as a lawyer, and no objection that he preferred to represent himself.

Judge Pratt had only three lawyers to pick from in assigning Nimrod a defender. Only three men had been licensed to appear on Judge Pratt's Benton County Attorney Roll. A licensed lawyer in those days was simply one who had a particular judge's permission to appear before the bar and argue cases in that judge's court. It did not take a law license to engage in non-trial work. Anyone could open an office and advise others about the law or assist them in preparing legal papers and affairs. Thus, there was a marked difference between an office lawyer and a trial lawyer, between a counselor and an advocate.

In 1852, the three authorized trial lawyers in Benton County were John T. Fortson, George E. Cole, and Andrew J. Babb. As already noted, Fortson served on Nimrod's grand jury and was among Nimrod's detractors. Cole might have been a good choice. He was also a schoolteacher, a good orator, and a territorial legislator for Benton County. Nevertheless, as the judge had put it, Babb was Nimrod's "only chance." Pratt was not about to have a first degree murder case tried in his court without lawyers on both sides—whoever those lawyers might be, whatever might be their competence, and no matter what the accused wanted.

The next stage in the arraignment process required that the defendant be given a copy of the indictment and a copy of the names of those summoned to petit jury duty. But as stated in the court minutes "Defendant by his counsel…waived" that right. Not much is known about attorney Andrew Jackson Babb. He never filed a donation land claim. Eight months after the trial, Babb became involved in the so-called "Elliott Cutoff" venture—an enterprising attempt to spur growth in the southern Willamette Valley by creating a southern passage into the Valley for migrants coming along the Oregon Trail. Some of the promoters, including Babb, rode east to meet the westward flow of settlers. Babb convinced one of the wagon trains to follow him along the cutoff. But report had it that Babb, frightened by Indians, abandoned the train in mid-route and left the migrants to find their own way. That deportment would prove to be consistent with his steerage in Nimrod's behalf.

The arraignment process then called for reading the indictment in open court. The indictment was obviously drafted most hurriedly. It omitted key words to understanding and was a legalistic catastrophe that went far beyond the legalese typical of the times. It was chock-full of repetition, peppered with "saids" and "aforesaids," and laced with "then-and-theres," all packaged in one recipe—a single turgid sentence that went on and on for two pages. Because prosecutor Boise wrote it, presumably he was the one who read it aloud before the courtroom audience. In doing so, perhaps, he suffered word by word the shame of his composition. If his candor was at all equal to history's glowing account of his ability, then Boise would have been the first to confess the abomination.[8]

Nimrod had no copy to follow. The indictment was the official statement of the precise crimes charged by the government against him, against which he would have to defend. It was part of the question to be put to Nimrod when asked how he would plead to the allegations therein. It was the most serious accusation a civilization could muster—a retaliation that sought death for death.

> The Grand Jurors of said Territory, within and for the said County of Benton, upon their oath present that Nimrod OKelley of said County, on the twenty first day of May in the year of our Lord one thousand eight hundred and fifty two, at and in the County aforesaid, in and upon one Jeremiah Mahoney, in the Peace of the said Territory of Oregon then and there being, and purposely and of deliberate and premeditated malice, make an assault and that the said Nimrod OKelley, a certain gun then and there charged and loaded with gun powder and forty leaden shot- - - - - (which gun in the said Nimrod OKelley in both Hands of him the said Nimrod O'Kelley then and there had and held,) to, against, and upon the said Jeremiah Mahoney, then and there, purposely, and of deliberate and premeditated malice, did shoot and discharge and that the said Nimrod OKelley, with the shot- - - - - - -aforesaid, out of the gun aforesaid, then and there by force of the gunpowder aforesaid shot and sent forth as aforesaid, the said Jeremiah Mahoney, in and upon the left breast- - - - - - -of him the said Jeremiah Mahoney,

then and there purposely, and of deliberate and premeditated malice, did strike, penetrate, and wound giving to the said Jeremiah Mahoney, then and there with the shot- - - - - - -aforesaid, so as aforesaid shot discharged and sent forth, out of the gun aforesaid, by the said Nimrod OKelly, in and upon the left breast of him the said Jeremiah Mahoney, three-mortal wounds of which said mortal wounds the said Jeremiah Mahoney, aforesaid, on the said twenty first day of May, in the year one thousand eight hundred hundred and fifty two aforesaid, at and in the County of Benton aforesaid, did die, and so the Jurors aforesaid, upon their oath aforesaid do say, that the said Nimrod OKelly the said Jeremiah Mahoney, in manner and form aforesaid, purposely, and of deliberate and premeditated malice, did kill and murder against the people of said Territory- - - - - - -and contrary to the form and effect of the Statute in such case made and provided

The body of the text in the indictment abruptly ended. The record is void of any final page; and if there ever was one, it was, to be sure, good riddance.

Boiled to its dregs, the indictment read thus: "Nimrod OKelley…on the twenty first day of May…did shoot…Mahoney…giving…wounds of which…Mahoney did die, and…OKelley…purposely and of…premeditated malice did kill." Tucked away in those dregs were the necessary pieces of what the prosecution had to prove: a corpse, a shooting, a malicious intent, and then, the causal connection that bound victim, killer, and plan all together into a single affront to society—murder.[9]

Judge Pratt then asked Nimrod, "What plea do you desire to interpose to the charges contained in the indictment?" Nimrod said, "Not guilty." Pratt ordered that the plea be entered in the record, and then adjourned the proceedings until the next day at nine o'clock.

The contest in the case of the *Territory of Oregon v. Nimrod O'Kelly* was now official. Unlike the ash stakes in Nimrod's land claim, which were rotting and temporary, the stakes at trial were the most permanent thing about life. At stake here was death—two deaths—one done, one to come.

Notes

1. The first volume of the *Decisions of the Supreme Court of the Oregon Territory* lists Reuben Patrick Boise and Alexander Campbell as co-counsel on the first two cases reported in that volume. If Campbell took a part in Nimrod's trial, he would have been a deputy prosecutor because Boise was the official attorney for the second judicial district. District Attorney Boise traveled with Orville C. Pratt for criminal trials on the circuit of counties within the district. Boise was undoubtedly at the reins of Nimrod's prosecution, and, as the saying goes among lawyers, Campbell rode shotgun. Even though today each county has its own prosecutor and "districts" have ceased to be a political subdivision, we still refer to county prosecutors as "D.A.'s"—*district* attorneys.

2. See note 3, Chapter 13. Today, Cynthian is the city of Dallas; Deer Creek is Roseburg; Jackson Creek is Jacksonville; Takenah is Albany—all within Oregon. Pratt's judicial district now is presided over by almost one hundred trial judges. Judges no longer travel

circuits. Their courts are stationary, yet they are still called "circuit court Judges."

3. Whether Pratt was a leader or not in the "Clique" is controversial. The view that Pratt played a leading role was instigated by the publication of an 1852 satire, "Treason, Stratagems, and Spoils." But whether or not a leader, Pratt's involvement in political partisanship is unquestionable.

4. The twenty-two grand jurymen called for service were Jacob Hammer, George Belknap, L.D. Gilbert, John T. Fortson, Isaac Foster, Jesse Ownbey, Harrison Douglas, Prier Scott, John Sylvester, Jacob L. Halter, Johanon Carter, James N. McAffee, Rowland Chambers, Lazarus Vanbebber, Joseph Hughart, G.N. Roberts, O.C. Motley, Luke Mulkey, John Trapp, C.R. Rouse, John Wrenn, and Thomas Norris.

5. "Ministers of the gospel" would not include clergy other than Christians; more specifically, Protestants; and arguably still more specifically, evangelical Protestants.

6. No record is kept of grand jury proceedings. All that is known is that the prosecutor called nine witnesses to testify: James E. Barclay, William Barclay, Jeremiah Criss, Richard Irwin, Mary Jane Mahoney, Thomas B. Richardson, Green B. Smith, N.A. Starr, and Isaac Winkle.

7. Section 64 of the Criminal Procedure Act in the Bluebooks required the court "to assign counsel to defend the prisoner, in case he cannot procure counsel himself." The Hamilton Code and Twenty Acts compilations do not contain any such enactments, but the procedure of appointing defense counsel had become well established by custom, especially in death punishment cases.

8. Boise had been a lawyer five years, and arrived in Oregon about eighteen months before the trial. Pratt appointed him to serve as district attorney. Over the years, Boise became a man of prominence in Oregon law. He later served in the territorial legislature and the constitutional convention for Oregon statehood. Five years after the trial, President Buchanan appointed him to the territorial supreme court.

9. Observe that the indictment described the crime as simply "murder." The Twenty Acts did not specify the *degrees* of murder. This strongly suggests that Prosecutor Boise, like Justice of the Peace Abiather Newton, was not yet dealing with the newly distributed Hamilton Code, where homicide was broken down into "murder in the first degree" and "murder in the second degree." On the other hand, Judge Pratt during the course of the trial brought the case and the charge into conformity with the new Hamilton Code compilation. Pratt was undoubtedly one of the first officials in the territory to receive the newly printed book. This was another indicator that Nimrod's trial seems to have taken place at the point of transfer from one set of laws to another. See note 3 in Chapter 12.

15

Trial—Second Day

June 30, 1852

The next day, Wednesday, at nine o'clock in the forenoon, the trial reconvened. Supper would be cold for those who stayed to the end of this long day's *doings*. The day began when Judge Pratt's "minutes and Records of yesterday's proceedings" were read, approved, and signed by him. This would have been the time for the lawyers to ask for deletions or additions to that record. No corrections were proposed.

Request to Change Venue. Judge Pratt wrote that the first new business for Wednesday was the calling of the petit jury panel. But Nimrod's recollections were different. According to Nimrod, somewhere about this time he pressed the court on other matters, one of which was a motion to change the place of trial. The court record does not reveal any such request. There is no doubt that Nimrod felt strongly that south Benton County residents, especially his neighbors in the Long Tom, Jennyopolis, and Bellfountain areas, were prejudiced against him. After the trial he expressed his fears in these written words:

> [It is] lamentable…to see hundreds of men all arrayed against one man with unrelenting zele with unmitigated determination to destroy me…Nefarious and clandestine plans and ambition was levyed at me…Their conspiracy is to undermind my family and devastate my habitation…They say now if they can get the old man hung or put in the states prison they can soon sift his family like wheat.

Others also confirmed the atmosphere against Nimrod. Spectator John Thorp wrote, "there was a determination in the people of Benton to hang O'Kelly and a determination in Pratt to accommodate them." Two of Nimrod's most intense foes, Richard Irwin and Isaac Winkle, wrote that, if Nimrod were freed, "other murders will be committed, either by O'Kelly or by the enraged feeling of the settlement upon O'Kelly & done in the shape of a mob."

The value of a venue change was demonstrated in a Polk County murder case just a few months before the killing of Mahoney. Four men were separately tried for killing Serenas Hooker. Three of them were tried in Polk County—two were sentenced to hang, and one given a three year prison term. The fourth man, however, was acquitted after his trial was moved to another county.

Afterward, Nimrod wrote that he had prepared for trial a written petition to have his case tried elsewhere. He recalled giving the petition to his lawyer, but Babb did not present it to the court. Instead, Babb "withheld [the petition] until after the trial; he then handed it back to me." Because the writing was "kept out of the way," Nimrod made his motion orally. "I repeated verbally that I wanted a change of venue."

According to Nimrod, Judge Pratt "observed it looked bad to see a man trying to move his trial out of his own county." But Nimrod "was unwilling to accede."

Pratt persisted. "I would advise you to let the trial proceed in this county." Now it was Nimrod's turn to persist. "There had been all kinds of foul means employed to excite the people against me." To which Pratt countered, "Men will talk—that signifies nothing."

Thus, instead of overruling the motion, Judge Pratt simply deflected it. No record was ever made of it having been offered. The account of the attempt is based solely on Nimrod's own recollections—the memories of a mind beset by seventy-two years and the *lorn lost*. Yet, every sump—spring full or autumn dry—has its source.

Request to Postpone Trial. Next, Nimrod spoke out again in open court, saying he was not ready to go to trial. Apparently, he did this on his own, and not through Counsel Babb. Once again, the source is Nimrod's own memory, not the court record, which was silent on any attempts to postpone. If Nimrod's recall was correct, he reported to the court that "there were six of my witnesses not present…Two of them live on Tualitan plains, two at Umpqua, and two in Polk county." He subsequently learned, "there were only two of them summoned, and that, too, the day after the trial." He then stated to the court, "I could not safely go into trial without said witnesses."[1]

Pratt responded, "That depends upon what they will swear." The matter ended there. Once again Pratt had dodged a ruling. Suffice it to say that any delay of the proceedings would not meet with Pratt's notions of swift justice or his personal schedule. A special term of court had been called, at a specific time, specific place, and for specific ends. Neither a delay in time nor a change of place would be allowed to waylay those ends.

Selecting a Petit Jury. According to Judge Pratt and his daily trial journal, the first item of court business on the second day was "calling the panel of Petit Jurors." Twenty-two persons answered this second call of the roll. On the previous day, twenty-three had been present.[2] By law, twenty-four were required to serve on the panel or venire. From this pool, twelve would be chosen. With only twenty-two present, Pratt had to order Sheriff Starr to take from the spectators two good and lawful men. These recruits were called "the tales." The "Juries" chapters of the Twenty Acts and the Hamilton Code authorized the use of talesmen. The originally called panelists were called "veniremen."

Sheriff Starr went into the onlookers and conscripted J.P. Friedley and Jacob Slagle to serve. Having now stretched the panel to twenty-four, it was then necessary to shrink them back down to twelve. The Twenty Acts and the Hamilton Code required Clerk Hovey "to write the name of each panelist, on a separate ticket, and put the whole into a box." Then, in open court, Hovey was required to "draw, by chance, twelve names out of such box." After the trial, the defense contended that this procedure was not followed.

Unfortunately, the procedure that was allegedly followed appears nowhere in the records. Perhaps no names were put in a box. Perhaps the sheriff, clerk, or the court simply picked faces from the twenty-four. Whatever the procedure, neither Babb nor Nimrod made any objection at the time of trial; or if they did, Judge Pratt's daily journal did not record any such objection. These persistent failures to preserve events in the record were devastating blunders, as the future would tell.

With a panel of twelve in the jury box, the selection process was still not over. The prosecution and the defense were now entitled to question and challenge each of those chosen. But here again, the court record is vague. Nimrod wrote that he "was not once asked if I objected to any of the jury." He also said Babb told him that "two men, then on the jury, had offered him [Babb] $700 to exert himself to have me convicted and executed. And the same two men were allowed to remain on the jury, until I insisted on their being set aside." Again, the only record of these challenges was Nimrod's reminiscences.

At least one man, who ended up on the jury, could have been successfully challenged for cause by the defense. Almost two months after the trial, Sheriff Starr swore in an affidavit that when he served summons on T. M. Read to appear as a petit juror, Read said in earnest that Nimrod "ought to be hanged." Not only should this have banned Read from the jury, it also supported Nimrod's claim that he was tried in a hostile atmosphere.

Certainly, the defense should have asked if any of the panelists had read the June 1 issue of the *Statesman*. That newspaper reported Nimrod was the culprit, that he claimed far more land than he was entitled to, and, worst of all, that he had killed another man back in Missouri. But, here again, the record does not show any interrogation as to news articles read or as to any other mind-sets against Nimrod.

The court's only record pertinent to the jury selection process stated simply, there "came as a Jury to try the issue…twelve good and lawful men of the County." Job S. Hayworth, William Knotts, and Jacob Martin were apparently the older members; they were in their forties. Thomas M. Read, who had already prejudged Nimrod, was thirty-nine.[3] Younger Oregonians on the jury were Samuel L. Leneve, James H. Stewart, and G.P. Wrenn, all in their twenties. These seven were land claimants under the Donation Act. The remaining five had never staked claims.[4] Elias D. Keys was listed as a county taxpayer, because taxes were assessed on personal property as well as real property. The ages, businesses, families, and locations of Abraham Acock, B.F. Chapman, M.W. Ellis, and Henry Powell are a mystery. They had neither claims nor property to tax in Benton County. To be a juror, one had only to be a Benton County voter, not a landholder or taxpayer. It was not to Nimrod's advantage that four of the twelve jurors held no property and paid no taxes. Hired-hand drifters without land or place might not yet give full feeling to a pioneer's deep need to settle, shape, and defend homestead.

Judge Pratt called for the twelve jurymen to stand and raise their hands to the Almighty:

> You solemnly swear…without respect to person, or favor, or fear, you will well and truly try and true deliverance make between the Territory of Oregon and Nimrod O'Kelly the prisoner at the bar, whom you shall have in charge, according to the evidence and the laws of this Territory. So help you God.

Twelve voices muttered "yea," and with that, all court folk were in place. The evidence could now begin.[5]

The Testimonial Record. Pratt's daily journal did not and was not required to summarize the proof given at trial. The court record simply reported that the jury "proceeded…to hear the allegations and proofs of the respective parties." Without official court reporters, the lawyers had the choice of summarizing the testimony in their *bills of exception*. If such summaries were kept in the Nimrod case, they were never filed as court records and none have been found.

Who the witnesses were and what they had to say can be pieced together from various unofficial accounts—letters, affidavits, and articles written in the days, months, and years following the trial by those who were there. The most specific account was the affidavit of petit juror Miletus W. Ellis. It was sworn to before Clerk Hovey fifty-four days after the trial. Ellis described it as "an abstract from minutes which I took in the process of the trial." The "minutes" are gone, but Ellis's "abstract" of those minutes listed eight named witnesses and "several" unnamed witnesses.

Nine days after the trial, the *Oregon Weekly Times* published an article about the proceedings, reporting that "the following brief summary of the facts" was taken "from the memorandum of A. Campbell, Esq. prosecuting attorney." Probably, the Campbell "memorandum" consisted of notes taken in preparation for a bill of exceptions if one was needed. The memo has not been found, and the *Times* article is the only record of it.

Those served with subpoenas provide some clue as to who might have been called as witnesses. Also, the coroner report of what three witnesses had to say at the inquest is a fair indicator of what they repeated as testimony at the trial. And, the letters of trial spectators J.P. Welsh, J.C. Alexander, and John Thorp indicate the nature of some of the evidence presented, as does Nimrod's own writings.

The Swearing of Witnesses. Euro-American law has always operated on the notion that folks are more apt to be truthful when they vow to be. Witnesses called to testify in Nimrod's case had three choices as to how they would solemnize their vows. They could place a hand on a Bible and "swear upon the Holy Evangelists of Almighty God," or "solemnly swear"(without the book), or "solemnly, sincerely, and truly declare and affirm" (without book or oath). All of the witnesses in Nimrod's trial would likely have chosen an oath upon a Bible. But whether book or no book, oath or no oath, witness honesty was largely induced by law's own vow—Speak the truth or be jailed.

Proof of a Homicide. In order to first establish that a crime was committed, prosecutors Boise and Campbell would have called James "Sib" Barclay, Jeremiah Criss, and young Tom Richardson to testify—just as they had testified at the coroner's inquest, then again in Abiather Newton's justice court, and a third time before the grand jury. Now they appeared a fourth time before the petit jury. It is a wonder to know how much of their testimony came from rehearsal and how much from heart. Be that as it may, their composite testimony was that at seven or eight o'clock in the morning on Saturday, May 22, 1852, Missus Mahoney told them that her husband had been gone all night and asked them to see if they could find him. They found his body about a half-mile away, not too far from Nimrod O'Kelly's cabin. The body was lying in a dry slough bed with a huge hole in the chest. There was no shotgun or any other weapon in sight. Criss established the probable time of the killing when he testified that he had heard a shotgun blast from the direction of O'Kelly's cabin on the previous day, Friday, May 21, between noon and two o'clock.

These three witnesses, along with all of the other prosecution witnesses, were apparently present in court to hear one another's testimony. Nimrod would argue later that procedure tainted their separate accounts:

> The court let them all stand together in the court. One would hear what the other swor and then go up and swear as near the same as he could.

The potential problem of witnesses conforming their testimony justified keeping walls between them—a thing in law called "sequestering." But Nimrod's complaint apparently did not come during the trial, and, as far as the record indicates, Babb made no motion to exclude prospective witnesses from the courtroom. So, nothing more came of it.

To further show a homicide had occurred, the prosecutors called Isaac Winkle and Richard Irwin. It was easy to get the two confused. Winkle was on the coroner's jury and Irwin was the coroner. Irwin was the owner of a store and post office, and Winkle lived right across the road from the store. Their buildings composed the wayside called "Jennyopolis." Winkle was illiterate, so Irwin had occasion to write letters in both of their names. They too were present during each other's testimony and were able to confirm each other on the evidence. Coroner Irwin testified as to the condition of the corpse. His testimony would have been in keeping with his letter sent to the newspapers just two days after the killing. There he described the wound in these words:

> the charge being shot—slugs or buckshot, 37 shot and 3 or 4 slug wounds being counted by the coroner's jury—the whole charge taking effect in the left breast, ranging across his breast to the point of the right shoulder. Many of the shot took effect in his neck and throat. the slug or buckshot took effect a little above the left nipple, ranging inward, the wounds of which were probed 6 inches deep.

Juryman Ellis, confusing Irwin and Winkle, reported that the testimony of "Coroner Winkle" confirmed that the chest wound "extended from the nipple to the chin glancing across the breast."

The Identification Evidence. Next, the prosecutors sought to connect Nimrod to the killing. Either Winkle or Coroner Irwin swore that the shot found in the chest and the shot found in the unfired barrel of Nimrod's double-bore shotgun were both mixed loads of the "same two sizes" of shot. John Loose, a spectator, had a slightly different recollection of the testimony. Loose said the witness testified that the load was a mix of "shot and slugs." In either case, the point was that the load mix in the corpse matched the load mix in the unfired gun barrel. It was a clever rig for hitching the accused to the victim—clever, but needless makeweight in view of the fact that Nimrod freely admitted his shotgun was the one that fired at Mahoney.

Prosecutor Boise would have also sought to prove Nimrod's motive to kill—anger at Mahoney's land intrusion. Here, Jeremiah Criss undoubtedly repeated his inquest testimony that Nimrod forbid Mahoney from passing across the land to get timber, and warned Mahoney that he did so at his own risk. Young Tom Richardson repeated his testimony that Nimrod asked him to convey a warning to Missus Mahoney to advise her husband to move off. Sib Barclay was also asked about any warnings that Nimrod may have made. But, according to Nimrod, Barclay "refused to testify that I had made any threats against claim jumpers." Barclay may have developed misgivings while toeing the fine line between persecution and prosecution.

Mary Jane Mahoney, a widow of forty days, also testified. Most likely, she had her five-month-old baby with her. The widow would have been dressed in black from bonnet to button shoes. According to the Alexander-Welsh letter of 1852, she testified that when she and her husband first met Nimrod, he warned them that he would have his gun when next they met. She also testified, according to Juryman Ellis, of hearing from across the prairie the shot that killed her husband. What she had to say was not the main reason Boise called her to the witness chair. As the widow, she had to be given the courtesy of a voice in the trial of her dead husband's killer. The jury and the crowd expected it. Even the spurrings of Judge Pratt had to rein up for this lament. But it went beyond mere homage; tactically, prosecutors knew full well the advantage gained from the picture posed before the jury—the widow, in the box, in black, and in mourning.

Forty days ago, Nimrod faced his victim for the last time; here now he faced the widow for the first time. How would he react? The *Oregon Weekly Times* article reported, throughout the trial, Nimrod "seemed little affected" and "showed little concern." It characterized him as having a "suspicious hasty temper" and as "soured against the world." What beset Nimrod in those days made life "irksom and bitter," to use his own words and spelling. But now in the quiet tableau of widow and killer eye to eye, broken only by the cries of a now fatherless baby, maybe Nimrod's hardened heart rued the dreadful reach of violence.

To further identify Nimrod as a murderer, prosecutor Boise called Mary E. Norris to the witness chair. The Norris family had a house near Boonville, about midway between Marysville and Jennyopolis and seven miles north of Nimrod's cabin. Her front window looked out on the Gold Mines Road. According to Ellis, she testified seeing "Mr. O'Kelley pass towards Marysville" on the day of the killing. That was all she had to offer.[6] Boise wanted to argue that if Nimrod had innocently killed, why was he running north? Why did he not stay and offer himself up to Sheriff Starr, Justice of the Peace Hinton, or Coroner Irwin—all of whom resided in south county? The inference was standard and time honored: The guilty seek to escape.

On that premise, Greenberry Smith had important details. Greenberry was an old acquaintance of Nimrod. They probably shared a few campfires during the 1845 migration, when Nimrod was sixty-five and Greenberry twenty-three. It was not clear who called Greenberry as a witness. He had been subpoenaed by both sides—twice by the prosecution, and once by the defense. According to Juryman Ellis, Greenberry testified on Nimrod's behalf, stating that Nimrod came to his house on the night of the killing, "and said his life was in jeopardy & he did not know but he might be pursued and killed." His reason for running north, therefore, was because he feared his neighbors to the south. Nimrod told Greenberry, "he was on his way to the Judge and needed protection."

Now the door was open for questioning by prosecutor Boise, whose cross-examination would have made it clear why the prosecutor was just as anxious as the defender to have Greenberry in the witness chair.

Tell us, Mr. Smith, where is your house? How far north are you? Greenberry would have replied he lived twelve miles north of Marysville and about twenty-two miles from Nimrod's place.

But you say Mr. O'Kelly said he was on his way to the judge. Where was the nearest judge? And Greenberry would have said Justice of the Peace Abiather Newton lived back upriver near Marysville.

So, indeed, when you saw him, he was on a course away from the scene of the crime and away from the nearest judge, correct? Greenberry would acknowledge that as true.

Why did he go so far? Why did he not stop at Marysville and report to Abiather Newton? Perhaps, Greenberry ventured an opinion, Nimrod was confused and needed a friendly face, a fellow 1845 migrant, someone to trust.

But, where do J.C. Avery, William Fooks Dixon, and John Stewart live? In Marysville, would have been Greenberry's reply.

Were they not also friendly faces to be trusted? Like you and Nimrod, were they not also 1845 migrants to Oregon? There is, of course, no way to know if Nimrod's flight was laid open by the blade of that specific examination. But most assuredly, in one way or another, his flight would have been exploited by the prosecution. Was he escaping a mob or the law? Was he seeking help or hideaway? Why was he headed north, twelve miles beyond Marysville? Indeed, according to Ellis, Greenberry had to testify that he urged Nimrod "to go back and give himself up."

But aside from the mere implication of guilt by the act of fleeing, Greenberry's testimony included Nimrod's expressed confession that he had shot and killed. Abiather Newton was subpoenaed for the same reason. He too testified that Nimrod came to his doorstep and confessed. Juror Ellis wrote that Abiather swore, "at his house on the 22nd of May Mr. OKelley came there and pointing to a gun sitting against the fence stated that is the gun I killed Mahoney with."

Confession is the most telling proof of all, and Boise would make sure it was fully exploited. That is why it may seem odd that Boise did not offer into evidence Nimrod's written declaration filed on June 3, in which he freely confessed to the killing. Surely, a confession etched in ink would be even more telling than an oral admission conveyed by witness hearsay. But Boise probably felt that Nimrod's oral confessions to Greenberry and Abiather were convincing enough, without the jury seeing a written confession seeking to justify the killing as self-defense or an accident. While hearsay law allowed Boise to offer the declaration to convict Nimrod, the law did not allow Nimrod to offer the declaration to acquit himself. Anything an accused said out of court could be offered *against* him, but not *for* him. Consequently, it appears that Nimrod's written justification never became part of the trial and was never seen by the jury.

Accident or Self-Defense. The real heart of the controversy was excuse. So far, the prosecution's evidence had simply established what Nimrod had already confessed: There was a killing and Nimrod did it. More critical issues remained. Did Nimrod act maliciously? Was the killing planned? Was Nimrod justified in killing? On those issues, Nimrod's written declaration suggested two separate reasons for the killing. On the one hand, the declaration read:

> [Mahoney] continued coming towards me saying if I did not mind I would get it [the gun in Nimrod's hands] threshed out over my head...[He kept] sidling up towards me in a stooped position.

These allegations indicate a shooting in self-defense. The declaration went on to say:

> [T]he gun went off in my hands...I have no recollection of even cocking the gun, but held her down at arms length.

These allegations indicate an accidental shooting.

If Nimrod pursued both arguments at the trial, it would have been a tactical blunder. Either he *did not deliberately* pull the trigger, or he *did deliberately* pull it in order to protect himself. While conceivably one might accidentally shoot an attacker and thereby be a lucky defender, that theory would be a long reach for the biscuits. Jurors were part of the process because they brought common wisdom to law's complexities. Horse sense dictated that Nimrod would do himself no good by straddling the fence with one ear on the ground of purpose and the other on the ground of mistake.

Prosecutor Boise refuted the potential self-defense claim with several items of proof. Juryman Ellis reported, "Several of the witnesses state on the examination of the body of the deceased that they saw nothing near him by which to protect himself and that his hat was still on his head when found." According to Ellis, witness Winkle testified that "Mahoney must have been… some twenty or thirty yards from where the gun was discharged." The *Oregon Weekly Times* reported the distance as fifteen to thirty yards. On the other hand, Nimrod's written declaration described the distance as "about ten steps apart," when "he continued coming towards me." But the *Times* article said that Nimrod's claim that Mahoney was closing ground was "disproved by the strongest circumstantial evidence." Then too, Winkle testified that the chest wound was "glancing across the breast," implying the victim was not directly face to face with his killer.

During Winkle's or Coroner Irwin's testimony about the chest wound, Judge Pratt made a comment that greatly upset at least one of the court spectators. John Thorp recorded his trial observations and shock at the actions of the court.

> The manner in which he [Pratt] acted in the case of the Coroners evidence was sufficient to chill the Blood of an honest man, making the Evidence to say that the wound went inward & downward toward the ground as the Body lay, instead of that which the witness stated.

Apparently, the slant "downward toward the ground" would suggest Mahoney was down and Nimrod was over him at the time of the blast—certainly not the posture of someone simply defending himself. If Pratt made that interpretation, not only was it in conflict with the evidence, it was an intrusion that undermined his required impartiality. Only spectator Thorp reported the matter, and nothing more was made of it.

In any case, Nimrod's own written declaration tended to discredit self-defense. He wrote that his gun was discharged at Mahoney "before getting near enough to me to get hold of the gun." And, Nimrod said nothing about any weapon in Mahoney's hands. The law was clear. The force used to legally self-protect must not be excessive, and the force defended against must threaten immediate harm. Defensive action had to be protective, not avenging. And it had to be a last resort. Deadly force could not be used to stop a mere punch in the nose, verbal abuse, or distant threat.

Nimrod's potential self-defense theory was on soft bottom; he might have been better off fording on defenses like accident and the lack of malicious premeditation. The prosecution had no hard evidence that Nimrod had his mind set on harming Mahoney. Proof of motive, flight, and a few idle threats were soft circumstances. At that shallower crossing and on the firmer footing of reasonable doubt and of a voluntary surrender, Nimrod might have reached more forgiving shores.

Defense of Property. A more cloaked issue snuck into the trial when it was let fall that Nimrod too was a victim: Mahoney was allegedly claim jumping. Settlers understood that anyone who sought to grab another's claim could be dealt with harshly, even to the point of inflicting serious bodily harm. It may not have been the law, but it was folk justice on the frontier.[7] Claim jumpers, like horse thieves, were despised. Until the courts became more efficient in dealing with trespassers, bloodshed was frequently tolerated self-help in enforcing boundary lines—particularly in a land rush where the rap of the gavel could not be heard above the boom. Although the vanguards of order had arrived in Oregon Territory, the older practice still had roots.

On the other hand, some would contend that if Nimrod did not use his claim, he might forfeit any liberty to protect what he left unused.[8] However, the feeling against claim grabbers was so strong that even a land hog was held in greater favor. In December 1852, a newspaper in the Puget Sound area defended a land hog, declaring that while a land grabber taking from a land hog "is justified by a technicality of law...yet what honorable person would desire to be the neighbor of such a person." Differences over the balance to be struck between the greed of jumping and the greed of hoarding reached political levels. At a town meeting in Oregon City in 1847, 152 gatherers pledged not to give their votes to any candidate for public office who favored claim jumping. Shortly thereafter, claims associations were organized, whereby members vowed to stand together under the principle that an intruder against one was an intruder against all.

Thus, the Nimrod O'Kelly trial presented an unsettled situation on defense of property in a homicide case. There were no legislative mandates on the matter. The general rule in the States prohibited the infliction of serious body harm simply to protect land boundaries. If that had been the rule for Nimrod's trial, then any evidence about land borders, rightful claims, and land intrusion would have been irrelevant. But contrary to developed eastern law, frontier jurymen would be hungry to know: Was Mahoney squatting on

Nimrod's claim? How much did Nimrod claim? Was he hogging 640 acres or more? Was he entitled to only 320 acres? Was he married? After being in Oregon for seven years, why was his wife not at his side? Had he deserted her?

No doubt these inquiries, probed in depth, would have prolonged the trial. An impatient Judge Pratt would have preferred to exclude evidence on that digression but, at best, was only able to hold it to a minimum. The jurymen heard enough of it, however, to take it into their deliberations. The newspapers reported that Nimrod took more acres than allowed and Mahoney took only a portion of that excessive claim. According to Nimrod's account of the trial, "Bartley" swore at trial that Nimrod claimed "six sections of land"—six square miles. Justified or not, jumping or not, hogging or not, like it or not, the defense of property became an issue at the trial.

The Tardy Letter. While under arrest earlier in Marysville, Nimrod's reaction to a letter was used as crucial evidence against him at the trial and became heavily contested thereafter. On Sunday, the day after the killing, a letter from Texas was delivered to Nimrod, still in custody at the home of William Fooks Dixon. According to J.P. Welsh and J.C. Alexander, the "letter, of which much has been said…was lying in the P.O. for several days previous to any knowledge of the murder, this can be attested by the P.M."[9] Upon reading the letter and in the presence of his captors, Nimrod spoke words to the effect that "had he received the letter one day sooner it would have saved all this trouble," and the "killing would never have happened." At least three persons overheard the remark: Noah Starr, Deputy Sheriff Silas M. Stout, and Fooks Dixon. Prosecutor Boise called both Noah and Silas to testify about what they heard Nimrod say. Fooks was not called as a witness.

The relevance of Nimrod's remark is not easy to see, but the jurymen attached great significance to it. Apparently, the prosecutors offered the remark to show premeditation: By his words, Nimrod was admitting that the letter would have put an end to his intentions; thus suggesting that days before the killing, he had a plan to kill. Under that interpretation, the letter content was immaterial. Accordingly, the prosecution did not offer the letter itself into evidence. The jury need not know what the letter said, but needed only to know what Nimrod said in response to it.

Knowing the content of the letter, however, might have provided the jury with a different interpretation of the remark. The letter was dated March 7, 1852, and had found its way from Quitman, Wood County, Texas, in eleven weeks. It was from Mary Ann Fitzgerald and began, "Dear Father…," and near the end stated, "Joseph & Mother O.Kelley & Family I suppose will Start for Oregon in April next." Along about the same time, a second letter had been delivered to Nimrod. It was from his alleged son, Charles L. O'Kelly,[10] and dated March 28, 1852. After some opening cordialities this second letter stated:

> [Joseph] is now A Bout Redy to start to you in ten or twelve days he has got 2 waggons & team plenty he is going to fech Mother & her family…My Children is at Joseph now on A farwell visit I will write you A gaine as soon as they start an I git the first Letter from them on the rode I expect it will be A Bout the first of May.

Both letters indicated the critical fact that Nimrod had wife and family. If Nimrod had received those letters prior to that fatal day, "the killing would never have happened," because it would have shown entitlement to 640 acres and persuaded his intruders to abandon their trespasses. His reaction to the letter then, was to show that it could have changed their intentions, not his. Mahoney would have left peacefully. Fooks Dixon later wrote that if he had testified, he would have explained that this was the context in which Nimrod made his offhand remark. But the prosecutors did not call Dixon, and neither did the defense.

To be sure, there were those who shrugged off the contents of the letter as part of a scheme. The "Mother O'Kelly" referred to did not necessarily mean a wife. It could have been an aunt, grandmother, or some other matriarch. The doubters were unshakeable in their belief that Nimrod was nothing more than an old bachelor or a family deserter. According to Nimrod:

> Five or six protestant preachers…made it high treason for me to say I had a family and every time I got a letter from my family it would raise as heavy an excitement as if I had stold a horse. It would be in all their mouthes he has got another forged letter to make people think he has got a family.

No doubt, Nimrod's view was magnified by his situation. He was, after all, a troubled man in trouble—not the kind of man to be readily believed. Nevertheless, at trial, he was entitled to give an explanation for what coaxed his response to the letter. Both letters were apparently offered into evidence because they were both added to the court file. They were, however, either rejected by Judge Pratt or abandoned by the defense. Without the letters' contents, jurymen were left with the notion that Nimrod's plan to kill would have been stopped by the letters.

Quite apart from court doings, receiving daughter Mary Ann's letter was poignant. The day following the killing would have been a dismal Sunday for Nimrod. He was under arrest and facing charges of murder, a future trial, and a potential hanging. On such a day, a letter from a loving, sensitive, and sympathetic daughter must have been fresh rain on parched earth.

Dear Father, we are at this time in good health and hope this will find you enjoying like blessings. Your kind letter of the 30th Oct. last came to hand…We was almost [most?] overjoyed to hear from you…and was proud to think that you had written to us under your own hand. A few years Since and we were almost infants in your presence. But all have changed. We have now become parents ourselves…We Sympathize with you in your present lonesome condition so far distant from your friends and relatives. We can easily…imagine your lonesome Solitary abode in Oregan…[Y]ou have acquired more for yourself & family by going to Oregan than you all would have acquired in your lifetimes in Missouri & Arkansas. We are perfectly Sensible of all the privations and hardships which no doubt you have been compelled to undergo in such a length of time in a Strange Land alone and among Strangers.

Her letter ended on this promising note:

We are now consoled with the thought that this State of bereavement or long Separation…will not last much longer…Your affectionate and ever loving children until death.

The jurymen knew nothing of family or a daughter's love. They were not given the words.

Other Potential Evidence Not Given at Trial. Available records indicate that at least eleven witnesses testified for the prosecution. While the record shows that an equal number of defense witnesses showed up, apparently none testified. Letters, affidavits, and articles written by spectators, jurors, newspapers, and Nimrod himself say nothing about any defense testimony. Greenberry Smith, Abiather Newton, R.B. Hinton, and S.M. Stout, who were summoned by both sides, did testify. What the defense witnesses would have sworn to had they testified is left to surmise. Fooks Dixon, David Stump, and Benjamin Nichols were acquaintances, who shared with Nimrod the 1845 migration to Oregon. Nichols had known Nimrod since 1812 in Tennessee. Stump signed Nimrod's last will and testament as a witness just the day before trial. Dixon had been at Nimrod's side since his arrest. Their testimony, had they given it, might have been simply to swear to Nimrod's good character. But, apparently, the jurymen did not hear one word from any of these men.

L.G. Hoge could also have been a witness. A month and a half after the trial, Hoge signed a written statement attesting that "previous to the murder by okelly [he made?] statements to me about his neighbours that they wished to trample on his rights." All Hoge had to offer was hearsay and makeweight—a repetition of Nimrod's allegations of a conspiracy to provoke abandonment of his claim. Hoge was not subpoenaed until the second day of trial. Either a defense decision was made not to call on him, or the judge decided to disallow his testimony, or Hoge ignored the subpoena and did not show up.

Most of the other witnesses called by Nimrod were southern Benton County residents and not likely to be friendly toward him.[11] What use Nimrod thought he could make of these neighbors is unclear. He may have summoned them for either confrontation or expectation—that is, to challenge them as foes or to chance from them something favorable or kind. But a court of law was no place to pick a fight or to go fishing. Investigation was to be done in advance of trial, albeit preparation time was a measure of which Nimrod claimed to be short. Whatever the reasons, defense witnesses came but apparently did not testify because of either Babb's advice, Boise's objections, or Pratt's spurring the case along.

Curiously, among all of those who were summoned as character witnesses for Nimrod, not one was a French Prairie Catholic. If Nimrod was interested in having his good character conveyed to the jury, folks like John McLoughlin, godfather Joseph Gervais, or a Catholic priest would have been logical—but, perhaps, not tactical. Nimrod was still the only Catholic in all of Benton County. How a Benton County jury would react to Catholic testimony was dangerous guesswork.

Another witness who could have been called in Nimrod's behalf, but never subpoenaed, was John Loose (sometimes spelled "Luce"), who had been one of the coroner jurymen. One week after the trial, J.C. Alexander, a concerned Benton County settler, reported that he talked to a "Mr. Loose," who apparently examined Nimrod's double-barreled shotgun soon after the killing. Loose said he "found but light load of powder in the other barrel." Loose was surprised at the testimony for the prosecution that there was a mix of "slugs and shot" in the gun, when in fact "it was agreed by the jury of inquest that they were shot." The critical point here for the prosecutors was that a hunter would not load his gun with slugs just to kill crows; slugs were used for bigger prey. A light load and no slugs would have borne out Nimrod's claim that he was carrying the gun on the day of the killing to hunt crows, not men. The jury never heard from Loose.

No one testified concerning Nimrod's mental state at the time of the killing. But after the trial, many asserted that Nimrod was "feeble in mind & body." Alexander and J.P. Welsh wrote that it was "well known that O'Kelly is not a man of sound mind," and that he was "constantly kept in such a state of mind that a slight personal provocation might easily lead him to commit a rash act." Nimrod, of course, did not and would not bring himself to fall upon that excuse. If there was going to be any claim of madness, it would have had to be interposed by a compassionate and wise court. Nimrod's conduct at the trial, however, would not have stirred Pratt to such initiative. On the contrary, Nimrod agitated instead of stirred. Pratt may have been inclined, but he was not convinced. In later years, he wrote:

> [W]hile my mind struggled with the sympathies excited by the old man's age, I was compelled to yield to the conviction that he was but *too guilty*.

Nimrod was not allowed to testify at his trial. Consistent with traditional rules of evidence throughout the nation, litigants were barred from offering themselves as witnesses, even in trials where their lives hung in the balance. The "Evidence" chapter of the Oregon Code of 1854 had a roundabout way of codifying the rule:

> Section 3: No person offered as a witness shall be excluded by reason of an interest in the event.

> Section 4: The last section shall not apply to a party to the action.

Two reasons accounted for that ban: Litigants (especially the criminally accused) were most likely to be incompetent liars; and furthermore, litigants and their agents already had plenty of voice in the proceedings by way of jury selection, opening statements, motions, objections, and final arguments. A decade later, Oregon lawmakers recognized the unfairness, if not unconstitutionality, of that prohibition and decreed:

> All persons without exception…may be witnesses; therefore, neither parties, nor other persons who have an interest…are excluded.

That 1862 enlightenment did Nimrod no good in 1852.

On the other hand, Nimrod may not have felt any special desire to testify, inasmuch as he spoke up on many occasions throughout the trial. He wrote that he was obliged to interject because he did not have "counsel that I could place confidence in," and because he "was loaded down with irons…to keep me from writing." In rising from his chair, his outbursts would have been heralded by the clanking of cuffs and hobbles. Those interruptions would have put him nose to nose with a presider who did not brook delay. Nimrod wrote of those confrontations:

> My enemies…say if you had not exposed judg pratt openly it would be much better for you. Judg pratt is a strong man he can influence the people…Is judg pratt and his family and reputation to be defended and mine and my family to be bloted forever and me not permitted to say a word in my own defense…?

Closing Summations. Judge Pratt's minutes record that the jury then heard "the arguments of counsel." Nowhere was it reported what those arguments contained or how long they took. Prosecutor Boise's summation, much to the satisfaction of the court, would have been simple, short, and highlighted by these essential points:

There can be no doubt that the prisoner shot and killed the victim. The prisoner confessed that several times. He loaded his shotgun with man-killing slugs. The victim had no weapon. His hat was still upon his head when he was found dead. He was as far off as thirty yards and at least fifteen yards when he was fired upon. The prisoner threatened to do the victim harm, several times. He admitted that a certain letter could have stopped his plan to kill had he received it earlier. Immediately following the killing, the prisoner did not report to the sheriff or to the widow or to anyone nearby, instead he ran as far north as twenty-two miles. There may have been a land boundary dispute between him and his victim, but that is still no reason to kill; and, in any case, the size of the prisoner's claim was false and greedy. That the gun may have gone off accidentally is not supported by any proof except the prisoner's own naked, self-serving contention. On the contrary, all of the evidence leans toward a deliberate, planned, malicious, unjustified, inexcusable killing—murder in the first degree.

As for the defendant's closing argument, Nimrod wrote that he "had not the first man to speak a word for me." That attorney Babb made no summation at all to the jury is hard to believe. If he spoke, perhaps he refuted the distance between O'Kelly and the victim when the shot was fired, arguing that it was closer than fifteen yards. Perhaps Babb pressed the fact that the victim had threatened to take the gun from O'Kelly and thrash him with it, that O'Kelly had to protect himself against the younger man. Perhaps Babb urged strongly that Nimrod did not mean to shoot. Perhaps Babb was smart enough to emphasize that the accused did not have a duty to prove accident, rather it was the prosecution's duty to prove intent. Perhaps Babb explained that O'Kelly fled because he feared reprisal from his neighbors, and that many of those neighbors sought a means to seize his claim by subtle encroachments. Perhaps Babb emphasized that O'Kelly turned himself over to the justice of the peace at Marysville, that he freely admitted the killing, and that his own volunteered confessions were the only real proof connecting him to the death. Perhaps, Babb was clever enough to have constantly reminded the jurymen of O'Kelly's seventy-two years, his military service in defense of the nation, and the fact that, in southern Benton County, O'Kelly was isolated from his family, friends, and religion. Perhaps Babb capped his argument with the most important point of all: the jury must not convict of first degree murder if they had any reasonable doubt about O'Kelly having maliciously conceived a plan to murder.

Perhaps Babb made this summation. Perhaps. But it is more in keeping with the record to assume that such coverage was, at best, not within his competence and, at worst, not within his heart. He was a lawyer whose passing of the bar in Pratt's court was less than three months old. The best that may be said in defense of Babb is that he had but one day to prepare for a first-degree murder trial. Although he was the judge's choice, he was not the accused's choice and likely not his own choice.

Nimrod himself may have been allowed to speak to the jury, but his skills would have been no better than Babb's. There may have been one other who spoke in Nimrod's behalf. Somewhere in the course of the trial, J.C. Avery rose to be heard in court and in his own backyard. He was never subpoenaed as a witness, and there is no account of him having given sworn testimony. But Nimrod reported that Avery did speak and did so with apparent feeling.

> In the midst of all this clangor of envy and prejudice JC avery speak loud and said how does it look to see an old man forced in to trial in this manner. As he speak these words I saw large tears flowing from his eyes he was the first man in which I saw remorse.

Nevertheless, Nimrod felt that the cut of Avery's words was dulled by his conflicting loyalties.

> Here was an awful difficulty stood in the way which prevented him from saying a word for me: That was judg pratt and JC avery was great friends and in great colligation in politics.

Avery and Pratt indeed were fellow Durhamites. Pratt was probably a guest in Avery's home during the trial. So, whatever plea Avery made in Nimrod's behalf, it may have been choked with restraint. He stood between compassion on the one hand and partisanship on the other. Then too, Nimrod may have sensed the hypocrisy of one who showed passion for mercy, yet aversion to liberty; Avery was an advocate of slavery.

The Court's Instructions to the Jury. Judge Pratt's journal reports the jurymen then heard the "charge of the court," that point in the trial when the judge instructed the jurors about the law and their legal duties. So far, the day had been packed with some preliminary motions, the calling and selecting of a petit jury, the hearing of the testimony of at least eleven witnesses, and the final summations of the parties. Rather than adjourning at this point, Pratt chose to instruct the jury and to send them off to deliberate on their verdict. It had been a long day that now promised to be much longer.

There is no official record of what Judge Pratt instructed at this time, but no doubt his schedule pared his charge to a core. He would have intoned a litany of standard duties, which included reaching a unanimous verdict, doing so dispassionately, and basing it upon the evidence presented and nothing more. Under the Hamilton Code, he had to explain three different kinds of homicide. If Nimrod killed deliberately and with premeditation, that would be *first degree murder* punishable by death. If Nimrod killed without prior deliberation or premeditation, yet with malice and intent to kill, that would be *second degree murder* punishable by life imprisonment. If Nimrod killed without malice, as for instance "upon a sudden quarrel," or without any intent to kill, yet still without justification or excuse, that would be *manslaughter* punishable by imprisonment from one to ten years.[12]

Pratt's instructions may have gone on to describe justifiable and excusable homicides. Accordingly, Pratt should have told the jurymen that if they found Nimrod acted to save himself from "great bodily harm" and "danger so urgent and pressing" that the killing was "absolutely necessary," then that would be self-defense warranting a verdict of not guilty. If the jury were to find Nimrod acted "without any intention of killing" and within "the bounds of moderation" and the death resulted "unfortunately" and by "misadventure," then that would be innocent mistake also warranting a verdict of not guilty.[13]

Most assuredly, Pratt's instructions would have been short, but not as short as the instructions attributed to Judge Cox of Idaho, in 1878.

> Gentlemen of the jury, if you believe what the attorney for the plaintiff says, you will have to find for the plaintiff; if you believe what the attorney for the defendant says, you will have to find for the defendant; but if you are like me and don't believe a damned word that either of them says, I don't know what in hell you'll do.

Unlike Judge Cox, Pratt knew that in cases of no persuasion one way or the other, the party with the burden to prove must lose. Pratt would have known the prosecution carried that burden and that a failure to persuade meant an acquital. While Pratt probably provided this much instruction, he may have failed to take it one step farther. According to spectator John Thorp, Pratt failed to tell how heavy the prosecution's burden was and what had to be done to overcome it. Thorp reported Pratt neglected to emphasize that in order to convict, the jury had to be persuaded *beyond any reasonable* doubt. Thorp wrote:

> Refusing or Rather neglecting to give in charge to the Jury that their minds must be freed from doubt…, is a neglect of duty in the court that must have been intentional and is proven by his language to Avery, for had he stated to the Jury that the Evidence must be such as to free their minds from all doubt, that the Jury could never bring a verdict for murder in any degree

The alleged failure to give this highly critical instruction was not recorded in any bill of exceptions. Accordingly, it could not be claimed as an error for appeal purposes. Once again, the failure to preserve an official account of events strangled Nimrod's chances and led him toward a strangulation of a more vivid nature.

Before Pratt sent the jurors off to deliberate, he should have instructed them to elect a foreman. But the court's daily journal does not show the name of any petit jury foreman, even though it did give the name of the grand jury foreman. Nor does the verdict form designate any juror as foreman. There was no petit jury foreman, either because Pratt neglected to give that instruction, or because the jury neglected to follow it. It was late. Matters were moving along rapidly.

Jury Deliberations and Verdict. The court minutes recited that the jurymen "retired in charge of a sworn officer to consider of their verdict." They probably went into Avery's house for privacy. The day had been long. Folks were tired. Although daylight was long lasting at that time of year, some of the jurymen were a three or four hour ride from family and supper. Night came a half-hour after sundown and would make travel dangerous without a full moon.

According to Judge Pratt, the jury "after a short absence returned into court the...verdict." Here it is important to acknowledge that Pratt did not note that the jurymen returned *with* the verdict, rather he wrote that they "returned" the verdict to the court. This could be read to mean that the jury verdict was delivered, but not necessarily that the jury delivered it. The reading may be technical, but subsequent contentions made events at this point highly critical. It was later argued that when the verdict was eventually rendered, it was not delivered in "open court"—meaning it was not rendered in the presence of the jury or defendant or both.

If so, then the sequence of events could have been this—the jury retired to consider their verdict, Pratt called a court recess, and Nimrod returned to confinement. The jury then reached a verdict much sooner than expected, and Pratt and Nimrod had to be rounded up. The jury grew impatient in the late hour, with dark coming and bellies growling, thus the judge gave some or all of them permission to leave before Nimrod returned.

The jury's written verdict seems to confirm some such happenings. Although Pratt's record recited that the verdict was "signed by all of the Jurors," most of the twelve signatures on the verdict form appear written in the script of the same person. The similarities of the handwriting are unmistakable. Furthermore, signatures of some of the jurors that appear on other documents are quite unlike their alleged signatures on the verdict. The swift verdict and early departure of jurymen would also help explain why no foreman was designated.

If neither Nimrod nor the jury were present during the rendering of the verdict, then that would be an extreme break with tradition and an affront to the accused's rights. It was no mere technicality. High on the list of ceremonial necessities—where rights and rites join—was the face-to-face reckoning between the accused and his condemners. But Judge Pratt's official journal did not record whether jurymen or Nimrod were or were not present for the verdict. Neither does the journal say whether any adjournment of court took place while the jury deliberated—although a recess would seem to be a matter of course. Nor does it say that the defendant left the court or that an objection was made at trial about the absence of the accused or any jurymen. All it does say is that the jury deliberations were "short," and that the jury "returned into court the verdict." Allegations that the accused and his jury did not come together for deliverance were destined to be unearthed in the future.

But like their deliberations, the jury's verdict was short and predictable:

> We the jury find the Defendant Nimrod O. Kelley guilty of murder in the first degree in manner and form as charged in the indictment.

Appended thereto were their twelve purported signatures. Whereupon "the court adjourned," wrote Pratt, "until tomorrow morning at eight o'clock."

It was not a good night for sleep. Summer heat had begun. Bugs were at hatch. Perhaps some who witnessed the trial were kept awake by second thoughts. Certainly, one soul, convicted of murder and locked in a shed, would toss upon a tick filled with straw and a fate sealed by law.

Notes

1. The record verifies some parts of Nimrod's contention. He did attempt to serve six witnesses outside of Benton County. Two from Polk County were successfully served with subpoenas by the Polk County sheriff. Another, from Clackamas County, was also served the day after the trial commenced. The returns of service upon the others were reported as "not found" by the Clackamas County sheriff, and consequently those requested witnesses were not present, as Nimrod observed.
2. The panelist missing on Wednesday could have been David Carson, who might have been ailing. Born in Ireland, he was at age fifty-two the oldest juryman on the panel. He died two months after the trial.
3. Thomas M. Read was among the first settlers in Benton County. He and Nimrod were both 1845 immigrants who had started out in the same wagon train as single men. Undoubtedly, they had previous dealings with each other. Read is not to be confused with Thomas D. Reeves, who served on the coroner's jury. The lives of Tom Read and Tom

Reeves ran parallel. Aside from the similarity in their names, both filed claims in Benton County in 1846. They were approximately the same age, and both married in Benton County in 1846 to pioneer women named Nancy.

4. To be sure, not all pioneers were lured west by the call of free land. Judge Pratt himself never made a land claim. Such men apparently saw success in something other than tilling the soil. Settling a frontier offered opportunities at labor, business, government, mining, logging, and, for some, merely a place in which to be.

5. The jury panelists not chosen included the two talesmen recruited from the crowd, Friedley and Slagle, plus ten veniremen: Charles Allen, Charles Bayles, G.W. Bethers, Jesse H. Caton, D.R. Hodges, Isaac King, Lucius Norton, Washington Patterson, Morgan Savage, and B.W. Wilson. All of the dismissed were nevertheless paid fees of about four dollars each for having answered the call. The two talesmen received nothing. Venireman David Carson, or whoever it was that did not report for duty on Wednesday, was paid his fee nonetheless.

6. Missus Norris was a descendant of Daniel Boone. Her husband, Tom Norris, had been on the grand jury that indicted Nimrod. Boise felt that her single item of evidence was important enough to subpoena her, just the day before the trial began. She did not testify before the grand jury.

7. Under Oregon's Twenty Acts, the law on defending property seemed clear—a murder might be justified in defense of habitation, but only against an intruder who "endeavors by violence or surprise to commit a...felony," or who enters "for the purpose of assaulting or offering personal violence" (Section 14 of "Crimes and Punishments"). Even if Mahoney was grabbing Nimrod's *legal* claim, there would be no license to just up and kill him. Intruders were not open game—not unless they threatened "felony" or "personal violence." Mere trespass was not violent, nor a felony. The common law of the states back east was fairly the same as Oregon's Twenty Acts definition: Killing could not be used to protect a claim from jumpers. But here was where it was critical to know whether the Hamilton Code had as yet been distributed and assimilated in Oregon (see note 3 in Chapter 12). Section 78 of the Hamilton Code completely replaced all prior laws dealing with "Crimes and Misdemeanors," and was silent on any definition for defense of property. Without legislative mandates or judicial precedent, Oregon judges were now free to fashion how far settlers could go in defending their property. Judge-made law would tend to follow the unwritten customs of folk law. On a frontier beset by squatters and land rush, violence in the protection of borders was a practice readily, albeit not openly, accepted in trials.

8. The growth of mining introduced a different attitude about land and its boundaries. Miners returning from gold fields brought back more than dust. They brought back grit—a zeal that defied borders in order to remove the land. Miners did not look at the land as place. They saw it as resource. They came to the land for one thing only, and settling down was the least of their intentions. They took and went. They had no use for land lying fallow. Whether claimed or unclaimed, vacant land was open for digging, panning, sluicing, and scouring. Government and law encouraged their need to follow the color, the vein, the glory hole, the stream. And so, those who had gone off to take land into their pokes, returned with it and with a different feeling about the rights in unused land.

9. By the spring of 1852, the number of branch postal stations had grown. It is not known whether the letter had been delivered to and was resting in the Avery Post Office in Marysville, Irwin's Jennyopolis Post Office, the Nesmith Post Office farther north, or the Oregon City Post Office still farther north.

10. It is possible that Charles' letter was the first received, on May 22, but not likely. If its path wended the route directed by its sender, it would have taken longer than seven weeks to arrive. It came from Cassville in Barry County, Missouri, and was addressed to Nimrod at

"Origan Sitty Origan territory via New Orleanes San Fransisco, please postmaster forward this Letter." Mail directed to Oregon Territory through the U.S. Post Office, as of October 20, 1851, came only as far as Astoria at the mouth of the Columbia River. From there, delivery became the responsibility of the territorial government. Mail by sea from the east came to Astoria semi-monthly. Oregonians suffered so much delay and loss of mail that on October 20, 1851, the Oregon territorial legislature petitioned Congress for improvements. The Mary Ann letter, mailed two weeks earlier than Charles' letter, more likely was first to be received.

11. Aside from Stump, Nichols, Dixon, and Hoge, and not counting the witnesses jointly subpoenaed by the prosecution, the defense summoned fourteen other witnesses: John Gibson, John Thomas, Rachel Newton, John Fiechter, Robert Grimsley, William Coyle, Gideon Richardson, Missus Jacob Slagle, Missus William Porter, Adam Zumwalt, Henry Noble, Jacob Hammer, Thomas Reeves, and David Butterfield. Except for Stump, Nichols, Gibson, and Zumwalt, they all appear to be Benton County residents—six of whom were near neighbors.

12. The earlier Twenty Acts had set forth only two kinds of homicide and punishment—for murder, punishment was death; for manslaughter, a maximum seven years imprisonment and a $10,000 fine. The Hamilton Code added the prospect of life imprisonment for second degree murder. But Oregon had no penitentiary, Benton County no jail, and jails in other counties were too insecure and too inhumane for lifetime incarceration. The choices were simply these—old man O'Kelly would have to be set free, jailed for a short time, or killed. The new charge of second degree murder with its mandatory life imprisonment was simply not a meaningful choice.

13. Oddly enough, the Hamilton Code gave no definitions for justifiable or excusable homicide. The phraseology quoted in the text is taken from the Twenty Acts. Over the decades, lawmakers have made many attempts at reclassifying the various attitudes taken by those who kill. Today the Oregon Revised Statutes call for at least seven classifications of homicide.

16

Trial—Last Day

July 1, 1852

It was Thursday, the third and last day of trial. In three more days, the nation would be seventy-six years old. Judge Pratt convened court promptly at eight o'clock that morning, an earlier start than usual. Pratt had an agenda. Political, commercial, and judicial business had to be put in order before heading to Astoria to catch an ocean clipper. Most likely, the crowd in Avery's yard was thinner. The *doings* had lost their drama. What remained was foregone. Stock and fields had been too long without tending.

The previous day's minutes were read aloud. No one objected to the content, which bears repeating—No one sought to amend Pratt's record keeping! Accordingly, the journal was signed by Pratt and thus solemnized. The reported facts would be binding on higher courts. Truth would now be measured by the record, not by the reality.

Before yesterday's adjournment, defense attorney Babb, in response to the guilty verdict, filed a hastily written motion asking the court to withhold judgment and to retry the case before a new jury. Two reasons were given: "1st The record of said conviction is informal and insufficient. 2nd the verdict of said Jury was against the weight of evidence." Babb gave no details. He simply claimed the jury had made a baseless decision and the judge had kept a measly record of it. Pratt would have taken no offense at the motion, nor would he have paid it any mind. A motion from a party for a new trial was routine sputter, the final growl of a loser sulking away. Nevertheless, at the close of yesterday's business, Pratt had dignified the motion by taking the matter into consideration overnight.

Now, here, the next morning, Pratt's first act was to announce that he had been "advised" on the motion, and had "fully considered" it. Motion denied. No new trial. No more delays.

Spectator John Thorp was bothered by what he heard at this point, and felt obliged to note, "something was wrong." According to Thorp, Pratt had expressed "great astonishment at the verdict." Nevertheless, Pratt refused to grant a new trial. Thorp was himself astonished:

If he [Pratt] was satisfied that the Jury had found contrary to Evidence, why not grant a new trial. Was he not placed on the Bench to administer Justice. Was he not Sworn and did he preserve that oath when he had stated that the Jury could not find for murder.

Pratt's denial of the motion for a new trial opened the door for more routine. This time it was prosecutor Boise, who moved the court to enter "Judgment against said Nimrod OKelley, upon the Verdict of the Jury." Judge Pratt then asked Nimrod and his counsel Babb "to show cause why Judgment and sentence should not be passed upon him." It was at this point that Nimrod would have had more to say. Perhaps, it was here that J.C. Avery made his plea on Nimrod's behalf. All that is known for certain is that Pratt ruled that no sufficient cause was shown to arrest the proceedings.

The motions at this stage dressed the doings in dignity, protocol, sobriety, office, and form. But no amount of *going-through-the-motions* could dull the edge of the blade poised for striking. It was about to cut deep. Nimrod was asked to rise. The clanking of chains would have rung across the morning mist rising there. When all was quiet, Pratt delivered the judgment of the court in keeping with the jury's verdict.

"Defendant Nimrod O'Kelly is guilty of murder in the first Degree." Pratt then intoned the sentence of the court:

> It is further ordered and adjudged by the court that the said Defendant Nimrod O'Kelly be taken hence by the sheriff of said County of Benton and be by him the said sheriff kept and detained in safe and secure custody until Tuesday the twenty fourth day of August A.D. 1852, and until the hour of Eleven o clock in the forenoon of that Day last aforesaid, and that said Nimrod O'Kelly be taken by the said sheriff or his lawful deputy or successor in office on the day and at the hour in that behalf last aforesaid from the place of confinement of him the said Nimrod O'Kelly to a Gallows to be by said sheriff or other officer aforesaid for that purpose rected at the County site in and for said County, and there hanged by the neck until he the said Nimrod O'Kelly be dead.

For mercy's sake, death on the gallows would hopefully come quicker than the sentence commanding it.

Nimrod sat back down. There was no more to say. His chains were heavier than ever. The judge's reckoning pinched out the last spark upon the wick at which the hopeful were transfixed, no matter how sure the coming of darkness. Nimrod was to be killed. He would have fifty-four days to put his house and soul in order.

The 1852 overland migration to Oregon would not begin arriving in the Valley until September. Nimrod was scheduled to die in August. If he had family and if they were in that migration, he would never see them again.

Apparently Pratt took no account of farewell or family. The judge paused long enough for Nimrod to reflect upon the crux of the sentence before intoning its afterpiece. It too gave reason for pause:

> And it is further ordered and adjudged by the court that the said Territory of Oregon have Judgment against the said Nimrod O'Kelly for the costs of pros-ecution and have Execution thereon against the Goods and Chattels Lands and Tenements of said Nimrod O'Kelly pursuant to the form of the statute in such case made and provided.

Not only did the sentence take Nimrod's life, it took his land as well.[1]

Prior to trial, the Benton County Fee Journal and Judgment Docket book had listed costs in the murder case of *Territory of Oregon v. Nimrod O'Kelly* at $111.38.[2] Four days after the trial, the county commissioners approved these added trial fees—$16.00 to Sheriff Starr for "opening court" four times and for attending trial three days; $15.50 to Deputy Sheriff Stout for "opening court" two times and for attending trial three days; $15.00 to Clerk Hovey for attending trial for three days; $50.00 to "R.P. Boise, Esq." for prosecuting the case; and $96.00 to "Hon. O. C. Pratt" for presiding as judge.

The Hamilton Code chapter on "District Judges" authorized expenses and a special fee for judges holding special terms—$5.00 for every day of travel and court presidence, plus expenses for room, board, and travel. The commissioners' minutes stated that the $96.00 "due the Hon. O. C. Pratt be subject to the order of J.C. Avery." The probable reason for payment to Avery instead of Pratt is that Avery had furnished the room and board to his fellow Durhamite, and had advanced Pratt his fees and travel expenses. Pratt had no time to wait for the commissioners to make payment.

The commissioners' minutes also reported payment of $6.90 to Coroner Irwin, and $24.00 to the twelve coroner jurors for their work at the May 22 inquest, even though the inquest was a dubious legal procedure. And the commissioners approved payment of $64.40 to twenty-two grand jurors, about $54.00 to the twelve petit jurors, and $56.00 to eleven veniremen.

If all of these expenses could be deemed "costs of prosecution," they to-taled over $500 and did not yet include fees and travel expenses for the wit-nesses. Nimrod's land claim was the only potential source for a payment this large. Although his claim was still in jeopardy from squatters, now it was endangered by a bigger intruder—Benton County.

And that was not all. There were still other and much bigger costs. The expense of keeping Nimrod in custody would far exceed the judicial costs. Charges for guarding and attending the prisoner from May 22, 1852, through the end of the trial came to about $258. By August 24—the date set for the hanging—there would be at least another $500 to pay to the guards, and this did not include the price for their food and lodging. While these custodial outlays were arguably not "costs of prosecution," there would be those who would urge that Nimrod should pay for his confinement as well.

On April 5, 1853, the Benton County Commissioners approved the payment to "A.J. Babb, Esq." of $60 for his service as court-appointed counsel. The nine-month delay in paying for the accused's defense was either because Babb took that long in bringing himself to make the request, or because the commissioners took that long in bringing themselves to honor it. Of course, expenses of the accused's own defense counsel would not qualify as "costs of prosecution"—although one could make sport of that.

Two more costs to the county marked the doom already descended, and the doom yet to fall. Both were charges for lumber. Isaac W. Winkle was to be paid $2.00 for making Mahoney's wood coffin; William Matzger was to be paid $9.56 for the lumber used in constructing Nimrod's gallows. Coffins for the dead were much cheaper than gallows for the damned. As for the grim business of hanging, there would be additional costs for an executioner, another box, and diggers.

According to a list compiled by Sheriff Starr, Benton County had 207 taxpayers at the time of trial. That being so, the prosecution, custody, and hanging of Nimrod was about to cost each taxpayer more than $6.00 a piece—unless Nimrod's assets were enough to defray some of that assessment. Nimrod now had many more detractors—taxpayers who would benefit by taking his claim from him.

Murder and justice had one thing in common—an enormous price to pay.

Notes

1. Pratt's sentence was mandated by law as to the death punishment and the taking of property. Section 35 of the "Crimes and Misdemeanors" chapter of the Hamilton Code stated: "the court shall render judgment against such convict for the costs of prosecution, and award execution thereon against the goods and chattels, lands and tenements of said convict."
2. The pretrial costs included $1 paid to each of the witnesses in Abiather Newton's Justice Court proceeding. The sheriff and deputies were paid 25¢ for each witness subpoenaed, plus 10¢ for each mile traveled in making service. Clerk Hovey was paid 10¢ for each court paper filed and recorded, and 25¢ for every 100 words copied by him as a scrivener.

17

Post Trial Stirrings

July-August 1852

The throes of justice had barely faded when some swooped in for the leavings. Just five days after the trial and before any printed news of it had reached the public, men gathered near Nimrod's cabin to peck at the pieces of boundary. The claims of Nimrod O'Kelly, Jeremiah Mahoney, Asa Stark, Jeremiah Criss, and Robert Grimsley all came together in huge overlaps. One of those claimants was now dead, and another was scheduled to die. But death did not simplify matters. A widow lived on, claiming her share. Another future widow, supposedly on the horizon, compounded the problem. In addition, the county now drove its stake on account of court costs owed. New claims searchers would soon be arriving daily. Lines and corners needed an immediate resolve, but territorial surveyors were still a long way off.

And so, a citizen survey was the reason for the gathering organized by Richard Irwin and R.B. Hinton—they were the two who had instigated the earlier coroner inquest at the same spot just six weeks before. John Lloyd, Dave Williams, Tom Reeves, Bill Porter, John Loose, and Isaac Winkle were also there—they had all served on the coroner's jury. "Sib" Barclay was there—he had been a witness four times. Aaron "Doc" Richardson would not have missed the surveying of Nimrod's borders. Stark, Criss, and Grimsley, the overlapping claimants, must have been there. But the widow Mahoney was not. Reportedly, "fifteen men" attended.

Needless to say, Nimrod stayed put in Marysville under guard and in irons. Perhaps that was why J.C. Alexander was invited to attend. He was not from the Long Tom neighborhood. He lived north—on the edge of Marysville. His presence, as a representative of Nimrod's interests, was a show of square doings. Neither the surveyor general nor the county had a hand in calling this citizen vigilance. On July 16, R.B. Hinton wrote a letter to Nimrod that began:

> Sir on the 6th of July the citizens in the neighborhood of your claim met at your house for the purpose of surveying and marking off your claim to prevent people from intruding on it.

When they met on Nimrod's claim, the gatherers found two new intruders who had already pitched camps at Nimrod's spring. In a countryside with more seekers than acres, vacating land was like uncorking a vacuum into which those without roots were sucked. Irwin's letter went on to state that the neighbors bade the intruders to strike their tents and leave—which they did. There was something slippery, however, about a letter that began with a gentle bit and kind reins, yet came from those who in the past had been a spur in Nimrod's flanks. The letter went at great length to couch its purpose in neighborly care and concern for Nimrod. A few lines later, the hand of friendship was again extended: "We further bound ourselves to protect your claim from all intruders." At the end of the letter, that pledge was reduced to solemn certification:

> We the citizens of Benton Co. and neighbors of N. OKelly we do hereby certify…to protect [the claim surveyed] for the benefit of his heirs or to whom the law may give it to.

As a final cordiality, Hinton stated: "I would have wrote to you earlier but a lack of time prevented me."

If Nimrod was pleased to read that his neighbors had made a turn of heart and were now caring for him, he was in for an awakening. The heart of the letter reported where his neighbors re-drew the lines and corners of his claim: "Beginning at the South-East corner Running West 200 rods thence North 260 rods East 200 rods thence South to the Beginning." Those borders would have fired Nimrod's cheeks and dropped his jaw. A tract of land measuring 200 by 260 rods was far from the one he had staked at 320 by 320 rods. His neighbors had given him about one half of what he had staked—325 acres instead of 640 acres. They were promising to protect him from intrusion, while at the same time intruding. Richard Irwin and Isaac Winkle in an August 17 letter verified Hinton's survey description, characterizing it as generous in that it gave

> OKelly his house and all his improvements and 5 acres more than what he was entitled to making in all 325 acres and not Joining lines with Mahoney by 600 feet or with any other settler by near the same distance. Showing to the whole settlement that Mahoney was not on OKellys claim.

J.C. Alexander, the one representative from outside the Long Tom neighborhood, saw the homemade survey differently. On July 30, he wrote his account of that day. It began: "By request of Mr. Irwin & others after the sentence of OKelley I went up to help lay of his claim." Alexander reported his findings in a sketch and in these words:

We found the S.E. corner & the Sight tree on the S. line as Mr. OKelly had described them. I found many of the neighbors already acquainted with the corner & the line, & we all agreed as to the lines…I was surprised to find all but some 160 acres of the Section of OKelley, claimed by four different men. Two houses were on the Section and a third if not [on] the section, very near the line. One claim took the field.

At the bottom of Alexander's statement, he sketched a simple map of his eyeball survey. In another letter written two weeks later on August 18, Alexander stated, "It is a notorious fact that N. O. Kelly's claim had been

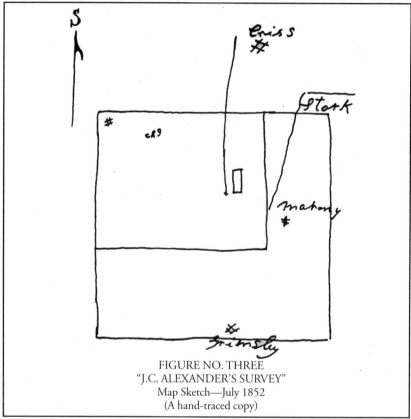

FIGURE NO. THREE
"J.C. ALEXANDER'S SURVEY"
Map Sketch—July 1852
(A hand-traced copy)

Figure No. Three. The map is upside down; north is at the bottom, thus making the upper left-hand corner the southeast point of beginning of Nimrod's claim. The larger square signifies a full square-mile section. The smaller square apparently was meant to represent a 320-acre, half section. The smallest square is probably Nimrod's field. Nimrod's cabin is in the upper southeast corner as represented by a "#" mark. The other "#" marks represent the houses of Grimsley, Criss, and Mahoney. The other terminal lines probably represent indefinite borders of the Criss and Stark claims. A small squiggle appears a short distance west of Nimrod's cabin and is unidentified. Conceivably, it is the letters "srg" representing the spring.

trespassed upon by the Deceased Mahoney & others until there was scarcely any left to him."

Alexander and Nimrod's neighbors saw ends differently because they came from different beginnings. Alexander began with the reckoning that Nimrod had a wife, who would one day be in Oregon; while the Long Tom settlers held to the notion that, after seven years alone in Oregon, Nimrod was either unwed or a deserter. The trial had fixed Nimrod's future, but his land title was a long way from being fixed.

The people of the territory did not read about Nimrod's trial until ten days later, when the *Statesman* and the *Oregon Weekly Times* first reported it. Many who witnessed the trial, and many more who had heard of it, were disturbed by the outcome, feeling that something wobbled in the wheels of justice.

J.C. Avery took a quiet hand in seeking to undo the sentence of the court. Three avenues were open—one each in the three branches of territorial government. In the judiciary, an appeal to a higher court could be made. Through the executive branch, a petition for reprieve might be tried. In the legislature, there was ordinarily no recourse, but Avery, being a member of that body, thought the time was ripe to try. Certain factors came together to make it inviting. Governor John P. Gaines had called a special session of the territorial legislature to assemble on July 26 in Salem. Citizen lawmakers did not take kindly to extra sessions in the summer, when shops and crops needed tending. That resentment added to the profound hostility that had developed within the Democratic legislature toward their new Whig governor. Democrats were in a mood to challenge the governor and the Whig judges. The struggle between the three branches for the upper hand had surfaced in the so-called "location quarrel," a contest over what town should become the territorial seat. In such a stir, the Democratic lawmakers might be receptive to seizing the reins of executive pardon and judicial review, and to giving Nimrod a new trial through the dubious means of legislative enactment. Nimrod's case set sail upon a voyage into politics.

For whatever it was worth, from his Benton County confinement Nimrod wrote a petition to "both houses of the legislature of the Territory of Oregon," urging them to

> take my case in to consideration and give me to get justice where as I do know that I have not had justice done me in my trial by which I am now under the sentence of death. There is many facts that if I could prove them & that would clear me entirely. And if I could get a new trial I do know that I could prove some of them. But if this honourable body will not grant me a new trial I humbly hope they will intercede for me to his excellency the governor to get a pardon for me. Pleas excuse my unworthiness.

Nimrod wrote his petition on July 28, but unfortunately it arrived too late. It was sent on the day that the Democrat legislators at Salem abruptly adjourned in token disdain for the Whig governor's attempt to assemble them. The special session lasted only three days. Gaines might have the power to convene, but the legislators had the power to adjourn. They quickly did so, once the governor had finished with what was in his craw. To show the governor who was in charge of Oregon laws, they did so by passing none.

In an August 17 letter to Governor Gaines, Richard Irwin, on behalf of himself and Isaac Winkle, seized the opportunity to show their reproach for the discourtesy shown the governor by Avery and the Democrats, and to connect it, somehow, to O'Kelly—a case soon to be on the governor's desk.

> Mr. Avery as soon as OKelly was sentenced. Remarked to me that he was Glad that you had the "Extra Session called." That he would try and have a Bill passed. If you did not Reprieve OKelly. Commuting his Sentence to the Penitentiary for Life! The Legislature met! *Passing no Bills*! Adjourned! & came home condemned by this community! & I hope By the whole Territory!

When news reached Nimrod that the special session had withered, undoubtedly his spirits withered as well. On August 7, he filed his last will and testament with County Clerk Hovey. But Nimrod's supporters were not done yet and proceeded to the next branch of government. A petition to Governor Gaines was circulated. Curiously, this entreaty did not ask for full pardon, but instead requested that the governor

> suspend…[Nimrod's] execution until the next session of the Legislature of this territory in order that his punishment may by act of the said Legislature be changed from death to imprisonment.

The petition clung to the erroneous notion that commutation was a legislative, not an executive, function. That the legislature could take from him the power of executive clemency would not have set well with the governor.

This *imprisonment petition* told the governor that Nimrod was "71 years" old, "feeble in mind and body," and before trial was "unassisted" and had only a "few days" and no "means or opportunity to prepare." The petition went on to explain the misunderstanding of Nimrod's remark when he read the letter from his daughter in Texas.

> It was testified by one witness that the prisoner had said substantially that had he…received a letter from his family previous to the killing of Mahoney the killing would not have happened…[T]he evidence induced the jury to find the prisoner guilty of Murder in the first degree…[S]ince the trial…it has come to light that in the same conversation in which he used the expressions…he gave the following explanation, to wit, that if he had received the letter…Mahoney and others would have left his claim and ceased to trouble him.

In other words, Nimrod's comment did not mean that the letter would have stopped his plan to kill, rather he meant that it would have stopped Mahoney's intrusion. Nimrod's supporters felt so strongly about this that they devoted one half of the petition to its explanation. On August 16 in a joint affidavit, petit jurymen Jacob Martin, Miletus W. Ellis, and Henry Powell swore before the Benton County Clerk, A.G. Hovey, that if they had heard this explanation of Nimrod's remark at the trial, they would not have found first degree murder. Five more affidavits, statements, or letters to the governor from William Fooks Dixon, James L. Mulkey, juryman Powell, J.P. Welsh, and J.C. Alexander dwelled upon the letter and emphasized Nimrod's misunderstood remark.

Five copies of this imprisonment petition were circulated by D.W. Russell, Greenberry Smith, Edward Ryburn, G.H. Murch, and J.L. Mulkey—they were the first signers and the names under which the petitions were officially filed. Altogether, there were 117 signatures on the imprisonment petitions.[1] Although invoked on Nimrod's behalf, Nimrod himself would not have bowed to the petition's prayer for imprisonment. Nimrod saw hypocrisy in it and wrote:

> One Methodist class leader this day came to me and said in the most sanctimonious form, OKelly, I will assign the petition for you to go to the penitentiary because I think it is the best for you. If you get a free pardon you will go home. You will not be safe. I do this for your good…Is it not lamentable…? They are so blinded with prejudice that they do not know it. But I do pity them. We see them get down on their knees…and their eyes rolled up to heaven and…implore the majesty of heaven to have mercy on the distressed and the oppressed…Then they will go and sign a petition for me to hang or be sent to the states prison.

There were other petitions to the governor filed on behalf of Nimrod that were more to his liking—petitions for full pardon, petitions for freedom. That plea may have been more to the governor's liking as well—not because he was inclined to honor it, but because it honored him—as it sought his mercy and not the mercy of the legislators. It was not just Nimrod's life at stake here—also at stake was power.

The *full pardon* petitions were apparently circulated by J.D. Boon, James Shiel, and Robert "Doc" Newell. J.D. Boon was an 1845 immigrant who traveled with Nimrod in the Stewart wagon company. He was also a Methodist minister, a fact not acknowledged by Nimrod in his commiserations. Boon was also the Oregon Territory Treasurer. As such, his support for full pardon ought to have weighed heavily. It was the first hint that Oregon dignitaries were taking note of Nimrod's case.

The Boon petition had thirty-one signatures, including some repetitions of signatures appearing on the imprisonment petition. Men like J.C. Avery, J.C. Alexander, D.W. Russell, and G.H. Murch signed both petitions and thereby urged both the release of Nimrod and his imprisonment. From a distance that might seem inconsistent, but up close it was sound tactics. Free him, it said, but at least do not kill him. Talent in politics belonged to those who never closed a gateway. Zealots, unwilling to compromise, went down paths of all-or-nothing-at-all, a rigidity that could cause more victims than victories. While Nimrod could afford righteousness, his supporters could not.

Shiel's petition for full pardon had twenty-eight signers, who described themselves as "citizens of the Mission of St. Paul's and vicinity, Marion County—the neighborhood in which O. Kelly formerly resided." These were the Catholic friends he had made in that locality, and at least three of the signers were priests. It is the first record that Catholics were taking a hand in Nimrod's recent troubles.

The Newell petition for pardon was signed by thirty-four "citizens of Marion County," representing a waning group of retired trappers who had settled at French Prairie. Many had been *engagés* for the Hudson's Bay Company. Robert "Doc" Newell was a former mountain man who, along with Joe Meek, opened the final leg of the Oregon Trail to wagon travel and family migration.

The total number of signers on these three full-pardon petitions were ninety-three. This brought the total number of petitioners on Nimrod's behalf to 210, granting a few duplications. In addition, William Fooks Dixon on August 14 certified that two other petitions "in favor of a Pardon," which contained from 150 to 200 "names of Persons belonging to Benton County," were missing. Dixon stated that he had given these petitions to a "Mr. Allison" to take to "Rev. Mr. Spauldings," and apparently they were lost en route or at destination.[2]

Grievance petitioning was a grant preserved in the Bill of Rights and a well-worn path from the citizenry to government leaders. Methods for gaining signatures included canvassing cabin-to-cabin, circulating at a congregation, or tacking on a message board at a local store. A petition probably was not posted at Richard Irwin's Jennyopolis store. There were no Nimrod supporters in that vicinity. But it was posted at the Boonville store just four miles north on the same road. According to Irwin, he learned about the Boonville petition and the pardons campaign "from those who signed the Petitions… and told to me in the store whilst passing up and down the Road." But another possible source of his information was suggested by Thomas Norris and

A.C. Whitley. Norris and Whitley, along with Greenberry Smith and others, had founded the settlement of Boonville. On August 16, Norris and Whitley wrote the governor:

> We had a Petition in favour of Nimrod OKelley signed by some 14 Persons the said Petition has been Stolen or taken from the Store of Mr. Whitley where it was left for Subscribers names I Suppose Dear Sir that this petition was taken By Some of his enemys as there is a good deal of Predguce against him.

If Irwin did have access to the words of the petitions—whether by theft or gossip—he was nevertheless grossly mistaken or deliberately false as to their contents when he wrote Governor Gaines on August 17: "Many Petitions are now in circulation in this (Benton) and in Lane, Linn, Marion Polk & 'French Prarie.'"[3] In fact, none of the petitions on record represented that they were circulated in Lane or Linn counties. Irwin went on: "The Petition says 'that three families' besides 'Mahoneys' was and are on OKelly Claim That OKelly has but '40 acers' left." None of the known petitions stated that there were intruders, or that intruders had squeezed Nimrod back to forty acres. Irwin further misrepresented that the petition called Mahoney "a Quarlsome man." None of the petitions ever mentioned Mahoney. Irwin went on to mis-state: "[T]he petition says that OKelley did not have a fair trial, because that he was a 'Catholic.'" None of the petitions expressed or alluded to religion or to prejudices. One of Irwin's objections, however, rang true:

> The question may be asked who are the 'getting up' & signers of the Petition. All in this county says J.C. Avery got out the Petition & has the same now in circulation in this and in different counties; getting men women & children to sign the same.

Some of the petitions did contain the signatures of women and a few children.[4] Children were, of course, improper petition signers. A twelve-year-old girl might be old enough for marriage, but not for addressing her government. But adult women ought to have been a different matter. Lumping them in as unqualified petition signers was an old bias fed by false logic, imagined danger, and aloof premise. The logic was this: Women, having no capacity to serve as jurors and to convict criminals, ought not be allowed to express an opinion on the fate of those convicted. The danger was this: If women could be petition signers, then next they would be seeking the right to vote on juries, followed by the right to vote in elections, followed by the right to get votes in elections. The premise was this: Office, votes, verdicts, and petitions were the business of menfolk.

Equally offensive to Irwin, Winkle, and the other Nimrod detractors was the fact that the petitioners went, not only beyond the bounds of gender and maturity, but also beyond the bounds of Benton County. Irwin's letter reported to the governor that signers included

> miners & Packers that travels the Road & In the 'French Prarie' amongst the Catholics…So your Excellency can see that the Petition is not confined to this county as it ought to be.

Accordingly, with regard to their own forthcoming, contrary petition (called a "remonstrance"), drafted at Doc Richardson's house, Irwin and Winkle pledged to the governor that the remonstrance would have no signatures

> but male citizens…leaving women & children entirely out!…[and] the names of none but actual citizens of the county! Believing that your Excellency will pay no attention to any Petition except that…will come only from the citizens of this county.

Some of Nimrod's foes carried Irwin's point even further. They urged that southern Benton County remonstrators should carry greater impact than northern county petitioners. Sheriff Starr wrote Governor Gaines and furnished the names of Benton County taxpayers broken down into north and south residents. Starr explained it this way:

> I herewith transmit to you the names of the taxpaying of said County divided into two classes…OKelley lived some eleven miles south of Mary's river and consequently the murder was committed in the southern portion of the county. This I do in order that you may be able to Judge whether his neighbors or others are the petitioners.

The division between north and south county rested upon the notion that Nimrod's near neighbors were better fixed or more entitled to know what to do with him. But it was also a schism that would separate the county for many decades on many issues—including the Civil War.

Starr's two lists showed a total of 207 taxpaying males on the 1852 Benton County tax rolls. A number of Benton County adult men, who signed in Nimrod's behalf, were not on either of the sheriff's lists. Irwin accused these non-taxpaying petitioners of being drifters and strangers—"miners & Packers that travels the Road." But this did not necessarily follow. Five of the twenty-two grand jurymen and four of the twelve petit jurymen likewise were not listed as taxpayers. All jurymen were required to be voters and residents of the county, but not necessarily taxpayers. Some of Nimrod's petitioners could have been hired hands, tenants, and townsmen who lived in Benton County, but had never staked a land claim there. Property taxes were levied on land, livestock, and furnishings—things most likely held by families that had settled an acreage. While drifters had no land stakes or family ties, they nevertheless had stakes in and ties to a frontier opened by birds of their feather—the pathfinders, missionaries, and mountain men. Still, some complained that, without dirt in their nails and sweat in their dirt, drifters were footloose with nothing to hold them to the countryside into which they were petitioning to release a murderer.

The remonstrance called Nimrod a "cold blooded murderer," and his supporters "designing persons." It urged Governor Gaines "to protect us from such lawless designs." Four undated copies of the remonstrance were circulated. One copy circulated by—or at least filed by—John Loose contained forty-four signers. About half of those names can be identified as residents in the Bellfountain settlement or were members of the Methodist class in that area. Many of the signers were men in the Belknap, Gilbert, Hawley, Newton, and Starr families, including Justice of the Peace Abiather Newton. Possibly, this copy of the remonstrance was circulated at a Methodist camp meeting that assembled at Marys River near the Newtons in the first week of July 1852.

A second copy of the remonstrance, filed under the name of N.A. Starr, contained sixty-two signatures. Most of these signers were south Benton County names, many of them in the Long Tom, Jennyopolis, and Starrs Point areas. Widow Mahoney's full signature appears thereon, even though she was illiterate and had signed other documents with an "X" mark. Nimrod's intrusive neighbors all signed—Stark, Grimsley, and Criss. Other nearby neighbors were signers—William and Sib Barclay, "Doc" Richardson, John Porter, John Fiechter, and, of course, Richard Irwin. Two of the petit jurymen appear on this copy of the remonstrance—William Knotts and Thomas M. Read. Their signatures on the remonstrance do not match their portended signatures on the verdict.

Just as there were middling positions among Nimrod's supporters, there were also middling positions among his detractors: Don't kill Nimrod, but at least don't free him.[5] How many other petitioners for liberty or remonstrators for death would have been willing to reach an accord at the middle ground of imprisonment, if that option had been presented to them? Then too, perhaps, these crossover signers may have been those without conviction, those who were neither retaliatory nor conciliatory, those taken by the power of signature—followers who sought to please and were moved by the need to join anyone who took the time to offer pen, ink, and a line on which to sign.

The third was filed as the Taylor remonstrance. It had fifteen signers, including R.B. Hinton and coroner jurors John Lloyd and William Coyle. Petit juryman Abraham P. Acock also signed.

The fourth and final copy was filed as the Gage remonstrance, after Samuel Gage, the probable circulator. On the Gage remonstrance there were seventeen signers, including two more petit jurors—Miletus Ellis and J.S. Hayworth. Ellis was another crossover compromiser. He also wrote two separate statements in favor of second degree murder and imprisonment.[6]

Some of the Gage remonstrators were residents near the Boonville area.[7] That location was right in the shadow of where the reckonings for and against Nimrod met—the no man's land between north and south Benton County. The J.D. Boon full pardon petitioners and the Gage remonstrators were neighbors. It was in Boonville that a petition in favor of Nimrod was stolen from the Whitley store.

The total number of signatures on all four copies of the remonstrance was 138. In spite of Irwin's emphatic assurances to the governor that the "Remonstrance will be presented to your Excellency with the names of none but actual citizens of this county!" And, in spite of the fact that some of the remonstrances began, "We the undersigned citizens of Benton County," someone subsequently had identified and marked at least nineteen signers as "Out of County Benton" residents.

Of the eighteen nearest neighbors surrounding Nimrod's claim, not one of them petitioned in Nimrod's favor. Practically all remonstrated against him. Irwin and Winkle wrote that the neighborhood had "enraged feeling," was potentially "a mob," and was capable of "other murders" if "Okelly is…set at liberty." That "enraged feeling" was no doubt fostered by the lowly regard of Nimrod as a family deserter, a liar, a menace, a lazy subsister, a maverick, and a religious misfit. But one other motivation—party politics—was beginning to drive remonstrators and petitioners as well. Oregon politicking was in its early formation and, like hunting and fishing, was a pastime for the menfolk. Few made a living at politics. Most played at politics. Nevertheless, political intrigue was a breeze at the base as well as the boughs of almost any kind of bickering. Not even Nimrod's simple pleas could escape its sway.

In the beginning, the Oregon Provisional Government was free of national party politics, but territorial government brought with it the need to ally with either the Democrats or Whigs. Oregon's first territorial governor, Joseph Lane, had been a man of the people—an appointee of President James K. Polk, a Jacksonian Democrat. The leadership of Polk and Lane, over rugged pioneers, was at once compatible—a slick hitch of team and wagon. Accordingly, the Oregon frontier took its lead from the Democrats.

When Lane resigned the governorship in the summer of 1850, Whig President Zachary Taylor appointed his successor. Taylor's first choice was a young, backwoods, Illinois lawyer, who would have been a workable choice, but Abraham Lincoln turned down the offer. Taylor's search then took a 180-degree turn. He appointed John P. Gaines, who took the reins as governor in August 1850. Like Lane, Gaines had been a military officer; but where Lane served on the battlefield, Gaines served in camp as a general's aide. Dignified, vain, and given to stiff collars, Gaines's bearing was a stark contrast to the rugged style of Lane. At lead harness they were as different as a high horse and plow horse. Gaines was the first, and would be the last, Whig governor in Oregon history.

After Illinois attorney Abraham Lincoln declined to take an appointment as Oregon's territorial governor, Whig President Zachary Taylor selected John Pollard Gaines for the position in 1850. Governor Gaines postponed Nimrod's first hanging date for just one month. At odds with Democratic territorial legislators, he championed a failed attempt to keep the territorial capitol in Oregon City rather than moving it to Salem. Nevertheless, after his gubernatorial term he permanently settled in Salem. *Oregon Historical Society #9180*

While the governor office was eastern spoils, territorial legislators were elected by Oregonians. Territorial governors were not the people's choice; they came to rule, not to pioneer. Gaines and his family arrived in Oregon by clipper ship, not by covered wagon; and from their Oregon beginning, the frontier had not been kind. Two daughters died of yellow fever at sea on the way around the Horn. In the summer of 1851, the wife died at Oregon City in a fall from a horse. Then a young son died. Nevertheless, widower Gaines met the frontier aloof to its denizens and stubborn to its challenges. He stayed an easterner in the West. He brought bearing and propriety to the frontier, no matter how galling it may have been to those who lived in dirt-floor cabins. Farm-folk lawmakers and an urban-elite executive were on separate trails headed for a crossing.

And cross they did. Under the influence of a tight band of frontier Democrats—the Durhamites, who were led by an abrasive newspaper editor, Asahel Bush, and whose members included Reuben Boise, Joseph Avery, and Orville C. Pratt—the popularly-elected, territorial legislature wasted no time in targeting Whig Gaines.

The most thunderous clash between them was the so-called "location quarrel"—a struggle over which city should be the territorial capital. Should it stay in Oregon City, the seat of the Provisional Government, or should it shift upriver fifty miles to Salem? The overwhelming number of legislators favored Salem. Gaines insisted on Oregon City. Oregon City was the home of the federally appointed officers—Governor Gaines, Secretary Edward Hamilton, U.S. Attorney Amory Holbrook, Chief Justice Thomas Nelson, and Surveyor General John B. Preston. As the terminal at which the annual trail migrations and oceanic shipping met, Oregon City reflected eastern industry, politics, fashion, and society. It was a Whig city and held to urban views. Salem, on the other hand, had mission origins and was surrounded by rural interests. Near the middle of the Valley's southward growth, Salem reflected Oregon's frontier life. Salemites and the Democratic lawmakers felt that, while Oregon City had become the tie to the nation, it had let wither the bonds to its own.[8]

Aside from the location quarrel, there were other political skirmishes. A few days before Nimrod's trial, Gaines had exercised executive clemency in another case. He released Enoch Smith, whom Democrat Pratt had sentenced to hang for encouraging a murder. Democrat Asahel Bush in his *Statesman* newspaper took Gaines to task for that mercy. On July 3, the *Oregonian*, a Whig newspaper, under the headline, "Blood I Will Have Blood," struck back and assailed Bush for assailing Gaines. Those two papers were the cannons for the warring factions. Gaines, the Whigs, and the *Oregonian* were targets for the *Statesman*, while Lane, Pratt, the Democrats, and the *Statesman* were targets for the *Oregonian*.

Nimrod's quest for clemency was on a dead reckoning with the fire between these opposing forces. His supporters had first tried to outflank the chief executive by a direct appeal to the Democratic legislature. Now that the petitioners turned their plea to the Whig governor, the remonstrators were quick to cozy up to the governor by casting those legislative attempts as political. The Irwin-Winkle letter to Gaines stated that Benton County citizens

> hope that our laws will be maintained & not millofied as Mr. Avery & a few of his Satalights in this country wish too. 'Avery' was not elected upon the 'Territorial quarrel' But upon Local matters altogether…[T]his county is on the side of Law & order & Its citizens are your friends.

Lawyer John T. Fortson, who had been a grand juryman in Nimrod's case and who had married into the Belknap family, tried to strengthen the political implications. On August 12, 1852, Fortson wrote the governor about the petitions favoring Nimrod:

> I shall rank myself as a personal and Political friend…[T]hese Petitions are gotten up and circulated by your Political enemys for a partisan effect not as it purports

to be prompted by mercy…[I]t seems that every stratagem is resorted to, for the purpose of assailing your administration and the Whig Party.

Like many issues in politics, the location quarrel and the Enoch Smith pardoning debate were mostly for show, not for content. Underlying those battles was the struggle for power, not perfection. Partisanship was the game being played in territorial government while Nimrod's trial was afoot. It was a vortex into whose pull not even a killing—leagues away from the intrigue—could escape.

The petitions, remonstrances, statements, affidavits, and letters began to flow into the governor's office in mid-August. A file on Gaines' desk was labeled, "1852—Pardon Papers of Nimrod O'Kelly." The file thickened and awaited the governor's action while Nimrod waited in irons. Carpenters put a finish to the gallows in the streets of Marysville. While file, prisoner, and scaffold waited, Orville C. Pratt did not. He had left the Valley for Astoria at the Columbia's mouth, where he boarded an ocean clipper bound for the Atlantic coast by way of Panama. The *Statesman* estimated that seafaring Pratt would be within four days arrival of New York when Nimrod would hang.

In that same short four day span, Governor Gaines had much to think about. The petitioners numbered over two hundred. The remonstrators numbered almost one hundred and forty. This would be a much harder call than the Enoch Smith pardon. Enoch had not murdered. He simply encouraged murder. Five hundred petitioners had favored Enoch and only twenty-five remonstrated against him. Popular decisions were always easier to make. Nevertheless, as popular as the Enoch pardon might have been, it drew reproach. If criticism could be mustered for taking the noose from the neck of an abettor, then what would be the outcry against mercy shown to one who pulled the trigger? And how much greater would be the outcry if no compassion was given to an old-time pioneer who was trying to protect his claim? Was Fortson correct? Was this pinch another Democratic ploy to undermine his governorship?

In the midst of this predicament, Gaines was undoubtedly relieved when, in his file, he found "Petition A," called so because someone had marked it with that letter in the upper left-hand corner. Petition A had thirty signatures—all Clackamas County citizens and neighbors of Governor Gaines in Oregon City. It urged the governor "to interpose" in Nimrod's behalf, and gave reasons why Nimrod "would not merit the punishment of death." First, "there might have been some provocation." Second, Nimrod was of "advanced age…being seventy two years old." And finally, the situation called for, "mercy to his family from whom he has been separated for many years, but who are now in the mountains and daily expected to arrive in Oregon."

The influence of this petition came not so much from *what* it said, but rather from *who* was saying it. It was an impressive list of signatures. First of all, the petition's circulators were apparently Amory Holbrook and James K. Kelly—prominent frontier lawyers. Holbrook was the nation's highest-ranking law official in the territory, the United States Attorney—one of the seven top officers appointed by the President. Holbrook had often served as the prosecutor in major territorial criminal cases, including the five Cayuse Indians charged with the Whitman Massacre. Winning Holbrook to Nimrod's side was, needless to say, a surprise and a tactical victory. Whig Holbrook's word would mean a lot to Whig Gaines.

James K. Kelly, now Nimrod's lawyer, was probably responsible for Holbrook's recruitment. Andrew Jackson Babb was out of the picture. The signature of Nimrod's trial lawyer nowhere appears in the "Pardon Papers" file.

James Kerr Kelly replaced Nimrod's trial lawyer, Andrew J. Babb, during the appellate and clemency proceedings, and thus debated against prosecutor Reuben P. Boise in the Nimrod case, albeit the two were political allies and joint codifiers of Oregon's statutory laws. Later, Kelly followed Boise's path as Chief Justice of the Oregon State Supreme Court. *Oregon Historical Society #4506*

Babb's counsel had ended with the final decree of Pratt's sentence—"hanged by the neck until...dead." With those words, Babb, like Pratt, had distanced himself from the Nimrod case. Likely, it was J.C. Avery who brought Kelly to the defense. They were fellow Democrats, who served in the legislature together and may have joined forces at the special legislative session in Salem at the end of July. Why Kelly took on the task is not clear, but he may have been coaxed along by an attraction to name and roots. Whatever the reasons, Kelly went to work for O'Kelly. At age thirty-three, Kelly's career was just beginning. In the years ahead, he was destined for eminence in Oregon history.

The thirty signatures on Holbrook and Kelly's Petition "A" included some of the most noted citizens in the territory. There was Matthew P. Deady, lawyer, legislator, law compiler, and eventual jurist. His name on Petition

"A" was most significant—he and Avery were a part of the inner Democratic clique, and together they had the ear of clique spokesman Asahel Bush, editor of the *Statesman*. Other signatories included: F.S. Holland, Clackamas County Clerk; Sidney W. Moss, Oregon City's first hotel operator and Oregon's first purported novelist; John B. Preston, Oregon's Surveyor General; Joseph N. Prescott, Mayor of Oregon City; Robert Moore, Mayor of Linn City; Paine Page Prim, future Oregon supreme court judge; George H. Flanders, sea captain and merchant; George Settlemeier, pioneer nurseryman; Edward Dupuis, pioneer stage operator and store owner; Forbes Barclay, medical doctor and former Hudson's Bay physician; and "the white-headed eagle," John McLoughlin. All carried Nimrod's banner.

Even more influential than their reputations was the fact they represented a political cross-section. Moss, Preston, and many of the signers were Whigs. Others were Democrats. Likewise, the co-circulators, Kelly and Holbrook, were a Democrat and a Whig, respectively. There were apolitical signers as well, such as Barclay and McLoughlin.

Gaines could rest easier knowing his decision was not enmeshed in political partisanship. Petition "A" freed him to address the grievance on its merits. Unfortunately, his own political instincts were not so easily suppressed. Those instincts told him to take the high ground—neutrality. Like the legislators, he decided for indecision. The judges made the mess, let them have the first fling at fixing it. Clemency ought to be a last resort. And so, Gaines chose to straddle the fence. By simply postponing, he would offend neither side. Nimrod would still be scheduled to hang, and that ought to please Irwin, Fortson, Winkle, and the remonstrators, but Nimrod would be given more time to go to the judges and get them to take a second look, and that ought to please Avery, Kelly, Holbrook, and the petitioners.

Although the territorial capital had been transferred to Salem, Gaines continued to operate out of Oregon City where he felt the capitol ought to be. Accordingly, his postponement order would have been dispatched from Oregon City, nearly ninety miles by the Gold Mine Road from Marysville, where the trap door was already being tested. Gaines recorded his decision on August 21—just three days before the hour set for hanging. Three days and scores of miles was a hard ride, but the message was received in time. It must have furrowed the brows of both those who were on edge to see a hanging and those who clung to the edge of that despair.

The governor's postponement set the noose aside until the 24th day of September 1852. The clock was not stopped, but only reset. Like the moon and its tide, the noose would be high again in merely thirty days. The petitions and pleas had not bought life or freedom; they merely bought time—a very small piece of it. Nimrod's life was simply moved from one brink to another.

Notes

1. Ten signatures appear on the Ryburn copy, eleven on the Russell copy, twenty-four on the Murch copy, thirty-four on the Smith copy, and thirty-eight on the Mulkey copy.
2. It is not clear in the record whether these two petitions remained lost or were found and included in the reported documents. Presumably, "Spaulding" was the Reverend Henry H. Spalding, a survivor of the Whitman massacre. Spalding now lived directly across the Willamette River in Linn County at Brownsville. Why petitions for "persons belonging to Benton County" were sent to Spalding, who was ill disposed to Catholics, is unknown, while yet providing a possible explanation for why the petitions were missing.
3. This August 17 letter, much cited throughout this chapter, was signed by both Richard Irwin and Isaac Winkle, but Irwin was the scribe because Winkle was illiterate. It was misdated "1850," but clearly had to have been executed in 1852, shortly after the trial.
4. The Greenberry Smith copy of the imprisonment petition appears to have at least eight women signers. There are also six Chamberlin family names listed, almost all apparently written by the same hand. Three "Berry" family names are listed. Three Hodges family names appear, one of them signed "M. Hodges Junier." The eleven names on the Ryburn copy of the imprisonment petition are all Ryburns, men and women. There are also women's names on the Mulkey copy of the imprisonment petition.
5. Two of the signers of the Starr remonstrance had also signed the Russell copy of the petition urging imprisonment instead of death. Their names appear to be "H.N. Moss[?]" and "Japtha[?] Walling." The consistency in being both a petitioner and a remonstrator is not at once apparent. Moss made his position more clear by appending the words "against re-prieve" behind his remonstrance signature. Apparently, he and Walling were against killing Nimrod, but also against freeing him. There were a few other such crossover signers. The signature of William Taylor on the Loose remonstrance appears to be the same signature as on the Murch imprisonment petition.
6. Thus, of the twelve jurors who convicted Nimrod, two petitioned for Nimrod, four remonstrated against him, one straddled the fence between petition and remonstrance, and five stayed clear of what they had done.
7. See Figure No. Four, "Southern Benton County Topography," 1852–53, in Chapter 20.
8. The course taken by, and the aftermath of, the location quarrel is more fully detailed in the text accompanying notes 1–4 in Chapter 18.

18

Pursuit of the Judges

September 1852

For 1852, estimates of those jumping off at the Missouri for Oregon and California were as high as seventy thousand—the largest migration on record. Swollen ranks of wealth seekers bound for California gold fields exceeded farmers eyeing the Willamette by five to one. As the trains ground through the Plains and Rockies, cholera-polluted waterholes took an exceptional toll of lives. A few days after Nimrod's postponed August execution date, the first of the main body of Oregon migrants began to trickle into the Valley. By late September, the trickle would become a flood that would peak sometime in October.

But in early September, there were likely seven thousand wagons still rolling on the Overland Trail. At least twelve thousand travelers had taken the fork to Oregon and were strung out from Fort Hall on the upper Snake to The Dalles on the Columbia. Somewhere between the head and tail of that five-hundred-mile serpent of wagons and livestock were supposed to be Nimrod's wife and children. It was rumored that messengers rode back along the column to find the family, to tell them of Nimrod's plight, and to urge them to speed their journey if they wanted to see him before his September 24 hanging. The errand was neither practical nor likely; a family would be hard to find among so many, along so much trail. Then too there was still the gnawing question: Was there ever a family?

Meanwhile, those focused on Nimrod's plight may have taken no note that Harriet Beecher Stowe's novel about escape from slavery was touching a nation's conscience. Nor would they have noticed a thirty-year old quartermaster, Lieutenant Ulysses S. Grant, serving quietly in their midst on the Oregon frontier under an equally obscure Captain George McClellan. Nor could they have predicted that these events would come together back east, where the rest of the nation was inching toward a violence that would one day reach across the continent to touch the Nimrod story.

Down the street from the Stewarts or wherever he was kept, Nimrod may have glimpsed the gallows—a patient sentinel of death now biding its time as a plaything for children. In the beginning, a gallows was just any place high enough to dangle boots above ground. As civilization progressed, so too the gallows gained civility by higher scaffolding so that necks would be dropped down instead of pulled up—snapped instead of choked. Eyeing one's own gallows during a month-long postponement was a strangulation of still another kind.

If Nimrod's sentence and gallows were meant to deter frontier homicide, it apparently failed. Murder continued to occur. While Nimrod's friends and foes were out rounding up signatures, thirty-five year old Adam Wimple killed his thirteen-year-old wife in Polk County. Wimple went berserk, put the body of his girl bride under the floorboards of his house, and set it afire. In short order, he was captured. Then in late August, he escaped from the Polk County jail. But a posse soon caught up with him. Like Nimrod, he was tried for murder. Like Nimrod, he was found guilty. Like Nimrod, he was sentenced to hang. But unlike Nimrod, Wimple escaped once more. Four days later, they caught him for the third time, and civilization erected the Wimple gallows, just thirty miles north of Nimrod's.

With the Marysville scaffold already in place and gaining dust, taking Wimple south for his execution could have saved money. But Judge Thomas Nelson's order was that Wimple was to be hanged in Dallas, and Judge Pratt's order was that Nimrod was to be hanged in Marysville. It made sense to have one central place for killing manslayers, but a territorial penitentiary had not yet been erected. Furthermore, justice done had to be justice seen. If death was to be a damper, then each county needed to give time, money, and ceremony to the killing of its own in plain view of its own.

From his makeshift confinement, Nimrod could have peered out across Marys River and down the road south toward his claim twelve miles off. His acres there were vacant now, his fires gone cold, his animals gone wild. Maybe freedom beckoned him, when along that road he saw a steady flow of prospectors headed south to the Rogue and Umpqua valleys. Once again, gold had been found—this time in southern Oregon. The rush may have been steel to Nimrod's flint. But if any spark caught tinder, it would have been snuffed by his years and his righteousness. Escape was not within him. As others shanked off along the trail, Nimrod could only watch through chinks and dreams.

Prior efforts in Nimrod's behalf with the legislature in July, and with the chief executive in August, now turned to the judiciary in September. While the outside world paraded news of migration, novels, slavery, murders, and gold, Nimrod's new lawyer, James K. Kelly, appeared before Chief Justice Thomas Nelson in Oregon City with a motion urging the territorial supreme

In 1850, Whig President Millard Fillmore appointed Thomas Nelson as Chief Justice of the Oregon Territory Supreme Court. Nelson denied Nimrod's plea for appellate review of the trial conviction and voted to affirm the death sentence. Nelson stayed on the Oregon Frontier for just three years. *Oregon Historical Society #37492*

court to review Nimrod's case. In Oregon in 1852, the trial judges and the appellate justices were the same three people. The Territorial Act of 1848 created three district judges and then made them supreme justices to sit on high in review of their own trial decisions. Judge Pratt's rulings would be upheld or overturned by the concerted judgment of Chief Justice Nelson, Justice William Strong, and Justice Pratt himself. If a single justice could be persuaded that his brethren's trial court decision was questionable, then Nimrod could at least get his hanging postponed again until the full, higher court could hear formal arguments and affirm or reverse the lower judgment.

There was no use going to Pratt for sanction. For one, he would never yield to a review of his own decisions. For another, he was by now on the Atlantic Ocean. That left Justice Nelson or Justice Strong. Strong lived in Cathlamet, 180-river miles northwest of Marysville. Nelson lived in Oregon City—ninety trail miles north of Marysville. And so it was that Kelly went to Oregon City to convince Nelson that Pratt may have blundered. Kelly had to wait until Nelson returned from Polk County and the murder trial of Adam Wimple. Finally, on Thursday, September 9, 1852, just two weeks before the second hanging date, Kelly made his argument to the chief justice, but then had to wait again, because Nelson took the matter under advisement.

Unfortunately, Nelson had more than law to think about in deciding Nimrod's case. Once again, politics had to be weighed as well. Ordinarily, judges stayed clear of such partisanship, but the major issue of the day—the *location quarrel*—had created such a stir that even the supreme court had been caught in its gyrations. The quarrel was over where to locate the territorial capital city—Oregon City, the base of Whig and federal governance, or Salem, the center of Democrat and pioneer leanings? The mounting debate between the factions reached a bitterness sometimes verging on violence. In the streets of Oregon City, *Statesman* editor Asahel Bush and Governor

Whig President Zachary Taylor appointment William Strong as Associate Justice of the Oregon Territory Supreme Court in 1850. Strong granted Nimrod's plea for appellate review of the trial conviction and voted against the death sentence. Strong took permanent residence in the Pacific Northwest and was active in the founding of Washington Territory. *Oregon Historical Society #24951*

Gaines reportedly had a couple of encounters involving drawn pistols and threatened canings.

And so it was that the popularly elected Democratic legislators had challenged the federally appointed Whig governor in the legislative session of December 1850. The lawmakers had assembled in Oregon City and passed the "Location Act," making Salem the capital city, Portland the location of a new penitentiary, and Marysville the site for a university. Oregon City was deliberately snubbed and given nothing at all. The change required the governor, the supreme court, and other territorial leaders to move their offices forty miles upriver away from ocean shipping and eastern ties and into the Valley's rural center.[1]

However, Gaines contended the Location Act was a nullity. This was because the bill contained more than "one object" in a single piece of legislation, which was contrary to Section 6 of the Oregon Territory Act, wherein it was stated, "every law shall embrace but one object." Singularity of purpose was required in order "to avoid improper influences, which may result from intermixing in one and the same act such things as have no proper relation to each other." There should have been three separate bills for locating the capital, penitentiary, and university.

Nevertheless, one year later in December 1851, Democrat legislators stayed true to their enactment and held their annual session in Salem. The governor and a handful of Whig legislators, however, stayed in Oregon City. That was when the judicial branch of government was called into the fray. With the executive and legislative branches at loggerheads, the supreme court was asked to decide whether the 1850–51 legislature had overstepped its power when it piled too much into one enactment. The two Whig appointed judges—Nelson and Strong—sided with the governor and Oregon City, and wrote long supporting opinions in the case of *Short v. Ermitinger*. On the other hand, Judge Pratt, the Democrat appointee, ruled that the legislature had acted within its power in locating the seat, jail, and school. That it was done in one act and in one vote was insignificant because the objects all had "proper relation to each other."

Normally, this would simply be a case of a victory for the two-to-one majority. But here was the rub—Nelson and Strong had convened court in Oregon City in order to make their decision, while Pratt had gone to Salem to hold court and make his decision in court. Section 9 of the Territory Act required the supreme court to hold court "at the seat of government of said territory." So, where was the seat of government—Salem or Oregon City? And where should the court sit, in order to decide where it was proper to sit?

It was a fly in honey, and it got more and more sticky.[2] The court had no one to blame but itself. Instead of staying together—that is, Nelson and Strong going to Salem to render their decision a second time in order to remove doubt—the court got caught up in political maneuvering and pompous stonewalling. Chief Justice Nelson was highly intelligent, having earned a college degree at age seventeen; yet, his written opinion in the location quarrel was indicative of the bullheadedness pervading the issue on both sides:

> [W]e are told that as a matter of expediency, as an indication of respect to one of the co-ordinate departments of the government, we ought…to go to Salem, even if the assembly contravenes the law of Congress…[W]hat good purpose could it serve…? It would be a mere piece of useless formality…and I entertain too high an opinion of [the legislators]. I for one will never demean them so far as to suppose they are to be "pleased with a rattle, and tickled with a straw."

It was a pettiness unworthy of the judiciary, whose very purpose as a third branch of government was to rise above bickering, to tend the rules within which debate must play out, and to safeguard the survival of law after the heat of partisan zeal.

In the struggle for the upper hand in childishness, the Salem legislators matched the judges sop for sop. Their reaction to Judge Nelson's opinion was swift. They enacted a bill that pared down the bounds of the chief justice's trial district. Henceforth, Nelson could only try cases in his Whig stronghold—Oregon City and Clackamas County. Pratt, on the other hand, was bestowed wider reign by being given Nelson's previous region in Marion and Linn counties, including Salem.

Repercussions of the location quarrel were felt on the far side of the continent. The U.S. Attorney General in Washington City wrote Oregon's Secretary, Edward Hamilton, expressing regret "that there has been a division in your Councils." In May 1852, about the time Nimrod shot Mahoney, Congress put an end to the location quarrel by ruling that Oregon's Location

Act was valid. A Democratic House and Senate vindicated the Democratic Oregon legislative assembly. Salem was to be the territorial seat, Portland would get the penitentiary, and Marysville the university. Oregon City got no pork. The Whigs were reined back from the feeding trough.

When word of the congressional ruling reached the Oregon frontier shortly after Nimrod's trial, Governor Gaines called the previously mentioned special session of the legislature at Salem. At the session, he expressed his compliments to the lawmakers and announced his cooperation. More in a pique than in politeness, however, he tactlessly suggested that the lawmakers should reenact all of the legislation they had passed in their Salem session last winter. Reenactment was necessary, he said, because Salem was not the seat until May, when Congress had made it so. Under the cover of congratulations, Gaines had sought to dig up the carcass of a quarrel that Congress had buried. The bullheaded do not lose gracefully.

As reported before, the lawmakers' strongest expression of contempt for Gaines and his request for reenactment was to waste the specially called session by doing absolutely nothing. Immediate adjournment was their trumpet of victory. Unfortunately for Nimrod, this meant his request for mercy was trampled beneath the feet of a sore loser and swaggering winners. At the lawmakers' next session, the disrespect and pettiness would continue. One of the legislative bills deliberately referred to the chief executive as "*one* John P. Gaines," instead of the more courteous *Governor* John P. Gaines.

By September 1852, although the location quarrel had ended, deep wounds remained. Gaines had yet to bring himself to move to Salem, and the judges still made decisions within the fumes and bile of the battle's leavings. Nimrod's case was in the middle of a shoving match. Two other previous controversies compounded the problem.

In October 1851, Judge Pratt had held W.W. Chapman in contempt of court, and banished him from appearing before the bar as a lawyer. Chapman was, at that time, a founder of the *Oregonian*, a Whig newspaper. Chapman took his case to Nelson and Strong; those Whig appointees restored Chapman's law license and reversed his contempt conviction. Needless to say, Pratt was irate. Political blades within the judiciary were further honed in December 1851, when Chapman appeared before the Oregon City bar as the lawyer arguing against the legality of the Location Act. While Pratt chose not to attend those arguments because he felt Salem was the proper venue, he may also have been absent because of pique—Chapman was not allowed to argue in any court of his.

Still another controversy divided the court—the "Battle of the Blue-books." Throughout most of the 1840s and up to 1850–51, Iowa territorial laws were the adopted laws for Oregon. Those Iowa laws were contained in either one of two books—both were blue in color, one slim and the other thick. The Oregon Provisional Government in 1843 had adopted the Little Bluebook. Then, in September 1849, the Oregon Territory legislative assembly adopted in one enactment the Big Bluebook, Iowa's revision of its earlier statutes.[3] Consistent with their positions on the Location Act, Governor Gaines and other Whigs maintained that the Big Bluebook was illegal because its sweeping adoption of the entire Iowa Code embraced more than one object. The Democrats felt otherwise. The two codes were so much alike that application of one or the other was, as lawyer Matthew Deady observed, about as important as "which end shall an egg be broken." But once again, substance ceased to be the issue where power was at stake. Democrat Pratt favored the Big Bluebook, and Whig appointees Nelson and Strong tracked with the Little Bluebook. The matter would eventually be largely put to rest when Oregon finally got around to publishing its own code of enactments, in the Twenty Acts and then later the Hamilton Code.

And so it was that in September 1852, the scars and open wounds of the location quarrel, the Bluebook Battle, and the Chapman escapade were barely healed and closing when Nimrod's case came before Judge Nelson. Whig Nelson may have preferred to approach the case on its merits and to avoid petty infighting, but nevertheless, here before him, making a case for a murderer, was Democrat James K. Kelly. *What were Kelly's motives?* He was one of the pro-Salem lawmakers, and one of those who had stripped Nelson of jurisdiction in two counties. To make matters worse, Joe Avery and his fellow Durhamites were at the forefront of the Salem proponents, now called the "Salem Clique." Avery's support of Nimrod was one more suspicious connection. The thickets through which Nelson had recently come were briars where clear thinking was stuck.

Two other connections, however, could have eased his mind. First, Democrat Kelly was here asserting the errors of fellow Democrat Orville C. Pratt. Second, also appearing in O'Kelly's behalf was U.S. Attorney Amory Holbrook, a Whig.

The chief justice took his time finding his way through intrigue and into the refuge of law. He took Nimrod's case under advisement on September 9, but did not issue a written decision until September 15. In part, he may have savored the case because he had nothing else to do. Indeed, he may have been flattered to have the work. Months before, he went to Salem in

Marion County on his routine circuit to conduct trial work. While there, he learned abruptly that he had no court business. Pratt had already taken care of the county's cases, and a spiteful legislature had restricted Nelson's district to just one county—Clackamas. Turned out to judicial pasture at the early age of thirty-three, Nelson would have had lots of time to dawdle over fewer decisions.

The chief justice's week-long deliberations produced an opinion that was printed in the *Oregonian* on Saturday, September 18, 1852. It measured one full column—two feet long—and dealt point by point with each of five errors that lawyer Kelly said Judge Pratt had made. Kelly had pressed the point that Pratt's court procedure was wrong—first, when it did not give Nimrod notice of the trial date ten days or more in advance; second, when it did not record that a grand jury had authorized any indictment; third, when it neglected to have the petit jurymen randomly selected; fourth, when it took the verdict without the accused's presence; and fifth, when it punished Nimrod with the costs of the trial.

Nelson's ruling on the second assignment of error was that the record was sufficient to imply that a valid indictment must have been returned against Nimrod. As to Kelly's fifth assignment of error, concerning court costs, Nelson, like a horsetail at flies, simply waved off the challenge with a phrase—court costs were "the mere incident of the proceedings" and not an unauthorized punishment.

As to Kelly's first, third, and fourth assignments of error, Nelson observed that nowhere in the written record did it appear that the prisoner was denied ten days notice of the trial, that the jury was illegally hand-picked, or that the prisoner was absent when the jury rendered its verdict. When the record is silent, a reviewing court must presume that timely notice was given, that the jury was randomly selected, and that the reckoning was face to face with the accused. Fairness to the accused is paramount, but there must be fairness to the system as well. Error must appear affirmatively in the record by way of objections raised and rulings made. In short, lawyer Kelly was stuck with his forerunner's failures. If there were errors, they were not Pratt's; they were Babb's. Nelson saw no reason why the supreme court should review the case. No writ of error would issue. Nimrod would hang in nine days.

Judge Pratt, the legislators, the governor, and now Justice Nelson had refused to help. Nimrod was left with one final resort—Judge William Strong. That recourse had an obstacle. Strong had to be found. He lived beyond the Valley in a remote part of Oregon Territory. Finding him might be difficult because his jurisdiction encompassed what today are parts of Oregon, Idaho, and Montana, and all of Washington. Those hinterlands were said to be the largest judicial district ever assigned to an American judge. Then, too, even if he could be located in time, there was no reason to think he would see the law any differently than Nelson, his fellow Whig.

The search for Strong would have to start at his home in Cathlamet, near the mouth of the Columbia River. Strong settled there partly because it was mid-ground between his district's major white settlements—the clusters at Astoria, Fort Vancouver, and Puget Sound. But he also chose Cathlamet because the land beckoned to him. He was the only early territorial judge to stake a claim, and would be the first to stay and make the frontier his home after his judgeship ended. Nimrod might have liked his chances with this man who embraced land and place.

Cathlamet was one hundred miles downstream from Oregon City—twenty-five miles north on the Willamette, then seventy-five miles west on the Columbia. The trip would require at least two nights down those rivers by bateau on tide-affected waters. The return upstream would take much longer. Even if Strong could be found at home and persuaded to issue a writ, calling off the hangman and his noose would be skin tight. The gallows at Marysville and the judge at Cathlamet were separated by some three hundred river miles, to and fro. The hanging date and the outset of the search were separated by just nine days.

When Kelly and Holbrook were given word of Nelson's refusal, they wasted no time in setting out to find Strong. Their best route was by water. They may have hired Indian paddlers, packed a bateau with a week's provender, and shoved off down the Willamette. On the other hand, for some or all of the round trip, they might have hitched aboard a paddle wheeler. The speed of steamboat travel, a new form of transport on the Columbia and Willamette rivers, would have more than made up for any delay in waiting for a scheduled departure.

Apparently, Kelly and Holbrook began their mission within two days of Nelson's September 15 decision, because on September 17, Asahel Bush wrote a letter from Oregon City to lawyer Matthew Deady in Lafayette, Oregon, saying:

> Nelson refused the writ of error in O'Kelley's case. Kelley & Holbrook have gone down to see Strong. They are confident he will grant it. I shall not be surprised if he does. It is reported that old Gaines says he will not pardon.

But Deady was not so confident about Strong's decision, and he had a dire forecast. In a September 20 reply to Bush, Deady wrote:

And Nelson didn't grant that writ of error! Well I supposed he would not. Strong will not either. I was rather desirous they should. Won't Gaines pardon him? Perhaps, and more than probable he will try and slide the responsibility upon the legislature. If so I would not prejudge the matter beforehand, but I am quite confident they will neither arrest or change the penalty of the law.

On Wednesday, September 22, two days before the execution date—with no word from Kelly and Holbrook on their search—John Thorp, a Polk County territorial legislator, wrote Governor Gaines urging "the great necessity of your interference to save the condemned." Thorp reported he went to Salem to see the governor personally, but the governor was not there. Apparently, Democrat Thorp could not suppress this untactful, yet irresistible, jibe. Gaines was still situated in Oregon City—his pride had not yet succumbed to the law that required him to move to the new territorial seat. Thorp's plea to Gaines was seized by a desperation that had no time for courtesy. His lack of finesse also extended to Judge Pratt. Instead of the technical errors politely assigned to Pratt by lawyer Kelly, Thorp's letter to Gaines made a direct attack on Pratt's character. Thorp watched the trial and was repulsed by what he had seen.

> Something was wrong…[T]here was a determination in the people of Benton to Hang OKelly, and a determination in Pratt to accomodate them…Regardless of what your Enemies may Say or do…Save the old man from an untimely and disgraceful end.

Gaines took no action. In the two days preceding the execution date, the governor showed no signs of any further clemency. He was done with the matter. Judge Strong was Nimrod's sole taper of light, now sputtering on the last of its wick.

Meanwhile, Kelly and Holbrook finally had found Judge Strong somewhere in his wilderness district. Their "court" appearance before the justice may have been at Strong's Cathlamet home, or Fort Vancouver, Astoria, along the Cowlitz, at tidewater, or by some forsaken rock or meadow spring. Wherever, in the face of the energy expended, Strong would have been impressed, and hard pressed to not send these searchers back to the Valley empty-handed. And indeed, he did not. Sometime in the period September 17 to 22, William Strong granted a writ of error in Nimrod's case. Understanding the need for haste, he wrote no opinion. He was familiar with cases like Nimrod's—it fit a pattern. Later, Strong reminisced:

> There were a good many homicides. I think I tried some eighteen homicidal cases, and most of them arose from disputes about land under the donation law.

Another factor may have given Nimrod's case an edge—Strong had need for favor as well. About this time, Strong and other leading citizens north of the Columbia were concerned that the government of Oregon could no longer serve their interests.[4] Accordingly, as of September 1852, Strong was actively seeking to split up Oregon Territory and form a new government north of the Columbia River, called "Columbia Territory." A request to Congress had already been drafted, but it would carry much more weight in Washington City if it came from Oregon's established political leadership, rather than from secessionists. Strong needed the support of Oregon territorial legislators in the forthcoming December 1852 legislative assembly. Needless to say, the last persons Strong expected to see coming out of the woods seeking him and his favor were two of the foremost leaders in territorial politics—the future Democratic president of the Oregon legislative council, and the Whig U.S. Attorney.

Sometime during this period, Strong and Kelly had put their heads together on the Columbia Territory proposal. Kelly did not oppose it—albeit he did not think too much of its political chances, nor did anyone else. It is possible that the subject was discussed when Kelly and Holbrook met with Strong on the O'Kelly case. Favor was sought, and barter may have been in the favor. There is no way to know how each of these interests may have played off on the other. Politics was not ordinary when dealing with the sanctity of human life. Still, the facts are that Strong granted a writ of error in Nimrod's case. Then, a few months later, the Oregon legislature voted overwhelmingly, and surprisingly, in favor of a memorial to Congress urging the creation of Columbia Territory, without any partisan outcry from Holbrook's Whigs or Kelly's Democrats.

To everyone's amazement, Congress quickly obliged. In March 1853, a new territory was created. Congress did all that Strong and his allies requested, except for one thing. Some in Washington City felt that *Columbia Territory* might be confused with the *District of Columbia*. Thus they renamed it, apparently feeling the new name would not be confusing—Congress dubbed it *Washington Territory*. Indeed, it made for head scratching!

Strong, Kelly, and Holbrook all got what they wanted. That the new Washington Territory may have sprung from causes that included the Nimrod O'Kelly case is a fact too faint to be confirmed, but not so far-fetched as to be fancied.

Thanks to Strong, Nimrod would have his case reviewed by the territorial supreme court. The hanging was en route to indefinite postponement—but there was one final hitch for the halter. The message to stay the execution

A pioneer journalist and editor for the *Oregon Spectator, Weekly Union,* and *Corvallis Gazette*, Thomas Benton Odeneal also served as Benton County's clerk, auditor, and justice-of-the peace, and Clerk of the Oregon Supreme Court. He was the only witness to record events directly from Nimrod and his contemporaries. *Oregon Historical Society #098092*

had to get from Strong to Sheriff Starr, the hangman in Marysville. If Kelly and Holbrook had found Justice Strong at his home in Cathlamet, then they had to carry the writ of error 180 miles against the currents of the Columbia and Willamette rivers. Whether by bateau, steamship, or overland by horseback, the record strongly suggests that timing was worn to its threads. As the execution date closely approached, the letters of Bush, Deady, and Thorp, and articles in the *Spectator* and *Oregonian,* expressed the belief that no stay of execution had been granted, and Nimrod was still scheduled to die.[5]

The race against time—soon colored somewhat by legend—is gleaned from the many occasions that the story was passed along. The first time it was written down—thirty-four years afterward—two noted pioneer journalists joined for the telling. Thomas B. Odeneal on his deathbed told the story to Samuel A. Clarke, who reported it in the August 1, 1886, *Sunday Oregonian.*[6] Clarke was an *Oregonian* editor and historical writer. During the 1850s, Odeneal had been the editor-publisher of a series of Benton County newspapers, as well as Clerk of Benton County. As a contemporary of Nimrod's, Odeneal was the last remaining reporter who was privy to, and who could present an account of, the full saga of the county's most famous manslayer.

Clarke reported that when he and Odeneal met in 1886, Odeneal was "weak and rapidly failing, but the mind was clear…; there was no weakness of intellect and he well knew the end was not far off." In advance of relating the story to Clarke, Odeneal

> had refreshed his memory from his county records…Those who knew Mr. Odeneal, moreover, will remember that in matters of the kind he preserved an accuracy of detail that few men equal. He was careful in preparing any fact with exactness.

Before continuing with the Clarke-Odeneal story, the status of Nimrod's captivity must be understood. Something about pioneering made it averse to bondage—those who pulled up stakes to go fancy free understood better than most how *choice* was as life-sustaining as food, drink, and shelter. To go, or to stay put, was an independence fought for, a freedom won, and a right inscribed. Although some pioneers might not hesitate at bigotry or hangings, they would balk at cagings. Patrick Henry's famous mandate, choosing death over loss of freedom, was not mere elocution; it was a cherished priority. Indeed, Oregon pioneers, just five years hence, would vote to bar the residency of blacks, yet also bar the enslaving of them.[7] Nimrod benefited from that aversion to captivity—Aunt Polly Stewart had released him on occasion from his irons and cage. That trust was destined to grow.

Samuel Asahel Clarke wrote the seminal story of the Nimrod tale, two decades after Nimrod's death, as taken from an interview with T.B. Odeneal. Clarke was editor or publisher of the *Oregonian, Salem Statesman,* and *Willamette Farmer,* and librarian of the General Land Office, Washington, D.C. *Oregon Historical Society #015735*

Shortly after the trial, somewhere in the first week of July, it was thought best to put the convicted murderer in custody of a county law officer. On July 6, the county commissioners made Deputy Sheriff Silas M. Stout the jailkeeper, albeit there was no jail. Stout and Nimrod were fellow-Tennesseeans. Stout continued the credit given by the Stewarts, earned by the prisoner, and tolerated by Stout's boss, Sheriff Starr. The leash had been looser still after Gaines postponed the execution in August. Once the veneer of maverick-recluse had worn off, Nimrod was seen as not so menacing after all. On the contrary, he appeared to be a law-abiding, God-fearing man, proud of his word and loyal to the trust placed in him.

The cost of Nimrod's keep, even under Deputy Stout's custody, continued to be a severe county expense. The thirty-six days in which the Stewarts bedded, boarded, and bound Nimrod cost the county about $330 or $9.00 per day. The sixty-four days in which Deputy Stout had Nimrod cost the county about $390, plus $24 to Missus Martha Huffman who served a meal from time to time. That still averaged as much as $6.50 per day. After the August hanging was put off, the continued tap of the county treasury for custody costs seemed unfair to Benton County citizens. If Governor Gaines wanted to postpone matters, then the territory, not the county, ought to pay for those delays.

That's when Prier Scott, Aunt Polly's brother, came up with an idea to the county's liking. Scott, who had been a grand juryman at Nimrod's trial, had just begun a blacksmith business in Marysville. Nimrod was a blacksmith. Scott could charge less for the keep because he could turn the jailing into a servitude, and then into a business profit. On or about September 7, Nimrod was once again transferred back to citizen keep within the Scott-Stewart clan. Scott's charges for Nimrod's keep were under $6.00 per day—considerably less than his sister's earlier charges, which had included boarding some guards. It was a kinder situation for Nimrod. Scott and Nimrod had traveled together on the 1845 migration in the company of Avery, Dixon, Greenberry Smith, the Mulkeys, and the Stewarts.

A smithy could not master iron while enslaved by chains. With Sheriff Starr's approval, Scott let drop the prisoner's hobbles and cuffs. Nimrod worked free at Scott's anvil, and forged hope and resolve at Scott's fires. He was probably as familiar to townsfolk as was his gallows; both were daily sights on the streets of Marysville—the doomed and the tool of doom. That familiarity would have worked its spell. The more familiar Nimrod became, the more difficult it would be to see him dead. It was much easier to kill a stranger.

Then too, the growing regard for Nimrod, at least among Marysville citizens, may have been fueled by the fact that Widow Mahoney, formerly in grief, was now in bliss. On September 10, less than four months after her husband Jeremiah's death, she married John Thomas, an Englishman. The newlyweds made their home at the widow's cabin, where she and her new husband persisted on the borders staked by her dead husband. Widowing and then surviving were a tandem of harsh realities for a woman to cope with alone. With an eight-month-old baby on a frontier where women of a *marrying-kind* were scarce and worth doubling the size of a land claim, a second husband was sure to follow.

And so it was, while Kelly and Holbrook were hurrying upriver in the fourth week of September to get Justice Strong's message to the hangman, Nimrod was a Marysville worker under watch, but not under lock. He was essentially free to come and go. The Clarke-Odeneal story put it this way:

> [T]here was no jail…in Benton County so…[the sheriff] told the old man to go home and be sure to be on hand when wanted. All the time up to his final…re-sentence, he seems to have been about 'on his own recognizance'…
>
> The evening previous to the day appointed for his execution he appeared in town, went to the sheriff and tried to deliver himself up. But no, the sheriff said he had no use for him until 11 o'clock the next morning…Before he went the old man asked to see the arrangements made for his 'taking off.' He didn't want them to make a poor job of it, so he looked at and passed a favorable opinion

on the gallows…The next morning he ate breakfast and then strolled carelessly down to the spot the sheriff had made ready for him.

The sheriff shook hands with O'Kelly the next morning and many of his friends dropped in on him to see him off in good style. The court had given the sheriff the discretion to do the hanging somewhere between 11 A.M. and 1 o'clock, P.M.…O'Kelly found it tiresome business hanging to the ragged edge of despair, as it were. He had received the congratulations of his friends and the last offices of the church and was thoroughly resigned to his fate, so did not care how soon he met it…[T]he prospect of death was not alarming; he believed he was changing to a better world and had no regret at leaving this.

On this scheduled day of execution, September 24, the sheriff delayed as long as he could. It was well that he did. "At the last hour," Clarke wrote, "a reprieve came." Nimrod was saved for the second time.

The Clarke-Odeneal article must be tempered by Clarke's penchant for drama and Odeneal's aging memory. Although essentially confirmed as to its central drama, their account is at odds with more reliable documentation as to a few minor details.[8] On the other hand, Odeneal had the advantage of live reporting, and he was the only journalist to have met and talked with Nimrod. His description of Nimrod was consistent with other inferences in the record:

> a type of a past generation of mankind…tall in form, commanding in appearance, venerable in aspect, with flowing gray hairs and patriarchal beard…was well informed in a common way…had no fear of dying…a pleasant talker and not a bad hearted man.

From the scaffold high above the crowd, Nimrod walked down. His troubles were far from over—he still had a supreme court and, perhaps, another jury to convince. But those distant prospects could not overwhelm the relief at stepping away from the edge. The stairs downward had to be far better looking than the stairs upward, taken just moments before.

Notes

1. Governor Gaines foolishly had triggered this legislative response in a prior address to the legislators, saying that, while they had the power to name the capital city, he and the federal government in Washington City, led by a Whig President, controlled the purse strings. Gaines threatened to withhold money for government construction in any place but Oregon City, whereupon the rebellious pioneer lawmakers, in an exercise of insolence, enacted the Location Act.
2. Contrariety, once started, went even further. The Democrats argued that until voided, the Location Act had to be followed. In other words, the court had to obey legislative dictates and meet where the legislature ordered the seat of government to be located—Salem. Any legal decision rendered in Oregon City, even one that would correctly declare Oregon

City to be the true capital seat, would be ineffective because the court was not at the outset convened in the legislatively declared capital. The Whigs argued that the court need not follow void acts, that an enactment is void by virtue of law, not by virtue of a court having determined that it violates law. As Nelson put it, "The court does not make the law void; it only settles the question and removes the uncertainty." In other words, a given law is void whether a court says so or not; it's just that no one knows whether the law is void until the court says so.

3. The official title of the Little Bluebook was *Statute Laws of the Territory of Iowa, 1839*. The Big Bluebook was the *Revised Statutes of Iowa, 1843*. See note 3, Chapter 12.

4. In the location quarrel, legislative representatives north of the Columbia River were among the few who favored Oregon City. When Congress settled the dispute and moved the capital seat farther south, settlers north of the Columbia felt their ties slipping still farther away. The northerners argued that a trip to the new Oregon capital cost more time, effort, and dollars than a journey from St. Louis to Boston and back. In view of the newly developed railroad transportation system east of the Mississippi, that exaggeration was not far from wrong.

5. Strangely enough, the clerk of the Oregon Territory Supreme Court, Allen P. Millear, wrote that Justice Strong's grant of the writ was dated Friday, September 17, and that a stay of execution by Millear's office was issued on Saturday, September 18. These dates are highly suspect and extremely unlikely. If true, then there would be only two days between Nelson's denial of the writ and Strong's granting of it. That would mean that Strong must have been readily available in the Oregon City area—a fact contrary to reports of other keen observers. As of Friday, September 17, one week before the execution, Asahel Bush was unaware of any decision by Strong when Bush wrote Matthew Deady that Kelly and Holbrook "have gone down to see Strong." As of Saturday, September 18, six days before the execution, neither the *Statesman* nor the *Oregonian* reported Strong's decision; to the contrary, the *Oregonian* published Nelson's denial. As of Monday, September 20, four days before the execution, Deady in writing to Bush had no word of Strong's decision. As of Wednesday, September 22, two days before the execution, legislator Thorp, who had been at the territorial capital seat the day before, was not aware of any stay of execution because he pleaded with the governor to do just that. More likely, Millear's dates were post-dated. Kelly and Holbrook had no time for record keeping. Their mission probably took them directly to the gallows at Marysville without any stop at Millear's office, whether it be in Oregon City or Salem. The recording of Strong's writ and the issuance of Millear's order to stay the execution would have had to wait. Millear was a record keeper, not a timekeeper. The problem was time, not recording. Stopping the hanging with Strong's writ was more important than going through formality. A record can always go back in time; a hangman cannot. That seems to be what happened here—the hanging had to be stopped; the paperwork was done later to make it look right.

6. The Clarke-Odeneal article is a crucial resource in putting together the Nimrod O'Kelly story. It was not an easy find—preservationists had "lost" it. The article was originally printed on page two of the August 1, 1886, *Sunday Oregonian*. In copying a full run of the newspaper since its inception, modern microfilmers neglected to reproduce that page two. Consequently, researchers will not find the article in any library microfilm reels. Most research libraries simply do not keep newsprint copies of the *Oregonian* as far back as the 1880s. The *Oregonian's* news morgue has packaged and warehoused its old newspapers, making them inaccessible. The only other known research copies of the now rare page two are located in the Multnomah County Library in Portland, Oregon, and the University of Oregon Library, at Eugene, Oregon. A clipping of the article can also be found pasted on the inside front cover of an original 1880 edition of Oregon Reports, Volume One, in the

collection of the Paul Boley Library of Northwestern School of Law, at Lewis and Clark College, Portland, Oregon.

7. Article I, Sections 34, 35, of the original Oregon Constitution, 1857.

8. Samuel A. Clarke wrote that Nimrod "came from Ireland"; not true. Clarke wrote that Nimrod "was educated for the priesthood"; not true. Clarke wrote that Nimrod "was educated at some college belonging to the church"; not true. Clarke wrote that Nimrod "spoke several languages"; not likely. Then too, Clarke or Thomas B. Odeneal was slightly askew regarding dates—a shortcoming all too familiar in reminiscences. For example, the 1886 article reports that the incident occurred in "1854," but a more logical time, as will appear later, and one in keep with all other documented events, would place the Odeneal story at the September 24, 1852, execution date. The Clarke-Odeneal article also speaks of the reprieve as coming from the territorial governor. But, as shall be seen, the narrow escape makes more sense in the context of the Kelly-Holbrook last-ditch mission to Strong, and then to Starr. If so, then it was not a governor's reprieve that came, rather it was a judge's writ of error followed by a stay of execution.

19

Review and Reunion

October-December 1852

The territorial supreme court was scheduled to review Nimrod's case at its annual term in December 1852, more than two months away. But the delay promised to be even longer than that—much longer. Asahel Bush was quick to see the problem looming. He set it forth in the *Statesman* on the day following Nimrod's aborted execution:

> There are but two judges composing that court in the Territory, and as the application for a new trial will be based upon the same points which have already been argued before them, and in respect to which they disagreed, they of course cannot agree in December, unless one of them changes his opinion. In case they then disagree, no new trial can be granted; nor do we see how the sentence of death already pronounced can be lawfully executed; as, of course, judges disagreeing as to the right of a rehearing, could not agree to appoint a day for execution.

Bush was correct when he observed that an appellate majority was necessary to overturn a lower court decision. Thus traditionally, without the vote of two appellate justices, Nimrod's hanging sentence had to be affirmed. But Bush's continued reasoning operated on the false notion that a majority was also necessary for setting a new date for execution of the sentence. It was the affirmed trial judge—Pratt—who had that power of scheduling.

Nevertheless, Bush was on the right trail; he just took the wrong fork. He was correct in predicting extreme delay, but the impediment would be for different reasons. On February 4, 1851, the territorial lawmakers had passed *An Act to Govern the Practice of the District and Supreme Courts.* The Hamilton Code, section 34, read:

> Whenever the Supreme Court shall be equally divided in opinion on hearing an appeal or writ of error, the cause shall stand continued until all the Judges are on the bench.

That rule made it clear that if Strong and Nelson remained at loggerheads, and if Pratt did not show up in the territory before the end of December, Nimrod's review would have to be postponed once again—this time indefinitely. In spite of that prospect, the noose and scaffold stayed in the streets of Marysville on the chance Justice Strong might succumb to Chief Justice Nelson's way of thinking. Like a buzzard with head hung low and perched in patience, the gallows bided its time.

Disappointed Benton County spectators, who had hankered to witness a hanging, needed to wait only two weeks to see another just thirty miles north in Polk County. Adam Wimple was scheduled to hang there on October 8. Seeing Wimple hang would be much more rewarding. This was the villain who killed his child wife. His trial had been a fair test of his guilt; the capable Matthew P. Deady had represented him. Judge Nelson, in Pratt's absence, was called in as the trial judge and would have been thorough and slow in his presidence. Then too, there was no public outcry in Wimple's favor. In contrast to the O'Kelly trial, where lawyer, judge, and emotion had left an unpleasant taste, the Wimple hanging was served upon a table of just desserts.

There were, of course, those who were belly full of hangings—a fairly common spectacle throughout the nation—and had no hunger for the hideous. They might come to pay respect, but not to be gratified. That might have been the case with Benjamin Nichols, Nimrod's old-time acquaintance.[1] Reluctantly, Nichols might have felt obliged to see Nimrod off, whereas Wimple's parting was good riddance. As Wimple was carted to the noose on the road in front of Nichols' porch, Wimple, seated on his coffin, reportedly called out, "Ben, ain't you coming down to see me hung?" And Nichols said, "I've seen enough of you, Adam." Indeed, the vengeance taken or the homage paid at the two dramas were moods apart.

Another who may have missed Wimple's execution was A.G. Hovey. Supreme Court Clerk Allan P. Millear had issued a written order commanding Benton County Clerk Hovey to send to the territorial supreme court a true copy of all trial court records and actions taken in the case of *Territory of Oregon v. Nimrod O'Kelly.* Consequently, on the day of Wimple's execution, Hovey was busy with the large task of copying each word of the trial court papers. He copied the one-page verdict. He copied the written motions of attorneys Boise and Babb. He copied Judge Pratt's court minutes. He copied his own orders to the sheriff to summon grand and petit jurors. He copied the

Albert G. Hovey in his later years.

indictment. In all, there were about fourteen pages Hovey had to ink by dip and scratch, and then dispatch to Millear with a certification that the papers were "true, full, and entire." In those copies rode the success or failure of Nimrod's case before Oregon's highest tribunal. The keeping of records was becoming a central feature in the Oregon frontier's rising justice system.

Aside from being a court clerk, Hovey was a twenty-two-year-old school-teacher, who was now preparing to be a lawyer. A usual education for law study was to become a lawyer's apprentice or clerk, called "reading the law." On the other hand, some of the more elite lawyers had prepared for their careers by attending college lectures. The three men of law who had gathered to fashion a writ of error for Nimrod were all college graduates—Kelly went to Princeton, Holbrook to Bowdoin, and Strong to Yale.

But on the Oregon frontier, there were neither colleges nor law libraries. Students in Oregon learned by attending trials, reading forms, filing papers, and running errands, chores that infused the law's primary fulfillments—uniformity, consistency, and predictability. They were lessons that taught the value of precedent—holding to the past, sticking to the trail. In short, copying. Hovey, surrounded by law papers, learned by immersion, recitation, and repetition. For the time being, Nimrod's fate was in the hands of mechanics, not architects.

Sometime in late October 1852, a covered wagon pulled by a team of oxen rolled and bumped its way down the hoof-beaten, muck-ridden, center street of Marysville. The scene would have looked something like this: Two men rode or led horses alongside the wagon. A third man would have been at the wagon reins. Two grown women—one grandmotherly, the other in a family way—were probably seated on the buckboard as well. From the back of the wagon, a toddler may have peeked out over the tailgate. Perhaps a milk cow was tethered to the tailgate and a young miss slogged along with a hand on the side rail—the wagon pulling steps from each of them.

Uncombed, bitten, and hungry, the seven bore all the signs of six months of punishing travel. Grime made tatters at the hems of skirt bottoms. Bonnets needed thread and scrubbing. A wave of brine ringed the men's hats. Bones and muscle rippled beneath the oxen's hides—hides drawn taut at top and hanging loose at bottom. From the wagon's fixings, swayed buckets, ladles, grease horns, lantern, and butter churn. And, as the wagon clinked, clunked, squeaked, and sloshed with the endless roll of the wheels, heads bobbed in rhythm. Layered on all was dust.

The wagon passed in review of Marysville's storefronts and citizens, and was to them a hard reminder of a misery once shared. Every year at this time, the Overland Trail migrants straggled into the Valley towns. This particular caravan would have drawn an especially large crowd—and many whispers. Likely as not, the wagon came to a halt at Marysville's latest carpentry work, causing one of the horsemen to lean down from the saddle, point to the gallows, and ask someone in the crowd if it was for the man, O'Kelly. On being told it was, the horseman would have swallowed, drawn a breath, and asked if O'Kelly had gone up yet. On being told Nimrod and his gallows had yet to come to a reckoning, the horseman would have breathed again and asked where the man was jailed. On being told there was no jail and Nimrod was doing smithy work for Prier Scott, the oxen would have put shoulder to the yoke once again and moved on to find the blacksmith shop.

As the party inched those final steps in their ordeal, the joy of expectation was no doubt laden with foreboding. They had come two thousand miles and six months over rugged, barely charted terrain to find their family patriarch near rope's end.

Realization for the people of Benton County was a slow pour at first. For some, it was corked by stubborn denial, but gradually all came to know they were looking at the family of Nimrod O'Kelly. There they were—rubbed raw, tuckered down, footsore, and at bottom provender—but nonetheless flesh and blood, just as Nimrod had insisted for over seven years. It was not all of Nimrod's family. Charles O'Kelly and Mary Ann Fitzgerald, the letter writers, were not there. Son Charles had written:

> I am not Able to Come at this time & I have no out fit sofishent to come I think Joseph is fitted out very well to Come but the Emigration is the Longest that has ever bin to Calaforni & origan & I am A frade their teames will perish on the way on the A Count of so many going they will eat the grass up so the hine waggons wont get through...there is A Bout 25 waggons in his Company...I may come nex spring if I Can git oxen A nuff

But three of Nimrod's sons had made the trip in this crowded year on the trail—Benjamin Garrett O'Kelly, Joseph Bell O'Kelly, and Nimrod O'Kelly, junior. There was also an unmarried daughter, Sarah O'Kelly, and a daughter-in-law, Matilda E. O'Kelly, wife of Joseph and pregnant with their second child. The toddler was Nimrod's granddaughter, Sarah P. O'Kelly, Joseph and Matilda's first born. And, finally, and most importantly to the validity of Nimrod's 640 acre claim, there was Sally O'Kelly—Nimrod's wife.

Faces of immigrants were not easy to read for age. Weather, dust, and strain put years to countenance. In readying to see her husband after seven and one-half years, Sally may have done her best to finger-comb tangles and spit-wash hands—choosing in the end to hide hands and hair in apron and bonnet. Unfortunately, when they reached the blacksmith shop, they learned that Nimrod was no longer indentured there—a letdown to which they had become quite hardened. The whole of the trip from the Missouri taught migrants that over each ridge came still another horizon.

Sheriff Starr had moved Nimrod from Scott's keep, not because the sheriff was unhappy with the liberties Scott had given Nimrod, but more likely because the sheriff was concerned with Nimrod's safety. It would never do for Nimrod to be at large in Marysville's streets after Pratt's sentence was thwarted once again by the lawyers. Certain south county citizens would not have *cottoned* to Nimrod's second slipping of the noose. Immediately following the September 24 stay of execution, Sheriff Starr had transferred Nimrod's keep from Scott to "Ownbey," whose family cluster lay six miles southwest of, and away from, the exposure in Marysville.

If the O'Kelly family search took them to the Ownbey claims, they may have had another letdown. Sometime around October 18, Thomas P. Adams became Nimrod's next custodian. Exactly when and where the O'Kelly family finally caught up with their patriarch is guesswork. Suffice it to say, if they reached Marysville after October 18, they would have met Nimrod on the Adams' claim.[2] Whenever and wherever the O'Kelly family finally caught up with Nimrod and his shifting bondage, the drama of that moment can only be imagined. Perhaps he was found at some wintering-in chore, like ricking hay, stocking the larder, or bucking firewood. Certainly a prouder Nimrod would have preferred to greet his family on the gift of land that he had carved out, fought for, and was now ready to pass along.

The long-sought rendezvous was likely reduced to weary smiles, awkward embraces, and tears. His two older sons were twenty-nine and twenty-one when Nimrod left Missouri. Benjamin, the oldest, now thirty-six, had a few more lines in his face. Joseph, now twenty-eight, had married and had one child, with another coming. Benjamin listed himself as a shoemaker; Joseph, a blacksmith. Nimrod had never before seen Joseph's wife, Matilda, who was a Nuckiber from Newton County, Missouri. Nor had Nimrod seen his two-year-old granddaughter, Sarah.

Nimrod's daughter, another Sarah, was six or seven when he had left Missouri. Now, at thirteen or fourteen years, she had grown up, and, on the frontier, was *of a marrying kind*. There were three Sarahs in the party. Nimrod's wife was also a Sarah. Fortunately, she was called "Mother O'Kelly" or "Sally," or else there would have been a muss with mother, daughter, and grandchild all answering to the same call.

Sally O'Kelly was about fifty-nine years old, some thirteen years younger than Nimrod. Born Sarah Bell, she had been raised in the Great Smoky Mountains of Tennessee.[3] She was nineteen when they wed in Cocke County, Tennessee, in 1812 or 1813, depending on which record to believe. Nimrod and Sally's first child, Charles, was born in Cocke County in 1813. War with Britain was then waging, and Andrew Jackson was busy in that countryside recruiting his Army of the Cumberland. Did Nimrod become a husband, father, and soldier in that order? Many, now forced to believe he was a family man, still doubted he was ever a soldier.

Sally had been without her husband for over seven years. She had not seen him, heard him, or touched him. She could not read the words he may have sent, and she could not write him the words she may have felt. Sally Bell, raised in the Great Smoky Mountains, was not schooled. Now, here in the *kalapuya* grasses of the Willamette Valley, she stood facing her husband of forty years. After a long time coming, their heads, grayer and graver now, were at last cradled against each other.

Over the years, Sally and Nimrod had begat their share of children. Four made the overland journey, and at least two stayed back east. Undoubtedly there had been more. After forty wedded years, Sally had seen more pregnancies than just those six. Nimrod's letter to Congress in 1851 reported he had nine children. His last will and testament, recorded just a few months prior to the family reunion, gave his land to

> my three children that are in their minority at this time…my son John O'Kelly in his eleventh year, Sarah O'Kelly in thirteen year going into fourteenth…my son Nimrod O'Kelly eighteen years of age.

Apparently, eleven-year-old John did not survive the trip. A later census and other documents did not show any "John O'Kelly" in Oregon. The 1852 migration was riddled with cholera and other diseases. Some put the estimates of death along the 1852 trail at five thousand, mostly children, and as many as thirty graves per day. There was no way of knowing the exact number of bodies buried in that netherland between the States and its far northwestern colony. Certainly, John, the youngest of Nimrod and Sally's children, would have begun the trip. Possibly, he arrived in Oregon and died there before government records were instituted. Whenever it came—whether in the Ozarks, in the Valley, or in the space between—death was never good news and would have marred the reunion still further.

The most awkward greeting in that reunion may have been the one between the two Nimrods—Nimrod the elder and Nimrod the younger. After eight summers and seven winters of separation, they may not have recognized each other. Nimrod junior, age nineteen, was now full grown, beyond his cuffs, and later described as six feet tall, with light complexion, blue eyes, and brown hair. Nimrod the elder would have remembered a young pup still growing, not yet to cracking voice or chin fuzz. Conversely, the younger Nimrod would have remembered his father as taller, straighter, and stronger. One shrunk and one grown, they were now eye-to-eye. In a crowd, father and son might have passed each other without so much as a "how do." At a time of deep passage for each of them, they had not been there for one another.

Perhaps keeper Adams, with Sheriff Starr's approval, allowed Nimrod the liberty and proud moment of leading his family to his land claim—the seed for and the fruit of their years of separation. Alone, Nimrod would not have dared to go beyond Boonville and into south Benton County—the neighborhood he had fled. But in the company of his family and under the auspices of the sheriff, who lived in south county, it was worth the risk. Nimrod would have brought himself ramrod straight as he rode past Isaac Winkle's place and past the men gathered on the stoop of Richard Irwin's Jennyopolis store. It was strut—a show of land to the family, a show of family to the doubters.

Father and sons undoubtedly traced the four miles around the claim's edge. The heirs had to see the stakes and carry forth the legacy. In circling the claim, they would have seen the continued encroachments of Criss, Stark, Grimsley, and the widow Mahoney, now Missus Thomas. The tour may also have taken them to the dry slough bed where the journey to the gallows began. Perhaps, Sally joined the boundary walk. She was, after all, an owner in her own right of one-half of the claim. It would take awhile before Sally fully grasped the piece of independence this new frontier offered women.

In the 1851 Benton County Assessment Rolls, Nimrod was reported to have seven cows, five sheep, thirteen hogs, and one horse. The stock now roamed somewhere on the *kalapuya*. The county had not levied on any of Nimrod's property to pay prosecution costs—not while the appeal was still pending. A first order of business next spring would be to round up the stock. The family's two oxen and milk cow, if she had gone dry, would be given open range and would add to the spring round up. Some of Nimrod's cats may still have been about, albeit well on their way to becoming feral. Nimrod's garden and home field suffered and would not feed seven for winter. Indeed, wintering over on the claim would not have been the kindest way to bide the cruelest season. But the family would have to make do with what Nimrod had left them.

The sons may have camped in tents and lived out of the wagon, leaving the cabin to the three women and child. The inside of a claim cabin, aged more than half a decade, would have ripened into the smells and infestations of rot, insects, and varmints. Its upkeep would have borne the marks of an old man's disrepair and five months of emptiness. It was, as Father James Croke would describe it ten months later, a "most miserable hovel." In short, Nimrod the subsister had little to show for six years of being there. His claim was uncertain and by no means ready to receive a family.

Like salt in open wounds, the winter of 1852–53 added agony to misery. Said to be one of the "worst winters" in Oregon history, there were torrential rains, snow, and ice storms. High water at Oregon City washed away one of Doctor McLoughlin's sawmills. Up river, the Long Tom went over its banks; there would have been days when all seven O'Kellys stayed to the cabin on high ground surrounded by flooded swash and swale. Nimrod may have been the eighth O'Kelly huddled there. His keep at Adams' place was just ten miles away, and with the weather making prisoners of the whole countryside, it is likely Adams gave Nimrod freedom to visit his family at will—a reason, perhaps, why Adams charged far less than the other keepers.

To brave those winter evenings, Nimrod and his family would have stoked up the fire for a last bit of heat, light, and story. The hearth was a core where family came together—a place to read, to dry, and to cook. Most always there would be an iron kettle with steaming water for scrubbing or pouring a cup. And, there was another isle of homely joy in those hard days and nights—Joseph with help from his father and brothers may have fashioned a cradle for his second daughter, Mary Ann. In that cruel winter, Matilda gave birth to the first O'Kelly born in Oregon. Indoors, there was family, freedom, fireside, and forget; while, outside, the land and the law never ceased to beat upon the walls.

By late 1852, the federal land surveyors had finally reached the *kalapuya* prairies of Benton and Linn counties. Severe winter meant that operations in Nimrod's area had to wait until spring. In the meantime, down river at Oregon City, the home of Surveyor General John B. Preston was the site of Governor Gaines' second marriage. Neither the governor nor the surveyor general, both Whigs, had yet made the move to Salem. It was too late to do so. Their terms of office were about to end, because Franklin Pierce, a Democrat, had been elected the fourteenth President of the United States. The Whigs were out.

That set the situation for a series of twists showing how a life and history turn upon threads. Orville Pratt's regular term as a frontier judge in Oregon was due to end in mid-December during the final days of Fillmore's presidency. But Fillmore, the Whig, was not about to return a Democrat to the vacancy. The lame duck appointed Charles F. Train of Massachusetts to be Oregon's third judge. Train, not Pratt, would cast the deciding vote in the case of the *Territory of Oregon v. Nimrod O'Kelly*. But Train was not yet in Oregon when, in mid-December, lawyer Kelly for the defense and prosecutor Boise for the territory presented their arguments to Chief Justice Nelson and Associate Justice Strong. The court's conclusions were predictable. The Christmas 1852, edition of Asahel Bush's *Statesman* reported:

> The Supreme Court adjourned on Wednesday…The judges disagreed in O'Kelley's case, and also in a number of cases taken up from the second district [Pratt's]…If Mr. Fillmore's new appointee, judge Train, arrives soon we understand an adjourned term will be holden for the disposal of these cases. Otherwise they will go over to the next regular term, which will be holden by Judges appointed by President Pierce.

Had Pratt not gone east, he would have been in Oregon to break the loggerhead and send Nimrod to heaven, hell, or oblivion. Now tie-breaker Train might side with Strong to give Nimrod a new trial, but it would never be known because Train declined to accept Fillmore's appointment. The privilege of appointing a substitute for Train would now pass to the new President, Democrat Pierce, who would be inclined to reappoint Democrat Pratt.

The future of Nimrod and the O'Kelly family, huddling in a hovel in a far-off corner of one of the nation's territories, was at the mercy of more than a harsh winter. Spoils, whims, denials, and maneuverings at the opposite edge of the continent were equally tormenting. Who would sit in judgment to weigh Nimrod's case? First it was Pratt, then Train, then Pratt again. Then too, who would be replacing Whigs Nelson and Strong?

Once again, Nimrod's life had not been saved—only delay had been purchased. But then, each delay for a man in his late years was a lifetime.

Notes

1. Benjamin Nichols knew Nimrod from back in Cocke County, Tennessee. They were both in the 1845 migration, and in the future Nichols would have occasion to sign an affidavit in Nimrod's behalf.
2. See Figure No. Four in Chapter 20 concerning the apparent locations of Nimrod's keepers. The Ownbey clan had three different land claims belonging to the father, Nicholas Ownbey, and his two sons, Jesse and William. Like Prier Scott, Jesse Ownbey had been one of the grand jurymen in Nimrod's case. The record does not reveal which Ownbey was Nimrod's keeper. Whether the family found Nimrod at Ownbey's or the Adams' place depended on when the family arrived in Benton County. Benjamin O'Kelly reported that they came to Oregon on October 10, 1852, but arriving in that vast territory could have

many entries—crossing the Rocky Mountain divide, leaving the Snake River, reaching the Cascade foothills at The Dalles, coming to trails end at Oregon City, or rolling to a halt in Benton County. Ownbey kept Nimrod for twenty-four days, while the Adams custody lasted some eighty days. The transfer from Ownbey to Adams appears to have been for monetary reasons. Adams gave the county a better bargain. Ownbey, like previous jailers, charged as much as $6.00 or more per day for board and keep. Adams' keep averaged $3.40 per day.

3. Some research shows Sarah (Sally) O'Kelly's maiden name to be *Burk*.

20

Survey, Freedom, and Wait

1853

The year of 1852 had seen Nimrod weather more than rain and hard winter. He had faced a hangman's noose twice. He was enslaved, his tether passing from keeper to keeper. He was beggared before judges, a governor, and lawmakers. He was shamed before his family. And, worst of all, he had taken the life of another human being. It was a year that came and went like a terrible, angry grizzly. The start of 1853 made no better offing. In the midst of a hard winter, Nimrod's fate was still undecided and in the hands of unknown judges yet to be chosen. The hanging was postponed indefinitely. What was to become of the gallows during this time? Taking the unused scaffold apart would signify that Nimrod had won. Leaving it as a permanent structure would brand Marysville as a place of doom. Like lye soap, a gallows was cleansing, but it had to be rinsed away forthwith. Kill, but do not linger on it.

The delays had their effect upon Benton County's treasury. The county commissioners were learning it was cheaper to kill a prisoner than to keep him. They took a hard look at the mounting costs of Nimrod's room, board, and guard. At their meetings of July, September, October, and December 1852, the commissioners had authorized payments of almost $1,350 for the custody of Nimrod O'Kelly since his arrest on May 22, 1842.[1] Payment of the bills was no small matter. According to Sheriff Starr's report to the governor in the summer of 1852, there were slightly more than two hundred taxpayers in Benton County. The custody had already cost each taxpayer almost $7.00 on average and promised to continue for another year.

Nimrod was not the only ward of Benton County. Henry Shepherd was insane and had no family. Just as there was no Benton County jail or territorial penitentiary, there was no asylum for the custody of "lunatics." Thus, the commissioners ordered Sheriff Starr to hold a public auction for the "services for taking care of said Shepherd." That was the way custody was handled; the care of lunatics and convicts was bought and sold. But, unlike slaves where the highest bidder paid for a purchase, with lunatics and convicts the lowest bidder was paid for storage. Aside from that difference, both auctions treated humans as merchandise, bondage, and thrall.

The county costs for Shepherd's custody set the stage for the entry of Doctor T.J. Right. At the April 5, 1853, commissioners' meeting, Doctor Right "proposed to cure the said Shepherd of his insanity for the sum of one hundred dollars or failing to cure him to charge only for medicine." The commissioners accepted the offer. Just like lawyering, doctoring did not require a license and anyone could hold forth as a practitioner of cures. But Dr. Right was no traveling snake-oil showman, albeit he did have something of the rogue in him. It is not known whether Right cured Shepherd; suffice it to say that not long afterward, Right dropped the business of medicine and took up the business of law enforcement. As a future sheriff and hangman of Benton County, his path was on a dead reckoning with Nimrod's.

Unlike Nimrod's keep, Shepherd's keep carried a means to defray the county's costs. In September 1853, the commissioners authorized the sale of Shepherd's property. No attempt was made at the time to do the same with Nimrod's assets, because the success of the prosecution and the validity of Pratt's sentence order were still in the hands of unknown judges.[2] Instead, the commissioners sought a different solution. They went to the territorial lawmakers and argued that Nimrod's custody ought to be charged to the taxpayers of all of Oregon and not just to the citizens of Benton County— reasoning that if the territorial supreme court and the governor had let well enough alone, Nimrod would have been dead by now. Accordingly, in January 1853 the territorial lawmakers passed "An Act for the Relief of Polk and Benton Counties," which in part authorized the payment of $630.32 to Benton County, "to remunerate said county for keeping Nimrod O'Kelly, who was...respited by the Governor."

The territorial relief, however, covered less than half the costs of Nimrod's past keep and did nothing to resolve Nimrod's future keep, which portended to be long and costly. A new course had to be devised. Why not tether Nimrod to his word? Why not put him on his claim with his family and hold him to his promise to show up when needed? Trust is what his paid keepers had been giving, so why not make it official? On January 10, 1853, Adams' term as keeper was brought to a close, and Silas M. Stout, now the new sheriff, took custody of the prisoner. This lasted only five days, because Stout and the commissioners made a quiet decision. The minutes of the April 5, 1853, commissioners' meeting gave a brief hint of the new course that had been taken in January: Stout was reimbursed for five days of keep and two dollars "for taking bail bond." For the remainder of 1853 and on into 1854, no further expense appears in the commissioners' journal for caretaking Nimrod. Apparently, Nimrod was released from custody on bail.

The procedure was more than odd; it was downright extraordinary for three reasons. First, the bail was set by the county commissioners and not by the courts. Second, government paid the bail and not the prisoner. Third, the bail was set for a first degree murderer, already convicted and under sentence of death. Needless to say, this was *far and fancy doings,* even for the frontier.

The actions of the sheriff and the commissioners could be read as an invitation for Nimrod to leave Oregon. Certainly, many problems would have been solved if the convict simply went away. The courts could take the appeal off the docket; the county would have no further expense; the intruders would have their land contests favorably resolved in the face of the abandonment; the neighborhood would be rid of its misfit; the sheriff would no longer have the unpleasant duty of killing a grandfatherly man; and Nimrod's family would still have their patriarch for the tail end of his days. Nothing bad could come from his fleeing Oregon. But escape had one major opponent—Nimrod himself. There would have to be hair on a frog before Nimrod would abandon his land, risk the loss of his word, or let slip his righteousness.

When the floodwaters receded in the spring of 1853, Nimrod's sons grew anxious. Under the Donation Land Claim Act, the free gift of public land was set to expire on December 1, 1853, a little over a half-year away. That deadline promised a heavy surge of claim searchers in the migration now afoot. Many on the Oregon frontier were not yet aware that back in Washington City on February 14, Congress had moved the deadline ahead two years to 1855. Unaware of this extension, Joseph and his wife Matilda would have been in a hurry to carve out 320 acres of free land. Benjamin, a bachelor, was entitled to 160 acres. Nimrod junior was still too young to make a claim.

Just to the east of Nimrod's claim, some vacant bottomland was still available along the Long Tom and Willamette rivers; and then, too, Nimrod would have been pleased to give up acres to his sons. But none of that was to the sons' liking. They had spent the winter in witness of rivers spilling their banks. Future surveyors would record that the area of Nimrod's claim was "subject to be overflowed by the Long Tom River." To a family farmer, that concern was huge; to a solitary hunter, it meant little. Even Nimrod described his claim as "overflowed land," and acknowledged there was "8 or 10 much better places in 2 miles" of his claim. Furthermore, flatland was strange to Nimrod's sons. They were hill folk raised in the holts and hollows of the Ozarks, Cumberlands, and Smokies.

And on top of it all—there were the stares and silence. The overlapping claims were chasms, not bridges, between Nimrod and his neighbors. On the stoop of the nearby Jennyopolis store, the Nimrod family probably received few words and no smiles. An agony of peace prevailed as everyone waited for the surveyors and the judges. Whatever may have been their reasons, Benjamin and Joseph O'Kelly chose to reject their father's choice of neighborhood. They searched farther up the Valley.

Five miles south, at the new town of Starrs Point, the neighborhood included Samuel F. Starr, the former sheriff and now postmaster; Joseph White, a saw mill operator; and R.B. Hinton, the justice of the peace at the coroner inquest over Mahoney's body. All had been remonstrators against Nimrod.[3] So, Benjamin and Joseph went farther south and found what they were looking for in the Lancaster area of Lane County—an easy day's wagon ride on the Gold Mine Road from their father's claim. The brothers' claims were side by side and took 480 acres. Joseph and Matilda improved and settled their claim on May 1, 1853. Although Benjamin had filed his claim four days prior to that, he did not settle the claim with improvements until much later. In an August 15, 1853, letter to the surveyor general, Benjamin gave this explanation for his delay:

> Dear Sir Mr. Survair Ginerarl…I Benjamin G.O.Kelley have taken a claim of land joining my brother…have not got my house up yet as to make it my plce of resadence as yet but I am still working on my place allican and want to get my huse up and moove on it shortly. I have beter than 2 acres fenced.

As a single male and the eldest, Benjamin undoubtedly felt obliged to stay down river to help his folks. In early September 1853, Benjamin finished his claim cabin and began to stay there on occasion. Teenage sister Sarah went to Lane County to live with her brothers instead of staying with her parents. Nimrod junior also set out to build his own fires. The 1854 Census of Jackson County—in far southern Oregon beyond the Valley—reported a nineteen year old "Nimrod O'Kelly" living there alone. Gold had been discovered in Jackson County, and it seems Junior had taken to the fever. By autumn of 1853, all fledglings had flown the nest. The 1853 Benton County Assessment Roll for Nimrod's Long Tom claim listed two horses, twenty-five sheep, and thirty-eight hogs. It also listed two souls—Nimrod O'Kelly and "one female." Sally and Nimrod were now alone surrounded by unknown borders.

On Saturday, August 6, 1853, a solitary horseman wearing a Roman collar rode up to the door of Nimrod's cabin. Father James Croke was the first missionary priest to make an official circuit into the southern Oregon settlements. In a letter to Archbishop François Norbert Blanchet, dated August

9, 1853, and written from Jesse Applegate's home in the Umpqua foothills, Father Croke wrote:

> I found old O'Kelly on his claim fourteen miles south of Marysville. As my horse was tired and as it was approaching Sunday, I thought it better to remain with him in order to have an opportunity of saying Mass on Sunday. His house is a most miserable hovel, and so small that I'd scarcely find a corner to fix me up an altar. I succeeded, however, in arranging a few boards against the wall, and having spread upon them my altar cloths and ornaments celebrated the first Mass that was ever said in this part of the country. All the neighborhood are very bigoted against the Catholics, and hold O'Kelly in abhorrence. He received the Sacraments of Confession and Communion, and appears to me to be a very good old man. His wife and children are Protestants, but very well disposed towards the Catholic religion. His wife, in fact, believes in it, and is reading Catholic books.[4]

On his way back from southern Oregon, Father Croke stopped again at Nimrod's cabin. And, later from Salem, Croke wrote to the Archbishop on Wednesday, October 26, 1853, saying he had baptized "old O'Kelly's...wife." Upon his return to Portland, Croke made the following entry in the Portland Catholic Registry:

> The 23rd day of October 1853 we the undersigned missionary priest of Oregon having first received her solemn abjuration of Protestantism, have admitted in the bosum of Holy Roman Catholic and Apostolic Church Sarah OKelley (aged about 60 years) residing in Benton County Oregon, in the presence of Nimrod O'Kelley.

As of autumn 1853, the number of Catholics in Benton County had doubled—from one to two. Nowhere in Croke's writings does he report that Nimrod was a convicted murderer awaiting the supreme court and gallows. But in the mind of Catholic authorities, particularly Archbishop Blanchet, there must have been the thought that here was a manslayer needing to give penance and gain absolution.

Nearly a year earlier—in November or December 1852—surveyor George W. Hyde, an axeman, and two chainmen had passed along near the southern edge of Nimrod's claim. They sighted, slogged, and bushwhacked, while toting chain, level, plumb, solar compass, and other tools of their trade. The general survey of the territory that began eighteen months before at Portland had finally made its way to south Benton County. Hyde and his crew had been the forward patrol in a series of three surveys. Hyde's job was simply to fix the townships—squares of land six miles long on each side.

Using that grid, a second crew of surveyors, led by James E. Freeman, came through Nimrod's countryside a few months later, cutting each township into thirty-six square mile sections. The land was being sliced up like cornbread. At the corners of each of these square mile sections, Freeman placed stakes, large stones, or rock cairns. Near these markers, witness trees were blazed to help locate the posted corners. These sectional cross-hairs would now form the vital *points of beginning* for the descriptions of private land claims. No longer would lakes, trees, river bends, gullies, or buttes be used as points and edges in uncharted lands. Now land would be parceled in keep with charted grids—precise artifice, not fickle nature.

Once the township and sectional survey teams had finished their work, a third survey was in order. This chore had to retrace the matrix and make a "Surveyor's Walk and Description of the Countryside." The field notes of the walking surveyor located physical features, such as houses, fields, fences, towns, forests, prairies, streams, lakes, swales, and sloughs.

In Nimrod's immediate vicinity, the walking surveyor noted that he headed "West on S. boundary of Sec. 35," and then turned north to walk the line separating sections 34 and 35. Shortly, he passed within "3 links [of] O'Kelly's house"; thus as he walked the line, his left shoulder would have passed within two feet of the log wall of Nimrod and Sally's hovel.[5] The surveyor then returned to the south border of section 34, and proceeded westerly along that border, where he came upon the Jeremiah Criss claim, which was "over half mile wide as pointed out by himself." Criss's boundary formed the "E. boundary of Asa Stark's claim." The surveyor then indicated in his field notes that Stark or Criss, or both, pointed out that their mutual boundary "bears N. 40 chs." Forty chains would have taken the Criss and Stark claims over two thousand feet into the western portion of Nimrod's claim.

Apparently, the surveyor had no conversation with the O'Kellys. Walking through the north side of Nimrod's claim, the surveyor noted "Mahoney's house" south of him, and "Robt Grimsley's" north of him. By these indications, those abodes could also have been on land claimed by Nimrod. The surveyor was not aware that the house he described as "Mahoney's" was now the home of John Thomas and his wife, Mahoney's widow.

The field notes confirmed that the borders of Criss, Stark, Grimsley, Mahoney, and O'Kelly were like fingers clenched in a fist. But the positioning of claims was not the business of the walking surveyor. None of the survey teams conducted surveys of private claim borders. Contended borders were reported occasionally for the purpose of orienting the countryside, not for deciding the superiority of claims.

The written work of the township, sectional, and walking surveyor teams were delivered to Surveyor General John B. Preston in Oregon City. He then amassed all of the work into official topographical or "field" maps—one for

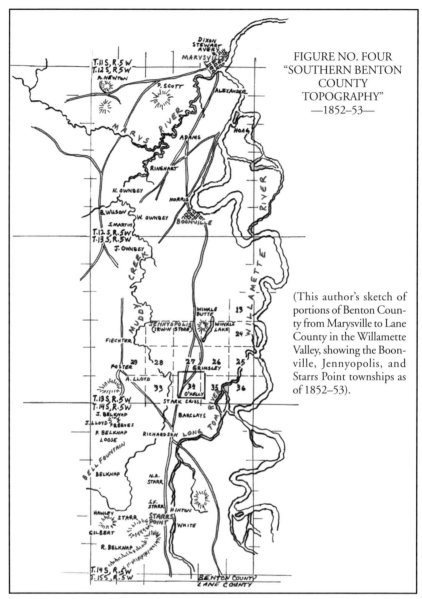

FIGURE NO. FOUR
"SOUTHERN BENTON
COUNTY
TOPOGRAPHY"
—1852–53—

(This author's sketch of
portions of Benton Coun-
ty from Marysville to Lane
County in the Willamette
Valley, showing the Boon-
ville, Jennyopolis, and
Starrs Point townships as
of 1852–53).

Figure No. Four. Nimrod's claim does not appear on the topographical township maps of that
time. Nimrod's claim borders are here superimposed, based upon his own (unofficial) survey in
his notification file. General locations of other key claimants also are provided. Each "section"
equals one square mile. Bear in mind that these field surveys are one-and-a-half centuries old
and the courses of rivers, creeks, and roads change over time—e.g., the large bow of the Willamette River at Boonville, just like Boonville itself, no longer exists.

each township. Nimrod's township plat was finished on March 18, 1853, and designated, "Township No. 13 South, Range No. 5 West"—or *T.13S, R.5W* in surveyor brevity. It meant that Nimrod's township was thirteen townships south of the Willamette Stone in Portland, and five townships west of that stone's north-south meridian. Herein, for convenience sake, *T.13S, R.5W* is called the "Jennyopolis Township." Nimrod and Sally's claim occupied most of section 34 of the Jennyopolis Township. The Stark and Criss cabins were in the adjacent township to the south, conveniently the "Starrs Point Township." The "Boonville Township" was situated immediately north of Jennyopolis.

The three surveys having been completed, the door was now open for settlers to file notifications of their claims. This filing entailed more surveys—the settlers' own private surveys of what they had claimed. Once the countryside had been sufficiently carved up by preemption, the surveyor general could then construct another set of maps called "claims maps" (cadastral survey), showing private land borders. This second set of township maps was destined to be many years away. The future claims maps and the 1853 topographical maps were the difference between realty and reality.

Nimrod was the first settler from the Jennyopolis Township to file a notification of claim. This convicted manslayer, under sentence of death, travelling far north to Oregon City to make the filing at Preston's office, was three weeks ahead of other claimants.[6]

On March 30, 1853, twelve days after the survey completion, the condemned murderer, apparently without guard, was in the office of the surveyor general, one hundred road miles from home. Nimrod had been there on the same errand over six years ago, when filing his original claim in the office of Frederic Prigg, the Provisional Government Land Recorder. This time, in Preston's office, the process was much more orderly. There were printed forms from back east with blank spaces to be filled in, and Nimrod had prepared a private survey of the 640-acre claim that accorded with the government's survey grids.[7]

While his claim still covered the same 640 acres, Preston's description of it was a far cry from the one Prigg fashioned for the Provisional Government. Those differences told something of the changing ways in which land was beheld. It was more than just the difference between the older "rods" and the newer "chains." Where the Prigg description referred to natural landmarks, such as the "head of a lake," the "mouth of the Long Tom Bath," "two butes on the California Trail," and the "brink of a ravine," the new description read:

beginning at a point 8.25 chains North, 11.00 chains East of the S.W. corner of
Sec. 35, T.13S. R.5W running thence North 80.00 chains, West 80.00 chains,
South 80.00 chains, East 80.00 chains to the place of beginning containing 640
acres.

From the eye of an eagle looking down, no one could see townships, sections, or chains. On the other hand, from maps, no one could soar and see the
earth's folds. And so, when asked, "What is *land*?"—Prigg and Preston and
the laws that guided them were as different as eagles and angles.

Nimrod's "Notification" was given file number "2087 " and dated March
30, 1853. "Notification" under the Donation Act had other requirements besides giving a precise description of borders. The time of commencement had
to be specified in order to start the clock on "four successive years [of]…con-
tinued residence and cultivation." Accordingly, Nimrod signed an affidavit,
swearing "he has personally resided upon and cultivated" the claim "continuously from the 1st day of May 1849." Nimrod swore to *continuous* use, full
knowing his claim was vacated for five months while he was in custody in the
latter half of 1852.

Two months later, on May 26 and 28, 1853, Joseph C. Alexander and
Joseph C. Avery made separate trips to Oregon City to confirm Nimrod's
starting date. They swore Nimrod "personally resided upon and cultivated
said tract…on or about the 6th day of May 1849." In both of their affidavits,
however, in describing the duration of Nimrod's residency, the word "continuously" in the printed form was deleted by penstroke.

Nimrod, Alexander, and Avery chose to use the year "1849"for a starting
time. Why not 1847? Nimrod had filed his original claim with the Provisional
Government in December 1846. A four-year succession beginning somewhere in 1847 would have expired well before the killing and custody. But
for some reason, "1849" was the year sworn to by all three men. That time of
commencement would create serious problems if the surveyor general were
to rule that "residence and cultivation" of the land claim could not include
Nimrod's confinement period.[8]

To perfect a 640-acre claim, Nimrod also had to prove he was married.
His affidavit of March 30 swore he married Sally O'Kelly "on the ___ day of
___, 1813, in Cork [sic. Cocke] Co. Tennessee." The day and the month were
left blank. Benjamin F. Nichols, in Dallas, Oregon, may have been the only
man in all of Oregon who had known both Sally Bell and Nimrod in their
early years in Tennessee. On April 7, 1853, Nichols vouched that

from credible report…Nimrod O'Kelly and Sally Bell, were married in said
County of Cocke and State of Tennessee somewhere about the year A.D. 1812,

and I believe from report that they are now living together in Benton Co. Oregon as man and wife.

That kind of hearsay testimony was about all that could be hoped for in proof of marriage. Nichols signed the affidavit with his "X." That he could not read what he had signed, and that his scribe was nowhere identified or required to attest to the accuracy of the recording, was a gap in procedure that was of no bother when illiteracy was so prevalent.

Nimrod thought the wedding year was 1813. Nichols put it "somewhere about…1812." On April 14, one week after Nichols affidavit, Nimrod wrote the surveyor general:

> I made a mistake in the date of our marriage. We was married in the year 1812. I know now what made me make the mistake. I have been often asked of late what year my oldest son was borne and being accustomed to answer them in 1813 this is what led my mind to 1813 as I done it through inadvertence…You will pleas alter the three into a two.

Nimrod's earnest attention to this irrelevant and minor detail is curious. The *fact* of marriage and not the *time* of marriage was the essential point to the surveyor general. Indeed, it was common for some donation land claimants to stake their claims first and then marry. Furthermore, Nimrod did not bother to fill in the month and day of his wedding. Why, then, did he deem it so important to correct the year? It may have been that in those times a first child and marriage in the same year put tongues to wag. Their eldest son Charles was born in 1813. Children were supposed to be the *fruit* of union, but sometimes were rumored to be the *seed* of union. Sally may have urged her husband to hush the whispers and turn away the glances.

Nimrod's letter of April 14 also reported that his neighbors were still persisting in their interference with his claim.

> I set my stakes to the proper place before I started down to oregon city but my family tells me they saw a man go to them in two hours after I left. Then they went to see and they was puld up and taken off…[The] letter I shewed to you will shew to the world that they all knew well the very spot where my beginning corner was by their own handwriting.[9]

About three weeks after Nimrod's filing of notice under the new survey, Mary Jane Thomas, the widow of Jeremiah Mahoney, made the trip to Oregon City to do the same. She filed a "Notification of Claim" and "Settler's Oath" on behalf of her dead spouse. Richard Irwin and Jeremiah Criss accompanied her and swore affidavits before the surveyor general in her behalf. The three signed their attestations on April 22. The widow signed with her "X. " Her private survey clearly showed a conflict of claims. Although the filing of

Nimrod's application preceded hers, that made no difference. What counted was not a race to the land office, but rather a race to the land. Nimrod's affidavits put him on the land since at least 1849. His opponent's affidavits gave Mahoney a start no sooner than March 1852. Accordingly, the surveyor general summarily rejected the claim of Jeremiah Mahoney, now deceased, because of the prior claim of Nimrod O'Kelly.

That rejection could have been appealed to the courts, but it never was. A few weeks after the rejection, Mahoney's widow and her new husband, John Thomas, moved off the claim and became townsfolk. J.C. Avery may have had a hand in that apparent surrender. Thomas borrowed money from Avery and took out a mortgage on Lot No. 11, Block 2, in Marysville. But that was not the last of the Thomases. Their cabin in the Jennyopolis area remained, and they would be heard from again.

Beneath all of this paper work, there seethed resentment. *A convicted manslayer under sentence of death was running loose over the countryside and winning a piece of it from his victim.* These liberties were unquestionably a rub upon the sore of those who felt he should be dead by now.

In the autumn of 1853, immigrants began their annual arrival. Unclaimed land in Benton County was growing scarce—so much so that new settlers began taking the low lands east of Nimrod on the Long Tom and Willamette rivers, lands rejected by Nimrod's sons earlier in the year. Into these low lands came the families of Caspar Kompf and the James, Thomas, and Patrick Kinney brothers. Kompf was the father-in-law of Richard Irwin, proprietor of the Jennyopolis store. The Kinney brothers, like Irwin and Mahoney, were from Ireland.

On September 27, 1853, Irwin wrote Surveyor General Preston on behalf of these newest immigrants and requested a clarification: The new neighbors wished to settle, but could not tell where existing claim borders lay. An old trouble had grown, big enough to threaten new settlement in the Valley. Although the section lines were now mapped on paper and marked on the land, where were the official claim lines? The surveyor general's claims maps could not be readied for many years—not until all private claims were filed and conflicts resolved. Until then, inexact squatter stakes, when not decayed or "puld up," were the only clue.

As a postscript in his letter to Preston, Irwin asked about the price of goods for sale in "your Mercantile House…I start 2 teams down next week for Blacksmith Tools, Iron & other merchandise & will Instruct them to give your House a call." Preston had supplemented his income with a private wholesale business. Did Preston take the time to resolve the border problem identified by Irwin? Did Preston sell tools and iron to Irwin's store? Were Preston's public service and private business connected? The record does not show what Preston's response was to Irwin's letter; but one month later, the land boundary problem was apparently solved, because that was when Kompf, Irwin's father-in-law, filed his notification of claim on the lands in question. A few months after that, the Kinneys, Irwin's countrymen, did the same.

Nimrod's problems with the law were a long way from over. Criss, Stark, and Grimsley were still conflicting claimants, and now more neighbors appeared to be new foes against him. Even more critical, the territorial supreme court was waking up after a political nap. Nimrod's attention would have to turn from the threats to his land, to the menace to his life.

Notes

1. The largest payments went to keepers John Stewart ($176), Prier Scott ($100), Ownbey ($144), Thomas Adams ($271), and S.M. Stout ($410). In addition to these costs, there were additional payments of $156 to the guards. Other expenses included meals, a flannel shirt, tobacco, a door lock, handcuffs, hobbles, and chains.
2. Any attempt to seize and sell Nimrod's land claim had added complications. Shepherd was not a married man; Nimrod was. That half of a husband's claim belonging to his wife could not be levied upon to pay the husband's expenses. Any doubts about that had been laid to rest by Oregon lawmakers in a bill passed in the 1851–52 session at Salem. Until the surveyor general split Nimrod's claim and assigned one half to wife Sally, the sheriff had no way of knowing which half of the claim to auction off, and no bidder was about to pay cash for an unseen half of an unperfected claim.
3. Like Boonville, Jennyopolis, and many small communities of that day, Starrs Point was less than a town. Some called it "Lick Skillet." It was simply a center where farmers came for store goods, mail, millwork, the granary, and cracker-barrel chawing and jawing. No doubt, the citizens of Starrs Point favored hard work, scorned "subsisters," and embraced the words of ex-President James Monroe, who said the "hunter or savage" was "incompatible with progress," and "must yield to civilized life." In 1874, the Starrs Point settlement became a chartered town and changed its name to Monroe.
4. Edwin V. O'Hara, author of the *Pioneer Catholic History of Oregon* (pp. 175–76, 188), recorded the name "O'Reilly" instead of "O'Kelly" in Father James Croke's quote. But a typed transcript of Croke's actual letter at the Archdiocese of Portland has Croke using the name "O'Kelly." Croke reported Sally "reading…books," yet she signed her name with an "X" on documents. Her illiteracy can be concluded from the fact that if she could not write her name, she must not have been able to read it; and if she could not read her own name, she probably was unable to read much of anything else. There may be possible reasons for the conflicting "illiteracy" on the one hand, and "reading" on the other: Croke may have been simply presumptuous; or Sally may have been the beneficiary of someone else reading aloud; or Sally may have been ashamed and shamming.
5. In addition to the "Southern Benton County Topography" map in this chapter, see Figure No. Two in Chapter 11, and Figure No. Six in Chapter 29. A survey "chain" is 66 feet long (4 rods). There are 100 "links" in a chain—a link being almost 8 inches.
6. John B. Preston, a Whig, had not relocated to the new capital in Salem. The 1852–53 territorial lawmakers passed a resolution instructing Delegate Joseph Lane in Washington

City to have Congress force Preston to move to Salem, but nothing came of it. Only territorial offices were required to be at the capital seat; the surveyor general was a federal officer. Furthermore, Preston knew, as a lame duck, that any move on his part would be short-lived. It was just a matter of time before new President Franklin Pierce and the Senate would get around to the spoils of appointing new officers in faraway corners.

7. Perhaps Nimrod's friend, David Stump, had given him a hand with the private survey. The two had traveled in the 1845 migration, and David had been a witness to the writing of Nimrod's will. David Stump was a surveyor by trade, and a "George Stump" was the Benton County Surveyor in 1850–52. Records do not indicate whether George and David were related.

8. In Nimrod's favor was the fact that, when settlers like Avery went off to the California gold mines for many months, such absences were not deemed to interrupt residence on Oregon lands. Would the surveyor general view a criminal confinement in the same way? And what if the courts subsequently decided that Nimrod's confinement was not warranted because he was innocent? Would that affect the stream of habitation?

9. The letter Nimrod referred to was either the one sent to him by R.B. Hinton on July 16, 1852, or the J.C. Alexander statement of July 30, 1852, both of which referred to the informal survey taken by Nimrod's neighbors after the trial. See Chapter 17.

21

Spoils

1853

I n the spring of 1853, while Nimrod's sons and other new emigrants searched for land to claim, a new U.S. President on the other side of the continent foraged in the spoils of victory. Whig Fillmore was out, and Democrat Pierce was in. The nationwide dole included filling the vacancies in Oregon's offices—Governor Gaines, Secretary Hamilton, U.S. Attorney Holbrook, Chief Justice Nelson, Associate Justice Strong, and Surveyor General Preston all had to be replaced. These easterners would not be missed by frontier Democrats, who, like cubs in the wild, were leery of strangers.

Since the infusion of federal governance in 1848, almost all of Oregon's officers and judges, Whigs and Democrats alike, had been lured to Oregon by the carrot of appointment. Oregonians had their bellies full of imported leadership. On April 1, 1851, the pioneer legislature passed a resolution informing the President, "there are many respectable individuals in Oregon capable of discharging the duties devolving upon the judges as well as filling any other office." President Franklin Pierce was accommodating. As counseled by Oregon's congressional delegate, Joe Lane, who in turn was advised by newspaperman Asahel Bush, patronage would be keyed to local Democrats. The cadre of Oregon's top leadership was about to be totally changed, with one exception—Democrat incumbent Orville C. Pratt.

In the office of Secretary of the Territory, an 1846 Oregon pioneer, George Law Curry, replaced George Edward Hamilton. Curry had been the editor of several Oregon newspapers, served as a legislative and court clerk, and was a compiler of Oregon's Twenty Acts code. His wife, Chloe Boone, was a great-granddaughter of legendary Daniel Boone. Curry was destined to have a long leadership role in the remaining years of Oregon Territory, and would one-day play a part in the Nimrod O'Kelly story.

For U.S. Attorney, President Pierce replaced Amory Holbrook with Benjamin F. Harding, an 1849 immigrant. He was part of Asahel Bush's clique of Democrats and would strengthen those bonds by marrying into Bush's family. Among lesser federal offices Pierce took his broom to those corners in a clean sweep of Whig dominance. Local frontiersmen Joel Palmer, John Adair, A.C. Gibbs, and Asa L. Lovejoy were among the many new appointments to federal Indian affairs, customs, and the post office. Most pertinent to Nimrod's situation was the ouster of James B. Preston as the surveyor general, replaced by J.K. Gardiner.

The biggest prize, of course, was the empty chair left by Governor Gaines. Pierce filled that space with Lane, who had been Oregon's original territorial governor. Back in 1850, after the Whigs replaced Lane with Gaines, the citizens of Oregon promptly elected Lane to serve as their non-voting delegate to Congress. Now, in 1853, Lane's retaking of the governorship seemed a fitting touch to the seesaw of regimes back in Washington City. But Lane's reappointment as Oregon's chief was short-lived, lasting only three days. He accepted on May 16, and resigned, May 19, because Oregonians reelected him to the Oregon delegate post in Congress. Lane opted to honor the wishes of the people, not the President.[1]

Upon Lane's second exit from the governorship, Secretary Curry automatically ascended to the head of the territory. Curry would act as governor for six months until Pierce got around to making another appointment. For his next pick, Pierce was no longer willing to accommodate local leaders. Instead, Pierce sent John W. Davis of Indiana to serve as governor. Davis did not arrive in Oregon until December 1853. As far as Oregonians were concerned, Davis was just another import untested by pioneering and unfit to bell the cat.

The one remaining non-judicial officer on the replacement list was the U.S. Marshal. That turnover was most telling, for it signified more than any other the changing face of the Oregon frontier. As sheriff in the Provisional Government and as marshal in the territorial government, Joseph Lafayette Meek had been the chief law enforcer in Oregon for a decade. His term was twice as long as any other officer and came under the good graces of three former Presidents—Polk, Taylor, and Fillmore. He had trekked and trapped his way in the Oregon and Rockies backcountry long before white settlement began. In words of his own special whimsy and bravado, he had roamed the Pacific Northwest when "Mount Hood was just a hole in the ground." That tenure put him beyond the current trend toward party politics.

But growing feelings against Meek went deeper than the absence of party loyalties. Joe Meek was a wilderness man, a drinker, swearer, fighter, a coarse man with little schooling. Worst of all, he was a *squawman*. He had had two former Indian wives and was now wed to a third. His robust manner was no longer in step with the new civilization. More than any other officer, now or then, mountain man Meek betokened the passing frontier.

The record does not show that the paths of Joe Meek and Nimrod O'Kelly ever crossed. But words that had been used to describe Nimrod might have fit Meek: "He was of a past generation of mankind." In the spring of 1853, both men found themselves on a waning trail. Meek had served his times, and his times were done. President Pierce appointed Oregonian and clique member James W. Nesmith to the office of U.S. Marshal. Meek was put to pasture on his farm on the Tualatin Plains. Nimrod too was headed for pasture, albeit of a more drastic sort.

With the non-judicial offices now refilled, President Pierce turned to the three vacant bench seats. The President's broom here was the most telling whisk of all to Nimrod's future. Justices William Strong and Thomas Nelson had resigned, as was expected of all Whigs. Justice Pratt's court term, on the other hand, had merely expired, and he was in line to be reappointed. Indeed, he expected to move up to the chief justice's chair, a position he had sought for a long time.

Nearly three years earlier, in September 1850, he had been in Washington City to lobby for the chief justice robes, but the Whigs gave it to one of their own—Nelson. Now in 1853 with a Democrat President, Pratt's chances were near certain. As a Democrat, local Oregonian, and member of the clique, Pratt was the one incumbent likely to withstand the purge. He had a brief scare when lame duck President Fillmore appointed Charles F. Train to succeed him. When Train declined the appointment, President Pierce took the reins and did what was expected—he made Pratt the chief justice. Pratt and Nimrod would have taken the news differently. What was robe for the breast of one, was rope at the throat for the other.

Not all was as it seemed, however. The consent of the Senate on Pratt's appointment had reached a surprising impasse. Senator Stephen A. Douglas of Illinois opposed Pratt's reappointment, even though previously Douglas had been the one who recommended Pratt to then President Polk. The *Oregonian* ran a series of articles that shed possible light on Douglas's turnaround. The articles accused Pratt of having resigned from the West Point Military Academy on account of dishonesty, of having run a gambling business before coming to Oregon, and of accepting money from the Hudson's Bay Company while on the Oregon bench.

Additionally, the articles described Pratt as exhibiting "sly cunning, moral dishonesty, unparalleled egotism, overbearing selfishness, and utter destitution of principle." The language, however, needed to be taken in several contexts. For one, Oregon journalism was given to and had become notorious for barbs, bombast, and abuse. For another, the *Oregonian* was openly

Democratic President Franklin Pierce appointed George Henry Williams in 1853 as Chief Justice of the Oregon Territory Supreme Court, replacing Thomas Nelson. Williams wrote the appellate opinion denying Nimrod's appeal. As district judge, he re-sentenced Nimrod to his third and final trip to the gallows. Williams later became the U.S. Attorney General, and was President Grant's candidate for Chief Justice of the U.S. Supreme Court. *Oregon Historical Society #230*

a Whig newspaper and an enemy of the clique. Then too, lawyer W.W. Chapman, one of the founders of the *Oregonian*, had a personal feud with Pratt stemming from the contempt-of-court charge.

Whatever may have been in Senator Douglas's craw, President Pierce obliged him and withdrew Pratt's reappointment. Pratt's defeat was a lone victory for the Whigs in a sea of Democratic appointments, and a crushing blow to Pratt's ambitions. Little could he have foretold that his denial of a new trial and his issuance of a death decree in Nimrod's case were to be among his last decisions as an Oregon judge. In spite of his defeat, Pratt returned to Oregon, set up a law practice with one of Nimrod's former prosecutors, and over the next few years attempted unsuccessfully to return to Oregon's political scene. His steps in Oregon government were halted, but his tracks remained. Oregon had yet to deal with his past rulings, including those made in Nimrod's trial. While Pratt's voice as a judge may have been silenced, as a citizen he still had future things to say about Nimrod's case.

President Pierce and the Senate sent George Henry Williams to lead the Supreme Court of Oregon Territory. Williams was a judge in the newly formed State of Iowa. Senator Douglas, the same man who had undermined Pratt's appointment, recommended Williams. Oregon's new chief justice was thirty years old.

Meanwhile, Pratt's original associate justice chair went to Cyrus Olney, a Willamette Valley settler and immigrant of 1851. To the third and final seat on the territorial supreme court, President Pierce appointed "Mordecai" Deady—a replacement for Associate Justice Strong. In Oregon, no one doubted that "Mordecai" was meant to be *Matthew P.* Deady of Lafayette, Oregon. Deady came to Oregon in 1849 and was president of Oregon Territory's upper legislative house. He was a member of the clique and, thus, in close association with political puppeteers Asahel Bush and Joe Lane. While the ousting of Justice Strong was a vote lost for Nimrod, the appointment of Deady was likely a vote regained. Deady had been one of the signers on "Petition A" for Nimrod's full pardon. Furthermore, on September 20, 1852, Deady wrote, "I was rather desirous that they [Nelson and Strong] should… grant [Nimrod's] writ of error!"

With Williams, Olney, and Deady seemingly in place, the new territorial supreme court went right to work, meeting in Portland in June 1853. At that term, a few cases were heard and decided. For reasons unknown, Nimrod's case was not among them, even though urgency in the matter was obvious—a condemned murderer was, after all, moving around at large. A

possible reason for skipping over Nimrod's case was that deputy clerk Allan M. Seymour stubbornly refused to deliver court files to the new justices. Seymour was apparently not yet convinced of the new judges' credentials. Then too, perhaps, he questioned holding court in Portland instead of Salem. On that, Seymour may have been correct. Lawmakers did not authorize a Portland term until six months later. Whatever Seymour's reasons, his refusal ran afoul of the court's patience. The judges jailed him— some say, in a saloon. His eventual compliance may have come too late to docket Nimrod's case.

How might the future have gone for Nimrod if Seymour had obeyed the court immediately? How would the Williams-Deady-Olney slate have decided Nimrod's fate in the summer of 1853? That slate was never given another chance to hear the case, because authorities back in Washington City took a renewed interest in this mysterious "Mordecai" Deady.

In 1853, Democratic President Franklin Pierce appointed Cyrus Olney as Associate Justice of the Oregon Territory Supreme Court, replacing William Strong. Olney withdrew from voting in Nimrod's second appellate review, and tendered his resignation from the court with the desire to be replaced by Matthew Deady. The resignation was denied. *Oregon Historical Society #3540*

Was he *Matthew?* Although no one named Mordecai contested the appointment and although all Oregonians understood Matthew was the man intended, President Pierce chose not to cure the mistake with a simple name correction. Rather, a new candidate was interposed.

In late October, Obediah B. McFadden, an import from Pennsylvania, stepped off the ship onto Oregon soil with the President's official commission, which appointed him as a replacement to Mordecai Deady's bench seat. Oregonians and particularly the clique were flabbergasted. A gross error had been made and needed correction. In March 1854, Pierce would rectify the mistake by sending McFadden to the newly created Washington Territory Supreme Court. The Oregon chair would be returned to Deady with a commission correctly recording him as "Matthew P."

In a matter of months, the repositioning of seats on the supreme court went like a game of musical chairs. The chief justice

Democratic President Franklin Pierce appointed Matthew Paul Deady as Associate Justice of the Oregon Territory Supreme Court in 1853, replacing Pratt, and then again in 1854, in place of McFadden. Having been temporarily replaced on account of a spelling error of his name, he was not given the opportunity to cast a vote (likely favorable) to Nimrod's appeal. *Oregon Historical Society #63119*

chair began with Nelson, then opened for Pratt, but was quickly taken by Williams. Pratt's associate justice chair went to Train and then Olney. Strong's associate justice chair went to Deady, then McFadden, then back to Deady. Although McFadden's stay on the Oregon bench lasted less than four months, he was there for the December

In 1853, Democratic President Franklin Pierce appointed Obediah B. McFadden as Associate Justice of the Oregon Territory Supreme Court, replacing Matthew Deady. McFadden served only five months as a short-term replacement for Deady. He cast the deciding vote affirming Nimrod's conviction and death sentence. *Oregon Historical Society #105359*

1853 term—the term in which Nimrod's case came up for review. Because of a spelling error and a clerk's contempt of court, instead of Deady sitting in judgment, Nimrod would have McFadden, an imported easterner just passing through, as one of his judges.

In all, some fourteen territorial offices were vacated and refilled by Pierce.[2] Not one incumbent was allowed to continue, and no one was there to build a bridge. With the ouster of the Whig officers, Oregon City ceased to have any lingering hold on Oregon politics. Territorial offices began to shift to Salem and federal offices to Portland. Asahel Bush moved his *Statesman* newspaper from Oregon City to Salem—a move that capped the slow christening of Bush's inner circle with the name "Salem Clique."

How all of this affected Nimrod's future was guesswork. The issues in Nimrod's case had nothing to do with party politics. When it came to politics, Nimrod might have said he *floated his stick no wise.* Nevertheless, his pleas were adrift in partisan undertow.

Notes

1. Subject to Senate consent, the President had the power to bestow offices in the executive and judicial branches of the territorial hierarchy. But in the legislative branch, the people had the power. Accordingly, territorial legislators and Oregon's delegate to the U S. Congress were bestowed by popular vote. One may only conjecture about Lane's motives in making himself simultaneously a candidate for governor and for delegate. It may have been a ploy. He took the governor job full knowing he preferred to continue his service as Oregon's delegate to Congress. Indeed, when he accepted the governorship, he was awaiting news of the vote in the delegate race. Perhaps he took the President's appointment in order to sport it in the delegate race as a feather in his bonnet. Then too, he may have taken the appointment as medicine for wounded pride—a payback to his successor. Years later he wrote: "I took care to have Gaines removed as a kind of compliment to me." Whether Lane meant "compliment" or complement, flattery or satisfaction, President Pierce may have been annoyed to find out that this appointment was used as either boost or balm.
2. Many of Franklin Pierce's 1853 appointments later became famous in national roles. In 1860, Joe Lane was the U.S. Vice Presidential candidate for the southern faction of Democrats. Benjamin F. Harding, James W. Nesmith, and George Henry Williams would one day be U.S. Senators from Oregon. Williams would go on to become the nation's top lawyer—the U.S. Attorney General. He was also destined to be named as President Grant's choice for U.S. Chief Justice.

22

The Judges' Last Word

Winter 1853–54

The time: December 1853. The place: Salem. The court: The highest in Oregon Territory. The case: *Territory of Oregon v. Nimrod O'Kelly.* The lawyers: Reuben P. Boise for the prosecution, and James K. Kelly for the defense. The judges: Chief Justice George H. Williams, Associate Justice Cyrus Olney, and Associate Justice Obediah McFadden. Had the spelling of a first name on a Presidential commission been correct, had Senator Stephen A. Douglas of Illinois raised no objection, and had a lame duck appointee accepted, the Oregon territorial supreme court would have been Matthew P. Deady, Orville C. Pratt, and Charles F. Train instead.

The hearing would be the first murder case ever heard before that court. A *hearing* meant exactly that—a listening, an oral argument. Difficulties in hand-scripting and pen-copying made written argument in the form of briefs a seldom used presentation. Oratory and elocution were the mainstay of judicial review.

Kelly and Boise were vigorous, yet friendly, adversaries. They were often allies, not combatants. They were both territorial lawmakers and about to enter legislative session in another part of Salem. Then too, they were working together as codifiers of a new compilation of Oregon's growing number of statutes. The Hamilton Code needed replacing. Kelly and Boise's effort—the *Oregon Code of 1854*—would soon be printed, and its 1855 amended version would remain the written law throughout the rest of territorial times. Furthermore, Boise and Kelly were Democrats. In Oregon's bicameral legislature, Kelly became Chair of the Council Judiciary Committee and Boise became Chair of the House Judiciary Committee. Both would one day be judges on the very court that they now appeared before as rival advocates. That was the way of lawyers—a strange mix of alliance and adversity. Lawyers cooperated in combat, and contested in collaboration. Indeed, a difficult breed to understand.

The Salem hearing before the supreme court was just fifty miles from Nimrod's claim. Knowing Nimrod's concern, and his love of a walk, he could have attended. But, unlike a trial, the defendant was not required to be present, and his lawyer probably advised him to stay home. His presence could operate against him—he was a convicted murderer wandering loose in open defiance of a judicial sentence specifically commanding that he be "kept and detained in safe and secure custody until" his execution.

Recognizance not only violated that order, it violated the traditions of crime and punishment. The failure of county executives to carry out court orders could have cast cold water on court charity. Judges could be persuaded to initiate leniency, but the affront of disobedient enforcers might overcome such compassion because of the need for dignity and decorum. The freedom and trust extended to Nimrod were factors best left out of any deliberations made by these judges, two of who were new to the ways of this far frontier.

Nimrod's case was one of a dozen heard in that December term. Kelly and Boise had to wait their turn to debate Nimrod's case.[1] It took awhile. In later years, speaking of long-winded frontier argument, Boise observed:

> When the speeches of the learned counsel had been concluded, being much longer than I had been used to hearing in the courts of Massachusetts, I became impressed with the fact that the arguments of lawyers lengthened as the distance from the seats of legal learning increased.

It made sense. As libraries and school training grew more distant, horse-sense oratory would tend to stray from what the law *is* and graze instead on what it *ought to be*.

When Kelly and Boise finished their court debate, they packed their papers into totes and lugged them down the street to where they would serve as lawmakers in the Oregon legislative assembly then in session. The judges, left alone to argue among themselves, would take considerable time on all twelve cases heard in that term. In his reminiscences, Chief Justice Williams spoke of such deliberations:

> I now recall one instance, when we sat down at a table in my residence at Salem to consider a case, and continued the discussion, with no little animation, until we adjourned for breakfast in the broad daylight of the next morning.

Indeed, under Williams' regime, even more wait than usual was necessary. As chief of the court, he put a new chore upon his brethren. Aside from a few cases that aroused public attention—where judges would sometimes write, and newspapers would occasionally publish those writings—territorial judges did not ordinarily put their reasons to readership. But Williams required that an essay detailing the reasons for the court's decision in each case would have to be written and published by the government. Henceforth, the formal reasonings would be as strong as the rulings they supported. These public essays were the beginning of Oregon's common law. The difference between common law and statutory law was the difference between law gleaned from reasoning and law imposed by decree.

The written opinions in those first twelve supreme court reviews began to trickle down from the court in late December 1853, and continued one by one through late January 1854. Chief Justice Williams wrote the opinions in seven of the twelve cases, Olney wrote four, and McFadden wrote one. Eight of the twelve appeals alleged error in rulings made by Judge Orville C. Pratt.[2]

In the ever-continuing game of musical chairs as to who would sit to decide Nimrod's fate, there was one final unseating. Associate Justice Olney decided to withdraw from the case. Olney's short and cryptic reason given for exiting was that he was "of counsel." In law jargon, this meant he had some prior involvement in the case. But nowhere in the record is there any mention of what that involvement was.[3]

The record does suggest, however, a reason for Olney's exit. McFadden's surprise replacement of Deady just six weeks before the supreme court was to convene had riled Olney's sense of fairness. Not only had his colleague Deady been done a grave wrong, McFadden compounded the wrong by not resigning once he discovered his appointment rested on a silly mistake over first names. Olney went so far as to question McFadden's "clearness of intellect," "legal knowledge," and "habits of studious application." Olney was upset and reacted with more than slurs. Not only did he feel that Deady would serve Oregon better than McFadden, he also felt that Deady would serve better than Olney himself. If McFadden did not have the decency to give up his chair to Deady, then he, Olney, would give up his own chair. Prior to the December term, Olney had tendered his resignation to delegate Joe Lane in Washington City on the condition that Deady would be appointed to fill his vacancy.

Chief Justice Williams agreed with Olney's self-effacement. In later years, Williams would write that Olney's "qualifications for a judge were not equal to those possessed by Judge Deady." Deady himself had a dim view of Olney's abilities and was "damned sorry that Boise does not occupy the place of Olney." Olney stayed on the bench until his resignation had enough time to be accepted back east. He heard cases in the December term, writing the opinion in four of them. On December 22, Lane relayed Olney's resignation to the U.S. Attorney General. With the new year, Olney may have concluded that his resignation had been acted on, and he no longer was an Oregon Supreme Court justice. Any vote rendered by him after his effective resignation would be annulled, thus jeopardizing the full court's decisions. Probably all three justices would have agreed that it would be better if Olney took no further part in deliberating cases after the new year—especially cases calling for the ultimate punishment.

On December 27, the *Statesman* reported no decision had yet been reached in *Territory of Oregon v. Nimrod O'Kelly*. At a time when ambition feasted upon spoils, Olney excused himself from the table. His was a modesty at which power and fame scoff, and for which history makes no reward.

As it turned out in the months ahead, President Pierce did not accept Olney's resignation. Instead, Pierce and Lane worked out a different solution. McFadden was reappointed to the supreme court of newly created Washington Territory, and Deady was reappointed to replace his replacement—McFadden—on the Oregon Supreme Court. Now Olney could remain on the Oregon court in good conscience. But word of that realignment did not reach Oregon until the spring of 1854, months after Nimrod's fate had been decided by a quorum of two, Williams and McFadden—two younger men imported from the east—one destined to be in permanent harness at Oregon's wagon, and the other hitched up for a short haul. Neither had pioneered. Neither had struggled to reach the frontier's edge. Neither had driven and defended corner stakes. At the dawn of their young careers, neither faced the dusk.

Chief Justice Williams wrote the opinion in Nimrod's case, and McFadden joined in it. The written decision was first published verbatim in Asahel Bush's *Salem Statesman* on January 10, 1854. Not much later, it was published in the back pages of the *1853–54 Council Journal of the Legislative Assembly*. Then, in 1880 it appeared in the first volume of the official *Oregon Reports* at pages 51 to 57 under the title *Territory of Oregon v. Nimrod O'Kelly*. For that reason, it has been called "Oregon's First Reported Murder Case."[4]

Defense lawyer Kelly had raised nine charges of error committed by Judge Pratt. Judge Williams' decision addressed them one by one. To begin, Kelly urged that the trial was a nullity because it was not held during a regular term of the district court. The regularly conducted Benton County court session had ended in early April 1852, almost three months prior to Nimrod's trial. Pratt took it upon himself to call a special, unscheduled term of court just to handle the Nimrod trial. Pratt had no power to do this, said Kelly. Yes he did, said Williams. Judges have the power to call themselves into session. The public benefits by saving money—money otherwise expended for prolonged and, perhaps, unnecessary imprisonment. Prisoners benefit by reducing "punishment without conviction." "Humanity and expediency harmonize" by allowing judges to call their courts into special terms.

Kelly's next assignment of error resorted to a minor technicality. He maintained that the indictment was defective because it did not describe the crime with the words "felonious killing." This, said Kelly, was the traditional way. Williams disposed of this quickly. It was no longer necessary under current statutes to label the crime charged with the word "felony."

Kelly was not done with the indictment. Even if it was properly worded, Kelly had argued, Judge Pratt's daily minutes, in violation of customary practice, "do not show that any indictment was found." The chief justice saw that as another technicality deserving short shrift. The presence of the indictment in the file was its own court record. No matter how traditional, it was unnecessary for Pratt to record in his journal that a certain record had been made when, indeed, it was plainly there in the record. Relevant to the last two denials of error, Williams wrote:

> Olden rules cease with the reasons on which they rested, and criminals cannot be allowed to take refuge from the judgments of our liberal laws in the cobwebs of an antiquated practice.

Kelly had then listed a more critical error: The county commissioners, not Sheriff Starr, should have picked the potential jury panel. The "Juries" chapter of the Hamilton Code unequivocally stated that the commissioners were to be the selectors. But Williams hastened to point out that Kelly's research had not gone deep enough. Tucked away in a different part of the code, in a chapter headed "District Judges," was an obscure enactment passed in 1851, "authorizing any of the district judges…to hold special terms." Section 2 of that act allowed the sheriff to summon jurors. It must have been an embarrassing moment for Kelly. As a recent compiler of all of Oregon's statutes, Kelly should have known better. Oregon's enactments at that time were, indeed, a mess. But mess is precisely what codifiers were supposed to straighten out and, certainly, not compound.

Kelly had posed five remaining assignments of error. In the opinion of the chief justice, all of them were without merit for the same basic reason—the record did not support the alleged facts. Kelly charged that Pratt did not give Nimrod the required ten days of notice in advance of the trial. Ah, but he did, said Williams. Pratt's daily journal recited that the trial commenced "after ten days' notice to Nimrod O'Kelly." Kelly alleged that the grand jurors had not been examined as to their qualifications to serve. Yes they were, said Williams. Pratt's daily journal stated that the grand jurors were "good and lawful men." This could only mean they must have been qualified; and to be qualified, they must have gone through a qualification procedure. Kelly made a similar charge regarding the petit jurors, saying they were "not regularly empanneled." Yes they were, said Williams. The daily journal recorded that they "came as a jury." If they *came as a jury*, it must be presumed that correct procedure was used in seating them as such. Kelly argued that Pratt allowed the verdict to be delivered without the jury being present in open court. No he did not, said Williams. The daily journal reported "the jury, after a short absence, returned into court the following verdict…" Finally, Kelly argued that Pratt allowed the verdict to be presented without the prisoner being present. Yes he was, said Williams. According to the daily journal, the prisoner was brought into court that day, and nowhere was it recorded that he was ever taken from the court or "remanded to jail" while the jury "took the case." Presumptively, "the prisoner having been brought into court, remained there until the verdict was delivered."

In all of these final five denials of error, the court's position stood squarely on an interpretation, not of what was done, but rather of what was "down"— written down. Judges Williams and McFadden, of course, were not at the trial. Indeed, they were not even in Oregon at the time. They had no idea of what transpired at the trial. They could not accept Kelly's account or Nimrod's word for what had happened. Nor were they going to call witnesses and take testimony as to what happened. Appellate courts did not conduct trials about other trials.

The only source for what occurred at the trial was the official written record—a daily journal of minutes prepared by the trial judge, the very person whose rulings were being brought under scrutiny on appeal. The lawyers in the case were free to record their versions of the happenings at trial in so-called "bills of exception," but these versions had to be prepared and officially entered in the record at the time of trial. Neither Boise nor Babb had apparently done this. How else then were the appellate judges to know what had occurred in Marysville eighteen months before? Williams had no other course but to resort to Pratt's own words and to the inferences taken from them. If Pratt was wrong in his recordings, objections should have been made and filed in the record as exceptions to the rulings of the court. None were. Williams laid out the procedure:

> Prisoners in our courts are provided with counsel…allowed to except to all the court says or does upon trial; and it is no hardship to say that, if they have any objections to the acts of the tribunal before which they are tried, they shall make these objections known to such tribunal, or forever after hold their peace.

Whatever may have been the reality, the facts upon which the territorial supreme court were compelled to operate were these—Nimrod had timely notice of trial; the grand jurors and petit jurors were qualified and duly selected; and the jury and Nimrod were present for the rendering of the verdict.

> We are called upon to presume error, simply because it is alleged…Wrongs are never presumed against private persons, much less should violations of law be presumed against a court.

The new chief justice was shoring up Oregon's substance with procedure. Gone were the days of informality. The frontier had to move toward a greater regard for formal record keeping. There must be principles, yes—but management as well. Once process was made due, then it had to be given teeth.

Not one word of Chief Justice Williams' written opinion mentioned the names Orville C. Pratt or Andrew Jackson Babb. Not one word spoke of overlapping land claims, land jumping, or land hoarding. Not one word mentioned the age of the prisoner. Nor was there any talk of families, nor of wives widowed or to be widowed. Nor of a corpse clutched over a gaping hole in its belly. Nor of blood soaked up by a dry slough bed. Humanity and substance were simply not the issue. Process and form were the issues. Like a smithy at his smoke and dousings, Chief Justice Williams put the red-hot iron of judgment to the cold hammer of order and icy anvil of law. *Law and order* was forged.

But in closing his written opinion, Williams did have this to say in a paragraph often quoted by future opinion writers:

> Criminal laws were made to prevent crime, and their firm enforcement by courts is a duty as plain as it is painful. Executive clemency may be interposed in one case and withheld in another, as a matter of discretion, but this decision must be followed hereafter; and if judicial compassion now bends the laws to suit a seemingly hard case, a door may be opened through which the midnight assassin and mercenary murderer may escape.

In this one passage, the heart of the man filters through the mind of the judge. Apparently, Williams had been made aware of pith and pity in Nimrod's case. The chief justice called his duty "painful." He mentioned "clemency" and "judicial compassion." He acknowledged that before him was "a seemingly hard case." But before him was not just Nimrod O'Kelly; before him were also the "midnight assassin and mercenary murderer." Those first pages of Oregon's common law had to set future standards. Specters of what might one day be were in control of what was to become of Oregon's first reported murderer.

The chief justice's final gavel came down in two words: "Judgment affirmed." McFadden agreed. With that, the judicial fate of seventy-three year old O'Kelly was sealed. Pratt had committed no errors of law. O'Kelly was legally convicted of murder in the first degree. The sentence should be carried out.

Notes

1. Reuben P. Boise appeared as counsel in three of the twelve cases. Alexander Campbell, Boise's assistant prosecutor at Nimrod's trial, appeared as counsel in five of them. Kelly argued in Nimrod's case and one other. Thirty-one lawyers were listed on the 1853–54 supreme court Attorney Roll; only they were allowed to argue before the bar of the Oregon Supreme Court.
2. The twelve written opinions were eventually placed in volume one of the official *Oregon Reports*. Those volumes, covering all decisions of Oregon's highest appellate court for over one and one-half centuries, now number about 340 volumes, containing well beyond 200,000 pages of case law. Anyone who defines the *common law* as "unwritten law" is at best naive and at worst a fool. Common law is the most written law.
3. If Matthew P. Deady, not Obediah B. McFadden, had been on the court, then Deady too might have excused himself, because Deady, like Cyrus Olney, had previous dealings in the matter. Deady had signed Nimrod's pardon petition to Governor Gaines. That would have left the chief justice alone to decide the case—an insufficient number to constitute a majority of the court. Nimrod's case would have been postponed once again until a new court was cast, and the next court change did not come along until 1857, over three years later.
4. There were prior murders and murder trials in Oregon that were not appealed, and, therefore, did not reach the status of common law precedent—e.g., the previously mentioned Whitman Massacre trial, the Adam Wimple trial, and the Enoch Smith trial. The first semblance of a murder trial on the Oregon frontier occurred in 1835 at Fort William on Sauvie Island, when Tom Hubbard killed Thornburgh; Hubbard was not convicted.

23

Putting the House in Order

Winter 1853–54

In Europe, the latest form of public transportation—a road of rails for wagons driven by steam—was being built through the Alps. In England, people were being protected from smallpox by inoculation with milder germs. In The Netherlands, baby Vincent was born to the Van Goghs. In Rome, Pope Pius IX decreed that Nimrod and Sally O'Kelly, John McLoughlin, Joseph Gervais, Archbishop François Norbert Blanchet, and all other Catholics must take it on faith that the virgin mother of Jesus was conceived without sin. In the United States, the Wells Fargo Company showed a profit in its first year of business. On the eastern seaboard, sparrows, imported from England to fight caterpillar infestation, were becoming an infestation of their own. In California, the largest tree in the world was discovered. In Missouri, widow Emerson sold several property items to her brother John Sanford of New York—the items were Dred Scott, his wife, and children.

Closer still on the Oregon frontier, a gold prospector discovered a wondrous lake at the top of the Cascade divide—it covered twenty-one square miles and lay inside a deep crater. On February 14, 1854, at Oregon City, Valentine Neal was lashed, shaven of all hair, then tarred because he was "skulking around" and making "incendiary threats." At Fort Vancouver, Washington Territory, Captain Ulysses S. Grant was reassigned to California where he later resigned from the military—Secretary of War Jefferson Davis approved his resignation.

While the world so turned, the news of the Oregon supreme court's affirmation of Nimrod's conviction also came around. How and when Nimrod was informed of the decision is unknown. Perhaps, lawyer Kelly took a steamboat up river to Corvallis, and then a horse to the Long Tom and Jennyopolis countryside. Perhaps, Nimrod read the January 10, 1854, *Statesman*, where the opinion was quoted in full. However it came, the news had to be devastating. Having been given free rein for over a year, Nimrod had grown accustomed to a sentence that had withered and a vengeance that had cooled. Life around the world and on the frontier had seemingly ignored his small corner.

The Valley Indians were faring no better than Nimrod—both faced extinction. Like Nimrod, their lives and their lands were slowly being eroded. Like Nimrod, they and their growing body of new neighbors did not mix. Neither recognized the other as civilized. The whites saw the nakedness and called them "savages." The Indians saw the furry bodies and faces and called them "animals." Sharing the Valley drove them apart. Yoked, they did not shoulder together.

The McHargue and Kirk families lived just across the Willamette River from Nimrod. Valley Indians sometimes came to their cabin doors for food. To allay the pesters, Missus McHargue laced food with pepper sauce. Missus Kirk's response, on the other hand, was to lock the door and hide under a bed until they went away. The McHargue-Kirk lessons were mirrored by the white government. Sometimes the government gave false promise; other times, it ignored its own laws—in short, it either gave pepper sauce or hid. The 1851 unratified treaty attempts had left a bitter taste,[1] and for the last three years, government had stayed under the bed.

Indian Superintendent Joel Palmer, sensing the growth of a more violent public attitude, took it upon himself to renew efforts at treaty making. But the Tualatin Bands of the Calapooyas were reluctant to make senseless agreement. Why try again what had been rejected in 1851? Why give what was already seized? Just as surely as one cannot push on a rope, invasion could not be shoved backward. Nevertheless, the Tualatin headmen were persuaded by Palmer's good heart and counsel.

On March 25, 1854, they signed a second treaty. Once again, they agreed to take domestic animals, tools, clothes, food, pots, weaponry, flags, blankets, and a reservation yet to be designated. Once again, they ceded almost 1,500 square miles in the Yamhill and Washington county areas. And, once again, back in Washington City, the Senate did not ratify. Nimrod would have understood the disappointment—he too was left empty handed at the cabin door after the bitter carrot of hope had been dangled before him.

The population of Marysville increased with each migration. The wave in 1853 brought 6,500 new Oregonians—most of whom settled in the central Willamette Valley. Marysville was now the head of navigation up the Willamette River. Unclaimed land in southern Benton County was almost impossible to find. Nimrod and Sally were surrounded—together with the intruding claims of Criss, Stark, Thomas, and Grimsley, the circle was completed by new claimants George Shultz, John Rickard, Caspar Rickard, L.B. Perkins, and James W. Compton.[2]

Burgeoning settlement and commerce gave the Marysville postal system a headache. Mail meant for Marysville, Oregon Territory, was too often sent to Marysville, California, in the Sierra gold country, and vice-versa. One of the town names had to yield. J.C. Avery obliged. He renamed his city after a phrase that the French-Canadians had given the locality long before Avery and Dixon set up camp there—the *coeur d'vallee*, heart of the valley, is what the engagés had called it. On December 20, 1853, while the supreme court still had Nimrod's case under advisement, Marysville became the *coeur d'vallee*—Corvallis. One of the first jobs for officials in new Corvallis would be to awaken the timbers of Marysville's sleeping gallows.

The hitch between Benton County and the O'Kelly clan was gradually coming undone. Sometime in early 1854, son Benjamin moved permanently to his own claim in Lane County next to brother Joseph and his wife, Matilda, now pregnant with her third child. Daughter Sarah had also moved to stay with her brothers. And now, with Nimrod's fate apparently sealed by the supreme court decision, Mother Sally—as a prospective widow—might soon be joining them.

Nimrod the son had surfaced in Benton County for a short time in March 1854, when he was accused of stealing or running off James Woody's horses and Noah Reeves' cow. But it was all blame born of running around halfcocked. The false accuser was Noah Reeves—kin to Tom Reeves, one of Nimrod the father's more hostile neighbors. The feud, it would seem, had seeped into the families. Although an apology for the mistake was printed, it was not the Reeves clan who stooped to make it. Son Nimrod did not stay in Benton County much longer—according to the 1854 Jackson County Census Roll,[3] he went off into the Oregon gold country.[4]

About five weeks after the *Statesman* reported the supreme court's approval of the homicide conviction, Nimrod reacted by publishing an "advertisement." He had approached the governor, legislators, and judges—all to no avail. Now he sought the public's support. In the February 18, 1854, Oregon City *Spectator*—under the headline "Gross Prosecution" and dated "Benton County, Oregon Territory, February 11, 1854"—the following appeared:

> I have been beset by the bitterest of enemies. I became an early settler in the Willamette Valley—the first in my neighborhood. My nearest neighbor, 12 miles distant, was J.C. Avery. When and where I settled, and still live there was none to dispute my choice of location. At present, there are no less than *four* jumpers upon my claim, and one of them within a stone's throw of my house. They have tried to drive me off my claim, to persuade me off, buy me off and lie me off and scare me off. I have withstood all manner of insults and slanders.

The rest of Nimrod's "advertisement" addressed his trial. Tellingly, he had begun his statement with the troubles that beset his land, rather than the troubles besetting his life.

When Mary Jane (Mahoney) Thomas, now living in Corvallis, heard that Nimrod's appeal had failed and he would finally hang, she figured her claim at Jennyopolis was given new life. After all, it was only fitting—Nimrod killed her husband and that ended the Mahoney claim; so, the killing of Nimrod for killing Mahoney ought to end the O'Kelly claim. As so often with poetic justice, it had the ring of truth without a core. Nevertheless, she tried for a second time to lay claim to the same parcel of land on which she had been rejected in the previous year.

The former claim had been filed in the name of her first husband, Jeremiah Mahoney. This time her second husband, John Thomas, filed the notification papers. His February 20, 1854, application stated he was born in England thirty-seven years before, that he was now an American citizen, and that he married Mary Jane Mahoney on September 10, 1852. Robert Grimsley and Asa Stark, two of the other alleged intruders, both swore affidavits

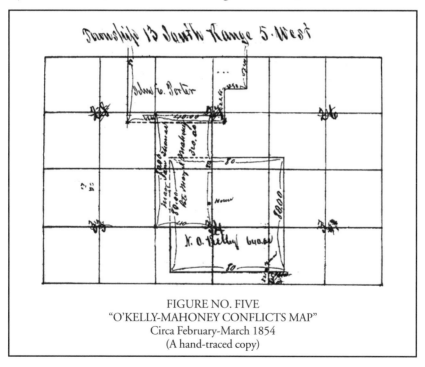

FIGURE NO. FIVE
"O'KELLY-MAHONEY CONFLICTS MAP"
Circa February-March 1854
(A hand-traced copy)

Figure No. Five. Special claims map in the John Thomas Notification File No. 3835 (rejected). This survey of portions of sections 26–28 and 33–35 of the Jennyopolis Township shows the overlap of the claims of "N.O. Kelley" and "Mary Jane Thomas—late Mary J. Mahoney." Also shown are the "houses"—Nimrod's (lower right corner of his claim) and Mary Jane's (near center of Nimrod's claim).

that Thomas had resided on the claim since at least November 20, 1853. The surveyor general next completed a special survey of the Nimrod and Thomas-Mahoney claims. The official survey map showed unequivocally that the 320 acre claim of "Mary Jane Thomas—late Mary Jane Mahoney" took up a vast segment of the northwest quadrant of the 640 acre claim of "N. O. Kelley," and, for that matter, a piece of the claim of "John E. Porter." On March 8, 1854, a letter from the surveyor general was sent to Thomas:

> Sir: Nimrod O'Kelly's Notification with proof of his "resid. & cult." from Feb. 1850 cover a quarter section of the south part of your claim: and as he was the prior settler, will of course supersede yours unless you show cause to the contrary.

That was the end of the matter; the record does not show that Thomas took any further action or bothered the O'Kellys again.[5]

Nimrod now wrote, "I have now proved up my land claim complete." But that was a *far holler* from the truth. There were still other conflicting claims. On the same day that Thomas was notified of his claim rejection, Berryman Jennings, the land registrar, penned a note in Nimrod's file—the claims of R.D. Grimsley, Asa Stark, and Jeremiah Criss were also in conflict with Nimrod's claim, and the "Surveyor General will survey the above claims." Although Nimrod did not seem to realize it, his house was still not in order, and there was little time to get it there. The hangman on the horizon was approaching with cart and coffin.

Notes

1. See the discussion in the early part of Chapter 11, plus note 4.
2. See Figure No. Seven in Chapter 29.
3. Each year, Jackson County, as well as other counties, took inventory of their citizens' property for taxation purposes. The taxing of both real and personal assets was a main source of government income. Not until 1913 did the Sixteenth Amendment to the U.S. Constitution permit the taxing of annual income.
4. Benton County's September 1854 census, in fact, would show a desolate O'Kelly claim in late 1854—no one living there—a dire omen!
5. Shortly after the second rejection of the Thomas-Mahoney claim, some of the main characters in the Nimrod saga were put together in strange company. This involved another complicated court dispute over a different piece of land in Benton County. In the civil lawsuit, Chief Justice Williams held in favor of defendant J.C. Avery and defendant Mary Jane (Mahoney) Thomas, but against defendant John Thomas. The lawyer defending was Orville C. Pratt.

24

The Last Efforts

Spring 1854

In 1854, at age twenty-seven, Joseph Gardner Wilson was about to become a married man, which may explain why he was behind in his work as clerk for the Oregon Supreme Court. Not until February 9, 1854, did he get around to the O'Kelly murder case and the issuing of the official court *procedendo*—a mandate to the lower court in Benton County "to repass sentence in the premises and proceed to final execution." Thirty days ago, the judges had rendered a decision; now it was capped by their official decree.

When the new Benton County clerk, James H. Slater, received the order, he further delayed, but finally entered it in the Benton County District Court records on March 6, another thirty days later. Nimrod's destiny at this stage was in the hands of clerks, their paperwork, and curious foot-dragging.

The *procedendo* order in Nimrod's case was an odd formality. Chief Justice George Williams wore two robes—as chief justice of the supreme court he was ruling that in his other role, as trial judge Williams of the district court in Benton County, he should proceed with the hanging. Yearling clerks may have seen no need to hurry in relaying a message that was talking to itself.[1] Whatever the reasons, no one seemed anxious to get on with the re-sentencing, even though the punishment for first degree murder—the most horrendous of all crimes—ought to have been a top priority.

Long before the paperwork was done, however, folks were aware of the supreme court decision. Word traveled fast in saddlebags, on the stoop, and over the fence. The *Statesman* had published the news forthwith. But, two months after everyone knew he was to be hanged, Nimrod was still free.

John W. Davis came to Oregon in December 1853, but was not sworn in as governor until April 1854.[2] He had never been in Oregon until President Pierce sent him there. He came by sea, not by trail, and he came to govern, not to settle. Like his predecessor, John P. Gaines, Davis began his duties among frontier folk who wished him failure. It made no difference that he was a graduate of a medical school. It made no difference that he had been the Speaker of the House of Representatives. It made no difference that, unlike Gaines, Davis was a devout Democrat. It made no difference that he had brought with him $40,000 of congressional money to relieve the Oregon budget. The Whigs resented him because he was a Democrat. The Democrats resented him because he was an imported leader. He would last in Oregon for just eight months.

But before he retreated to his native Indiana, Davis was entreated by Nimrod's supporters. Those who had not fallen to despair saw one last chance for Nimrod. A governor's clemency had been requested before without success, but this was a new governor, who may not have had popularity, but who, nonetheless, had power. The first to load and fire in Nimrod's behalf was Amory Holbrook. On January 24, 1854, Holbrook in Oregon City wrote to Davis in Salem, sending to him some of the 1852 petitions that were circulated in Nimrod's behalf. Holbrook called special attention to Petition "A"—signed by prominent officials, successful businessmen, and other Oregon leaders, including Matthew Deady, who was shortly to be reinstated to his seat on the very court that had mandated Nimrod's execution at the rope. Petition "A" was, however, eighteen months old and some of those leaders had gone to pasture—men like Holbrook himself, previously the U.S. Attorney and now a private citizen and practicing lawyer; John B. Preston, the former surveyor general and now in private survey practice in Oregon City; and John McLoughlin, now ailing in his final years. Any respect given them would have to come from honor, not clout.

Holbrook's letter concluded with a remark, partly obscured by faulty penmanship:

> Personally I have no interest in the matter, except that the sympathies of common humanity prompt us all to stay the [Sword?] of [vengeance?].

Tactically, it never hurt to seek the high ground of indifference from which to rain down a call for favor.

On February 11, Nimrod's lawyer, James K. Kelly, also wrote to Governor Davis and forwarded certain papers. He advised Davis that ex-Governor Gaines, still living in Oregon, had "additional petitions and also a brief abstract of the testimony as taken by one of the jurors." Kelly was undoubtedly referring to the affidavit of juror Miletus W. Ellis. Kelly went on to report:

> I have directed the son of Nimrod O'Kelly to call upon Mrs. Gaines & if possible procure them and lay them before you together with such others as he may be able to obtain. I feel anxious that the testimony should be placed before you, as I think you will be convinced upon an examination of it, that it was insufficient to warrant a conviction.

Whichever son it was, he was apparently successful in rounding up the Gaines' papers and joining them with the other documents now in Davis's growing file, marked "Pardon Papers of Nimrod O'Kelly."[3]

Early in February 1854, at least four new petitions were circulated, probably composed by lawyer Kelly or, perhaps, J.C. Avery. All were directed to "his Excellency the Governor of Oregon." All invoked "humanity and kindness as well as principles of Justice." All urged that Nimrod's situation was "one of those cases the law making power had in view when it placed the pardoning power in the hands of the Executive." All prayed for a full pardon and no compromising imprisonment. None mentioned the fact that Nimrod had been entrusted to his own care for over a year, that his family had now joined him, that his victim's intrusion upon his land had been verified by the surveyor general, or that he was now seventy-four years old.

The record does not show that any petitions circulated in Polk County or on French Prairie in Marion County. In Lane County, 122 signed, and in Benton County, 72 signed—almost 200 petitioners in Nimrod's behalf. Many of them were repeaters—those who had signed the 1852 petitions. The Benton County petitioners, for the most part, resided in the north and central portions of the county. Only two signers can be detected as residents in the south Benton County area of Jennyopolis, Long Tom, Starrs Point, and Bellfountain—they were Sally and Sarah O'Kelly!

Nimrod's sons, Benjamin and Joseph, circulated the two Lane County petitions. Nine of the 51 signers on Joseph's petition were women. Once again, there were those who protested that women's signatures had no business on a petition because they were not voters and because they were tag-alongs, simply doubling their man's *druthers*. The presumption that a wife would dutifully follow her husband's lead was a notion about which, just fifteen years before, Charles Dickens had written: "If the law presumes that, the law is a ass."

The grounds for executive clemency were broader than those allowed for judicial appeal. Mercy sees all; justice is blind. Judges bar public opinion; governors thrive on it. The trouble with the popular word in Nimrod's case was that it was carried not just by petition, but also by rumor. In his plea for amnesty, Nimrod had to counter the whispers that he had killed other men besides Mahoney. The *Statesman* in 1852 reported he "killed a man in Missouri and left there to escape the penalty." That story and its bloom took wings on the winds of talk.

Still at liberty, Nimrod traveled far north to Hillsborough on the Tualatin Plains in Washington County.[4] There he found two old acquaintances,

Benjamin Cornelius Sr. and Peyton Wilkes. Like Nimrod, they had come to Oregon in the 1845 migration. Hillsborough was a four-day walk-and-ride from the Long Tom and a hard journey in the dead of winter with the rivers swollen.

Wilkes and Cornelius both attested that they had known Nimrod in Missouri. Both signed their affidavits with "X" marks. The scribe for both affidavits was Nimrod. There is no mistaking Nimrod's clear penmanship, style, and grammar. On February 25, 1854, Justice of the Peace Thomas N. Latrin of Hillsborough took their oaths and subscriptions. Presumably, he read aloud to them what Nimrod had written. Cornelius swore in part:

> I had a lage and extensive acquaintance in missouri and I never heard of nimrod o kelly sen killing of a man in missouri neither did I ever hear a hint or suspected report…until I heard it in oregon and I am constrained to believe that it has been gotup and published by evil and malicious and designing men.

Wilkes swore in part:

> I lived in the same county in missouri [with Nimrod]…him and me both crossed the plains the same time and often times we ware both in the same company and I never heard it said or hinted or suspected that nimrod o kelly sen killed a man in missouri until I came to oregon and I am forced to believe it has been forged and published by evil and melicous men…it has also been reported that he killed a man on the plains but I was present at the time and I saw the begining and ending of the hole scrape it was nothing but a stratagem used by som designing men with an intent to take the old man o kellys horse from him to drive their cattle it is and will be a disgreace to them…I could mention their names if silence was not prudance.[5]

There was another witness who knew Nimrod in his past life. In the 1852 pardon papers to then Governor Gaines, L.G. Hoge had signed "A True Statement" dated August 16, 1852, at Marysville.

> I was aquainted the said okelly from the year 1825 to 1830 in the state of tenesee Mackmin Co. Knowed him to be an honest peaceable sitizen…I also believe if the said okelly had other council the jury would not have brought in a verdict of murder in the first degree.

Hoge was one of the few to openly blame Nimrod's trial lawyer, Andrew Jackson Babb.

Not all came to plead for Nimrod's release—on the contrary, Nimrod's foes wanted him dead. On March 15, 1854, a meeting of citizens of Benton and Lane counties took place at "Long Tom." Likely, they met at the home of Aaron "Doc" Richardson, just two miles south of Nimrod and Sally's cabin. The group elected officers and kept minutes. F.B. Ferguson was made chairman, and C.B. Brooks, secretary. Brooks's minutes did not reveal who or how many were present. Doc Richardson "arose and stated the object of the meeting"—to oppose the reprieve of Nimrod O'Kelly. Richardson's motion to circulate a remonstrance was carried. Richardson and Brooks then were appointed to a committee to draft the remonstrance, circulate it, and get it to the governor before pity prevailed. Three others also were appointed to the committee: C.B. Hinton, Joseph White, and R.B. Hinton. Though five men were assigned the work, no remonstrance was completed or entered in the governor's file.

While failing at their own effort, the group flayed the progress of their enemy. In accord with a motion passed at the meeting, the committee of five wrote Davis on March 15, 1854, asking the governor to send them a list of O'Kelly's petition signers, because:

> we believe their has been many persons names used on that petition without the consent or knowledge of them. Also that many who actually signed it were merely transient persons traveling to and from the mines—who knew nothing of the circumstances of the case, only as represented by interested individuals.

Beneath the reasons expressed was an attitude inferred—those who had to live with a problem should have the greater right in solving it. Outsiders were busy-bodies. Detached reflection was not as deserved as staked attachment. It was a rankle and a gnaw as old as society itself. Where were the borders of fair province? How narrow should be private matters? How wide should be the public interest? Territory or county? The Valley or The Long Tom? When should *big* stampede *little*? When should *little* shepherd *big*? The same fester was infecting the nation back east—the Union at cross with the States.

The Long Tom meeting had one final item on its agenda. It was moved and passed that the minutes of the meeting "be sent to the 'Oregonian,' 'Statesman' and 'Weekly Times' for publication." But the minutes were never published. Perhaps, Secretary Brooks never mailed the minutes; or, perhaps, editors reached independent decisions that the meeting was not worth the ink.

Among all of the voices raised for and against Nimrod, one stood out—a voice to be reckoned with—the voice of the judge who had taken the jury's verdict, passed judgment, and condemned Nimrod to die. Orville C. Pratt wrote Governor Davis on the matter of Nimrod's pardon probably as a response to the final back-breaking straw of a very humiliating year. In the spring of 1853, Pratt had received word that his reappointment as an Oregon judge had been withdrawn and he had been passed over. A year later, while licking his wounds and reading a newspaper, he perchance came upon Nimrod's "advertisement"—a public attack upon him, by a murderer no less.

Nimrod's advertisement appeared in the *Spectator* on February 18 and Pratt wrote Governor Davis four days later.

Pratt's public career had been ended by the powerful, but now a nobody was publicly criticizing him. The O'Kelly trial had been Pratt's last major trial as a presiding judge. He would have taken solace from the affirmation of that trial by the new appellate judges. He could not allow that swan song to be muffled by forgiveness of a begging convict. It was highly unusual for a judge to speak out against mercy, but silence was more than dignity could bear. Suddenly, he had much to say, and it would weigh heavily in the pardoning process.

> It is understood that an application has been, or is about to be made to you as Governor to pardon Nimrod O'Kelly who was convicted in 1852 in Benton Co. for the murder of Mahoney. I would prefer to be silent, but it is forbidden to me and I must speak to you earnestly and firmly in the premises, however unavailing it may prove. What I feel obliged to say, (& it is to you for the first time that I express it) is simply, that in my opinion the Executive clemency invoked on his behalf *is utterly unmerited, and if extended to him would do a positive injury not only to the dead Mahoney & his living murderer, but to the sacred cause of public justice.*

Pratt's emphasis expressed the absurdity that "clemency invoked" would do "injury" to the "living murderer." Did Pratt mean Mahoney's living *memory*? Or did Pratt carry the odd notion that his sentence of death was in Nimrod's best interest? Pratt's letter continued:

> I heard the testimony as it came from the lips of the witnesses, within a few weeks after the killing; and while my mind struggled with the sympathies excited by the old man's age, I was compelled to yield to the conviction that he was but *too guilty*; and, I assure you that I then thought, and now do as fully as then, that the verdict of the jury was *fully sustained by the evidence* and was only a just retribution for the commission of an awful crime. I am not insensible that many and good men are impressed with a sense of sympathy that may impel them to ask for Executive interference with the due course of the law…They must do as they please, and I will do what I am forced to *by a view of duty that I cannot forego if I would.* In a word then, had I the power to pardon him I could not with the knowledge I have, yield such a favor without feeling oppressed with the belief that public justice had been deprived of a rightful sacrifice through the more pressing importunity of mistaken friends. It is hard to say thus much, for reasons that cannot fail to be obvious to you, or any other correct thinking man; but, *I have been unable to do less.* I am dear Sir, Yours very truly, O.C. Pratt.

The letter rings throughout with the call to duty—"it is forbidden to me [to be silent]"; "I must speak"; "I feel obliged to say"; "I was compelled to yield to the conviction that"; "I will do what I am forced to by a view of duty that I cannot forego"; and "I have been unable to do less." It was as though he was driven by a force stronger than his own desire. At times, he seemed on the verge of compassion—"my mind struggled with the sympathies"; "I am not insensible"; and "it is hard to say thus much." In spite of such inner difficulty, he always returned to outer duty. Indeed, it was his official duty to enter judgment and render a death sentence based upon the law's mandate and the jury's verdict.

But it was not his duty to champion compliance with his orders. His trial duties had ended; he had ceased to be a judge. Something hidden beneath duty goaded his pursuit. He and Nimrod had been at odds from the moment of their first encounter at the trial.

In the months ahead, Nimrod wrote that others told him:

> If you had not exposed judg pratt openly it would be much better for you. Judg pratt is a strong man he can influence the people of every county against you,

Nevertheless, Nimrod openly belittled Pratt by contrasting their military service to country:

> Did judg pratt ever offer his blood upon the altar of liberty? Did judg pratt ever bare his bosom to danger? Did he ever rush at the mouth of cannons? Did he ever stand the iron hail to defend and protect the same laws that he wrested to take life and property from me to Gratify my enemis by which he thought to make himself everlasting popular and renouned for destroying one old Catholic?

Nimrod's invective was not finely dressed. He laid bare his heart. Pratt's heart, on the other hand, was decked in the finery of duty and cloaked in humility. Where righteousness openly parades, vindictiveness watches from shadows. But near the close of his letter to the governor, Pratt's nature is briefly exposed—"Public justice" should not be "deprived of rightful sacrifice."

Finery and front, whether in words or clothes, were important to Pratt. He was given to fashion. One autumn when riding the circuit, he had sought lodging at the home of Robert Kinney. Story has it that he was dressed in Spanish garb, the latest bib and tucker from California. His buckskin pantaloons with fancy fringe got soaked by rain and shrunk. They were no longer wearable. So, Missus Kinney quickly made the judge some trousers out of a bed tick. The judge cut a peculiar figure on the frontier in his sombrero, red waist scarf, and bedding trousers.

After being deprived of his judicial robes, Pratt re-entered partisan politics by seeking to unseat Joe Lane as Oregon's territorial delegate to Congress. It was as foolish a move as wearing a bed tick. Lane was much too popular among frontier Democrats. An incident in southern Oregon should have warned Pratt of what he was up against. He was holding forth and seeking votes at a saloon in a mining town. He wore a stovepipe, silk hat, and a "biled shirt with a stake- and-rider collar." The miners surrounding him at the bar were in their work clothes, having no trouble taking in his words as long as he furnished the rounds. George E. Cole, who saw the incident, described what happened next.

> One tall miner…drew out a long knife and took the silk hat off the judge's head, saying, "This stove-pipe is too high by a j'int." Suiting the action to the word he slashed it into two parts, and slapping the parts together, put it back on the judge's head. Pratt took this all in good part, and set up the drinks…Pratt had long, curly hair, black and glossy. The miner's next performance was to cut off a lock, saying as he did so that it was the "puttiest ha'r he ever seed," that he must have one lock for a keepsake, and that he hoped no offense to him, as he loved him. With that he threw his arms around the judge and gave him a good hug…Pratt took it all pleasantly. This somewhat nonplused the miner…as he remarked…that he would not take off the top rail of his "stake-and-ridered" collar…They parted…apparently the best of friends.

George Gibbs, surveyor and customs collector, had a dim view of Pratt, calling him "a swindler" and accusing him of having been "whipped publicly in San Francisco by Dr. [E.H.?] Griffin & only escaped it here by abject cowardice." But, no matter what may be said of Pratt's finery or faint heart, his advice would carry great weight in the mind of Governor Davis. Just like Pratt, Davis too had lost favor with the pioneers and felt the barbs of his political fellows. The Oregon bench may have been freed from Pratt's hold, but Nimrod was far from such riddance.

On April 16, 1854, Nimrod wrote directly to Governor Davis. It might have been called the letter of a crotchety old man were it not excused by the gravity of what awaited him. But Nimrod did not mention his fate, nor seek pity for it. He did not stoop or scrape. Rather he penned in relentless strokes, neither seeking forgiveness nor giving it. He wrote of "clandestine schemes," "deep rooted conspiracy," "unfair and inhuman trial," "cruel justice," and "unfeeling and invincible animosity." He had a lot to say about the religious prejudices that surrounded his claim and seeped into his trial:

> There has been five or six protestant preachers now for the last four years exciting and fomenting the people against me…The sheriff and his deputy both methodist preachers and had been exciting the people against me for two years saying all catholics was enemis to the government…that they worshiped imiges and that a catholic preast would pray a man out of hell for five dollars and that the chief employment of a catholic preast is to watch the people to keep them from reading the bible and to burne all the bibles that he can find to keep the people in ignorance and…makeing remarks what an impudent old catholic okelly is… What is it but prejudice that makes men envy each other for their politics and

their religion…? Yet all will boast of the…great freedom we enjoy…They say the catholic religion is hellish and damable but I do pity them.

He then went on to paint some rather fiery images of his enemies:

> Forked tung serpents is licking out their forked tungs at me from every part of the country.

> Awful darkness…envelopes the hearts of men and keepes them bound slaves to satan and filling up their wrath against the day of wrath.

> What is more darkening than prejudice is the smoke of the bottomless pit.

> With the tooth of the serpent and with the fang of the lion prejudice is the fruit of pride.

The wait and weight of two years hanging on the edge of an abysmal fate was taking its toll. The Clark-Odeneal account emphasized Nimrod's excessive devotion to religion, characterizing him as "infatuated," "zealous," and "bigoted," so much so "as to be almost a lunatic." He had been raised a Protestant—his grandfather, an Irish immigrant, was reportedly a minister in the Methodist Episcopal Church. In his current despair, Nimrod's new found worship and his older religious upbringing joined in his vented tirade.

In writing about his victim, Nimrod expressed no sorrow or apology:

> If they could have got mahoney to run me off of my claim of land before my time of continual residence was complete I would have forfeited all right to my claim of land and this is what they got mahoney there for. This formidable party that was conspired against me went and got mahoney and furnished him with provisions and cows to milk and team to work and bottle of brandy when he wished it. They built him a house near the middle of my land and promised to protect and support and justify him in all that he could or would do to harass and annoy me to run me off my claim.

The letter did not attack Judge Pratt by name, but it did cast a few stones at court allowances:

> These same men forged all the evidence that was against me. The court let them all stand together in the court. One would hear what the other swor and then go up and swear as near the same as he could…I was debared from all possible chance of geting counsel that I could place confidence in…I was loaded down with irons to the floor to keep me from writing.

Nimrod gave but fleeting credit to his public supporters:

> I had not the first man to speak a word for me. It was unpopular to speak truth in my favor. But when they saw the cruel injustice…it harrowed up some remorse in a few…men and women and they gradually increased by which means I still breathe and have been permitted to see my family.

He also noted the government's money problems that undermined his attempts at innocence and freedom:

> They say if that vile old catholic had have got an new trial he would have come clear without doubt and the hole expense would be on the county...Their is many men that would be in favor of me geting a new trial if they were not afraid the cost would involve the county.

Nimrod had things to say about the feud between himself and his neighbors. Each side of a feud burns with two inner fires—hate and fear. As for their hatred, Nimrod wrote:

> They say it is not sufferable to let an old superstitious catholic remaine in the neighbourhood without opposition.

As for his fear of their hatred, he said:

> I dare not to leave home only of a night when no one did know it. I knew they would burn my house down and swear that I had no residence.

As for their fear of his hatred, he believed:

> Okelly would have all the protestants all burned up a live if he could...They try to make people believe they are afraid of okelly taking their lives if he comes clear...Is it reasonable for men to fear vengeance when no vengeance is due to them?...If they ware not guilty they would have nothing to fear. Their fear rises from their own guilt.

As for his own hate, he wrote:

> Sir their is no mortal man that can stand before his God and say that I ever did take vengeance in my own handes. From my youth to this day I leave vengeance to God who will give every man his due.

For whatever it was worth, Nimrod also saw fit to state that his claim had finally been cleared.

> Now I have proved up my land claim complete and this same party that forged evidence to take my life also forged evidence to take my land but had a judg to deal with that had honor. He could not be suborned to their wishes.[6]

Undoubtedly the letter was not written under the nod of lawyer Kelly, because it lacked informed guidance. For one, its grouch and scold were not good tact for seeking favor. For another, it had no focus. The only hint of a request for executive action was tucked away and lost in the middle of his four page, one paragraph tirade:

> Sir if your excellency and his honor Judg Williams will order my case before the legislator the next session and put it in my power to force men to swear it will confere a favor on me and my family. Then I will be able to wipe this infamy that they so unrelentingly pore upon my head.

Lawyer Kelly would have known that Nimrod's fate was now entirely in the hands of the governor—the legislature was powerless. Nimrod was still a free man and seemed to be oblivious of the doom overtaking him.

Nimrod's letter was written on a Sunday from "Marren [Marion] County," where he was probably visiting on French Prairie. Perhaps he had gone to St. Paul, the closest place for a Sunday mass. Nimrod could have written the letter in nearby Salem, too, upon being denied personal audience with the governor.

Soon after writing the letter, Nimrod reportedly journeyed north to Milwaukie in Clackamas County—in this locality, his freedom would soon, and abruptly, end. His contact with the governor's office may have been the impetus, because Davis might have been astonished to learn that a convicted first degree murderer was still roaming the countryside. Order and good sense dictated that the doomed ought to be in the keep of the society that damned him. Perhaps then, the governor ordered the Benton County authorities to control their convict.

Whatever the cause, within the week following Nimrod's April 16 letter to the governor, Benton County's newest sheriff, Doctor T.J. Right,[7] went one hundred miles down river to Milwaukie, found Nimrod, took him into custody on April 22, and brought him back to Corvallis. The record does not show why Nimrod was in Milwaukie—a Willamette River town between Portland and Oregon City. There were no friends there, no religion, no land office. It could have been simply more of his wanderlust. On the other hand, perhaps he was not there at all. Sheriff Right was the one who reported finding Nimrod in Milwaukie, and the sheriff, it seems, had enough mischief in him to slightly enlarge upon the truth. This was the doctor who claimed he could cure insanity. As sheriff, some of his billings for expenses to the county were dubious and, thus, rejected. And so, with Nimrod on French Prairie just a few days prior, Right's search farther north into Milwaukie might have been a calculated extension. Right was paid by the day for such hunts.

His "bill for going to Milwaukie and bringing O'Kelly to Corvallis" appeared in the Benton County Commissioners' Journal as a seven day, round trip, at five dollars pay per day plus "$42 for Board and fare"—the "fare" including ferry crossings.[8] If Nimrod had been found on French Prairie, the trip would have been three days shorter, with fewer river crossings, and, of course, less pay.

Another bill from Sheriff Right to the county commissioners claimed $75, for "guarding and boarding Nimrod O'Kelly from April 22d to May 18th, 25 days at $3.00 per day." Nimrod had been without chains, jail, or guard for almost sixteen months. Now he and his keeper were a county expense again.

Two weeks after Sheriff Right took Nimrod back into custody, four young men rode into Corvallis. U.S. Attorney Benjamin F. Harding, District Attorney Reuben P. Boise, Deputy U.S. Marshal Joseph G. Wilson, and District Judge George H. Williams were on circuit and were greeted by Benton County Clerk James H. Slater and Benton County Sheriff T.J. Right. When these six men sat down to business, they convened the regular term of the Benton County District Court.[9] The docket was full. It had been accumulating since the last term, six months before, at what was then Marysville.

On the third day of court business, Wednesday, May 10, 1854, the case of *Territory of Oregon v. Nimrod O'Kelly* was called, and Nimrod was led into court. Perhaps he was back in shackles; the record does not say. Perhaps his family was present; the record does not say. Perhaps lawyer Kelly was at his side; the record does not say. Perhaps Avery, Dixon, Alexander, Stewart, or other friends were there; the record does not say. Perhaps Richardson, Winkle, Hinton, Stark, Criss, Grimsley, Irwin, and other foes were there; the record does not say.

There would be no arguments, no testimony, no deliberations, no final pleas—nothing to decide. Neither reason nor passion of the court was involved. Mechanism, not mercy, drove doggedly toward what had to be. No matter how ominous, it was all just formality. Supreme Court Justice Williams had already spoken. District Court Judge Williams had merely to listen and obey. There was no stopping an arrow in flight.

Prosecutor Boise rose and moved the court to impose sentence, just as he had so moved two years before. After two years of judicial handling, the judges were finally to be done with Nimrod O'Kelly. It was the last time that he would ever be in court. It was the third time he rose to hear the reckoning.

On the ninth day of June next, thirty days hence, at Corvallis, between the hours of eleven in the forenoon and three in the afternoon, prisoner O'Kelly was to be hanged by the neck until he was dead.

Notes

1. The contact between Clerk Wilson and Clerk Slater on Nimrod's case was the first of a many more links between these two men. Although from different political parties, their careers were destined to parallel one another, until one day in 1873, when they come together as Oregon's two U.S. Congressmen in Washington, D.C.
2. When John W. Davis arrived in Salem on December 2, 1853, he introduced himself by

presentation of his official oath of office, which had been taken back east. Davis then and there took the reins of governorship from acting governor George Law Curry, the territorial secretary. But not until April 1, 1854, did the territory received word that the Senate had confirmed Davis's appointment as governor. Thus, on that date, to make matters official, Chief Justice Williams again administered Davis's oath of office. So, who was Oregon's governor in December, January, February, and March? Formality and reality give different answers.

3. The need to amass the Nimrod papers into one file revealed the sorry state of record keeping in those times. Government officials clung to government records as though they were personal and private. Amory Holbrook, the ex-federal attorney, and John P. Gaines, the ex-governor, each had some of the Nimrod O'Kelly records. Other papers in Nimrod's case were lodged in the supreme court files and the Benton County files. Perhaps prosecutor Reuben P. Boise, trial judge Orville C. Pratt, defense lawyer Andrew J. Babb, territorial representative Joseph C. Avery, justice of the peace Abiather Newton, and Sheriff Starr also kept separate records. The wheels of the system suffered by the absence of a hub—some central record-keeping office, an archive.

4. Previously called "Columbia," then, "Hillsborough," and today, "Hillsboro."

5. The texts of both attestations (with some deletions) are quoted as written by the scribe. The lack of periods and capitals to separate sentences is truly representative of Nimrod's writing (see note 1, Chapter 10). Both affiants also swore that they had never been served with a summons to appear at Nimrod's trial. Nimrod had complained that witnesses he sought were never served by the sheriff. The Sixth Amendment to the U.S. Constitution guaranteed him the right to have attempted service on witnesses. However, it nowhere appeared in the record that Nimrod had issued summonses for the appearance of Cornelius or Wilkes. Once again, paper keeping did not support Nimrod's claims. As every researcher knows, records are a path to discovered history, but it is well to remind ourselves that a record is not itself full history. The facts of birth, marriage, testimony, or murder may be made official and certified by paper, but paper does not bear, wed, witness, or kill.

6. Here, Nimrod undoubtedly had in mind the notification claims of widow Mahoney and John Thomas, both of which were rejected by Surveyor General Preston and Surveyor General Gardiner respectively. Research does not show that these claims ever came before a judge in some judicial proceeding, which would be highly unlikely. Nimrod's reference to a "judg…that had honor" and "could not be suborned" was probably a reference to the surveyor general.

7. Sometime in early 1854, Methodist minister Silas M. Stout stepped down as sheriff and Doctor T.J. Right took over. The names of the first three sheriffs of Benton County were most fitting—Starr, Stout, and Right.

8. If Sheriff Right chose the west side route to Milwaukie, he would have crossed the Luckiamute, LaCreole, Yamhill, and Tualatin tributaries before crossing the Willamette. If he took the east side road, after crossing the Willamette, he would have had to cross the Santiam, Pudding, Mollala, and Clackamas tributaries. Either route would also have many swollen creeks at that time of year. Water crossings were a major factor in planning any long trip.

9. As indicated early in this chapter, James H. Slater and Joseph G. Wilson were both clerks, but at this proceeding, Slater would do the paperwork and Wilson served as sergeant at arms. Just as Williams had the double job of supreme court justice and district court judge, so too, Wilson was both the supreme court clerk and a deputy marshal.

25

Final Trip to the Gallows

May 1854

On Monday, May 15, 1854, five days after the re-sentencing, James C. Patterson wrote Governor Davis. His letter began in a style and respect current of the day: "Excellent sir permit me to address you…" Patterson had lived within five miles of Nimrod since the fall of 1853, and was familiar with the "movements of the people and their meetings." He went on to describe "the characters that have taken such a strong stand" against Nimrod:

> his worst enemies are people that have no regard for their Creator…they would rather choose his (the Lord's) day to collect and talk evil of Mr. O Kelly…[S]ome of them proposed to prove things to me that was the most eroneous things I ever seen or heard…They said they could prove that he claimed eight miles one way…to try to influence me against him…[S]ome of those men live immediately on the public road and one or two of them have little grog shops where they can catch every one that passes and say everything they can against him…[F]riends…have said but little. . . afraid if they say or do anything for him that some…would do them a private injury.

In concluding his letter, Patterson may have put a wee crook in the truth: "I am no ways related to this man neither am I interested in [anyway?] only for Justices sake." But Patterson *was* "interested," and almost "related." At the time, Patterson had or was about to begin his courtship of Nimrod's daughter, Sarah, who was fifteen years of age. A little over six months later, she and Patterson were wed at brother Joseph's house in Lane County.

On Tuesday, May 16, Nimrod wrote the governor again. Exactly one month had passed since he wrote his first letter to Davis. This second letter came six days after Judge Williams' death sentence, and was penned in "Corvalles benton county." Unlike his earlier letter, it began with more humility by showering *excellence* four times upon his reader.

> To his excellency Governor Davis Greeting excellent sir will your excellency condescend to permit me in my humble and condemned condition to address your excellency.

But, while Nimrod began on his knees, he did not take long to get on his high horse. He may have been going to die, but he would not go gently. He had written three times in the last three months, starting with his "advertisement" in the *Spectator* in February. Not once did he ask for mercy. The writings became progressively more righteous and rambling. His final letter raged against the growing dark, but according to T.B. Odeneal, that rage was no facade for inner despair.

About that time, Odeneal was working for Asahel Bush at the *Statesman* and had talked with Nimrod during his final days. In later years, Odeneal relayed his observations to S.A. Clarke, who wrote that Nimrod was "resigned to his fate," had "no regret," believed he was "changing to a better world," found it all "tiresome business," and "not alarming." And so, Nimrod's final letter to the governor was not so much a plea as it was a final affirmation from a dottering spirit. With no sorrow for his victim nor regard for the gallows awaiting him, Nimrod wrote:

> The only plan that…would have been esteemed and popular was for me to deny that I was a catholic as mahoney did. He said he was breed up a catholic but he was then nothing. If I had have used the same duplicity I could have been respected…But sir if a man either has to loose the favor of men or the favor of God which is he to choose?

Of all of the souls who may have deserved his gratitude, only one person received Nimrod's unqualified embrace.

> Would I honor my [ill?] father in his old age if I did not let the world know how this awful infamy was spit on me and my family.

That language suggests the father of seventy-four year old Nimrod was still alive. Other records would support that fact—Nimrod's father, Benjamin O'Kelly, applied for a Revolutionary War pension in 1850 and again in 1853. At the time of Nimrod's May 16, 1854, letter to Governor Davis, the father would have been ninety-three years old according to those applications. The May 16 letter fondly invoked his father's lessons:

> My dear old father taught me to be just and fear not and not make a refuge of lies. He taught me that all lies come from satan…But said he my son stick to truth. Truth will take you through all perilous conflicts of this life…Such admonitions have I received from my dear old father.

So strong were the lessons of the father on the virtues of candor that Nimrod the learner became Nimrod the messenger:

> I have taught the same to children and neighbors. My wife has also been faithful to inculcate the same. My children has also strictly observed our admonishing.

Candor for Nimrod was more than a virtue. It was a calling. Some might have tagged it as an obsession. Whatever it was, it longed for truths afar and was blind to truths at hand. He did not see; he sought. It made him a poor settler—but a good pioneer.

What happened next has received varied reports in history. The leading and dramatic version originated with an article written by Lawrence A. Mc-Nary in 1935:

> The presumption in the mind of the then sheriff, T.J. Right, possibly was that if the jury had been of the opinion that O'Kelly was married they would not have rendered a verdict of guilty, that is, if he were defending from intrusion the land to which he was lawfully entitled, the killing would have been justified. The sheriff, apparently without authority, opened the doors of the jail and gave O'Kelly his freedom…[T]he action of the sheriff would seem to be extraordinary.[1]

Indeed, it would have been extraordinary if it had happened that way. But it did not. What did happen was this—on May 14, 1854, Governor John W. Davis sat down at his desk to take up a file marked "Pardon Papers of Nimrod O'Kelly." It had grown thick on his desk. The most recent addition was news that Mister O'Kelly was now scheduled to die on June 9. Needless to say, Patterson's May 15 letter and Nimrod's May 16 letter were too late to reach that file on Sunday, May 14.

Davis may have separated the papers into two piles—those for and those against the pardon. The opposition pile was mostly 1852 filings, plus two new items—a letter from Mister O'Kelly's neighbors enclosing the minutes of their recent meeting, and a letter from the trial judge. Davis had heard of O.C. Pratt, and, as fellow Democrats, they may very well have socialized on the frontier or back in Washington City. Davis undoubtedly studied carefully all of what Pratt had written. Another new item in the opposition pile may have been the appellate opinion of the newly arrived judges, who were unable to find any pity within the law for O'Kelly.

The mass of papers in favor of the convict was what Davis could have expected in a claim for mercy: The pleas of friends, the contention of lawyers, and a tirade from the condemned, who, of course, had done nothing wrong. Davis would have noted with emphasis, however, that many who sided with O'Kelly were prominent Oregon citizens; that since the killing, O'Kelly had been joined by his family; and that he was entrusted with his freedom for eighteen of the twenty-two months since his conviction. But on the negative side, there was a hard fact—Davis could not see in the harangues of the convict's April 16 letter any contrition or saving grace. A condemned man showing no sympathy for the man whose chest he had torn open had a coldness

In 1853, Democratic President Franklin Pierce appointment John Wesley Davis as the Governor of Oregon Territory. Troubled by Oregon's provincialism, he remained in office just eight months before resigning and returning east—but long enough to consider Nimrod's second plea for clemency. *Oregon Historical Society #089974*

not easy to ignore. If one does not give pardon, how can one be given pardon? Why forgive the unforgiving?

Now it was time to bring these two sides to resolution. Other matters were at hand, and it was a Sunday, after all—a day of rest. As Davis sifted wheat from chaff, one circumstance may have struck him close to the heart—Mister O'Kelly was seventy-four years of age and had been opposed and preyed upon. The governor was fast approaching the age of sixty-five, and likewise had met nothing but resistance in Oregon. He was the oldest federal officer ever appointed to serve in Oregon. As a former physician, Speaker of the House, commissioner to China, and now a territorial governor, he, like O'Kelly, had come to close in Oregon. A job he thought would be a final feather in his cap turned out to be a thorn in his side. He came to serve, but was resented. He tried to help Oregonians in their desire for local leadership by proposing statehood, thus giving Oregonians the power to elect their own native officials. But his proposal met the same rejection as most of his other actions. The people, refusing to be steered by imported leaders, voted it down.

Davis would last just eighty more days as governor, resigning on August 1, 1854, after a mere eight months of service. When offered a farewell banquet, he refused. Like Nimrod's petition to him, his own letter of resignation sought pardon, and had these last words for his fellow Democrats in Oregon:

> I will be pardoned, I know, if I say a parting word, by way of admonition, to my political friends…[Y]ou can only maintain your supremacy by being united in your efforts; all sectional and personal considerations should be abandoned, at once and forever…[I]t is manly to differ but childish to quarrel because we differ.

That future resignation must have been a foment in the governor on that Sunday in May, when he leaned forward to focus on a different pardon. Here before him was an old man who had made a decision late in life to start anew, but had run into a dead end. Davis may not have agreed with Nimrod's anger, but he knew his hurt. The governor opened his Actions Journal—a daily log of decisions made by the executive. There, he penned the following:

> May 14th, 1854. Whereas…one Nimrod O Kelley was sentenced to be hung for the crime of murder, and the said Nimrod O Kelley having been recommended as a fit subject for executive clemency by numerous petitioners: Therefore in consideration of the premises and divers other good and sufficient reasons moving the Executive there unto, the sentence of the said Nimrod O Kelley is commuted to imprisonment at hard labor in the Penitentiary for the period of two years from this date.

It was over. Nimrod would not hang. The gallows could be tore down and the lumber used to build a library, hospital, school, steeple, or some better sign of a stumbling, but learning, civilization.

Note

1. Lawrence A. McNary's account was published in Volume 36 of the *Oregon Historical Quarterly*, and accepted and passed along by a number of respected authors, such as L.M. Lowell (1940), Lancaster Pollard (1957), Donald C. Johnson (1973), and Harriett Munnick (1979).

26

The Portland Penitentiary

May 1854

Word of Governor John W. Davis's Sunday, May 14, reprieve did not reach Corvallis until late Tuesday, May 16, at the earliest.[1] Sheriff T.J. Right, the hangman, would have been most pleased. As a doctor, he was committed to saving life, not taking it. But his relief would have been short-lived because there would be repercussions. Nimrod had to be taken to Portland at once. The final words of the governor's commutation order mandated "hard labor in the penitentiary for the period of two years *from this date*." The clock on the two-year sentence had been running since Sunday. Oregon's brand new penitentiary in Portland was as far as a four or five day wagon ride. But greater than the haste in getting Nimrod to Portland, was the haste in getting him out of Benton County.

The *Statesman* would not publish the governor's actions until a week later, but rumor of the reprieve would travel like wildfire. When it spread to the Jennyopolis, Long Tom, and Starrs Point areas, there might be fat in the fire. The new governor, imported from the east, had just taken a "cold-blooded murderer" down from the gibbet and *fixed* to release this "menace" upon law-abiding settlers in two years time.

Sheriff Right wasted no time in removing temptation. He rejected travel by river where there would be no place to hide. He opted for wagon, and quickly mustered horses and provender for nine days and three men. The need for a third man was a guard to spell him at watch, but also may have rested upon another consideration. Once danger was well behind them, the rest of the journey would need indulgence—medicine to ease the ache of wrenching an old man away from his family and freedom. Nimrod was said to be a man of temperance—poor company on the way, and lost company for the way back. No man should ride alone for nine days—especially when wayfaring at county expense. On very short notice, Sheriff Right got Bill Gird to ride shotgun. The Odeneal-Clarke account put it this way:

> As was customary in those days they laid in a comfortable stock of necessary commissary supplies and "wet groceries" to make the wagon and team work off right.[2]

While Corvallis still slept, three men and a wagon made long shadows at the crack of day as they sneaked and creaked down the main street. It was Wednesday, May 17. Gird and Right would be gone nine days. Their prisoner would be gone for two years.

The sheriff would have pushed hard on the first thirty miles, but after that, the remaining miles across French Prairie to Oregon City and then on down to Portland could slow to mosey by paying calls and *slaking a man's dry*. After all, this was no burial service. Nimrod had been snatched from the grave. His days of freedom deserved one last *hooray*, even if feted without his joinder.

Sheriff Thomas J. Right was fifty-five years old. Some folks spelled his name "Wright," but he preferred to sign it "Right." He settled in Benton County in 1853 and had no plans for land or wife. He chose town life where he was brash enough to believe that he could doctor lunacy and enforce the law. Wags might say he did more to enforce lunacy and doctor the law. Doctor Right would not balk at turning a chore into an outing, and then, as Sheriff Right, claiming it as an expense against the county.

Guard Bill Gird, age twenty-four, was a fledgling, who now found himself on wing with two old crows, both of a feather for soaring. The party was a generational misfit with no more in common than thirst for a good journey, and a general agreement that Nimrod should have been pardoned. Gird had signed Nimrod's petition for pardon circulated just four months prior, and Right might very well have done so were he not strapped by the neutralities of office.

Undoubtedly, after the first day of journey, chains were left in the wagon. On French Prairie, Sheriff Right would have allowed Nimrod some farewells. They may have stopped for blessings from the priests of St. Paul; for hospitality with friends at Champoeg, Fairfield, Butteville, and Parkerville; and for respects paid to Nimrod's godfather, Joseph Gervais, still alive. Fords, ferries and fences could have also slowed their travels.[3]

When reaching Canemah at the top of Willamette Falls, they could look down and see Oregon City, the aging maiden, immediately below them. Beyond were younger towns hugging the Willamette's shores—Linn City, Multnomah City, Clackamas City, and farther still, perhaps a glimpse of Oswego and Milwaukie, and finally, somewhere near the horizon, their destination's end, Portland. The top of the Falls was, indeed, the edge of contrast. Below was a clear pathway to the sea. Above were the settlements of French Prairie and the *kalapuya*—centers for farming, ranching, and those who slept the night. The cities on the lower shores were given to distant commerce—exporters,

importers, and all robust sorts attending—sailors, packers, marketers, steve-
dores, and those who used the night. Here, the evening would be alive with
medicine for the gloom of a trail's end—one last good table. Perhaps, Sheriff
Right put festivity aside long enough for Nimrod to settle accounts at John
McLoughlin's house—another place destined for a robust evening. After
McLoughlin's death, it became a "house of negotiable affections."

On the final day, a Sunday, the morning began without mishap. Perhaps
while Nimrod attended mass, Gird and Right continued to toast his last
hours of freedom. When the journey "reached the tall timber below Oregon
City," matters went awry. S.A. Clarke got the story from T.B. Odeneal, who
had talked to the participants:

> Here the "benzine" probably got too active and something gave way that had to
> be repaired. They ran against a tree and broke the wagon.

What followed has been written down many times over the decades since
first reported by Clarke. Lawrence A. McNary, who wrote of the story in
1935, was able to verify it from Governor Isaac Lee Patterson, who in turn
took it from Benton County lore.[4] According to Odeneal—as reported by
Clarke and supported by Patterson—the broken wagon was still miles from
the Oregon Penitentiary.

Nimrod, seeing that it was going to take some time to mend the wagon
and noting that the guards were still well stored by "benzine" and "wet groceries," offered this: "I will go on ahead and report at headquarters. You can
overtake me easily."

Sheriff Right was "not afraid to lose him…There was no way he could
escape from them if he desired ever so badly to do so."

And so, amazingly, Nimrod was allowed to go his way—on foot—alone—
to his punishment. He shortened his stride and stayed to the agreed route.
"But they never caught up."

Nimrod recrossed the Willamette at the Stark Street Ferry Station on
the James Stevens claim.[5] The ferry would have let Nimrod off in the hub
of Portland commerce. The Clarke-Odeneal story reported: "He got to the
river and crossed and spent some hours at the old hotel on the levee, that
afterwards became the American Exchange." The "old hotel" was the Canton
House—there on the steps, Nimrod waited for his guards, while inside Pres-
byterians may have been holding Sunday service. Portland's First Presbyterian
Church was organized in that building just five months before.

Right and Gird were probably having some anxious moments as they
traced Nimrod's route. With each passing mile, they may have wondered if
they would ever see him again. The legend was that Right, sometime about

then, had deliberately released Nimrod from custody.[6] It was, to be sure, not beyond the inclinations of either Right or Gird. Later that same year, Gird was prosecuted for the crime of interfering with the imprisonment of another culprit. Still, in Nimrod's case, the legend finds no basis in the original record. The sheriff, albeit a man of play, was also a man of law, who knew it was a crime to aid a prisoner's escape. And so, the most that can be said is this—what was beyond doing was not beyond hoping.

While Right and Gird did not give escape, they certainly gave opportunity. But if escape was any man's wish, it did not enter the mind of Nimrod O'Kelly. Just as he had been prepared to meet his Maker, so too he was resigned to serve his time. And so, he sat on the steps of the Canton House. But waiting was not among his virtues.

Clarke and Odeneal wrote: "He was anxious to have his time begin and end so that he could be at home and at work; so he asked the way to the state's prison and went on." He had yet to trudge sixteen blocks up Front Street—one last mile.

If his strides were made shorter now, it was not so much because he ached, but rather because he had but one last mile of liberty. And if he ached, he knew his years in cage would be time enough to let wither his shanks.

Front Street was Portland's riverbank road with all the signs of a port—wharves and slips, and cargoes coming and going. Like firs whose needles had fallen, the bare masts and yards of ships in dock made a dead forest on the Willamette. Church bells, school bells, ship bells, and wagon bells tolled the news of meeting, recess, sailing, or fire. A few of the newer buildings along the way were made of brick. On this street and down its side roads, Nimrod could have counted thirty-five shops, six saloons, several mills, and a whiskey distillery. There was a public school, academy, and bookstore, as well as tobacco shops, stables, boarding houses, blacksmiths, boat builders, and offices for newspapers, doctors, dentists, and lawyers. There was ice cream, chocolate, and cider to buy, daguerreotype photographs to have taken, and a baseball team to watch.

Portland was a far cry from "The Clearing" it had been when Nimrod first came through less than a decade ago. Six months later, lawmakers would make it the seat of a new county called "Multnomah." Nimrod was about to be walled within its energy for the next two years.

He followed Front Street south,[7] and near its end came to the top of a ravine within about three hundred feet of the riverbank. There, at the outskirts of Portland, between the Harrison and Hall street crossings, stood a large brick and stone structure—freshly built, with five vertical columns, two

Portland's Front Street, which ran along the west side of the Willamette River, was the heart of the commercial district when this photograph was taken in 1852. In this view looking south, note the mast of the brig *Henry*, docked at the shore. Two years later, Nimrod crossed the Willamette here and paused on the porch of the Canton House (fourth structure from the left), before proceeding alone off in the distance toward the Oregon Penitentiary. *Oregon Historical Society #13137*

stories high, and supporting a roof topped by a huge dome. The whole of it was massive. Nimrod had not seen anything like it since he had left the East. Its strength was, however, a facade. Inside, laborers were still constructing it—trying to make its pith live up to its shell. It was his next home.

When he tried to turn himself in at the gate, the keeper would have none of him. An avowed first degree murderer, duly convicted, seeking to be jailed at his own request was simply too irregular to be believed. *Go home, old man! Stop your foolishness! You got no papers. No guards. No chains. No sense. And no business here!* So, Nimrod once again sat and waited. Sometime along about then, deputies from Linn County may have ridden up with another convict for jailing. Records show that convict William Noble and convict O'Kelly arrived at the prison walls on the same day. A few months later, Noble would escape from the prison. Thus, on that Sunday in May 1854, the two convicts could have been a study in contrasts—one struggled against guard and chains to keep out; the other, without guard or chains, waited to get in.

By and by, "towards evening" according to Clarke and Odeneal, Sheriff Right and Guard Gird finally "came along to set up title to their prisoner, so that they could draw their per diem and mileage." For the sake of protocol, Right may have put Nimrod back in county chains, whereupon the new jailers would have replaced those fetters with territorial manacles and shackles. The exchange of irons was more ceremony than necessity, considering it bound over an old bird who had freely flown into the cage.

With Nimrod in new harness and on his way down new corridors, Gird and Right went out into the open air and began their way back to Corvallis. Rattles in the wagon were louder now because the load was lighter and the mood was silent. Potations may have started earlier that evening—if, indeed, they had ever stopped.

On his first night in prison, Nimrod looked out through bars to see the same stars that looked down on his family and his land. For the next two years, that night sky would be his only touch with liberty and union. His penalty began on Sunday, May 21, 1854—exactly two years from the day he shot and killed.

Notes

1. Nimrod and his future son-in-law, James Patterson, wrote the governor on the following Monday and Tuesday, but neither letter mentioned the governor's clemency. Nor did Tuesday's issue of the *Statesman* report the reprieve.
2. In the 1850s, one meaning for the word "grocery" was a place where alcohol was sold in quantities smaller than one quart. Such saloons had to be licensed. From that definition, the more colloquial term "groceries" referred to any spiritous drink.
3. In those days, the public way often crossed private land, making it necessary for graziers and farmers to either fence in or fence out animals. As the wagon moved closer to the towns and denser population of the north, road gates had to be opened and closed at an increasing number of claim borders. The mighty Willamette River had to be ferried twice to get to Oregon City, and then Portland. One of the ferries likely taken still operates today under the name "Wheatland Ferry." For a general overview of the route taken, see Figure No. One in Chapter 3.
4. Isaac Lee Patterson was born in Benton County and raised there in the 1860s and 1870s. Samuel A. Clarke had come to Oregon in 1850 at age twenty-two and first settled in Salem. He never met Nimrod, but got the story from Odeneal, who reportedly got the story from Nimrod and others on the journey (see note 7 in Chapter 18). The story was repeated for publication by L.M. Lowell (1940), Lancaster Pollard (1957), and Harriet Munnick (1979). All accounts undoubtedly originate from the two separate sources—Odeneal and Patterson.
5. It would cost Nimrod, a foot passenger, one dime to cross. Had he been on horse, one quarter. Presumably, Sheriff Right had given Nimrod coin for the passage.
6. See McNary's reported legend, note 1, Chapter 25.
7. Like all roads in 1854, except for some plank or cobblestone streets back east, Front Street was dirt, and might better have been called a dust or mud street depending on the weather.

A decade later, the southern extension of Front Street and its connection to the White House Road would be surfaced with tar, becoming known from then to now as MacAdam Avenue.

27

Prison and Home Again

1854–56

O n June 8, 1854, Sheriff Right filed a $128 expense claim for the nine-
day trip. It read in part:

> To T.J. Right for transporting & guarding Nimrod O'Kelly from Benton County
> to Penitentiary - - - - - - - - - - - - - - - - - - $92.00
>
> To per diem allowance for convict 9 days at $4.00 per day - - - - $36.00

The county commissioners denied the reimbursement. In the margin,
someone wrote, "not allowed." No reasons were given.

Perhaps, the commissioners learned of the sheriff's cavalier custody on the
trip. Why should there be pay for "wet groceries," for guards who lined their
gullets with "benzene," or for "transporting & guarding" a prisoner who all
alone turned himself over to the prison keeper? And worst of all, what proof
was there that the prisoner ever reached the penitentiary? Did Right simply
turn Nimrod loose?

The following document, however, appeared in the territorial penitentiary records: "Rec'd of the Sheriff of Benton County (May 21st, 1854) one
convict Nimrod O'Kelly for the term of two years. Joseph Sloan, Keeper." But
that receipt was a "duplicate" made on "January 8, 1855," over seven months
after the delivery of the prisoner. Apparently, Right either forgot to get, or
lost, the original receipt. As of June 8, 1854, Right had no formal proof of
what he had done with Nimrod. It was spark on tinder, and the smoke from
which fiery rumor and then legend were made. *The sheriff freed O'Kelly!* The
record does not show Right and Gird were ever paid for their nine-day escorting escapade.

Meanwhile, far down river in Portland, Nimrod's days stretched into
weeks, then months, without freedom. At the beginning, the cells in the new
penitentiary were not ready for occupation, so keeper Joseph Sloan confined
his charges in a wood-frame building called "Sloan's Hotel" not far away
from the new penitentiary. Without cells, prisoners had to be kept in irons—
hobbled in the daytime and tethered at night. A typical receipt for prison

purchases was a clue as to the iron endured—one set of shackles at $3.00; six pounds of chain, $1.80; four pounds of chain, $1.20; a twenty-one pound ball, $3.30. Smithy services for "puting on 2 Setts Shackles" cost $3.00.

At first, Nimrod had five fellow inmates; one half year later, there were eight. One of them raised a few eyebrows and put an extra furrow in Keeper Sloan's brow. Special care was needed, since Sloan's newest prisoner was a woman—Charity Lamb. Nimrod and Charity shared things in common. Lawyer James K. Kelly had defended both. They were the prison's only two homicide convicts—he, Oregon's first reported murderer; she, Oregon's first murderess. Both killed in the face of threat—a trespasser in one case, an abusive husband in the other. But there, commonality ended and imbalance and irony commenced. He had been convicted of *first degree* murder by jurors and judges, who called for his death, yet he was given two years of confinement. She was convicted of *second degree* murder by jurors and a judge, who begged mercy for her, yet she was confined for the rest of her life.[1]

Just as Nimrod huddled in cold stone and iron, so too his land, one hundred miles away, lay silent in its covers. What was to become of Nimrod's claim now that he was jailed? As soon as Nimrod was carted off to prison in May 1854, surveyors appeared once again to make detailed field notes of claim boundaries in the Long Tom area. When they saw that the O'Kelly borders were in conflict, they made no resolution, and left O'Kelly's lines to a special survey—a survey that would be postponed again and again over the next five years.

Less than five months after Nimrod's confinement, Father James Croke made his second annual circuit ride through southern Oregon. He gave this account of the atmosphere in south Benton County:

> Marysville…is, I believe, the most anti Catholic in Oregon—though that rabid opposition to everything Catholic which Characterizes many of its oldest settlers is principally confined to the farming community.

Croke spoke of how the Catholic religion was "incessantly ridiculed" and exposed to "rancorous hatred." While lamenting the loathing directed at his religion, Croke could not resist a bit of loathing of his own. He insinuated that the Protestants were "a motley crowd of brawlers," objected to being placed in the company of Jews and Mormons, and called Catholic tormentors "Ethiopians," who "cannot change their color." To be sure, hate infests all—those who give and those who receive.[2]

The choice between Protestantism and Catholicism tugged within the O'Kelly clan as well. On October 16, 1854, Benjamin O'Kelly, age thirty-eight, joined his mother and father in conversion to the Catholic Church. But sister Sarah remained Protestant. On November 30, 1854, she married James C. Patterson in a Protestant wedding conducted by "Minister/Elder Andrew Zumwalt." The ceremony was held at Joseph O'Kelly's house in Lane County. Brother Joseph and his family also remained Protestant—for the time being.

Other events evolved while Nimrod was imprisoned; Corvallis was made the territorial capital. The governor, legislature, and supreme court had to move their offices to the new seat of government. Even Asahel Bush, the official printer for Oregon, moved there, taking his private business, the *Oregon Statesman*, with him. Corvallis now had its first newspaper. Territorial lawmakers held their annual session there, but only long enough to pass just one enactment—a bill to return the territorial seat to Salem. Offices and newspaper moved back to whence they came. Corvallis was the capital for less than one year—from January to December 1855.[3]

Also during Nimrod's imprisonment, the Valley was boxed between Indian-settler wars—one south in the Umpqua-Coquille-Rogue river country, and the other north in the Puget Sound region and the interior Columbia Basin. Joseph O'Kelly was a volunteer private in that southern hostility, and James K. Kelly was a colonel in the northern hostility. The southern conflict subsided when the Rogue and Umpqua chiefs agreed to leave their ancestral lands and were made to walk 250 cruel and tormented miles through the Willamette Valley to new beginnings on the Grand Ronde Reservation.[4] Meanwhile, the northern conflict also saw ugliness in the Walla Walla country. Captured while under a flag of truce, Chief Peupeumoxmox was later clubbed to death, and his scalp, hands, and ears taken as trophies. Just a few days before, Indians had killed, scalped, and took the bearded face of Private William Andrews.

Neither Joseph O'Kelly nor James Kelly stayed with the military long enough to be present at those atrocities. Private O'Kelly mustered out of his company long before it disbanded. His wife was nearing the birth of their fourth child. He was needed to tend, not fight. Colonel Kelly left his command for the start of the December 1855 Corvallis legislative session. He was needed to make law, not war.

The flames to the north and south of the Valley did not ignite the Calapooyans, who made their homes within the Valley. As had Nimrod, they subsisted and kept to themselves. Yet, they were in the way. Doc Richardson insisted they were "troublesome" and would "provoke the whites"—they needed to be gathered up. Twice before, in 1851 and 1854, the Calapooyans were willing to move to new reserves. And twice before, the forked tongue of a new nation reneged on the treaties accepted. In spite of those rejections, the Calapooyan headmen were willing to make a third effort. This time, in March 1855, Congress ratified, and the Calapooyans abandoned all of the Valley in return for the promise of goods and services in the value of $155,000, plus land reserves at the headwaters of the Yamhill—the Grand Ronde Reservation.[4]

While months sped by outside, hours crawled by inside. By the beginning of 1856, Nimrod had spent over nineteen months in jail when his supporters began to stir again. On March 11, another pardon petition was filed with Governor George Law Curry, the fourth and last governor of the territory. The petition was signed by twenty-seven people—including T.P. Adams, one of Nimrod's former custodians in Benton County; J.C. Alexander, the man who took a rough survey of Nimrod's land immediately after the trial; J.C. Avery, one of Nimrod's most persistent supporters; James H. Slater, the court clerk for Benton County; and Nathaniel H. Lane, son of territorial delegate Joe Lane, Oregon's first governor. The petition gave no specific reasons for Nimrod's release, but rather made its appeal by "sentiments of humanity," "principles of Justice," and "kinder feelings of the harte."

While these appeals to compassion may have been a factor, more realistic reasons were afoot. The prison population was in a flux. Convicts came and went. Some served their short terms and were released. Many helped themselves to release. Oregon's first prison inmate, "Indian Charley," escaped, was re-captured, and escaped again. Three days before Nimrod's first Christmas in prison, two other inmates fled. Prisoner Jacob Williams, who arrived in the middle of Nimrod's term, proved elusive enough that his shackles had to be permanently riveted around his legs; yet he too was released before Nimrod. Poor prison conditions and the lack of funding were other problems. On August 28, 1854, Penitentiary Commissioner J.S. Dickinson wrote to Curry, sizing up the situation this way:

> I am sorry to have to inform you of the escape of two of our convicts last Saturday night…The usual precautions and vigilance was observed as far as I can learn on the part of the Keeper. We have circulated notices far and wide and offered a reward for their apprehension, and hope to succeed, but…it would seem a matter of doubt whether it would not be quite as well if they were all gone in the same way…I dont see clearly how they are to be retain[ed] or supported. [W]e are informed…that there is no money in the Treasury to pay past or future expense.

Prisoners bolted from their ragged situation, and commissioners wished for them to do the same. On September 26, 1854, Asahel Bush's *Statesman* labeled Nimrod's new home a "farce."

An acting governor for a brief interim in 1853 (replacing Davis), Democratic President Franklin Pierce appointed newspaper editor George Law Curry as Oregon's governor in 1854, replacing Joe Lane. Curry's wife Chloe was a descendant of Daniel Boone. Curry was the first Oregon chief executive to have been a pioneer (migration of 1846), and the last territorial governor before statehood. He was the third governor to consider executive clemency for Nimrod. *Oregon Historical Society #39019*

Accordingly, coaxed by fairness and prodded by expediency, Governor Curry acted. In the *Statesman* on March 18, 1856, the following one line story was tucked away:

PARDON—Nimrod O'Kelly of Benton Co. confined in the penitentiary for murder, has just been pardoned by Gov. Curry.

Nimrod's story had ceased to be newsworthy. His penalty was paid. The territory was done with him. He could now pick up his life and return to shooting crows or whatever he was doing four years ago, just before Jeremiah Mahoney came toward him in a dry slough bed.

On his return to Benton County, Nimrod faced change. For one, he would have been reminded of his age when informed that his granddaughter, Elizabeth, had borne a child back in Missouri. He was a great-grandfather now, and that may have put stoop to his gait. And there was change in the countryside as well. Telegraph lines were now strung between Portland and Oregon City. The first message on the wire was: "The weather is cold in Corvallis and the hills are covered with snow." At Corvallis, Nimrod would have noted that Benton County had finally built a jail. He would have stopped there to report his early release from prison to the proper county officials. The officers were all new. S.B. Fargo had replaced T.J. Right as sheriff. Fargo would have sulked; he was among those who two years before urged Governor Davis to let Nimrod hang. The new county clerk was T.B. Odeneal. Either then or some time soon, Odeneal and Nimrod had the talk that formed the basis for S.A. Clarke's 1886 newspaper article—the story that first put a page to the Nimrod legend.

As he left Corvallis, Nimrod observed another change. He found himself crossing Marys River on a plank bridge. Nimrod had not passed over a bridge since leaving Missouri.[5] Proceeding on up to his claim, he would have been struck by still more transformation. The fir groves had been turned to lumber. Where once had been a bolt of prairie, the countryside now was more fully stitched by fence and patched by field. Some swashes, swales, and creeks still corkscrewed through the landscape, but gone were the endless seas of wild flowers. Plow, livestock, and the invasion of bracken, blue-pod vetch, thistle, and dog fennel had eaten up the *kalapuya*. Draining and grazing had chased off the ducks, geese, beaver, muskrat, deer, and elk. Herders and harvesters had replaced the trackers and gatherers. Subsisting was no longer a way of life. The acres themselves were no longer free for the taking—the gift of land under the Donation Land Claim Act had expired on December 1, 1855. The carrot was mostly eaten.

What was left of Nimrod's claim was, perhaps, the only hint of what the *coeur d'vallee* once was. It was "uninhabited" and "in spoilation," according to the 1856 county tax assessment. Likewise, the earlier 1854 and 1855 assessors had found nothing to tax. Furthermore, when the county commissioners had ordered Sheriff Right in 1854 to satisfy prosecution costs out of Nimrod's properties, Right reported, "no goods or chattels to be found." This unoccupied state put the claim in jeopardy under the law of abandonment.

The O'Kelly family was aware of the problem. A few days after Nimrod had been carted off to prison, son Joseph O'Kelly had written to Surveyor General Gardiner:

> I wish you to give me some advise concerning whether it would make any thing against my Father or Mother or their heirs getting a right to the Section of land that is claimed by my Father if I was to move my Mother home with me where I could take care of her…[M]y dear old Father I suppose is sent to the penitentiary for 2 years…[W]hat would be best concerning me moving my Mother off of her land…?

The surveyor general responded: "in ordinary cases" it would not make a difference if "you ware to move your Mother to your house…but it would be safer in this case for your Mother to continue her residence on the claim." The thought, however, of a sixty-three year old woman alone in a hovel on 640 acres and surrounded by encroachers was too dire for contemplation— Mother Sally had long since gone to live with her sons, fifteen miles south in Lane County.

In walking his empty claim after twenty-two months of captivity, Nimrod would have been sore to see his neighbors still partaking of his acres—Grimsley at the northeast corner, and Criss and Stark in the southwest portion. In the northwest, there were signs of a more recent intruder—another one of Isaac Winkle's sons, Montgomery. The Winkle clan had tried to spread into the same general area as the Mahoney and Thomas claims of three and four years before. Like those previous attempts, the surveyor general rejected this Winkle expansion, because it conflicted both with Nimrod's prior claim and a prospective railroad right of way. The distant whistle of the iron horse was yet another foreboding of change. On his east border, Nimrod found another new claimant—George Shultz, who seemed to be overstepping the bounds. Although the glory hole had panned out, new scavengers kept sifting the seams.

Nimrod needed to sit down with Surveyor General J.K. Gardiner, whose office was in Oregon City. Whether Nimrod took that long trip once again is unclear. What is known is that Nimrod would have received the same response as all other claimants in those times when dealing with the surveyor general's offices. If Nimrod wanted to perfect his claim with a special conflict survey, there was a fee to pay. The promise of free land now had a cost. It was an exaction that enraged settlers. Nevertheless, Gardiner justified the fee on the grounds that his statutory job required him to make a quadrangular survey of the public's domain, but not to make individual surveys of private claims.

The Donation Land Claim Act was unclear in this regard. Section 6 provided, "it shall be the duty of the said surveyor-general to survey and mark each claim…at the request *and the expense* of the claimant" But a few lines later, Congress made it an obligation of the surveyor-general to specify the borders of conflicting claims—"Whenever a conflict of boundaries shall arise…the same shall be determined by the surveyor-general." Clearly, each claimant had to provide and pay for a private survey of what he claimed, which Nimrod had done long ago. But who was to pay for the expense of a special survey that decided "a conflict of boundaries?" To be sure, a seeker ought to pay the cost of specifying the gift sought, but the donor ought to pay the cost of specifying the gift to be given. Settlers felt strongly that no fee should be charged for the promise of free land.

Surveyor General Gardiner came to Oregon as an imported easterner—a stigma further enhanced by a rumor that he was "the town drunkard and has not drawn a sober breath within the memory of man." To make matters worse, Gardiner made it a practice to refer cases like Nimrod's to his predecessor's business office. Former Surveyor General John B. Preston had set up a private office in Oregon City just across the street from Gardiner's public office, and offered expertise as an agent to "prosecute cases of conflict of boundary before the Surveyor General." Although Democrat Gardiner and Whig Preston came from different political camps, they reached an accord in matters of commerce. The triumph of business over ideology has never been surprising.

Oregon citizens protested against what they perceived as greed in their imported surveyor generals, and sent complaints east to the General Land Office in Washington City to get Gardiner removed. Asahel Bush sought to have his father-in-law, John S. Zieber, replace Gardiner. It worked. Zieber took over as surveyor general in the late autumn of 1856—not in time, however, to solve Nimrod's springtime concerns. Shifts and shenanigans in the land office were among the many reasons why its business proceeded so slowly. Although there were some 7,500 claims under the now expired Donation Land Claim Act, only about 800 had been surveyed, processed, and approved as of September 1856.

Upon his homecoming, Nimrod found reason for disgust, frustration, and hopelessness. For years he had struggled with neighbors, judges, hangmen, keepers, and now surveyors and land officers. It was enough to *buster* a man.[6] He could no longer work or subsist on his land. His sons were not willing to do so. His wife was gone to Lane County. His claim was deserted and unfulfilled—no longer a hermitage, and far from being a heritage. He was a seventy-six-year-old great grandfather. Perhaps it was time to sit and be still.

But there was this—his life always had been a search, a migration, a moving on! He was old but not yet laid down. His beard was gray, but his legs were green. Nimrod pulled himself back up. If he could not get satisfaction in Oregon, if eastern leaders were too far off to hear the cry of distant voices, then he had but one trail to take. He would go to where his voice could be heard. He would walk back—far back—ocean to ocean—across the continent!

Notes

1. Had Charity Lamb maintained a balanced mind, she might have been pardoned after serving sufficient time in prison. But, alas, after eight years in the Portland Penitentiary, she was pronounced a lunatic, and, on December 8, 1862, transferred to the Hawthorne Asylum for the Insane, directly across the Willamette River from the penitentiary. Sometime after 1873, she died there.
2. Not all were anti-Catholic in Benton County. Just one week prior to writing his November 22 letter, Father Croke was in Corvallis, where he preached at three o'clock in the afternoon before what he called "a large and respectable audience." J.C. Avery made his house available for the sermon, though Avery was not Catholic. Father Croke called him, "the liberal-minded proprietor of Marysville." But Avery was not as "liberal-minded" as one might think; he favored the institution of slavery.
3. Section 6 of the Oregon Territorial Act stated in part: "All the laws passed by the legislative assembly, shall be submitted to the congress of the United States, and if disapproved, shall be null and of no effect." It does not appear that the move to Corvallis was submitted to Congress. The question for history then becomes—Was Corvallis ever really the capital city of Oregon as many historians have reported? The rules of law often confront the realities of history with dilemmas of that sort. What is true-in-law may not be true-in-fact, and vice-versa—e.g., because of the presumption of innocence, from the moment he shot Mahoney, Nimrod was a killer-*in-fact*, but not a killer-*in-law* until proven so. Likewise, Corvallis was the capital *de facto* when officials moved to and enacted on that location, yet arguably not the capital *de jure* until Congress was given the opportunity to veto the move.
4. The Grande Ronde Reservation had been established in the Coast Range at the headwaters of the Yamhill River. It took one wintry month to make the trek from south to north through the Valley, with the column setting out on February 22, 1856. Many settlers were not pleased to see a file of Indians entering, instead of exiting, the Valley. One observed, "the use of the plow and of the spade should be taught them, enough of the use of the latter, at least, to dig their own graves." During that wintry trek, a volunteer trooper could not contain his bitterness. He went berserk, shooting an Indian refugee in the back and killing him.
5. The Marys River bridge was one of the first in the Valley. The first spans were all built upstream on the smaller tributaries of the Willamette River. The Long Tom was bridged in 1870. The first bridge across the Willamette itself was erected in 1871 at Harrisburg, near the Joseph and Benjamin O'Kelly claims. Not until 1887 would the Willamette be spanned at Portland, where the river was widest. Indians did without bridges—canoes and horses were good enough for crossing. In Chinook jargon, *mamook chako illahee enati chuck* (bringing land over water) was the inventive phrase for the white man's bridge.
6. In Missouri, when a mule had too much kick, the skinners would run the animal until its wind gave in. From then on, a mule wheezed and sucked air, but was calm enough to work with harness. It was called a "bustered" or "bestered" mule.

28

Gone Withershins

1856–59

Legend has it that Nimrod O'Kelly, age seventy-six, went east in 1856 to Washington City in the District of Columbia. Respected writer Lawrence A. McNary reported it so in the twentieth century. But it is a difficult story to believe. McNary's account was partly based on a 1935 interview with Nimrod's eighty-four year old grandson and namesake, who came to Oregon fifteen years after the event, and who presumably heard the story from his grandmother, Sally O'Kelly. Most later journalistic reports stem from the 1886 *Oregonian* article by S.A. Clarke—as taken from T.B. Odeneal on his deathbed:

> It was late in summer, and O'Kelly was not a man so much of word as of action. He bade his newly found family a temporary farewell and started on foot for the City of Washington to claim his land of the head of the department. He had no spare means, and could not even afford a horse to ride. He traveled east alone and on foot, meeting and camping with emigrants all the way, who were coming to Oregon and California. He may have caught some chances to ride, and so have made better time, but certain it is that this gaunt, gray-haired man pushed his way on foot to the frontier, and then managed some way to reach Washington, where he presented himself and his cause before the general land office.[1]

Other facts are consistent with Nimrod's absence from Oregon in the summer of 1856. The Benton County Assessment Rolls for 1856 and 1857 continued to show Nimrod's claim to be vacant.[2] Likewise, the Benton County Census Rolls for 1856, 1857, and 1858 did not list any O'Kellys as residents of Benton County. On July 24, 1856, Father James Croke, on his third circuit through southern Oregon, visited Lane County where he received Nimrod's son, Joseph, into Catholicism. Joseph's vows and baptism were taken "in the presence of John Vallely, Sarah O'Kelly, Benjamin O'Kelly, and others." Nimrod's name does not appear. At the same gathering, Croke baptized Joseph's four children in front of the same recorded witnesses. Grandfather Nimrod's name does not appear. Surely, the patriarch of the O'Kelly clan—the first in the family to accept Catholicism, and the first Catholic in southern Oregon—would have been named if present.

If not present for his own son's conversion and the baptism of his grand-children, and if not residing on his land claim, then where was he?

Another incentive for returning east may have been because of what he always said he was—a soldier in the War of 1812. On March 3, 1855, Congress passed "An Act…granting Bounty Land to…Soldiers who have been engaged in the Military Service of the United States." Under the act, veterans of America's wars were entitled to a warrant for 160 acres of free public land. No cultivation or period of residency was required. The only *proving up* to do was a showing of military service. The land office in Oregon could not accept such proof. It seems this had to be done at the Department of the Interior in Washington City.[3]

But such confirmations are a weak knot against the tow of so incredible a feat. A three-thousand mile journey on foot by a seventy-six year old man, who just spent his last two years in a penitentiary at hard labor, had all the fuzz and fluff of a yarn spun—a story welcomed at fireside, but spurned at the bank. Still, imagination and truth are not necessarily incompatible. Sometimes the improbable occurs. While Nimrod's journey could not be confirmed at its source, it might be proven at its destination.

Lo and behold—in Washington City, Nimrod left tracks. In the Department of the Interior archives, there is a file under a cover jacket headed "Nimrod O'Kelly—75.058 issued Nov. 27th/57." Therein, Nimrod's signature unmistakably appears on documents he signed in the District of Columbia in 1857 and 1858, together with affidavits of others, including a U.S. Senator, attesting that Nimrod O'Kelly of Benton County, Territory of Oregon, had appeared before them on the east coast. The mind could now embrace the myth. The great-grandfather graybeard indeed had made his way three thousand miles across the continent.

The details of Nimrod's journey east can only be assembled from likelihoods—a frustration as true today as in 1886 when S.A. Clarke wrote:

> That journey across the plains, on foot, moneyless, old and perhaps infirm, as he was, was something I would like to tell of minutely, but the man is long ago deceased and Odeneal could gather only the plain statement that he actually went afoot to the East.

Although Clarke reported that Nimrod, "a man of no spare means," was "moneyless," he may have had a grubstake from John McLoughlin at Oregon City. Like Nimrod, McLoughlin was a septuagenarian, Catholic convert, and claimant plagued by land grabbers. As such, McLoughlin would have understood an old man's need to leave a legacy. When McLoughlin died one year later, his estate inventoried a list of debts owed him of "doubtful or no value," among which was an undated I.O.U. from "N. O'Kelley" in the round sum of "$100."[4]

And so it was that Nimrod O'Kelly went withershins—bent for sunrises and sharing campfires with pioneers headed for the sunsets he left behind. Once over the divide, he would have found the big sky now sprinkled below with sod houses of emigrants who had gone far enough. Nebraska Territory had been carved out of the Great Plains, and Iowa was now a state in the Union. Crossing "bleeding Kansas," Nimrod would have found himself headed directly into a gathering unrest—a nation at the brink of internal war. In Missouri, Nimrod undoubtedly stopped to winter over with his son Charles and family in the Shoal Creek Township of Barry County, deep in the Ozarks. It would have been at that time that he met his five-year-old grandson and namesake, who eventually came to Oregon.

In the spring thaw of 1857, Nimrod took to the road again. From the Valley through Missouri, his sojourn had been mostly afoot, interspersed by horseback. But on the final one thousand miles, he could ride the iron horse, and it is hard to imagine that he did not. A system of railroads now interlaced the nation on the east side of the Mississippi River. He would have joined the western rail terminal at Memphis, Tennessee. Trains raced at speeds of twenty-five miles in one hour, thus covering in one hour what horse-and-wagon took, at best, one day to do. Furthermore, the steam engine needed no rest. It traveled through the night with stops only for passengers, water, and wood. Nimrod had taken four to five months to come two thousand miles from the Valley. The remaining one-third of his journey to Washington City could have taken as little as three days.

Nimrod may have paused in his train travel at Greenville in Greene County, Tennessee. His brother Frank's son, Doctor T.K. O'Kelly, lived there.[5] Greenville was also just north of Cocke County where Sally and Nimrod were wed. Somewhere in his travels, most likely at Greenville, Nimrod met a man named Johnson, the former mayor of Greenville and now Tennessee's Congressman in the U.S. House of Representatives. Here in 1857, Congressman Johnson was campaigning for election to the U.S. Senate. His voyage upward on the political ladder was on a course that crossed Nimrod's continental voyage. Somewhere in Tennessee or Washington City, Nimrod gained the attention and counsel of Andrew Johnson, future President of the United States.

At Greenville and Cocke County,[6] Nimrod may have detoured from the train route to trek over the Smokies and into Buncombe County, North Carolina, to pay respect at the grave of his father. From there, he would have gone beyond the Blue Ridge Mountains to Granville and Warren counties in North

Carolina and Mecklenburg County in Virginia, where he was born and schooled by his mother, and where his illiterate father had owned considerable property, not the least of which were two human beings—slaves Sue and Barnett.[7]

From Mecklenburg County, Nimrod would have made his way north to connect once again with the rails. Washington City was another three hundred miles north by train.[8] Miles and miles of shiny wire flashed by Nimrod's train window. While horse and wagon might have taken weeks to go those final three hundred miles and while trains went the same route in mere hours, words along that telegraph wire could cover the same ground in seconds. Since his youth, Nimrod had been westering—going away from progress, backward to where time had been. Now, for the first time, he found himself headed into progress, forward to where time had passed him by. It made him older.

Nimrod undoubtedly had never seen a place quite like Washington City. Portland and Oregon City were small wicks against the blaze of Washington's costume, buggies, gaslight, gossip, and pavement. It was a city full of stand-up wait and sit-down hurry. Then too, there were so many *cheeked* men. It would be a few more years before the first bearded President would make face-hair fashionable. In the autumn of 1857, on the streets of Washington City, a frontier graybeard stood out.

The current President, James Buchanan, a Democrat, was a bachelor given to festivity—a stark contrast to the gloom of President Pierce's regime. But the liveliness was not all merriment—it was also quarrel, and bordered on violence. While Buchanan saw the depravity of slavery, he was a fence-sitter who abided the southern states in their insistence upon it. Within a few days of Buchanan's inauguration, a majority of the U.S. Supreme Court had decided there was nothing unconstitutional about people being property. If Buchanan's election stoked the fires of the slavery issue, the Dred Scott decision threw gunpowder on it.

Like Harriet Beecher Stowe's *Uncle Tom's Cabin* and John Brown's attack at Harper's Ferry, the Dred Scott decision awakened a grizzly. Nimrod could first see the tracks while crossing bleeding Kansas. The spoors grew fresher as he moved east through the southern states. Now, in the District of Columbia, he saw the beast. Secession, war, and the killing of citizens by citizens were just a matter of time. The sooner his business was done, the sooner he could give wide berth to what menaced. That was the way most Oregonians saw slavery—what was not business *in* Oregon, was of no business *to* Oregon. Oregonians wanted neither slavery nor the bother that went with it.

In Washington, Nimrod probably started his quest at the office of Joe Lane, Oregon's delegate to Congress. If so, Lane was not there—he was on his way back to Oregon because he sought reelection to a fourth term as delegate, and because Oregonians were about to vote for the fourth time on seeking statehood. The two men passed each other as ships in the night.

At this point, Nimrod likely went to Senator-elect Andrew Johnson, who then put Nimrod in contact with John H. Johnson, a Tennessee attorney practicing in Washington City. Allegedly, Nimrod had soldiered under the military command of still a third Johnson—Colonel William Johnson. It is unknown whether these three Johnsons were in any way kin. But it is certain that attorney Johnson assisted Nimrod in his paperwork, that Colonel Johnson was the link to Nimrod's military service, that Senator Johnson later became Nimrod's appointed agent, and that all four men were from Tennessee.

Attorney Johnson would not have been able to aid Nimrod with his donation land claim. The General Land Office in Washington was not receptive to helping *prove up* a claim located on the other side of the continent, where there was a local land office. But Nimrod's claim under the Bounty Land Act of 1855 was another matter. That act gave 160 acres of free land to soldiers who had served the United States in any war. Nimrod always boasted of his service in the War of 1812. Attorney Johnson went to work to find the proof. There, among files bound in red tape and almost one-half century old, he found it.[9] Once again, another of Nimrod's yarns was confirmed.

Payroll and muster roll records showed a "Nimrod O'Kelly" as a private in Captain Elihu Millikan's company of the Third Regiment, East Tennessee Militia, commanded by Colonel William Johnson. According to Nimrod, that company and regiment were within "general tailors brigade under the auspices of general Jackson of tennessee militia." Nimrod had enlisted at Dandridge, Tennessee, and served from September 17, 1814, to May 3, 1815, mustering out with pay of $60.53. Nimrod's service would have put him in time and place with General Andrew Jackson's Army of the Cumberland at the Battle of New Orleans, in December 1814 and January 1815—where, in Nimrod's words, he rushed "at the mouth of cannons" and stood "the iron hail."

On a form dated November 5, 1857, Nimrod stated he was "aged about 75 years," that he "was honorably discharged at Knoxville, Te," that his discharge was "either lost or destroyed," and that "Jno Johnson of Washington D.C. is hereby authorized to prosecute this my claim and to receive any warrant that may be issued thereon." Nimrod's signature thereto is unmistakable. Two citizens of Washington, D.C., swore Nimrod signed in their presence. The declaration, affidavit, and supporting documents were filed at the office of the Commissioner of Pensions, within the Department of the Interior. On November 27, 1857, Warrant No. 75058 for 160 acres of free public land was issued to Nimrod O'Kelly. A warrant was not a deed of title or a patent to any specific piece of land. It was a ticket that allowed the recipient free lands yet to be located and chosen. Nimrod could take his warrant west to the Long Tom and try to couple that warrant claim to his donation claim.

For the next three-and-one-half months, Nimrod's whereabouts are unknown. He finally surfaced again on March 10, 1858, when he was back on a train headed southwest through Lynchburg, Virginia, toward Greenville, Tennessee. When arriving at Greenville, he made a devastating discovery. His belongings had been looted somewhere along his rail travels. Clothing and some garden seed had been taken. Worst of all, Warrant No. 75058 was gone!

There was but one thing to do—he had to get a duplicate of the warrant. This meant returning to Washington and adding eight hundred miles to his travels. But Nimrod did not appear in Washington to report his loss until a few days before Christmas 1858. Nothing is known of his whereabouts or the reasons for this delay from March 20 to December 21, 1858—a nine-month period. Future events suggest that he stayed in the Greenville area, perhaps with kin and perhaps to mend tired body, mind, and purse.

On his return to Washington, he went back to attorney John H. Johnson, who now had become a justice of the peace. Although Senator Andrew Johnson was busy seeking the Presidential candidacy for the Democratic Party, he nevertheless took the time to meet with Nimrod and Peace Justice Johnson. From that meeting, Peace Justice Johnson composed a written "declaration" for the signatures of all three Tennesseans:

> On this 21st day December Eighteen hundred and Fifty-Eight, personally appeared before me…Nimrod O'Kelley…who, being by me duly sworn according to law declares that he is the identical person to whom Bounty Land Warrant number 75058 was issued…on or about the 27th day of November 1857…
>
> That between the tenth and twentieth day of March 1858 while on his way to the south by railroad, his trunk was broken open either at Lynchburg, Va., or Greenville Tennessee or between the two places and robbed of some clothing and garden seeds, which he intended to take with him to Oregon, & also the foregoing described warrant.
>
> He furthermore declares that he has never sold, assigned, nor voluntarily parted with his right to the warrant in question, and that he has this day filed a caveat in the Gen'l Lands office to prevent the issuing of a Patent to a fraudulent claimant. That he intends giving notice of the loss of said warrant according to law; and therefore, makes this declaration for the purpose of obtaining a Duplicate of the aforesaid lost Warrant.
>
> Jno. Johnson of Washington, D.C. is hereby authorized to receive my warrant and transmit the same to me or to the Hon. Andrew Johnson.

It was signed "Nimrod O. Kelly." The hand was a little shakier now, but the bold clear letters were unmistakably Nimrod's, and the Johnsons affirmed his signature:

We Hon. Andrew Johnson and Jno. Johnson, residents of Tennessee and Washington D.C. upon our oaths declare that the foregoing declaration was signed and acknowledged by the above Nimrod O'Kelley in our presence.

In the final paragraph, Justice of the Peace Johnson stated that he swore the "affiants," and knew them "to be credible persons." Thus, under this document, John Johnson wore four hats—scribe, witness, agent for delivery, and oath-taker.

The strongest reason for honoring the declaration's request was the fact a U.S. Senator signed it. Beyond that, there were questions. Should the Commissioner of Pensions, George C. Whiting, rely on a mere affidavit in putting two copies of a single land warrant into the stream of commerce? What was the validity of a document in which the oath-taker was the oath-giver? Why had it taken Nimrod nine months to report the theft to authorities? Furthermore, law required and Nimrod's declaration promised that a public notice would be given. That notice, however, was not published until mid-February 1859. Thus, citizens were not warned about the stolen warrant until eleven months after it was afoot in commerce.[10]

While Nimrod waited for government action, Oregon Territory did the same. Oregon's bid for statehood was before Congress. Oregonians had voted overwhelmingly in favor of being a free state, yet also in favor of barring "free negroes." The desire for neither slavery nor ex-slaves had confused the northern and southern factions in Congress, and put the debate on the congressional table for fifteen months, while Nimrod was in the east.

Finally, on February 14, 1859, Oregon became the thirty-third state in the Union. The Marine Band paraded in the streets of Washington City in celebration. Nimrod would have been among the first Oregonians to know of Oregon statehood.

Oregon had received its valentine from the nation, but Nimrod did not. On May 6, 1859, the General Land Office informed George C. Whiting, the Commissioner of Pensions, that a "caveat against the issue of a Patent" on the stolen warrant was on file in their office. Six days later, the file was apparently closed—with a final, illegible notation. The file was void of any duplicate of a veteran bounty land warrant issued to, or received by, Nimrod O'Kelly.

There was nothing more to do. Spring thaw had come. The grasses were alive again. The trail to the State of Oregon was open. He had left the Territory of Oregon three years ago. He was seventy-nine years old, and now faced the two-thousand-mile Overland Trail for the third time. He did so without the prize for which he had come.

Notes

1. See the latter part of Chapter 18, including note 7, for a discussion of the Clarke-Odeneal "Pioneer Days" article in the August 1, 1886, *Oregonian.*
2. Benton County assessment rolls for the remainder of the decade apparently no longer exist. The 1856 and 1857 rolls listed Nimrod's land at only 320 acres and valued it at $1,600.
3. Another motive also might have prompted Nimrod's return to the Atlantic Coast. His father had died, or was dying, back in Buncombe County, North Carolina. It seems that his father was alive in 1853, and gone by 1857—passing away sometime in that period. Purportedly, his father would have been ninety-five years old in 1856.
4. An even amount of precisely $100 was not apt to be the balance on any running account for accumulated purchases. On the contrary, a $100 debt suggests it was a single cash loan. The date of the loan is not recorded.
5. Doctor T.K. O'Kelly eventually moved to Missouri, where he became a prominent physician. Although the connections cannot be fully documented, this much is true—late in the 1800s, a man named Edward O'Kelly, son of a Missouri physician, killed a man in Colorado. Like Nimrod, he used a shotgun and was convicted and imprisoned. Like Nimrod, Edward gained public sympathy for his act and was pardoned. His victim, Bob Ford, had been the assassin of notorious hero Jesse James.
6. Before reaching Greenville, Nimrod may have visited Rhea, Meigs, and McMinn counties where, a quarter-century before, he and Sally had spent some years before moving on to Missouri. Those counties were at the heart of what came to be known as the "Bible Belt." Rhea County was the site of the famous "Scopes Monkey trial." With that kind of background, Nimrod's evangelistic writing style is understandable, while his Catholic conversion remains a puzzling inconsistency, the reasons for which are simply not available. But if frontier Christian appeal to the Indians is any indicator, then one may reason that Catholic missionary flare proved more attractive to the downtrodden than did the more somber thumpings of Biblical revivalism.
7. In June 1802, when Nimrod was 22 years old, his father donated one acre of land in Virginia for the building of a religious meeting house, "free and open for all orderly Christian society." That may explain Nimrod's liberal attitude toward denominations and, thus, help account for his puzzling shift from Protestant to Catholic.
8. Somewhere along this part of the journey, it seems that Nimrod picked up his brother Benjamin as a traveling partner. Brother Benjamin was actively seeking to have the government affirm the war pension of their father, who allegedly served in the War for Independence. The claim had been twice rejected. Now, in 1857, son Benjamin applied once again, this time on behalf of his deceased father's estate. Nimrod too was headed to the same pension department at the same general time. It is fair to suppose that they had met and came as one.
9. Establishing veteran bounty pensions in this period involved a great deal of research through poorly kept records. Veterans were required to wait in Washington, D.C., offices while papers were explored. Absent modern portfolios for paper storage, those early files were bound in red-colored ribbon. Thus came the modern term for bureaucratic excess and delay—"red tape."
10. On April 7, 1859, Harvey G. Robertson, publisher of the *Greenville Democrat,* a weekly in Greenville, Tennessee, swore he had printed a notice of the lost warrant "six successive weeks." The published notice reported the loss and was signed by "NIMROD O'KELLEY, Jno. Johnson, his Att'y." The date "Feb. 16" was printed on the notice.

29

Return to the Land

1859–64

Nimrod could have returned to Oregon by sea. But likely, he had nei-ther the $300 nor the stomach for 5,500 miles of seafaring. Sockets, sinew, and spirit willing, he most likely left the Missouri with the migration of 1859. Railroad tracks, telegraph wires, plumbing, gaslights, and talk of civil war grew faint, erased by the sound of the wind across the plains and the smell of a mountain timberline. When first he westered this way fourteen years ago, he was leaving home. Now, in 1859, he was going home. It was the difference between forging a trail that would never end, and following one that would.

Back in Oregon, most Valley residents would have yielded long ago to the reckoning that Nimrod, absent for three years, would never be seen again. So, when *it was heard he'd shanked fore and back* between the oceans, it must have dropped a few jaws. Just months short of his eightieth birthday, this graybeard was among the oldest, if not the oldest, pioneer to ever suffer the Oregon Trail, and he had done it three times.

Upon his return, Nimrod found the business of turning claims into pat-ents had not improved. The land office files in Oregon City were filled with unprocessed claims. W.W. Chapman had recently replaced John Zeiber as Oregon's surveyor general. On August 6, 1859, Chapman contracted the services of Benton County Surveyor L.A. Davis to measure the true lines of the Criss, Stark, Grimsley, and O'Kelly claims—the special survey that had been promised five years ago.

Davis found that the O'Kelly claim stood out as a parcel of what the coun-tryside used to be—nature had reclaimed it. On November 22, Davis report-ed the claim as having "no house" and having reverted to "prairie…subject to overflow from the Long Tom River." And not just nature intruded—Davis found that Grimsley, Criss, and Stark overlapped 245 acres of the O'Kelly's 640-acre claim. Had the Mahoney-Thomas claim still existed, Davis un-doubtedly would have found that well over half of Nimrod and Sally's land was overrun—just as J.C. Alexander noted seven years ago.[1] Davis reported the conflict to Surveyor General Chapman. But once again, forward came to halt. Chapman never got around to approving Davis's survey notes.

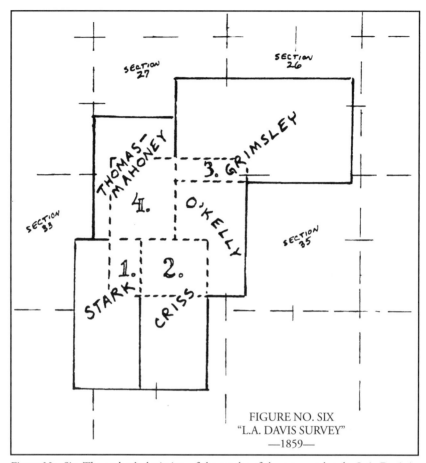

FIGURE NO. SIX
"L.A. DAVIS SURVEY"
—1859—

Figure No. Six. The author's depiction of the results of the survey taken by L.A. Davis in 1859—(1) the overlap between Nimrod and Stark is 58.8 acres; (2) the overlap between Nimrod and Criss is 127 acres; (3) the overlap between Nimrod and Grimsley is 59.3 acres; and (4) the probable overlap between Nimrod and Mahoney is taken from the Thomas notification File No. 3835. (See Figure No. Five.)

Just as Nimrod was troubled by conflicts within his own borders, so too his state and nation were troubled internally. Political parties in Oregon and the East were realigning. The Whigs and the Salem Clique were fading from power, a new Republican Party was forming, and Democrats were splintered between the Douglas Democrats and the Southern Democrats. In the 1860 presidential election, schisms and new coalitions assured the victory of an obscure Republican, who won with less than forty percent of the popular vote. Abraham Lincoln's presidency was final kindling to what smoldered. In

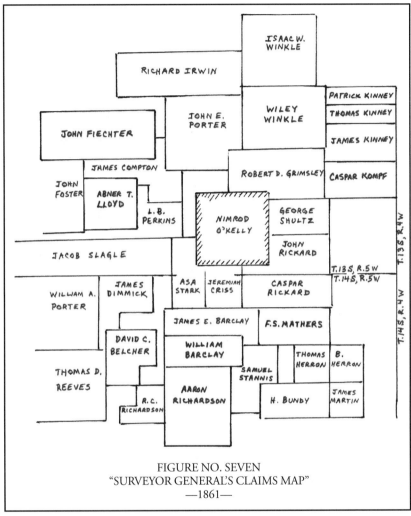

FIGURE NO. SEVEN
"SURVEYOR GENERAL'S CLAIMS MAP"
—1861—

Figure No. Seven. A hand traced portion of Surveyor General Pengra's claims (cadastral) maps of Jennyopolis and Starrs Point townships, October 26, 1861, fixing the donation claims in that vicinity.

the spring of 1861, news reached Oregon that the South had captured Fort Sumter and seceded from the Union.

President Lincoln appointed Byron J. Pengra as Oregon's next surveyor general. Among Pengra's first tasks was drafting a claims map for each of Oregon's townships. These plattings were not the same as the topographical township maps prepared back in 1853 by Surveyor General Preston. Claims mapping meant that the jigsaws of two decades of haphazard staking were finally going to be fitted into one picture.

In October 1861, Pengra's draftings had inked their way to the Jennyopolis township claims. Past cadastral surveys and fieldwork were on the drawing board before him. When his pen reached the southeast corner of the township, he saw that everything seemed to be in order in the Nimrod O'Kelly file. O'Kelly was an Oregonian prior to December 1850, and claimed no more than 640 acres. He was older than eighteen, married, and a citizen. While the 1859 Davis survey showed overlapping claims, that was no problem because Mr. O'Kelly was there first.

But one bother gave Pengra pause—had Mr. O'Kelly worked his claim for the required four consecutive years?[2] His continuing occupancy must have ended when he was taken into custody on May 21, 1852, for having killed a trespasser. Did he get in his four years prior to that? The notification files of the various claimants were full of contradictory dates for O'Kelly's starting occupancy. Surveyor General Gardiner had noted "Feb. 1850" as the commencement. In 1853, O'Kelly's notification witnesses, Avery and Alexander, wrote "the 6th of May 1849"; but then more recently Avery amended that to May 21, 1848; and Alexander amended it to June 20, 1848. O'Kelly himself initially swore to "the 1st day of May, 1849."

The pry that freed the tangle of dates was found in a musky old book penned by a drunken scribe—a page from the abolished Provisional Government's land record. That page, written fifteen years before by Land Recorder Frederic Prigg, was an imprecise description of land without benefit of any survey, and was more eyeball than ciphers, with measures *gimcracked* together by a claimant and a recorder who barely understood each other. But no matter how vintage, vague, or vacated, the book put Nimrod in claim as of December 8, 1846, five and one half years before his jailings began. Pengra was convinced. He inked the final decision onto the Jennyopolis township claims map. It depicted Nimrod's claim just as Nimrod had staked it fifteen years prior. Seemingly, Nimrod had won. But, as every Indian and pioneer had come to know, first decisions on the frontier were far from final.

Originally, section 13 of the Donation Land Claim Act stated: "All questions arising under this act shall be adjudged by the surveyor general." But on February 14, 1853, Congress added section 21 empowering the President to appoint two new federal officers for Oregon: "a receiver of public moneys" and "a register of the land office." Did that mean the receiver and the register now had the job of approving land claims? The question was taken to the Oregon Supreme Court in the case of *Keith v. Cheeny*. In July 1860, Nimrod's former prosecutor, now Associate Justice Reuben Boise, wrote the opinion: "The business of issuing certificates to settlers properly belongs to the office of register and receiver…they became in this business the successors of the surveyor-general." The surveyor general was still there to measure the federal lands, but his maps did not constitute a certification of private claims. Once again Nimrod was led to the trough, but not allowed to drink.

There were 8,000 claims now on file in Oregon's land office. Only 1,000 of them had been certified to the commissioner of lands back in Washington. Creation of the receiver and register offices had not done much to speed *proving up*. Throughout the nation, the business of turning over public lands to private ownership was notorious for backlog. Nimrod and Sally were made to wait on a process that came to be known as "doing a land office business."

On June 22, 1860, an event occurred that may have given Nimrod a reason to count his blessings. In the streets of Corvallis, a convicted first degree murderer, Philip George, was hanged from a gallows. Sheriff S.B. Fargo was the executioner, Doctor T.J. Right (the former sheriff, and now the coroner) pronounced death, and County Clerk T.B. Odeneal did the paperwork. This was Benton County's fourth attempt of a public hanging and the first success. If the beneficiary of the first three failures was in the crowd, he may have been the first to leave, carrying with him a mixture of sorrow and solace.

In 1861, other sobering events came in tandem. Nimrod's godfather, Joseph Gervais, died at his home on French Prairie. Gervais was eighty-four. Perhaps it was fortunate he died when he did, sparing him from seeing a disaster that swept chaos down the Valley that had been his home for half a century. Rains came and came again. For four months, six feet of water fell from the skies. Willamette River towns, including Champoeg, Orleans, Linn City, and Canemah, were destroyed. When the waters receded, driftwood was found as far as one mile from the river banks. The bloated bodies of humans and animals were strewn on the Valley floor. Needless to say, Nimrod's claim was not spared. Where intruders, trials, appeals, jails, paperwork, and delays had failed, nature succeeded with a reminder that, without her accord, no one could *keep* land. Floods dampened more than just field and store. Floods swept away fulfillment and drowned dreams.

During those years of war, hanging, flood, and wait, Nimrod startled friends and family with another unpredictable turn—he gave away half of the claim, 320 acres. His price?—one dollar! On April 14, 1863, somewhere near the time of his eighty-third birthday, Nimrod signed an "Indenture"[3] conveying one-half of a square mile to "Rev'd. Francis N. Blanchet, Archbishop of Oregon City, in the Roman Catholic Church." Although the indenture made no express designation, it came to be recognized that the portion conveyed was the *north* half of the claim, whereas Sally retained the *south* half.[4]

It was rumored that members of Nimrod's family were not pleased by the gift to Blanchet—Clarke and Odeneal reported that the children "could not invalidate it." J.C. Avery and E. Holgate witnessed the indenture, with no member of the family taking part. Nimrod's wife, Sally, did not sign the indenture and, therefore, retained her potential donation and *dower* interests in the north half. By common law, each spouse had an undivided life estate in portions of the real property of the other. Common law called those interests *dower* and *curtesy*, thus Sally had *dower* in Nimrod's north half, while Nimrod had *curtesy* in Sally's south half.

Family reluctance might have been a reason for a nine-month delay in placing the indenture on file in the Benton County deeds record. Exactly what prompted Nimrod to act as he did is unknown. A simple act of charity perhaps, no more and no less. Then too, he had killed a man—a horrible sin. The Clarke-Odeneal article in 1886 reported that Nimrod's gift grew out of a need for "life long repentance," and an "effort of conscience." They also labeled the giveaway as "an infringement on common sense," calling it "fanaticism." A less critical—yet still unkind—supposition for Nimrod's action might have been that he was in his dotage. One thing is certain—Archbishop Blanchet was there for the award whether it was alms, atonement, or affliction.

Back in the late 1850s, the Catholic clergy had begun to pay special continuing attention to the O'Kelly clan. Thus, on December 17, 1858, Father James Croke had written the Archbishop:

> I was anxious…about *Old Okelly's family* who live 14 miles north of Eugene City on the Corvallis Road—They are all Converts and wd require to be seen to as they are only partially instructed.

Unknown to Father Croke, Archbishop Blanchet had already taken an interest in "Old O'Kelly's family." In November 1858, the Right Reverend had used the Lane County home of Joseph and Matilda O'Kelly for three days, as a place from which to bestow sacraments on Catholic families. Nimrod was still in the East at that time. If he were ever to return, the Archbishop would have wanted to meet this miraculous old sinner who held steadfast to the last, pristine section of the *coeur d' vallee*. In 1863, destiny brought them together on a matter of business, not blessings, albeit some have insinuated that it was a mixture of both.[5]

Nothing in the record shows Blanchet dominating the negotiations. Indeed, Nimrod was as capable of pigheadedness as Blanchet was capable of bulldoggedness. If there was madness in Nimrod's giveaway, perhaps there was method in it as well. Nimrod's hold on the land was still a claim under conflict in the official books—conflict bogged down in bureaucratic beadledom.[6] The transfer now gave the O'Kelly south half an influential ally—the Archbishop of an enormous religious empire. Furthermore, the indenture expressly stated that the land was given "for the purpose of supporting and educating poor orphan children." Not only would the forces against Nimrod find it awkward to oppose a well-organized religion, they would be *crackbrained* to challenge support for society's waifs and urchins.

Of course, the indenture transferred nothing but a prospect. The acres still belonged to the federal government. Nimrod and Sally had yet to perfect their claim to a full 640 acres before Nimrod's giveaway of "half" could amount to 320 acres. In the path of that continuing pursuit, government in Washington recently had created one more crossing. Inking paper, like chasing horizons, always seemed to be followed by one more page to fulfill. With the Civil War in progress, the Union was not about to give away free land to rebels. An Oath of Allegiance had to be signed. For some it would not be an easy oath to take. Many pioneers had their roots in southern states. In Oregon, the center of southern sympathies was Benton County and, more particularly, the Jenny-opolis-Long Tom-Starrs Point area. The mayor of Corvallis was a secessionist, and the *Oregon Weekly Union* of Corvallis continued the pro-slavery notions of its predecessor—Joe Avery's *Occidental Messenger*. The *Weekly Union's* rebel advocacy was so strong that the federal government committed an extreme act of censorship—it ordered a close to the newspaper's operations.

When Lieutenant Philip Sheridan, the commander at Fort Hoskins in Benton County, was called back east to take a command in the Union cavalry, the Knights of the Golden Circle and certain Benton County residents con-spired to seize the fort. They also threatened to take over the Oregon arsenal, resisted any draft into the Union forces, and plotted assassination. Not far from Nimrod's claim, Confederate sympathizers attempted to haul down the Stars and Stripes at Starrs Point.[7] Citizens across the nation were forced into choice. Nimrod's state of birth, Virginia, was literally torn in two. While his state of former residence, Missouri, did not secede, its citizens came down on both sides. It is unknown on which side the Missouri O'Kellys fought, but in 1863 or 1864, a "Noah O'Kelly" was killed by a federal scout in Barry County, not far from Nimrod and Sally's old farm.

Amid the turmoil, where did Nimrod side? Was he with the Union and flag he defended in the War of 1812? Or was he with Tennessee, Virginia, and North Carolina—his Confederacy origins? Did he join with his pro-slavery and constant ally, Joe Avery, or with his lawyer, James K. Kelly, an anti-slavery

Unionist? Which influence was stronger—his upbringing in a slave-holding family, or his recent support from Andrew Johnson, one of the few prominent southerners loyal to the North, deemed a traitor by the South, and soon to become the U.S. Vice President? An Oath of Allegiance had to be signed at the land office in Oregon City, more than a two-hundred-mile round trip from son Benjamin's house in Lane County. Nimrod had made that journey many times. But now it was late in both the year and his years. Winter days grew shorter. Snow was in the mountains and in his beard. Nevertheless, he managed to make that week-long journey.

On November 19, 1863, Nimrod, age eighty-three, entered the land office at Oregon City. Register William A. Starkweather swore him to tell the truth and to sign the following print-form statement:

> I will support, protect, and defend the Constitution and Government of the United States against all enemies, whether domestic or foreign, and…I will bear true…loyalty to the same, any…law of any State Convention or Legislature to the contrary notwithstanding.

His signature, albeit shaky now, was bold and clear. Once again, the road seemed clear to *proving up.* But once again, he was given no satisfaction. Starkweather would not issue the certificate. The claim needed study. Nimrod's return to Lane County—empty-handed—was his last journey through the Valley. Sand in his glass was near bottom.

Nimrod and Sally had recently reached their golden wedding anniversary. They were living in Lane County and had no further use of Benton County. So, on August 26, 1864, they divided the south half of the Benton County claim into three acreages and signed two indentures. One deeded the uncontested eastern corner of the south half—"120 ac. more or less"—to their daughter, "Sarah Patterson of Lane County." The other conveyed the middle part of the south half—"100 ac. more or less"—to their daughter-in-law, "Jefelia O'Kelley of Clackamas County," the wife of Nimrod Junior since August 4, 1859. The transfers did not designate the husbands. Sons Joseph and Benjamin were excluded; they had their own lands. Benjamin signed both indentures as a witness. The menfolk were left out.

Apparently, the south half was to remain in the keep of the women in the family, just as envisioned by the progressive Donation Land Claim Act. Jefelia apparently paid nothing for her acres, while Sarah paid $500 for hers. Within eleven months of those transfers, Jefelia and Sarah sold their interests for $900 and $1,000 respectively. All that remained in the O'Kelly name was a claim to one hundred acres of the southwest corner, still contested by Stark and Criss.

Nimrod had yet to receive an official declaration from the Union government—a sovereign at war—granting his 640-acre claim. This flurry of conveyance was merely the transfer of the claim, not the land itself. And so, at dusk, Nimrod was simply contenting himself with the likelihood, that in the battle, albeit not yet the war, he had captured a flag. Even so, what did it matter? On the battlefield, what does a soldier seek? The battle or the field? Victory or prize?

The soldier was tired now. There would be no more journey—no more contest. Sometime during the month of November 1864, he stopped. It had been a long march. Nimrod O'Kelly was eighty-four years old when he died, and this has been his story.

Notes

1. See Figure No. Three in Chapter 17.
2. Under the 1853 amendment to the Donation Land Claim Act, Nimrod was provided another alternative. The successive four-year habitation requirement could be shortened to two years if Nimrod paid $1.25 for each acre claimed—$800 for 640 acres. Even if he had the money, he would have resisted paying for what was supposed to be a "donation."
3. Deeds in those times were often labeled "indentures," a word that came from still earlier times when papers that transferred land titles were torn in two—one half given to the grantor, one half to the grantee. Thus, the matching *indentations* formed by the tear were proof of the bargain. Public record keeping brought an end to this ceremonial practice, but the word "indenture" lived on until "deed" took its place.
4. Land office practice was to award the wife the more improved half, which, in the case of the O'Kelly's property, was the south half where Nimrod had maintained his cabin and field. It was understood that the north half was conveyed to the Catholics, albeit the indenture simply cited, "Nimrod O'Kelly's half of said claim."
5. Modern descendants of Nimrod relate the story, as handed down through the generations, that Nimrod took ill in his advanced years and was tended to by priests and their prayers. A convicted murderer was certainly a candidate for purgatory. He recovered from the illness, but it was during that time, or as a result of it, that he purged his sins with the gift.
6. In 1862, the O'Kellys and their neighbors were brought together for boundary conferences—a procedure for settling borders by agreement. Nimrod and Sally had separate conferences with Jeremiah Criss, Asa Stark, Robert D. Grimsley, and George Shultz. But as of mid-1863, the conflicts were not put to rest by those discussions. Notations in Nimrod's notification file read: "Papers on special file of Contested Cases," and "proofs forwarded to General Land Office with papers in contest between O'Kelly & others." Research has not revealed these "papers in contest" or what became of them.
7. Southern sympathizers attempting to haul down a U.S. flag in the face of Union protectors of that same banner was a frequent, petty eruption on America's borders, far from the heart of warfare. In Oregon, this reportedly happened in Jackson and Lane counties as well.

Epilogue

The Claim

The saga of Nimrod O'Kelly's sojourn—so much tied to what he had settled, strived, and slayed for—would be unfulfilled without knowing whether his claim ever ripened into a patent. On November 21, 1864, shortly after his death, his widow Sally sold the last acres of the Long Tom claim. Benjamin O'Kelly witnessed his mother's "X" on the indenture, and her jar was made $600 richer by the purchaser, Caspar Rickard.

On December 28, 1864, Surveyor General Byron J. Pengra drafted a more detailed plat of the 640-acre claim, which he continued to label "Nimrod O'Kelley." Pengra had no care for the fact that the claim had been trans-

A modern photo showing the east half of Nimrod's claim. *Kalapuya* grasses are gone under the plow. Swales, swashes, and sloughs have disappeared with drainage and flood control.

ferred by private agreements. The acres yet belonged to none other than Pengra's boss—the federal government—and that boss only did business with the original claim holder, whose efforts had to fulfill the legal requirements. The purchasers owned nothing until a patent to the O'Kellys was signed by the President, and then filed in the Benton County Book of Deed Records.

The principal proponents of the O'Kelly claim now became Archbishop F.N. Blanchet and the Rickard family.[1] Widow Sally, however, was not totally divested. Having never signed her husband's conveyance to Archbishop Blanchet, she still had a wife's potential right to a donation and dower in the north half. Eleven months after Nimrod's death, Blanchet went to Lane County to counsel the widowed member of his fold. On October 17, 1865, in the presence of A.A. Skinner and M.W. Mitchell, she deeded her "right of dower" to the archbishop for one dollar. Son Benjamin apparently was not present, for this time he did not sign as a witness to his mother's "X" as previously he had always done. Just like her late husband's indenture to Blanchet, Sally's deed

At the far left is Winkle's Butte from which Nimrod first eyed his desired claim. Nimrod's log cabin would have stood about where the farmhouse lies.

limited the transfer to a specific purpose—"supporting and educating poor orphan children."

Eight months later, in June 1866, Archbishop Blanchet ridded himself of the problem claim by selling the north half, clouds and all, to James Kinney of Benton County. Kinney paid "Two thousand ($2,000) gold coin." In the deed, Blanchet described himself as "trustee for purposes of supporting and educating poor Orphan children," but then he hastened to add the words "and otherwise." The land could be used "otherwise" than for an orphanage. Nimrod and Sally's conveyances did not say "otherwise." That subsuming word swept away the limits set by the original donors. No orphanage was ever built, and no "poor orphan children" were ever supported or educated on that Long Tom acreage. Nor was anything ever done about the non-fulfillment of the donors' purpose. Arguably, a land claim given for the express "purpose of supporting and educating" orphans did not necessarily mean that the orphanage had to be located there. But the question remained—did the O'Kellys understand that?

On May 31, 1866, Register Owen Wade and Receiver Henry Warren at the Oregon City land office finally capped the certification of the O'Kelly donation land claim. They accepted May 21, 1848, as the beginning of Nimrod's occupancy—a date that was precisely, and conveniently, four years prior to the day that Nimrod fled his claim for having killed another. But Certificate No. 2822 was no more than a certification of facts. It did not bestow title. Whether or not a patent should be issued was a decision passed along to the Commissioner of the General Land Office in Washington, D.C. While ordinarily that final passage would be clear sailing, Certificate No. 2822 had clouds. Wade and Warren noted in the margin of the certificate, "in contest between O'Kelly & others."

Another eight months passed. On February 4, 1867, a land patent came to the desk of the President of the United States for his signature and seal. If the President took the time to examine the patent— undoubtedly one of many documents laid before him[2]—he may have noticed it was a "Grant unto Sally O. Kelly, widow, and…unto the Heirs at law of the said Nimrod O. Kelly, deceased." That name, not an easy one to forget, might have held his eye. Ten years before, when the President was a U.S. Senator, he was in a brief alliance with this old voyager seeking bounty for his soldiering under Andrew Jackson.

Perhaps, President Andrew Johnson savored a moment of reflection on this old crow, whose flights had finally been overtaken and hauled down. Johnson knew what it was to be pursued. A hostile Congress sought his

"[H]e would com about my house almost every day and vilifie me for holding a full claim of land and me an old no count man without a family." Excerpts from Nimrod's letter to "Gov. Lane," June 4, 1852.

impeachment. Indeed, one of the leaders in that removal attempt was Oregon Senator George H. Williams, the same man who, as judge, sent Nimrod to the gallows for the third time. President Johnson may have had a nod and a smile for the patent before him—a posthumous trophy of land to a fellow Tennessean who, like himself, had been quarry for a hunt.

The signed patent was sent back across the continent to the Oregon land office. There it rested, undelivered, for many years to come. Without delivery and recording in the county records, title was still not conferred. Not even the President's authority could put an end to a mission that time and again had been reined back.

Two more years passed. On February 20, 1869, James Kinney sold the north half of the former O'Kelly claim for $2,000. The deed made no mention of an orphanage. The new owner, James Bruce, was concerned that the O'Kelly patent, now dormant in the Oregon land office, had included as grantees Nimrod's "Heirs at law." Furthermore, Nimrod's last will and testament, signed seventeen years before, left his land interests to his then-minor children. Nowhere in the chain of land conveyances had the children given up their descendant rights as heirs or beneficiaries. Nimrod's estate and will had not gone through a probate court. So, Bruce got quitclaim deeds from Sarah O'Kelly Patterson, Benjamin O'Kelly, and widow Sally.

As Bruce continued to cut the thicket from this title, his blade ran into hardwood—a chip off the Nimrod tree. Nimrod the son was more than passive in his resistance. On November 1, 1869, Nimrod the son filed a complaint against Bruce in the Benton County Circuit Court.[3] The son alleged a prior right to an undivided one-third of the north half of the claim and sought $2,500 in recompense. And so, a new conflict arose on the elder's old claim. This time the conflict would be handled differently. No one intruded, no one taunted, no one threatened, no one fired a shot, and no one died. Law was in place now, and conflict was solved with words, not swords. After a brief flurry of pre-trial motions, the $2,500 case bottomed out at a compromise. The son received $50, and Bruce a quitclaim deed.[4]

Another two years passed. In 1871, Nimrod and Sally's land claim had still not come to a close. One final technicality barred the way. The land office would not deliver the patent until a fee of fifteen dollars was paid. This final bother might have been comical by comparison to all else, were it not for the fact that the whole chain of title to the land was worthless without it. Until the fee was paid, there would be no delivery. Without delivery there could be no filing in the Benton County Deed Record Books. Without that recording, there would be no public notice. Without public notice, the hold on private ownership was the clutch of water in a fist.[5]

Who was to pay this fifteen dollars? Sally O'Kelly had already quit her claim to both halves. Sometime in 1871, the current deed holders sought to get the delivery from Register Wade. But Wade insisted the patent could only be delivered to the patent's named grantees—Sally O'Kelly or Nimrod's heirs. Apparently, the deed holders, led by James Bruce, prevailed upon Archbishop Blanchet to convince widow Sally to obtain the patent. On May 8, 1871,

Sally put her "X" on an informal letter to the "Surveyor General" at "Eugene City." The letter empowered "the Rt. Rev. F.N. Blanchet to obtain the Patent and Certificate to Nimrod O'Kellys land claim." However, the effort was rejected, because the surveyor general was not the appropriate office, because Eugene City was not where the patent was located, and because a casual letter from an illiterate, without notarization or witnesses, was hardly sufficient to anoint a messenger with agency to receive a critical document.

Consequently, a week or so later, Sally put her mark to a "certificate" stating that she gave to Blanchet "the power to draw away from the land office at Oregon City, the...patent, granted...to my husband, late of Benton County." It was done in the presence of two witnesses, one of whom was her son, Benjamin. Blanchet, an archbishop, was not about to run errands; he passed the chore along to one of his priests with a letter authorizing delivery to "the bearer." Strangely, Blanchet had written Wade a few days prior stating that he authorized Bruce to make the same pick up "on the condition he will pay you for me the fifteen dollars charge." Apparently, Bruce refused to pay and the priest likewise came without payment, because the patent was not turned over. It seemed that after all of the years of struggle, Nimrod's claim was going to be defeated by a fuss over $15.

A decade then passed. At eight o'clock in the morning on June 10, 1881, Clerk Bush Wilson decided to start his day by entering some documents into the Benton County records. Now, thirty-four years older than when he first came through the Long Tom countryside in search of a beginning, Wilson's blue-veined hand took, from the pile of papers at the top of his desk, a document that had finally worked its way to the surface. He then went to the huge, leather-bound volumes of Benton County Deed Records, reached to a top shelf, and drew down Book "N." He lugged the volume to his desk, flopped it open to page 439, and proceeded to dip and ink on that blank page each of some five hundred words from the document before him.

The Oregon land office had finally delivered the O'Kelly patent. It came fourteen years after the President issued it; seventeen years after Nimrod died; twenty-nine years after Nimrod killed; and thirty-five years after Nimrod had climbed a butte, looked down upon the *kalapuya,* and saw where he would spear his corner stake. Clerk Wilson fitted the massive Book "N" back into its slot atop the shelf. With that, the arch was bridged—the keystone at last in place.

Somewhere in the Valley is Nimrod's grave. It cannot be found. Perhaps it is just as well that stories should leave some mystery.[6] Calapooya lore had it that when humans died, they became *kahte*—clods of earth. And so, while this story told of the hunter's claim to land, the mystery is buried in the land's claim to the hunter.

> *Under the wide and starry sky*
> *Dig the grave and let me lie*
> *Glad did I live and gladly die,*
> *And laid me down with a will . . .*
> *The hunter home from the hill.*
> —Robert Louis Stevenson

Notes

1. The Rickard family eventually acquired the entire south half of Nimrod's donation land claim, thus the whole of Sally's 320 acres came together again, under the Rickard name. In the early 1870s, the Oregon and California Railroad would run along the western borders of Nimrod's old claim. The post office and whistle stop created there was called *Rickard*, no longer extant today.
2. By the Andrew Johnson era, a President's precious time had become far too valuable to expend in signing such routine papers; thus had begun the practice of a secretarial signing of the President's name.
3. This complaint provides the only known confirmation of Nimrod's death. It reported the month and year, but not the day: "on the ____ day of November 1864 the said Nimrod OKelly Sr. died."
4. James Bruce eventually acquired more acreage in the area, and became a successful and prominent Benton County citizen. Like Rickard, Bruce's name would be given to a post office and railroad whistle stop along the road and track on what was once the O'Kelly claim. The crossroad stations of *Rickard* and *Bruce* replaced the more memorable name, Jennyopolis—a place now ghosted. Rickard and Bruce are today likewise passé.
5. Even after private title is duly attached, the public maintains an exalted control. Eminent domain and its power stays with the public. When the public needs private property for public use, it can be taken back—condemned—without the private owner's permission, so long as just compensation is made.
6. To add to the mystery: About fifty miles on a beeline southeast of the old O'Kelly claim, there is a community site in the Cascade foothills along the McKenzie River road called "Nimrod." No one seems to know how it came by that name. A plaque on the wall of the Linn County Historical Museum in Brownsville, Oregon, (fifteen miles due east of Nimrod's claim, and thirty-five miles northwest of Nimrod the town) honors "Nimrod and Sarah (Burk) O'Kelley." Linn County is across the Willamette River from Benton County. The O'Kellys had little, if anything, to do with that county, so it too is puzzling. The plaque was a tribute made possible in 1995 by the work of their descendant, V. June (Blevins) Collins.

Appendix A
Nimrod's Age

Nimrod O'Kelly's age cannot be confirmed by any official birth document, since such records were not kept in our country's early history. Religious registers or family memories, notes, and papers were the usual sources for recording precise age in those times. Throughout this book, Nimrod's age is based on an April 1780 birth date. Thus, he would have been eighty-four when he died in November 1864.

Nimrod's birth date and age are taken from his sworn representation in the application form of his 1853 Notification of Claim, which also is consistent with information in the 1852 pardoning petitions sent to Governor John P. Gaines and signed by friends, sympathizers, and leading pioneers. Nearly consistent with that date and age are Nimrod's 1857 application form for a soldier's land bounty, and the 1850 U.S. Census (Seventh)—both documents show an age between one and two years younger. The 1860 U.S. Census (Eighth) shows him to be three years younger—i.e., born in 1783. Nimrod's 1860 affidavit in his Notification of Claim file has him reciting a birth date of 1786. His 1847 Catholic baptism record suggests a birth in 1787.

All of this documentation, of course, has a single, central source—the memory of its aging subject. Because generalization is more cautious, it may be more discreet to say that Nimrod was born in the early 1780s; that he was in his mid-sixties when coming to Oregon; that he was nearing his eighties when he journeyed to and from the East; and that he died sometime in his early eighties. The magnitude of his exploits, of course, does not suffer by this indefiniteness.

Old age in Nimrod's times and on the frontier was a wonder. To some extent it accounts for why so many people came to his aid. At most, only one out of every forty Oregonians was above the age of forty-five. Less than one out of a hundred was sixty-five or more. A septuagenarian or octogenarian on that early frontier was a rarity.

Today, about one out of every ten people is sixty-five or older. Now, more than age, we are impressed by our ancestors' week-long trips through the Willamette Valley and their transcontinental crossing of six months afoot. Modernly, there is nowhere that transportation cannot reach within a week or two. On the other hand, in Nimrod's time when long traveling was commonplace, his contemporaries would have admired his veneration more than his voyaging. Today, we grow older yet endure less.

Appendix B
Land Market Values

In the early 1850s, Benton County land assessors valued Nimrod's 640-acre claim at about $400. In 1866 and 1869, James Kinney and James Bruce each paid $2,000 for 320 acres of Nimrod's land. In 1878, Wallis Nash reported that many of the "level, easily-tilled bottom-lands" in the Willamette Valley would buy and sell at $40 to $60 per acre—thus making the O'Kelly claim worth about $32,000 when the Oregon land office delivered the patent on the claim in 1881. Today, realtors opine that Nimrod's one-square-mile section could be worth well over $2,000,000.

Appendix C
Federal Land Distribution

The State of Oregon contains almost 62 million acres of land. In 1850, when Oregon was a territory, the United States claimed it all. The Donation Land Claim Act, the first giveaway, lasted only five years, until December 1, 1855, and accounted for about 7,500 patents out of 9,000 claims filed.

Over the next century, other ways of distributing Oregon's federal lands were adopted. For every 100 acres, about 18 were homesteaded, about 10½ were bought (usually at auction), almost 7 were given to state and local governments, and slightly more than 6½ were taken up by transportation builders. On the other hand, about 4 acres out of every 100 were patented under the Donation Land Claim Act—approximately 2.6 million acres, and mostly in the Willamette Valley. Other miscellaneous distributions account for slightly more than 1½ acres per 100. Today, 52 of each 100 acres have never been distributed—the United States still owns more than half of Oregon.

Tucked away in the list, somewhere under either "miscellaneous" or "remaining federal lands," are Indian lands. The categorization is difficult to make because it is wrapped in debate. One view contends that Indian lands do not belong anywhere on a list of federal distributions. One cannot "distribute" that which was never acquired. By federal law, acquisition was supposed to be done by treaty—promises between recognized nations. Too often, the promises were ignored. In one such treaty, a chief of the Santiam Band of the Calapooya nation understood the exchange as promising the following:

> They will build a hammer house. A man will come who knows how to make all sorts of things…An iron house will be erected. Whatever sort of iron thing you may want, you will not have to pay for it. There will be a paper house. Your children will speak the paper.

But fourteen years later, another chief of the Santiam Band spoke again of those pledges of carpentry, smithy, and school buildings:

> We do not see the things the treaty promised. Maybe they got lost on the way. The President is a long way off. He can't hear us. Our words get lost in the wind before they get there. Maybe his ear is small.

So, did the United States acquire by trick or trade? If the former, then, can an ill-gotten acquisition be "distributed"? And, if the latter, then is a reservation a "distribution" of federal land? Whether called "conquest" or "broken promise," the takings in territorial times and early statehood left the tribes with about 8½ out of each 100 acres. By 1875, the reservations were reduced to slightly more than 6 acres per 100. Today, Indian tribal lands in Oregon have shrunk to about 1 acre in each 100.

Appendix D
Oregon's Image and Motto

The state of Oregon is sometimes reputed to be insular and isolated, at least more so than its neighboring states to the north and south. Perhaps, that estrangement was seeded by the two-thousand-mile, half-year, exodus by the earliest migrants on the Oregon Trail, followed by the establishment of their own Provisional Government. Accordingly, at the outset, the Latin phrase *Alis Volat Propriis* ("She Flies with Her Own Wings") was generally accepted as the motto of Oregon Territory, and then the State of Oregon.

But during the Civil War, the new state seal bore the motto "The Union." It probably did not occur to anyone that the two banners—one extolling independence and the other dependence—might have reflected different views on what statehood was all about. Not until 1957 did the Oregon legislature officially adopt the state motto: "The Union." Then, in 1987, the legislature changed its mind and restored the original territorial motto—"She Flies with Her Own Wings."

The swing between maverick and herd, between self-reliance and teamwork, between solitary and solidarity, is not so much contradictory as cyclical—not unlike the sway between risk and security. Indeed, Nimrod's path through the land and the law was indicative of that phenomenon, as he traveled back and forth between his own wings and his flock. Daniel Webster recognized the symbiosis between the two dynamics when he urged, "Liberty and Union, now and forever, one and inseparable."

Appendix E
Biographical Postscripts

The Judges

Judge Orville C. Pratt—While Nimrod was in prison, Pratt failed in his attempts to regain political office and ended up practicing law in partnership with Alexander Campbell, one of Nimrod's prosecutors. In 1856, Pratt left Oregon on the heels of a thwarted scheme.

He had attempted to lay hold of the assets of the renowned Ewing Young estate. Young, a rambling frontier stockman, had died in 1841 without heirs or a will. Consequently, his $5,000 estate was put in custody of the Oregon Provisional Government, which was created in part for just that purpose. Over a decade later, Pratt produced an Arizonan named Joachim Young, who claimed to be Ewing's son and heir; whereupon the territorial legislature authorized the transfer of the estate to Joachim. On the verge of turning over the monies, the legislators discovered that Pratt was the undisclosed beneficiary—in that he had persuaded Joachim to assign the claim to him. An incensed legislature negated the payment. Pratt took the matter to the judges, where he insisted the legislature could not renege on a prior approval. In short order, the Oregon Supreme Court approved the legislative nullification.

Not long after his ploy, Pratt departed for San Francisco. There he became a judge, millionaire, and owner of a ranch equivalent in size to eighteen one-square-mile, donation land claims. In 1877, his wife discovered he was having a romantic affair. He avoided prosecution for what was then the crime of adultery by consenting to a divorce and $750,000 in alimony. He then married the interloper. He also was involved in an unseemly gambling episode while in New York—he refused to testify at the trial on grounds that it might incriminate him.

He died in 1881, at the age of eighty. He had been at the forefront of Oregon's court-made law—a vanguard of order and decorum in the establishment of frontier law in need of form and beginning. On account of that pioneering, and despite the poor accounting of himself, the University of Oregon, in 1886, conferred upon him a posthumous Doctor of Laws degree.

Judge Thomas Nelson—After denying Nimrod's 1852 request for an appellate review before the Oregon Supreme Court, Nelson left Oregon for the same reasons that brought him there—the spoils of a new presidency. He returned to New York, where he practiced law until he died in 1907 at age eighty-eight.

Judge William Strong—After giving Nimrod his day before the Oregon Supreme Court, Strong was drawn into the affairs of new Washington Territory, which he had helped create. He served for a time on the Washington Supreme Court. During the Civil War, he moved to Oregon and took up a law practice in Portland. He died in 1878 at age sixty-four.

Judge Cyrus Olney—After trying to quit the Oregon Supreme Court in 1853, and after excusing himself from voting in Nimrod's case in 1854, Olney finally succeeded in resigning in 1857. As a member of Oregon's constitutional convention, he again absented himself and did not vote on the final resolution. In 1854, he and Thomas Dryer, publisher of the *Oregonian*, along with others, attempted the first known ascent to the top of Mount Hood. Dryer claimed to have succeeded. Olney could not bring himself to make that claim. Prior to his death in 1870, Olney had been using opium and chloroform habitually, apparently for what ailed him. His final withdrawal came when he died in 1870 at the age of fifty-five—nevertheless outliving his wife and all seven of his children.

Judge Matthew Paul Deady—Deady, who might have been the swing vote in favor of a new trial for Nimrod, but who was denied that role by a misspelling of his name, stayed on after statehood as Oregon's sole federal trial judge. He continued to be the leading compiler of Oregon's codes of law, and was a founder of the University of Oregon, the Portland Library, and a school of law in Portland. Deady died in 1893 at the age of sixty-nine, having been Oregon's most preeminent judge of the nineteenth century.

Judge Obediah B. McFadden—Soon after voting with Judge George H. Williams in affirming Nimrod's death sentence, McFadden moved to Washington Territory where he was more appreciated. His career there was long and popular, and included the chief justice position on Washington's supreme bench. He died in 1878 at age sixty-four.

Judge George Henry Williams—After affirming Nimrod's conviction and setting the third date for Nimrod's hanging, Williams went on to the most noted career of all. He became a U.S. Senator from Oregon and then the U.S. Attorney General, the nation's top lawyer, where he took a heavy hand in impeachment proceedings against President Andrew Johnson. Later, President Ulysses S. Grant nominated Williams for Chief Justice of the U.S. Supreme Court, but the Senate would not confirm because of his purported improprieties while Attorney General. In his later years, Williams was the mayor of Portland during a time when corruption in city politics reportedly was rampant. He died in 1910 at age eighty-seven.

The Lawyers

Alexander Campbell—In the years following his assistance as a prosecutor in Nimrod's murder trial, Campbell formed a law partnership with Orville C. Pratt in Multnomah City. Following the notoriety of the decision in *Joachim Young v. Oregon Territory*, Campbell left Oregon along with Pratt, resuming as *Pratt & Campbell* in San Francisco. Both men became California judges, and the partnership was dissolved.

Reuben Patrick Boise—The chief prosecutor in Nimrod's trial eventually became the Chief Justice of the Oregon Supreme Court. He was the oldest member of the Oregon Bar when he died in 1907 at age eighty-eight.

James Kerr Kelly—Nimrod's appellate lawyer was defeated in an 1866 attempt to become Oregon's governor on the Democratic ticket. But in 1869, he was elected U.S. Senator from Oregon, and in 1877 became the Chief Justice of the Supreme Court of Oregon. He died in 1903 at age eighty-four.

Amory Holbrook—Oregon's first U.S. Attorney assisted Nimrod by circulating a key petition for pardon and, along with James K. Kelly, by tracking down Justice William Strong in the back country. He later became the mayor of Oregon City in 1856, ran unsuccessfully for the U.S. Senate, organized Oregon's Know Nothing Party, and was editor of the *Oregonian*, 1862–64. He died in 1866 at age forty-six.

Andrew Jackson Babb—Nimrod's trial lawyer apparently married his second wife, Mary J. Matthews, in Lane County on or about July 22, 1855. After his escapade concerning the proposed Elliott Cutoff (see Chapter 14), he passed out of Oregon's recorded history.

The Custodians

Samuel F. Starr—Nimrod's first custodian, after quitting the sheriff's office, became a schoolteacher and chorister at the Bellfountain Methodist Church, and postmaster at Starrs Point, which evolved into the town of Monroe.

Silas M. Stout—Nimrod's second sheriff-custodian became a minister of the Methodist-Episcopal Church South in south Benton County—a pro-slavery, pro-South, arm of the Methodist Church

Thomas J. Right—Nimrod's third sheriff-custodian resigned not long after the county commissioners disallowed payment of his expenses for escorting Nimrod

to prison. Doctor Right then took a job as surgeon at the Indian agency in Tillamook County, where at age fifty-five, he settled down and married. Two years
later, he and Malcena, his child bride, moved back to Corvallis and entered the
drug store business while raising six children. He also returned to elected office
as county coroner, where it seems he was more content probing the dead than
punishing the living.

William Gird—Nimrod's deputy guard on the way to the Portland penitentiary
later became a noted horsebreeder in Oregon while Nimrod was still in prison.
Some evidence indicates that, when Nimrod was back east, Gird might have used
the O'Kelly claim for pasture at a wayside stable called "Twelve Mile House." For
a brief time, Gird moved his stables over the Cascade Range to Fossil, a town in
the John Day country. He returned to Benton County, but a creek near Fossil
still bears his name. Gird eventually moved again, this time to Albany, where he
became a saloonkeeper. He and other livestock fanciers gathered on occasion to
compare and race horses. Out of this common interest grew an annual event—
the beginning of the Oregon State Fair.

The Allies

Joseph Conant Avery—After Nimrod's release from prison, Avery began publication of the *Occidental Messenger* in Corvallis, a strong advocate of slavery. Avery
saw economic benefit for the nation in utilizing slave labor and he was oblivious
to its inhumanity. However, his compassion for persecuted Nimrod O'Kelly
made his pro-slavery stand ironic and hypocritical. Avery's territorial and munici-
pal leadership roles faded from prominence with the advent of statehood, Civil
War, and a new brand of politics. He died in 1876 at age fifty-nine.

Greenberry Smith—The man to whom Nimrod fled after killing Mahoney
became a noted banker, moneylender, and land baron. He acquired thousands of
acres in Benton and Polk counties, including an entire town. Greenberry signed
his first name as one word, not two ("Green Berry"), as has been suggested by
some authorities. He died in 1886 at age sixty-six.

Joseph C. Alexander—Many times, Alexander's signature appeared on Nimrod's
behalf. Alexander became Benton County sheriff in 1862, and the county's representative to the state legislature in 1868.

John McLoughlin—Aside from assisting Nimrod, McLoughlin was the sup-
porter of so many early pioneers that after his death in 1857 at age seventy-three,
he was dubbed the "Father of Oregon." Today, his home is a museum in Oregon
City.

James Croke—The priest who conducted the first Catholic mass in southern Oregon at Nimrod's cabin left the Northwest and became a vicar general in San Francisco. He died in the late 1880s at about the age of sixty. His 1889 obituary claims he assisted an unnamed Oregon murderer in gaining clemency; parts of the report can be read to suggest the Nimrod O'Kelly story. However, if claim was taken for aiding Nimrod in avoiding the hangman, that credit simply is not borne out by any court papers, citizen petitions, journalistic accounts, or Catholic records. While Croke did attend to Nimrod in his spiritual life, there is nothing to show that clerics took a lead in assisting him in his secular troubles.

François Norbert Blanchet—Some may question whether the Archbishop should be listed as an "ally." He never signed a petition in Nimrod's behalf, and his only dealings with Nimrod involved the transfer of half of the Long Tom claim for use as an orphanage that never came to fruition. Blanchet continued to serve as Oregon's leading pioneer Catholic prelate for fifteen years after Nimrod's death. Blanchet died at St. Vincent's Hospital in Portland in 1883 at age eighty-eight.

The Scribes

Thomas Benton Odeneal—At one time or another, Odeneal worked as an editor or writer with a series of short-lived newspapers, including the *Oregon Spectator, Occidental Messenger, Democratic Crisis*, and *Oregon Weekly Union*. Eventually, he became the founding editor of the more stable *Corvallis Gazette*, still published today. Odeneal also was active in various Benton County offices as clerk, auditor, and judge throughout the late 1850s and 1860s. He was the last Oregon Superintendent of Indian Affairs before the office was abolished in 1873. Near the end of his career, he served as clerk of the Oregon Supreme Court, and editor of volumes 9, 10, and 11 of *Oregon Reports*. Odeneal died in 1886, just a few days after S.A. Clarke interviewed him. The interview formed the basis of Clarke's 1886 *Oregonian* article, which was the first to describe Nimrod's narrow escapes and amazing travels. Despite Odeneal's quite ambitious resume, Clarke's admiration was capped by this rather faint praise: "Odeneal…was a man of mind and culture, and with a little more energy and force of character would have made a greater mark in life."

Samuel Asahel Clarke—At different times, Clarke served as editor of the *Statesman* and the *Oregonian*, two newspapers still published today. He became a railroad promoter, a published historian and poet, and librarian of the General Land Office in Washington, D.C. He died in 1909 at age eighty-one.

Asahel Bush—With the beginning of statehood and the outbreak of the Civil War, Bush faded from Oregon leadership. J.C. Avery and Bush, both Democrats and allies during territorial times, ran afoul of each other in later years in the game of politics. Their struggles within the party wore them down. Neither had the desire or energy to make the turn into the new national partisanships of the 1860s. Bush's parochial way and cliquish airs did not prepare him for the ideas of Unionism and national expansion. His hidebound look at matters reflected the insularity of the frontier—an image of Oregon that has lasted unto this day. During the Civil War, Bush sold the *Statesman* and turned to a financial enterprise, teaming with W.S. Ladd to form the Ladd & Bush Bank in Salem, at which business Bush prospered. Today, his home is a museum and park in Salem. He died in 1913 at age eighty-nine, having once been among the most powerful political puppeteers in Oregon's territorial era.

Albert G. Hovey—The court clerk who copied and kept the record for Nimrod's trial and appeal was chosen as one of Oregon's delegates to the 1860 Republican Party national convention in Chicago. Like most Oregon delegates, Hovey did not attend the convention, but gave his proxy to eastern Republicans, with instructions to cast a presidential vote for William Seward. After many ballots, the proxies led by Horace Greeley voted for Abraham Lincoln instead. Thus was Hovey's absence a factor in Lincoln's candidacy. In 1864, Hovey became a state senator in Oregon, and in 1891 he was elected mayor of Eugene, Oregon.

The Executives

Joseph P. Lane—His term in office as Oregon's territorial delegate to Congress far outlasted his stay as Oregon's first territorial governor. His influence on presidential appointments to Oregon offices had a deep impact on Nimrod's case and claim. In the 1860 national election, Lane was the vice presidential candidate on the Southern Democrat ticket. After Lincoln's victory and the start of the Civil War, Lane limped back to Oregon. Once a military hero and favorite son on the frontier, his pro-South stand during a time of Union rallying brought him no fanfares. Rather, he was marked a traitor and hanged in effigy. In Benton County, however, he was celebrated. His son, John Lane, fought for the Confederacy. After the war, his other son, Lafayette Lane, became a U.S. Congressman from Oregon. His grandson, Harry Lane, was mayor of Portland and a U.S. Senator. But Lane himself never made it back into the political graces of Oregonians. In 1867, he was baptized and confirmed a Catholic. He died in 1881 at age eighty.

John Pollard Gaines—After delaying Nimrod's first hanging date for one month, Gaines' governorship fell to the spoils system. Unlike most other unseated federal appointees, he and his second wife chose to remain in Oregon. He made a brief attempt at re-entering politics in 1855, running unsuccessfully against Joe Lane for the Oregon delegate seat in Congress. He died in 1857 at age sixty-two. Ironically, his final resting-place is in Salem, the town he had stubbornly refused to move to during and after the "location quarrel."

John Wesley Davis—Within a few months after changing Nimrod's punishment from death to two years imprisonment at hard labor, Davis quit the governorship and returned to his home in Indiana. He died in 1859 at the likely age of sixty-nine. His birth year is something of a mystery. Howard Corning says he was born in 1779, Malcolm Clark and George Himes indicate 1799, and George Turnbull says it was 1790. Turnbull's assigned birth for Davis (1790) seems most nearly in keeping with a chronology of Davis's achievements.

George Law Curry—When serving as Oregon's last territorial governor, Curry cut two months off Nimrod's two-year imprisonment. During Curry's governorship, a newly created coastal county was named for him. When Oregon gained statehood, Oregon lawmakers sought to have Curry serve as a U.S. Senator, but the effort was one vote short in the legislative balloting. From there, Curry's favor declined, and he returned to work as a newspaper editor. He died in 1878 at age fifty-eight.

Andrew Johnson—Like Nimrod, President Johnson narrowly escaped his pursuers. He was almost removed from the presidency in the year following his issuance of Nimrod's patent for the Long Tom claim. The House voted in favor of impeaching him, but the Senate fell one vote shy of the necessary two-thirds majority needed to remove him. Johnson finished the final year of his presidential term and died six years later in 1875, at age sixty-seven.

The Family

Benjamin Garrett O'Kelly—This son, apparently a bachelor all his life, stayed on in Lane County and died there at some unknown time.

Charles O'Kelly—The Missouri son, who wrote that he might one day come to Oregon, never did.

Joseph Bell O'Kelly—This son, with wife Matilda and family, left Lane County and crossed the Cascades to the Ochoco country of central Oregon, establishing themselves as early pioneers in the towns of Mitchell and Prineville. A streamlet there is named O'Kelly Creek. Joseph and Matilda died in 1882–83.

Nimrod O'Kelly, Junior—Like his father, Nimrod junior was indeed a rolling stone. After a stint in the southern Oregon gold fields and what appears to be an August 1859 elopement in Lane County before a justice of the peace, he and wife

Jefelia Clover moved to Washington Territory, where sons Jasper and Jefferson were born. By August 1864, Nimrod junior and his family were back in Oregon living in Clackamas County. On April 2, 1865, the two sons were baptized by a Catholic priest, apparently in Portland, even though both parents were listed as "non-Catholic."

Three days after the baptism and four days before the Civil War ended, Nimrod junior left the family to enlist in the Oregon Volunteers at Fort Vancouver for a three-year term. On the military muster rolls of Company D of the First Cavalry Regiment, he was described as "age 24, hight 6 feet, complexion light, eyes blue, hair brown, born Tennessee, occupation blacksmith." Following his military tour, he and Jefelia apparently moved to Scottsburg in Douglas County south of the Willamette Valley, where on October 20, 1868, they were baptized by a Catholic priest (but with no indication of abjuration or conversion).

In November 1869, Nimrod junior and his family were back in Lane County living with brother Benjamin and mother Sally. Apparently, by this time brother Joseph and family had moved to eastern Oregon. In October 1877, in federal district court at Portland, Nimrod the younger was found guilty of the crime of "disposing spiritous liquors to an Indian." Presiding Judge Matthew P. Deady gave the convict a choice of sentences: thirty days in prison, or one day in prison plus a $30 fine. The record does not indicate what choice was made. The 1880 federal census showed Nimrod and Jefelia living by themselves in Portland. He was listed as an unemployed blacksmith. By 1885 Jefelia was living in Portland with just two sons. Like Nimrod the father, Nimrod the younger was simply gone.

Jefelia Clover O'Kelly—Sometimes "Gefalia" or "Yefelia," a possible corruption of Ophelia, she seems to have outlasted all of her immediate O'Kelly in-laws. In 1885 she lived at 376 Water Street in Portland. The 1887 *Portland City Directory* listed her as a "housekeeper" living alone. The 1903 *Directory* showed her at 344 Front Street as a "widow." She died in Portland on December 16, 1919, at the age of seventy-four, according to an *Oregonian* obituary, which would have made her fourteen or fifteen years old when she married Nimrod junior and had her first child.

Sarah "Sally" Bell (Burk?) O'Kelly—The exact time and place of death of Nimrod's widow remains unknown. Customarily, she would have been laid to rest at her late husband's side. But circumstance may have parted them in death, just as it had parted them numerous times in their lives. Perhaps their marker or markers will surface one day, as has this, their story.

William Nimrod O'Kelly—This grandson of Nimrod the elder was the son of Charles O'Kelly of Missouri. He was the main source of information for

Lawrence A. McNary's 1935 article, "Oregon's First Reported Murder Case."
McNary wrote:

> A grandson and namesake of Nimrod O'Kelly is now living near Independence,
> in Polk County, and makes the statement that O'Kelly, several years after con-
> viction, visited relatives in Missouri…The present Nimrod O'Kelly states that
> he…heard from…[his grandmother] a recital of the circumstances.

In 1856 in the Ozarks, when five years old, grandson Nimrod would have
met his pioneering namesake during the elder Nimrod's long mission through
Missouri to Washington City. Like his grandpappy Nimrod and his uncle Nimrod, this third Nimrod had wander in his craw. In 1871, when he was twenty,
the youngest Nimrod made the journey to Oregon and to his granny Sally's knee,
where he heard her tales of his dead forefather—stories of the claim, the killing,
the trial, the conviction, and the near hangings. She must have fibbed when she
told him that Sheriff Right had set Nimrod free. Thus was McNary eventually
misled. Sally knew full well that her husband had been imprisoned at hard labor.
Perhaps the yarn was her way of keepsaking a more cherished memory within
their grandchild's mind.

William Nimrod died at Independence, Oregon, during World War II, some
seventy-eight years after his grandfather's death during the Civil War. The grandson's death certificate showed him to be "91 years old," and "a blacksmith." In
name, age, and trade, he followed and vanished along the ancestral path.

The Long Tom Square Mile

A final "character" must be traced, because it had the greatest sway in Nimrod's
story. The "being" evoked is the patch of land staked out by Nimrod. Gone are
the postal towns of Starrs Point, Boonville, and Jennyopolis. Gone are the denizens of that frontier. Gone are the swards, swales, and swashes. Gone is the claim
itself. But the land, needless to say, is still there. On paper it has been divided and
parceled out, but to the eye it is still an unbroken expanse of farmland with a few
roads, rails, fences, and wires to streak its surface. Where once was the *kalapuya*
are now crops. An aged farmhouse sits about where Nimrod's "miserable hovel"
would have been. A few old firs and cedars poke at the sky and are possibly old
enough to give testament to all here told.

Not far off, the Long Tom yet curls in its banks. Winkle's Butte still rises
above the near countryside, albeit it has been called "Irwin's Butte," and sometimes "Wagner Butte." Side roads in the area today are markers of those times
gone by—Starr Road, Barclay Road, Grimsley Road, Greenberry Road, and Bellfountain Road. The old Gold Miners' Trail is now State Route 99W, still labeled
the "Territorial Highway."

About twelve miles south of Corvallis on the highway, Bruce Road con-
nects from the west and Eureka Road from the east. Those two roads form a line

roughly marking the south border of Nimrod's old claim. Eureka Road appears to lie along the bottom of the "ravine" described in the 1846 Provisional Government land record book. Running parallel to and west of the highway are the rails of the Southern Pacific Railroad, which closely align with the west border of the old claim. Modern maps still carry the names "Rickard" and "Bruce" to designate the old whistlestops on that train route. No recognition has ever been given to the fact that Rickard and Bruce took their beginnings from a land claim pioneered by Nimrod O'Kelly.

The William L. Finley National Wildlife Refuge is located just west of the claim. Far from exact, but nevertheless about as close as can be, the refuge is a sample of the lay of the land in Nimrod's day. It covers six to eight square miles and includes the old donation land claims of Abner Lloyd, John Foster, John Fiechter, and Jacob Slagle. Fiechter's house, designed by Justice of the Peace Abiather Newton and built when Nimrod roamed that land, still stands in the refuge and is among the oldest structures in Oregon.

The Long Tom area has grown—without dying. Land can be wounded, but unlike Nimrod and his fellow denizens, land does not grow old. It simply evolves, grows anew. It is as close to a creator as one can get. It is creation. Our Indian friends have always had that right.

Chapter References

Chapter 1: The Inquest, May 22, 1852

BOOKS/MONOGRAPHS: Corning, *Dictionary of Oregon History*, "Willamette Prairie" "Willamette Valley"; Fagan, *Benton County*, 323–27, 332–33, 505 et seq.; McArthur, *Oregon Geographic Names*, "Long Tom River" "Marys River" "Monroe" "Jennyopolis" "Winkle Butte"; Lansing, J., *Portland*, 1–2; Victor, *All Over Oregon and Washington*, 179; Wojcik, *Brazen Overlanders*, 381 et seq.; WPA, *Inventory—Benton County*, A-43–45.

PERIODICAL: Boag, "The Valley of the Long Grasses," *Old Oregon* (Winter 1992):18 et seq.

NEWSPAPER: *Spectator*, "Gross Prosecution," February 18, 1854.

LAW: "Twenty Acts Code" (1849–50), Coroners, sections 5, 6, 11, 12, 14, 15, 17.

DOCUMENTS: "Benton County Commissioners' Journal, 1850–54," (July 1852 term) 27–28, 36; "Coroner's Inquest," re: Mahoney, May 22, 1852.

MAPS: Jennyopolis, Marysville, and Starrs Point township topographical maps, 1853.

PERSONAL CONTACT: Janice Barclay (wife of James "Sib" Barclay descendant), letter to author, September 9, 1994.

Chapter 2: The Migration, 1845

BOOKS/MONOGRAPHS: Clark and Tiller, *Terrible Trail*, passim; Douglas, *History of Southeast Missouri*, 798; Johansen and Gates, *Empire of the Columbia*, 251–52, 254–62, 270–71; Fawkes, *Journal of Walter Griffith Pigman*, 25; Randall V. Mills, "Oregon Speechways," in *American Speech*, 85; Newsom, *Western Observer*, 199; Paxson, *History of the American Frontier*, 45; Wojcik, *Brazen Overlanders*, passim, viz. 12, 379, 469.

NEWSPAPERS: *Oregonian*, August 1, 1886; *Statesman*, June 1, 1852.

DOCUMENTS: Benjamin Cornelius Sr. and Peyton Wilkes, affidavits, February 25, 1854; Nimrod O'Kelly, letter to Governor Davis, April 16, 1854.

Chapter 3: The Arrival and the Search, 1845–46

BOOKS/MONOGRAPHS: Applegate, *Recollections of My Boyhood*, 58–59; Blanchet, *Historical Sketches of the Catholic Church*, 21; Burnett, *Recollections and Opinions*, 181; Carey, *History of Oregon*, 446–51, 751; Corning, *Dictionary of Oregon History*, "Howison's Report" "Warre and Vavasour Report" "Willamette Mission, Methodist" "Mission Bottom" "St. Paul" "Bounty Laws" "Willamette Prairie" "Ferries"; Corning, *Willamette Landings*, 144–45; Fagan, *History of Benton County*, 323–26; Genealogical Forum, *Provisional Land Claims, Abstracted*, 79; Lang, *History of the Willamette Valley*, 288; Lockley, *Oregon Yesterdays*, 21; McArthur, *Oregon Geographic Names*, "Portland" "Salem" "Oregon City" "Linnton" "Marys River" "Corvallis"; McKay, *St. Paul, Oregon*, xi, 14; Munnick. *Catholic Church Records, [St. Paul]* xx, 1, 134, 143; O'Donnell, *An Arrow in the Earth*, 50–52; O'Hara, *Pioneer Catholic History*, 14–15; Victor, *Atlantis Arisen*, 108; Wojcik, *Brazen Overlanders*, 363–70; WPA, *Inventory—Benton County*, A-10–12, A-43–45.

PERIODICALS: Horner, "The Legend of Chintimini," *Oregon Magazine* (November 1924):7–8; Howison, "Report on Oregon, 1846," *QOHS* 14:1, 23, 25, 45; Vaughan and Winch, "Joseph Gervais," *OHQ* 66:331.

DOCUMENTS: "Oregon Provisional Government Land Claim Records," Nimrod O'Kelly, vol. 4, 107; James Shiel, et al., petition, August 16, 1852.

Chapter 4: Staking, Fall 1846

BOOKS/MONOGRAPHS: Fagan, *History of Benton County*, 369–70; Harris, *Look of the Old West*, 280–81; Oregon State Archives, *Echoes of Oregon*, 18–19; Snyder, *We Claimed This Land*, xiv–xv, and *Portland Names and Neighborhoods*, 15, 27–28.

NEWSPAPERS: *Oregonian*, June 3, 1852; *Statesman*, June 1, 1852.

LAW: *Organic Law of the Provisional Government of Oregon* (1845), Preamble, article III, sections 1, 3, 5.

DOCUMENT: J.C. Alexander, statement, July 30, 1852.

Chapter 5: Filing and Converting, Late 1846

BOOKS/MONOGRAPHS: Barnhart and Metcalf, *America in So Many Words,* 117–18; Boag, *Environment and Experience*, 101, 178 n.12; Carey, *History of Oregon*, 391, 399; Carstensen, *Public Lands*, xiii; Corning, *Dictionary of Oregon History*, "Polk County"; Dodds, *American Northwest*, 60; *History of the Bench and Bar of Oregon*, 19; Hulbert, *Frontiers*, 93–95; Johansen and Gates, *Empire of the Columbia*, 290; Munnick, *Catholic Church Records, [Oregon City]* Annotations A-3 "1846," *[St. Paul]* 150; O'Hara, *Pioneer Catholic History*, 15, 112.

PERIODICALS: Barker, "Estate of Dr. John McLoughlin," *OHQ* 50:162; Gatke, "Letters of the Reverend William M. Roberts," *OHQ* 23:182–83; Howison, "Report on Oregon, 1846," *QOHS* 14:1; Rockwood, "Diary of Reverend George H. Atkinson," *OHQ* 46:352; Vaughan and Winch, "Joseph Gervais," *OHQ* 66:358.

NEWSPAPER: *Spectator*, November 1, 1849.

LAWS: "Hamilton Code" (1851), Land Claims, 164–65; *Organic Law of the Provisional Government of Oregon* (1845), article III, sections 1, 2.

DOCUMENTS: "Oregon Provisional Government Land Claim Records," Nimrod O'Kelly, vol. 4, 107, J.C. Avery, vol. 1, 44, George Neal, vol. 1, 1, Greenberry Smith, vol. 7, 188.

Chapter 6: Improving and Subsisting, 1847–48

BOOKS/MONOGRAPHS: Banks, *An Oregon Boyhood*, 11–12, 44–45; Belknap, *Oregon Imprints*, 43; Boag, *Environment and Experience*, 47, 57–59, 61–62, 104, 107–8, 123; Bowen, *Willamette Valley*, 12–14; Cole, *Early Oregon*, 16–17, 29; Corning, *Dictionary of Oregon History*, "Bounty"; Dicken, *Making of Oregon*, 73–74, 76; Fagan, *History of Benton County*, 324; Harris, *Look of the Old West*, 280–81; Helbock, *Oregon Post Offices*, "Astoria" "Oregon City"; Lockley, *Oregon Yesterdays*, 27–28, 91–93; McArthur, *Oregon Geographic Names*, "Camas Valley"; Nash, *Oregon: There and Back*, 196–200, and *Two Years in Oregon*, 28–30; O'Donnell, *An Arrow in the Earth*, 54; O'Hara, *Pioneer Catholic History*, 176; Oregon State Archives, *Echoes of Oregon*, doc. 7; Parrish, *Historic Oregon*, 155; Ramsey, *Coyote Was Going There*, 119; Rawie, "History of the Carter Family," 74–75, 101–4, App. B, 98–102; Robbins, *Landscapes of Promise*, 74, 98–99; Russell, *Firearms, Traps, and Tools*, 360, 364–66; Shinn, *Mining Camps*, 222–24; Thomas, *Chinook*, "Camas"; Tobie, *No Man Like Joe*, 111, 126; Wojcik, *Brazen Overlanders*, 371, 382, 459, 465–66, 472; WPA, *Inventory—Benton County*, A-20, 12–13.

PERIODICALS: Bromberg, "Frontier Humor," *OHQ* 61:311–13; Davenport, "Recollections," *QOHS* 8:260; Gatke, "[Ketturah Belknap's] Bellfountain Settlement," *OHQ* 36:269; *Harper's New Monthly Magazine* (October 1882):766; Howison, "Report on Oregon, 1846," *QOHS* 14:51; Ingersoll, "In the Wahlamet Valley of Oregon," Rockwood, "Diary of Reverend George H. Atkinson," *OHQ* 46:352;

NEWSPAPER: *Corvallis Gazette-Times*, June 7, 1935.

LAW: *Organic Law of the Provisional Government of Oregon* (1845), article III, section 2.

DOCUMENTS: J.C. Alexander, statement, July 30, 1852; "Benton County Property Assessment Rolls," 1850, 1851; Robert Earl, "Reminiscences"; Nimrod O'Kelly, declaration (undated), filed June 3, 1852, and letter to "Governor" Lane, June 4, 1852.

MAP: Jennyopolis Township Topographical Map, 1853.

Chapter 7: The Neighbors, 1847–48

BOOKS/MONOGRAPHS: Banks, *An Oregon Boyhood*, 21–22; Bowen, "Oregon Frontiersman," in Vaughan, *The Western Shore*, 195–96; Cole, *Early Oregon*, 2, 9–22; Corning, *Dictionary of Oregon History*, "Bellfountain Settlement" "Robert A. Booth, Rev." "Scott-Applegate Trail"; Douglas, *History of Southeast Missouri*, 798; Fagan, *History of Benton County*, 323, 331–32; Friedman, *Tracking Down Oregon*, 115–17; Genealogical Forum, *Provisional Land Claims, Abstracted*, "Waman C. Hembree" "Amon Richardson"; Hine and Bingham, *The Frontier Experience*, 411–13; Karolevitz, *Newspapering in the Old West*, 26, 28, 130–31; Lockley, *Conversations with Pioneer Women*, 89; Macon, *Four O'Kelley Sons*, 4; McArthur, *Oregon Geographic Names*, "Skinner Butte" "Eugene," "Marys River"; Mintonye, *They Laughed Too*, passim; Nash, *Two Years in Oregon*, 196–97; Rawie, "History of the Carter Family," App. B, 98, et seq.; Wojcik, *Brazen Overlanders*, 418, 451; WPA, *Inventory—Benton County*, A-10–11, 14–16, 18, 26–27, 65–66, 71–73; Louis Wright, "Religion and the Frontier," in Hine and Bingham, *Frontier Experience*, 413–14.

PERIODICALS: Bromberg, "Frontier Humor," *OHQ* 61:271–74; Gatke, "[Ketturah Belknap's] Bell-fountain Settlement," *OHQ* 36:265, 267–74, 276, 281–83, 286, 289–90; Gatke, "Letters of the Reverend William M. Roberts," *OHQ* 23:175, 178, 182–84; Rockwood, "Diary of Reverend George H. Atkinson," *OHQ* 46:352–53.

NEWSPAPERS: *Corvallis Gazette*, December 31, 1880; *Spectator*, September 7, 1848.

DOCUMENT: Nimrod O'Kelly, letter to "Governor" Lane, December 5, 1851.

MAPS: Jennyopolis, Marysville, and Starrs Point township topographical maps, 1853; "Sketch of the Wallamette Valley…," Gibbs and Stadling, 1851.

PERSONAL CONTACT: Mary Jane Sorber (descendant of Robert Heron, Irish Bend pioneer), interview, August 25, 1994.

Chapter 8: Change, 1847–49

BOOKS/MONOGRAPHS: Applegate, *Recollections of My Boyhood*, 91; *Atlas of Oregon*, 16–17; Boag, *Environment and Experience*, 73, 80, 104–8; Carey, *General History of Oregon*, vol. 2:647 et seq.; Carstensen, *Public Lands*, xiii–xv; Corning, *Dictionary of Oregon History*, "Peter Burnett"; Dicken, *Making of Oregon*, 76; Fagan, *History of Benton County*, 368, 392, 422–24; Hine and Lottinville, *Soldier in the West*, 122; Dorothy O. Johansen, "The Land Base of Oregon's Economy," Genealogical Forum, *Donation Land Claims, Abstracted*, vol. 2:intro.; Johansen and Gates, *Empire of the Columbia*, 286; Lansing, *Juggernaut*, 17, 33, 121; Lockley, *Oregon Yesterdays*, 92; McArthur, *Oregon Geographic Names*, "Benton County" "Corvallis"; Nash, *Two Years in Oregon*, 35; O'Donnell, *An Arrow in the Earth*, 66 et seq.; O'Hara, *Pioneer Catholic History*, 147; Oregon State Archives, *Echoes of Oregon*, doc. 8, p. 16; Parrish, *Historic Oregon*, 154–55; Victor, *Early Indian Wars*, 503 et seq.; Wojcik, *Brazen Overlanders*, 379, 495; WPA, *Inventory—Benton County*, A-12, A-19–20, 37–39, 41–42.

PERIODICALS: Bromberg, "Frontier Humor," *OHQ* 61:326; Himes, "A History of the Press of Oregon," *QOHS* 3:353.

NEWSPAPERS: *Corvallis Gazette-Times*, June 7, 1935; *Spectator*, April 20, May 18, June 1, September 7, 1848.

LAWS: "Hamilton Code" (1851), Settlers on Public Lands, section 1, p. 246; *Act to Establish the Territorial Government of Oregon* (1848), section 14.

DOCUMENTS: "Benton County Circuit Court Fee Journal, 1851–1858," vol. 1, 1; "DLC Notification File No. 2087" (Nimrod O'Kelly); U.S. Seventh Census (1850), Benton County, Oregon, q.v. "John Kelly."

Chapter 9: The Land Law, 1850

BOOKS/MONOGRAPHS: Boag, *Environment and Experience*, 50–52 n.16, 116 et seq.; Carstensen, *Public Lands*, xiii–xvii, xxiii–xxv; Clark, *Eden Seekers*, 230–32, 237–39; Fogdall, *Royal Family*, 272–75; Gates, *Public Land Law Development*, 118–19; Hulbert, *Frontiers*, 86–95; Dorothy O. Johansen, "The Roll*[sic]* of Land Laws in the Settlement of Oregon," Genealogical Forum, *Donation Land Claims, Abstracted*, vol. 1:intro.; Dorothy O. Johansen, "The Land Base of Oregon's Economy," Genealogical Forum, *Donation Land Claims, Abstracted*, vol. 2:intro.; Lang, *History of the Willamette Valley*, 245–46, 261–62; Lansing, *Juggernaut*, 14, 41, 99, passim; Stegner, *Beyond the Hundredth Meridian*, xx; WPA, Inventory—Benton County, A-42.

PERIODICALS: Berquist, "The Oregon Donation Act," *OHQ* 58:21–23, 24–28, 31–33; Johnson, D.A., "The Donation Land Act," *Oregon Humanities* (Winter 1994):9–11; Johnson, D.C., "Oregon Territorial Supreme Court, 1849–1859," *Environmental Law* 4:16–26; Perry et al., "Spousal Letters of Samuel R. Thurston," *OHQ* 96:9, 11, 12, 44, 47, 74 n.99; Pisani, "Squatter Land in California," *WHQ* 25:284–85; Stoel, "The McLoughlin Land Grab," *Oregon Benchmarks* 7:2; Teiser, "William P. Bryant," *OHQ* 48:46–47, 49, 51–53.

LAWS: *Act to Establish the Territorial Government of Oregon* (1848), section 14; "Donation Land Claim Act," sections 1, 2, 3, 4, 5, 19, 26; *Organic Law of the Provisional Government of Oregon* (1845), article III, sections 1, 3.

Chapter 10: Letters to Washington City, 1851–52

BOOKS/MONOGRAPHS: Helbock, *Oregon Post Offices*, "Avery's" "Forks of Mary's River" "Jennyopolis" "Oregon City" "Starrs Point" map p. 136; McArthur, *Oregon Geographic Names*, "Corvallis."

DOCUMENTS: Nimrod O'Kelly, letters, to Congress, August 30, 1851, and to "Governor" Lane, December 5, 1851, and June 4, 1852.

Chapter 11: Crowding and Killing, 1850–52

BOOKS/MONOGRAPHS: Bancroft, *History of Oregon*, vol. 2:208–12; Beckham, *Indians of Western Oregon*, 44, 123–26; Boag, *Environment and Experience*, 42, 67 n.3, 174; Carey, *General History of Oregon*, vol. 2:548–54; Clark, *History of the Willamette Valley*, vol. 1:68–69; Corning, *Dictionary of Oregon History*, "Umpqua County" "Willamette Stone"; Fagan, *History of Benton County*, 369, 506–7, 518, 529–30; Genealogical Forum, *Donation Land Claims, Abstracted*, "Joseph Blackerby"(307) "William Barclay"(1467) "James E. Barclay"(1609) "John Fiechter"(3375) "Robert D. Grimsley"(3724) "Wiley Winkle"(3864) "Richard Irwin"(3865) "Jeremiah Criss"(4059) "Asa Stark"(4060) "Jeremiah Mahoney"(rejected) "Montgomery Winkle"(rejected); Genealogical Forum, *Provisional Land Claims, Abstracted*, "John Fiechter" (184); Helbock, *Oregon Post Offices*, "Jennyopolis"; Hine and Lottinville, *Soldier in the West*, 169; Hodge, *Handbook of American Indians*, "Kalapooian Family" "Joseph"; Dorothy O. Johansen, "The [Role] of Land Laws in the Settlement of Oregon," Genealogical Forum, *Donation Land Claims, Abstracted*, vol. 1: intro.; Dorothy O. Johansen, "The Land Base of Oregon's Economy," Genealogical Forum, *Donation Land Claims, Abstracted*, vol. 2:intro.; Johansen and Gates, *Empire of the Columbia*, 270–71, 307–8; Locksley, *Pioneer Women*, 206; Randall V. Mills, "Oregon Speechways," in *American Speech*, 85; O'Donnell, *An Arrow in the Earth*, 137–38; Rawie, "History of the Carter Family," App. C, 111; Shinn, *Mining Camps*, 224; Turnbull, *History of Oregon Newspapers*, 52–53, 55–56, 80; Ward and Maveety, *Pacific Northwest Women*, 93; WPA, *Inventory—Benton County*, A-5–6, A-43–46, 50; WPA, *Inventory—Linn County*, A-6–7; Zucker, Hummel, and Hogfoss, *Oregon Indians*, 66, 80–85, 179–80.

PERIODICALS: Gatke, "[Ketturah Belknap's] Bellfountain Settlement," *OHQ* 36:274, 280, 282; Gatke, "Letters of the Reverend William M. Roberts," *OHQ* 23:179.

NEWSPAPERS: *Oregonian,* "Horrible Murder," June 3, 1852, "Pioneer Days," August 1, 1886; *Spectator,* June 1, 1852, "Gross Persecution," February 18, 1854; *Statesman,* "Foul Murder in Benton County," June 1, 1852.

LAWS: *Act to Establish the Territorial Government of Oregon* (1848), section 1; *Johnson v. McIntosh, U.S. Reports* (1832), vol. 5; "Northwest Ordinance of 1787," article III; *Organic Law of the Provisional Government of Oregon* (1845), article I, section 3.

MAPS: "A Diagram of Public Surveys of Oregon," 1853; Jennyopolis and Starrs Point township claims maps, 1861; Jennyopolis and Starrs Point township topographical maps, 1853; "Sketch of the Wallamette Valley. . . ," Gibbs and Stadling, 1851.

DOCUMENTS: J.C. Alexander, statement, July 30, 1852; Richard Irwin and Isaac W. Winkle, letter to Governor Gaines, August 17, 1850 [1852]; Nimrod O'Kelly, declaration (undated), filed June 3, 1852, and letters, to "Governor" Lane, June 4, 1852, and to Governor Davis, April 16, 1854.

PERSONAL CONTACT: Janice Barclay (wife of James "Sib" Barclay descendant), letter to author, September 9, 1994.

Chapter 12: Peace Justice Court, May 1852

BOOKS/MONOGRAPHS: Belknap, *Oregon Imprints,* 40, 43–44; Fagan, *History of Benton County,* 371, 392, 527; Lansing, *Juggernaut,* 24, 41, 118–19 n.46; WPA, *Inventory—Benton County,* A-15, 42, 71.

PERIODICALS: Beardsley, "Code Making in Early Oregon," *PNQ* 27:6–12, 15–20, 22–23; Gatke, "[Ketturah Belknap's] Bellfountain Settlement," *OHQ* 36:280, 287; Hunt, "Law and Land in a Stateless Society," *Wisconsin Law Review* (1980):1212; Kelly, "History of the Preparation of the First Code of Oregon," *QOHS* 4:185–88; McNary, "Oregon's First Reported Murder Case," *OHQ* 36:360.

NEWSPAPERS: *Camp Adair Sentry,* October 15, 1942; *Oregonian,* "Horrible Murder," June 3, 1852; *Statesman,* November 11, 1851, "Foul Murder in Benton County," June 1, 1852.

LAWS: "Hamilton Code" (1851), Judicial Districts, 158–59; "Twenty Acts Code" (1849–50), Justices of the Peace, sections 1, 2, 9, Coroners, sections 1, 4, 11, 14, 16, Preliminary Proceedings, section 1.

DOCUMENTS: "Benton County Commissioners' Journal, 1850–54," 25, 27–29; "Coroner's Inquest," re: Mahoney, May 22, 1852; William F. Dixon, statement, August 23, 1852; Miletus W. Ellis, affidavit, August 23, 1852; "Justice Court Proceedings File," June 3, 1852; Nimrod O'Kelly, letter to "Governor" Lane, June 4, 1852.

Chapter 13: Pre-trial, June 1852

BOOKS/MONOGRAPHS: Bancroft, *History of Oregon,* vol. 2:155–56 n.28; Lang, *History of the Willamette Valley,* 591; Lockley, *Oregon Yesterdays,* 22–23.

NEWSPAPER: *Statesman,* September 4, 1852.

LAWS: "Hamilton Code" (1851), District Judges, special terms, 100–1, Juries, sections 2, 7; "Twenty Acts Code" (1849–50), Jurors, sections 2, 7.

DOCUMENTS: "Benton County Circuit Court Fee Journal, 1851–1858," vol. 1, 13–14; "Benton County Circuit Court Journals," 1852, 6, 21–26; "Last Will and Testament of Nimrod O'Kelly," June 28, 1852; Nimrod O'Kelly, letter to "Governor" Lane, June 4, 1852; Supreme Court file, *Nimrod O'Kelly,*

Appel. v. Territory of Oregon, Res., orders (venire) from Clerk Hovey to Sheriff, June 18, 1852; *Territory of Oregon v. Nimrod O'Kelly*, witness subpoenas.

Chapter 14: Trial—First Day, June 29, 1852

BOOKS/MONOGRAPHS: Adams, *A Melodrame Entitled "Treason, Stratagems, and Spoils,"* 3–4, 86–87, n.41; Bancroft, *History of Oregon*, vol. 2:159; Clark, *Pharisee among Philistines*, xxvi; Cole, *Early Oregon*, 1, 31–33, 66–69; Genealogical Forum, *Donation Land Claims, Abstracted*, "Reuben P. Boise"; *History of the Bench and Bar of Oregon*, 36–37, 259–60, 273–74; Johansen and Gates, *Empire of the Columbia*, 9; Lansing, *Juggernaut*, 4, 12–14, 27, 116 n.30; Nash, *Two Years in Oregon*, 186; Tobie, *No Man Like Joe*, 204; Turnbull, *History of Oregon Newspapers*, 80, 226; Woodward, *Political Parties in Oregon*, 51–57; WPA, *Inventory—Benton County*, A-41.

PERIODICALS: Bromberg, "Frontier Humor," *OHQ* 61:291, 312; Johnson, D.C., "Oregon Territorial Supreme Court, 1849–1859," *Environmental Law* 4:33, 40, 44, 45, 51; Menefree and Tiller, "Cutoff Fever," *OHQ* 78:42–44, 141–43; Pratt, "Twenty Two Letters of David Logan," *OHQ* 44:262; Teiser, "O.C. Pratt," *OHQ* 49:180, 185, 187, 191, passim.

NEWSPAPERS: *Oregon Weekly Times*, "Murder Trial in Benton County," July 10, August 28, 1852; *Oregonian*, June 4, July 7, 1853; *Spectator*, "Gross Persecution," February 18, 1854.

LAWS: "Big Bluebook" (1849), Criminal Procedure, section 66; "Hamilton Code" (1851), Juries, sections 1, 2, 3, 4, Judicial Districts, District Judges; "Little Bluebook" (1843), Criminal Procedure, section 66; *Nimrod O'Kelly v. Territory of Oregon*, 1 *Oregon Reports* 5 (1853), 55–56; 1 *Oregon Reports* 9, Attorneys—When Admitted; "Twenty Acts Code" (1849–50), Jurors, sections 1, 2, 3, 4.

DOCUMENTS: "Benton County Circuit Court Fee Journal, 1851–1858," vol. 1, 14; "Benton County Circuit Court Journal, 1852," 1, 6, 21–26; "Benton County Commissioners' Journal, 1850–54," 25, 35–36, 72; Matthew Deady, letter to Asahel Bush, September 20, 1852; John T. Fortson, letter to Governor Gaines, August 12, 1852; Nimrod O'Kelly, letters, to "Governor" Lane, June 4, 1852, and to Governor Davis, April 16, 1854; Supreme Court file, *O'Kelly v. T.O.*, trial court minutes, indictment; *Territory of Oregon Territory v. Nimrod O'Kelly*, indictment.

Chapter 15: Trial—Second Day, June 30, 1852

BOOKS/MONOGRAPHS: Bancroft, *History of Oregon*, vol. 2:155–56 n.28; Belknap, *Oregon Imprints*, 43; Fagan, *History of Benton County*, 323, 525, 526; Fisher, *Evidence*, 327–29, 860; Genealogical Forum, *Donation Land Claims, Abstracted*, various claimants; Lockley, *Oregon Yesterdays*, 90–91; WPA, *Inventory—Benton County*, A-10–11, A-13–14.

PERIODICALS: Berquist, "The Oregon Donation Act," *OHQ* 58:32; Bromberg, "Frontier Humor," *OHQ* 61:293; Hunt, "Law and Land in a Stateless Society," *Wisconsin Law Review* (1980):1209–10.

NEWSPAPERS: *Oregon Weekly Times*, "Murder Trial in Benton County," July 10, 1852; *Oregonian*, "Horrible Murder," June 3, 1852; *Spectator*, May 27, 1847, "Gross Persecution," February 18, 1854.

LAWS: "Deady-Lane Code of 1874," Oregon Civil Code, chapter 8, Title III, section 700, p. 251, Oregon Criminal Code, Title I, chapter XVI, section 165, p. 361; "Hamilton Code" (1851), Juries, sections 5, 7, 8, 9, 10, Crimes and Misdemeanors, sections 1–3, 38, 78, Oaths and Affirmations, p. 183, Practice, section 37; "Oregon Code of 1854," chapter IV (Of Evidence), Title I, (Of Competency of Witnesses), sections 3, 4, p. 111; *Oregon Revised Statutes*, Chapter 163 (1997); *Scott v. Cook*, 1 *Oregon Reports* 24 (1853); *Thompson v. Backenstos*, 1 *Oregon Reports* 17 (1853); "Twenty Acts Code" (1849–50), Jurors, sections 8, 10, Crimes and Punishments, sections 1–19.

DOCUMENTS: J.C. Alexander, statement, July 30, 1852; "Benton County Circuit Court Journal, 1852," 21–26; "Coroner's Inquest," re: Mahoney, May 22, 1852; Miletus W. Ellis, affidavit, August 23, 1852; Ambrose and Mary Ann Fitzgerald, letter to Nimrod O'Kelly, March 7, 1852; L.G. Hoge, statement, August 16, 1852; Richard Irwin and Isaac W. Winkle, letter to Governor Gaines, August 17, 1850 [1852]; Charles L. and Rebecca O'Kelly, letter to Nimrod O'Kelly, March 28, 1852; Nimrod O'Kelly, declaration (undated), filed June 3, 1852, and letters to Governor Davis, April 16 and May 16, 1854; O.C. Pratt, letter to Governor Davis, February 22, 1854; *Territory of Oregon v. Nimrod O'Kelly*, verdict; John Thorp, letter to Governor Gaines, September 22, 1852; J.P. Welsh and J.C. Alexander, letter to Governor Gaines, August 18, 1852.

Chapter 16: Trial—Last Day, July 1, 1852

BOOK: Fagan, *History of Benton County*, 380.

LAWS: "Hamilton Code" (1851), Crimes and Misdemeanors, section 35, District Judge, section 4, Fees and Costs, 146–52; "Little Bluebook" (1843) and "Big Bluebook" (1849), Criminal Procedure, section 89.

DOCUMENTS: "Benton County Commissioners' Journal, 1850–54," 24–25, 27–28, 35–36, 42, 72; "Benton County Circuit Court Fee Journal, 1851–1858," vol. 1, 13–14; "Benton County Circuit Court Journal, 1852," 21–26; Sheriff Samuel F. Starr, "Lists of Benton County taxpayers," ca. August 1852; *Territory of Oregon v. Nimrod O'Kelly*, motion for arrest of judgment, motion for judgment; John Thorp, letter to Governor Gaines, September 22, 1852.

Chapter 17: Post Trial Stirrings, July-August 1852

BOOKS/MONOGRAPHS: Bancroft, *History of Oregon*, vol. 2:172–73; Carey, *General History of Oregon*, vol. 2:469; Clark, *Eden Seekers*, 271–72; Corning, *Dictionary of Oregon History*, "Democrats" "Whigs" "Salem Clique"; Dodds, *American Northwest*, 68–69; Evans, *History of the Pacific Northwest*, 2 vols., various biographies; Johansen and Gates, *Empire of the Columbia*, 294–95; *Oregon Blue Book, 1993–94*, 343, 346–48, 379; Turnbull, *Governors of Oregon*, 22; Wojcik, *Brazen Overlanders*, "J.D. Boon"; Woodward, *Political Parties in Oregon*, 39–40, 45, 51–52; WPA, *Inventory—Benton County*, A-31.

PERIODICALS: "Bell Fountain Settlement," *OHQ* 36:286; Bromberg, "Frontier Humor," *OHQ* 61:292–93; Woodward, "Political Parties in Oregon," *QOHS* 12:37–38, 43, 49–50.

NEWSPAPERS: *Oregon Weekly Times*, July 10, September 4, 1852; *Oregonian*, June 3, July 17, August 7, 21, September 11, 1852; *Statesman*, June 12, July 10, August 28, September 25, 1852.

DOCUMENTS: J.C. Alexander, statement, July 30, 1852; William F. Dixon, certificate, August 14, 1852, affidavit, August 16, 1852, and statement, August 23, 1852; "Executive Actions Journal," August 21, 1852; John T. Fortson, letter to Governor Gaines, August 12, 1852; R.B. Hinton, letter to Nimrod O'Kelly, July 16, 1852; Richard Irwin and Isaac W. Winkle, letter to Governor Gaines, August 17, 1850 [1852]; Jacob Martin, Miletus W. Ellis, and Henry Powell (jurors), affidavit, August 16, 1852; Lewis L. Mulkey, affidavit, August 23, 1852; Thomas Norris and A. Whitley, letter to Governor Gaines, August 16, 1852; Nimrod O'Kelly, petition to Oregon Territorial Legislature, July 28, 1852, and letter to Governor Davis, April 16, 1854; Petitions to imprison [ca. August 1852], Mulkey et al., Murch et al., Russell et al., Ryburn et al., and Smith et al.; Petitions to pardon [ca. August 1852], Newell et al., petition "A," Shiel et al., Boon et al. (August 16, 1852); Henry Powell, affidavit, August 23, 1852; Remonstrances [ca. August 1852], Gage et al., Loose et al., Starr et al., Taylor et al.; Samuel F. Starr, letter to Governor Gaines [ca. August 1852]; J.P. Welsh and J.C. Alexander, letter to Governor Gaines, August 18, 1852.

Chapter 18: Pursuit of the Judges, September 1852

BOOKS/MONOGRAPHS: Bancroft, *History of Oregon*, vol. 2:139, 141, 142–43 n.8, 145–47, 159–72, 255–56 n.13; Carey, *General History of Oregon*, vol. 2:469–77, and *History of Oregon*, 497–9; Clark, *Eden Seekers*, 244–45, 251–52, 254–55; Cole, *Early Oregon*, 36, 39–42; Corning, *Dictionary of Oregon History*, "Ulysses S. Grant"; Fagan, *History of Benton County*, 526; Genealogical Forum, *Donation Land Claims, Abstracted*, "John Thomas" "Jeremiah Mahoney"; Grun, *Timetables of History*, "1852"; Dorothy O. Johansen, "The Land Base of Oregon's Economy," Genealogical Forum, *Donation Land Claims, Abstracted*, vol. 2:intro.; Johansen and Gates, *Empire on the Columbia*, 286–87; LeRoy, *Lairds, Bards, and Mariners*,

110; Lockley, *Oregon Yesterdays*, 91–92; Meeker, *Personal Experiences on the Oregon Trail*, 5, 15, 26–27; Mills, *Stern-wheelers Up Columbia*, 18–28; Newsom, *Western Observer*, 44; Spenser and Pollard, *History of Washington*, vol.1:281–84; Turnbull, *History of Oregon Newspapers*, 226.

PERIODICALS: Kelly, "History of the Preparation of the First Code of Oregon," *QOHS* 4:186–89; Johnson, D.C., "Oregon Territorial Supreme Court, 1849–1859," *Environmental Law* 4:35–50, 64–66; Strong, "Knickerbocker Views. . .William Strong," *OHQ* 62:64, 65–66, 72–73; Teiser, "Thomas Nelson," *OHQ* 48:214; Teiser, "O.C. Pratt," *OHQ* 49:180–83; Teiser, "William Strong," *OHQ* 64:296, 299–301.

NEWSPAPERS: *Camp Adair Sentry*, October 15, 1942; *Oregonian*, December 6, 1851; August 21, September 11, 18, 1852, August 1, 1886; *Statesman*, August 14, September 4, 11, 18, 25, October 9, 16, 1852.

LAWS: *Act to Establish the Territorial Government of Oregon* (1848), section 6, 9; *Organic Law of the Provisional Government of Oregon* (1845), article I, section 4; *Short v. Ermitinger*, Oregon Territory Supreme Court, 1851.

DOCUMENTS: "Benton County Commissioners' Journal, 1850–54," 24, 26, 29, 38–39, 42, 44, 54; Asahel Bush, letter to Matthew Deady, September 17, 1852; Matthew Deady, letter to Asahel Bush, September 20, 1852; House doc. no. 104, "Capital Location Controversy," 8–24; Supreme Court file, *O'Kelly v. T.O.*, Judge Strong's writ of error and supersedeas issue, September 17, 1852, and Clerk Millear's order to stay execution, September 18, 1852; John Thorp, letter to Governor Gaines, September 22, 1852.

Chapter 19: Review and Reunion, October–December 1852

BOOKS/MONOGRAPHS: *Adams and Blank Diary*, 12–13, 67–68; Bancroft, *History of Oregon*, vol. 2:159 n.36, 297; Banks, *An Oregon Boyhood*, 13–18; Boag, *Environment and Experience*, 43, 45; Clark, *Eden Seekers*, 251–53, 262; Cole, *Early Oregon*, 45; Evans, *History of the Pacific Northwest*, vol. 1:310n, vol. 2:402, 509; Fagan, *History of Benton County*, 392; Genealogical Forum, *Donation Land Claims, Abstracted*, "Benjamin O'Kelly" "Nimrod O'Kelly" "Joseph O'Kelly"; Grun, *Timetables of History*, "1852"; Dorothy O. Johansen, "The Land Base of Oregon's Economy," Genealogical Forum, *Donation Land Claims, Abstracted*, vol. 2:intro.; Lockley, *Oregon Yesterdays*, 92; McArthur, *Oregon Geographic Names*, "Dallas"; Meeker, *Personal Experiences on the Oregon Trail*, 5, 14, 26–30; Moynihan, *Rebel for Rights*, 30, 35; O'Hara, *Pioneer Catholic History*, 176; *Report of the Adjutant General, 1865–66*, 180; Winter and Thornbrough, *Letter of Dr. Thomas White*, 26; WPA, *Inventory—Benton County*, A-66.

PERIODICALS: Bromberg, "Frontier Humor," *OHQ* 61:291; Johnson, D.C., "Oregon Territorial Supreme Court, 1849–1859," *Environmental Law* 4:50–51; Sheldon, "Then and Now," *Oregon State Bar Bulletin* (November 1995): 35–38; Teiser, "O.C. Pratt," *OHQ* 49:184.

NEWSPAPERS: *Statesman*, September 25, October 9, 16, November 27, December 25, 1852.

LAWS: "Hamilton Code" (1851), Practice—District and Supreme Courts, section 34; 2 *Oregon Reports* 12, Attorneys.

DOCUMENTS: "Benton County Commissioners' Journal, 1850–54," 54, 58, 71–72; "Benton County Property Assessment Rolls," 1851; R.B. Hinton, letter to Nimrod O'Kelly, July 16, 1852; "Last Will and Testament of Nimrod O'Kelly," June 28, 1852; Charles L. and Rebecca O'Kelly, letter to Nimrod O'Kelly, March 28, 1852; William Nimrod O'Kelley death certificate, 1942; Supreme Court file, *O'Kelly v. T.O.*; U.S. Eighth Census (1860), Lane County, Oregon, Brice Precinct, Freedom P.O., dwelling and family nos. 750 and 751, q.v. "Kelly, B.G.C.," and "Kelly, Joseph B," 98; U.S. Seventh Census (1850), McDonald County, Missouri, dwelling and family nos. 106 and 107, q.v. "Joseph O'Kelly" and "Sarah O'Kelly."

Chapter 20: Survey, Freedom, and Wait, 1853

BOOKS/MONOGRAPHS: Bancroft, *History of Oregon*, vol. 2:167, 300; Campbell, "David Stump House," in D.A.R. *Oregon Historic Landmarks*, 30–31; Clark, *History of the Willamette Valley*, vol. 1:678; Corning, *Dictionary of Oregon History*, "Floods" "Methodist Episcopal Church South"; Fagan, *History* *of Benton County*, 380, 392, 398, 518; Genealogical Forum, *Donation Land Claims, Abstracted*, "Joseph O'Kelly" "Benjamin O'Kelly" "Jeremiah Mahoney" "John Thomas" "Caspar Kompp" "Thomas Kinney" "Patrick Kinney" "James Kinney"; Helblock, *Oregon Post Offices*, q.v. "Starrs Point"; Hulbert, *Frontiers,* 93–95; Josephy, *Indian Heritage of America*, 60; McArthur, *Oregon Geographic Names*, "Monroe"; Mintonye, *They Laughed Too*, 20, 30; Munnick, *Catholic Church Records, [Portland]* 7–8; Nash, *Two Years in Oregon*, 37; O'Hara, *Pioneer Catholic History*, 175–76, 188; Oregon State Archives, *Echoes of Oregon*, 6–7; Ransom, "Stories My Mother Told Me," 78–81, 82; Snyder, *We Claimed This Land*, xiv–xix; WPA, *Inventory—Benton County*, A-42, 71–72, 73.

NEWSPAPERS: *Oregonian*, "Horrible Murder," June 3, 1852; *Statesman*, February 12, 19, March 26, 1853.

LAWS: "An Act for the Relief of Polk and Benton Counties," *Oregon Laws, 1853*, 18–19; "Donation Land Claim Act" (1850), sections 4, 5, 6, 7, 19; *Moore v. Thomas, et al.*, 1 *Oregon Reports* 201 (1855).

DOCUMENTS: "Benton County Commissioners' Journal, 1850–54," 24–25, 28–29, 38, 42, 44, 54, 58, 71–72, 80; "Benton County Property Assessment Rolls," 1851, 1853; Father James Croke, letters to Archbishop Blanchet, August 9 and October 26, 1853; "DLC Notification File No. 2087" (Nimrod O'Kelly); "DLC Notification File No. 3835" (John Thomas); "DLC Notification File No. 2151" (Mary Jane [Mahoney] Thomas); Richard Irwin, letter to John B. Preston, September 27, 1853; "Jackson County Assessment Roll for 1854"; Benjamin O'Kelly, letter to Surveyor General, August 15, 1853; Nimrod O'Kelly, letters, to "Governor" Lane, December 5, 1851, and to John B. Preston, April 14, 1853; U.S. Eighth Census (1860), Shoal Creek Township, Barry County, Missouri, 906.

MAPS/SURVEYS/FIELD NOTES: Jennyopolis Township Claims Map, 1861; Jennyopolis, Marysville, and Starrs Point township topographical maps, 1853; survey field notes [Jennyopolis], T. 13S. R. 5W (1853); survey field notes [Jennyopolis], T. 13S. R. 5W (1859).

Chapter 21: Spoils, 1853

BOOKS/MONOGRAPHS: Bancroft, *History of Oregon*, vol. 2:294–95, 307, 308 n.30, 309; Clark, *Eden Seekers*, 251–52, 257; Corning, *Dictionary of Oregon History*, "George Law Curry" "Joseph Lane" "Benjamin F. Harding" "Asa L. Lovejoy"; Evans, *History of the Pacific Northwest*, vol. 1:350–52, vol. 2:632–35; Genealogical Forum, *Donation Land Claims, Abstracted*, "George L. Curry" "Benjamin F. Harding" "John Adair" "A.C. Gibbs"; Hendrickson, *Joe Lane of Oregon*, 62–63, 67–72; *History of the Bench and Bar of Oregon*, 26, 273–74, 282–86; O'Donnell, *An Arrow in the Earth*, 123; Scott, *History of Portland*, 326–27; Caroline Stoel, "Oregon's First Federal Courts, 1849–1859," in Buan, *The First Duty*, 17–22; Tobie, *No Man Like Joe*, 222–28; Turnbull, *Governors of Oregon*, "George Law Curry" "John W. Davis"; Woodward, *Political Parties in Oregon*, 52–57, 76–78, 79–81.

PERIODICALS: Johnson, D.C., "Oregon Territorial Supreme Court, 1849–1859," *Environmental Law* 4:51–60; Perry et al., "The Spousal Letters of Samuel R. Thurston," *OHQ* 96:50, 75 n.107; Teiser, "Matthew P. Deady," *OHQ* 44:76; Teiser, "Obediah B. McFadden," *OHQ* 66:29–30; Teiser, "Cyrus Olney," *OHQ* 64:312–16; Teiser, "O.C. Pratt," *OHQ* 49:179–80, 184–85.

NEWSPAPER: *Oregonian*, August 1, 1886.

LAWS: "Hamilton Code" (1851), Juries, section 2, District Judges, section 2; "Oregon Code of 1854," Act to Provide for Holding of Supreme and District Courts, pp. 63–64; 1 *Oregon Reports* 8.

DOCUMENT: Matthew P. Deady, letter to Asahel Bush, September 20, 1852.

Chapter 22: The Judges' Last Word, Winter 1853–54

BOOKS/MONOGRAPHS: Belknap, *Oregon Imprints*, 58 item-81, 64 item-101, 65–66 item-104; Bancroft, *History of Oregon*, vol. 2:307–8; *History of the Bench and Bar of Oregon*, 34, 35; Caroline Stoel, "Oregon's First Federal Courts, 1849–1859," in Buan, *The First Duty*, 20; Hendrickson, *Joe Lane of Oregon*, 63, 84–85; Lansing, *Juggernaut*, 3, 113 n.4; Woodward, *Political Parties in Oregon*, 76–77.

PERIODICALS: Beardsley, "Code Making in Early Oregon," *PNQ* 27:19–20, 22–24; Harris, "History of the Oregon Code," *Oregon Law Review* 1:196–200; Johnson, D.C., "Oregon Territorial Supreme Court, 1849–1859," *Environmental Law* 4:53–60, 63; McNary, "Oregon's First Reported Murder Case," *OHQ* 36:359; Teiser, "Obediah B. McFadden," *OHQ* 66:25; Teiser, "Cyrus Olney," *OHQ* 64:313–14; Teiser, "O.C. Pratt," *OHQ* 49:178.

NEWSPAPERS: *Statesman*, December 27, 1853, January 10, 1854.

LAWS: *Council Journal of the 1853–54 Legislative Assembly of Oregon,* q.v., *Oregon Territory v. Nimrod O'Kelly*; "Oregon Code of 1854" (Kelly-Boise compilation); 1 *Oregon Reports,* 8, 9, 17–73, viz *O'Kelly v. Oregon Territory*, 51–59.

DOCUMENTS: "Benton County Circuit Court Journal, 1852," 6; Supreme Court file, *O'Kelly v. T.O.*

Chapter 23: Putting the House in Order, Winter 1853–54

BOOKS/MONOGRAPHS: Bancroft, *History of Oregon,* vol. 2:25, 299 n.6; Beckham, *Requiem for a People*, 134–37; Boag, *Environment and Experience*, 84–86; Carey, *General History of Oregon*, vol. 2:568–69, 600–1, 713; Corning, *Dictionary of Oregon History*, "Methodist Church"; Fagan, *History of Benton County*, 424–26; Genealogical Forum, *Donation Land Claims, Abstracted*, "Jeremiah Mahoney" "John Thomas" "Nimrod O'Kelly"; Grun, *Timetables of History*, "1853–54"; Dorothy O. Johansen, "The Land Base of Oregon's Economy," Genealogical Forum, *Donation Land Claims, Abstracted*, vol. 2:intro.; Leroy, *Lairds, Bards, and Mariners*, 110; Lockley, *Oregon Yesterdays*, 22; McArthur, *Oregon Geographic Names*, "Corvallis"; Mills, *Stern-wheelers Up Columbia*, 53–54; O'Donnell, *An Arrow in the Earth*, 156, 166–68; Peterson and Powers, *Coos and Curry*, 89; Sauter and Johnson, *Tillamook Indians*, 34; Victor, *Atlantis Arisen*, 108; WPA, *Inventory—Benton County*, A-20; Zucker, Hummel, and Hogfoss, *Oregon Indians*, 83–86, 179.

PERIODICAL: Gatke, "[Ketturah Belknap's] Bellfountain Settlement," *OHQ* 36:291–94.

NEWSPAPERS: *Oregonian*, April 15, 1854; *Spectator*, February 18, 1854; *Statesman*, March 21, May 16, 23, 1854.

LAW: *Moore v. Thomas, et al.*, 1 *Oregon Reports* 201 (1855).

DOCUMENTS: "Benton County Property Assessment Rolls," 1854; "DLC Notification File No. 2087" (Nimrod O'Kelly); "DLC Notification File No. 3835" (John Thomas); "DLC Notification File No. 2151" (Mary Jane [Mahoney] Thomas); "Jackson County Census Roll," 1854, 45; "Lane County Agricultural Census," 1854, 57–58; "Lane County Assessment Roll," 1854, 18; Nimrod O'Kelly, letter to Governor Davis, April 16, 1854.

MAPS: Jennyopolis and Starrs Point township claims maps, 1861.

Chapter 24: The Last Efforts, Spring 1854

BOOKS/MONOGRAPHS: Bancroft, *History of Oregon*, vol. 2:322–23; Cole, *Early Oregon*, 67–68; Corning, *Dictionary of Oregon History*, "Joseph Gardner Wilson" "James Harvey Slater"; Davenport, *Best of the Old Northwest*, 115–16; Douglas, *History of Southeast Missouri*, 797–98; Fagan, *History of Benton County*, 392; Genealogical Forum, *Donation Land Claims, Abstracted*, "Benjamin Cornelius" "Peyton Wilkes"; Carstensen, *Pacific Northwest Letters of George Gibbs*, 46; Turnbull, *Governors of Oregon*, 27; Wojcik, *Brazen Overlanders*, 401, 510.

PERIODICAL: Teiser, "O.C. Pratt," *OHQ* 49:185.

NEWSPAPERS: *Statesman*, June 1, 1852, May 16, 1854.

DOCUMENTS: "Benton County Commissioners' Journal, 1850–54," 156–57; Charles B. Brooks et al., letter to Governor Davis, March 15, 1854; Benjamin Cornelius Sr. and Peyton Wilkes, affidavits, February 25, 1854; "Executive Actions Journal," December 2, 1853, and April 1, 1854; L.G. Hoge, statement, August 16, 1852; Amory Holbrook, letter to Governor Davis, January 24, 1854; James K. Kelly, letter to Governor Davis, February 11, 1854; Nimrod O'Kelly, letter to Governor Davis, April 16, 1854; Petitions, Amory Holbrook et al. (ca. August 1852), Benjamin G. O'Kelly et al. (February 9, 1854), Joseph B. O'Kelly et al. (February 9, 1854), Sally O'Kelly et al. (February 8, 1854), and Levi C. Phillips et al. (February 15, 1854); O.C. Pratt, letter to Governor Davis, February 25, 1854; Proceedings of meeting at "Long Tom," March 15, 1854, Benton-Lane county citizens; Samuel F. Starr, letter to Governor Gaines, ca. August 1852; *Territory of Oregon v. Nimrod O'Kelly*, witness subpoenas, and Supreme Court Mandate to the Benton County District Court, February 9, 1854.

Chapter 25: Final Trip to the Gallows, May 1854

BOOKS/MONOGRAPHS: Bancroft, *History of Oregon*, vol. 2:322; Carey, *History of Oregon*, 525 n.40; Corning, *Dictionary of Oregon History*, "John Wesley Davis"; Lang, *History of the Willamette Valley*, 814; Munnick, *Catholic Church Records, [St. Paul]* 73–74 annotations; Turnbull, *Governors of Oregon*, 27.

PERIODICALS: Himes, "History of the State Agricultural Society," *QOHS* 8:321; Johnson, D.C., "Oregon Territorial Supreme Court, 1849–1859," *Environmental Law* 4:11, 65–67; McNary, "Oregon's First Reported Murder Case," *OHQ* 36:362–63.

NEWSPAPERS: *Oregonian*, August 1, 1886, March 3, 1940, March 31, 1957; *Statesman*, May 23, 1854.

DOCUMENTS: "Executive Actions Journal," May 14, 1854; "Lane County Marriage Records, 1852–1869," vol. 1, 6; Nimrod O'Kelly, letter to Governor Davis, May 16, 1854; James C. Patterson, letter to Governor Davis, May 15, 1854.

PERSONAL CONTACT: Linda Brown-Kubisch, (State Historical Society of Missouri), letter to author, August 1, 1995.

Chapter 26: The Portland Penitentiary, May 1854

BOOKS/MONOGRAPHS: Boag, *Environment and Experience*, 111–12, 127; Carey, *General History of Oregon*, vol. 2:729; Corning, *Dictionary of Oregon History*, "Ferries" "S.A. Clarke" "Isaac Lee Patterson" "Presbyterian Church"; Corning, *Willamette Landings*, 32, 49, 55, 58, 70, 89, 94 et seq.; D.A.R., *Oregon Historic Landmarks*, 14, 16, 18, 20; Dimon, *'Twas Many Years Since*, vii, 36; Fagan, *History of Benton County*, 326, 392, 514; Bertha Hallam, "Medical School on the Hill," in *Land of the Multnomahs*, 141–43; Meda Zillah Johnson, "Bells 'Tolled' the Story," in *Land of the Multnomahs*, 252–53; Maddux, *City on the Willamette*, 31–33; McArthur, *Oregon Geographic Names*, "Girds Creek" "Fairfield" "Butteville" "Parkersville" "New Era"; Munnick, *Catholic Church Records, [St. Paul]* A-73–74; O'Donnell and Vaughan, *Portland*, 14; Scott, *History of Portland*, 140–41; Snyder, *Portland Names and Neighborhoods*, 133, 171; Turnbull, *Governors of Oregon*, 75–76; WPA, *Inventory of Benton County*, A-45–46.

PERIODICALS: McNary, "Oregon's First Reported Murder Case," *OHQ* 36:364; "Samuel A. Clarke," *Oregon Native Son* 1:456–57.

NEWSPAPERS: *Oregonian*, August 1, 1886, March 3, 1940, March 31, 1957; *Statesman*, May 16, 23, 1854.

LAWS: "Donation Land Claim Act" (1850), section 4; "Hamilton Code" (1851), Grocery License, section 3, p. 157.

DOCUMENTS: "Benton County Property Assessment Rolls," 1857; D.H. Lownsdale, deed to Penitentiary Commissioners, September 7, 1853, and survey field notes for Oregon Penitentiary, 1853; Joseph O'Kelly, letter to Surveyor General J.K. Gardiner, May 20, 1854, with the surveyor general's notation response; Nimrod O'Kelly, letter to Governor Davis, May 16, 1854; *Oregon Territory v. Gird*, Benton

County, 1854; Sheriff T.J. Right, expense claim to Benton County commissioners, for transporting Nimrod O'Kelly to Oregon Penitentiary, filed June 8[?], 1854; U.S. Eighth Census (1860), Benton County, Oregon, q.v. "Gird."

MAPS/SURVEYS: "A Map of the City of Portland," Talbot, 1868; Portland-Milwaukie Township Topographical Map, 1852; "Surveyed Portion of the Oregon Territory," Preston, October 21, 1852.

Chapter 27: Prison and Home Again, 1854–56

BOOKS/MONOGRAPHS: Applegate, *Recollections of My Boyhood*, 63–64, 68–69; Bancroft, *History of Oregon*, vol. 2:156 n.28, 167, 294–95, 323 n.4, 350–52, 644; Beckham, *Indians of Western Oregon*, 138–40, 144–45, and *Requiem for a People*, 153–66; Belknap, *Oregon Imprints*, 60; Boag, *Environment and Experience*, 46, 110–11, 123–27; Carey, *General History of Oregon*, vol. 2:513–14, 569, 584–85, 594–98; Carstensen, *Pacific Northwest Letters of George Gibbs*, 46; Clark, *Eden Seekers*, 267, 269, 280–84; Clark, *History of the Willamette Valley*, vol. 1:409–10; Corning, *Dictionary of Oregon History*, "State Penitentiary" "Charity Lamb" "Bridges" "Yakima Indian War"; Fagan, *History of Benton County*, 392; Genealogical Forum, *Donation Land Claims, Abstracted*, vol. 3:preface, vol. 4:"Montgomery Winkle"; Grun, *Timetables of History*, "1854–56"; Hendrickson, *Joe Lane of Oregon*, 83, 91–92 118–19, 120–26, 132; Dorothy O. Johansen, "The [Role] of Land Laws in the Settlement of Oregon," Genealogical Forum, *Donation Land Claims, Abstracted*, vol. 1:intro.; Dorothy O. Johansen, "The Land Base of Oregon's Economy," Genealogical Forum, *Donation Land Claims, Abstracted*, vol. 2:intro.; Johansen and Gates, *Empire of the Columbia*, 292; Lockley, *Oregon Yesterdays*, 83, 90; MacColl, *Merchants, Money, and Power*, 57; Maddux, *City on the Willamette*, 35–36; Munnick, *Catholic Records, [Portland]* 16, *[Roseburg]* 1; Preston E. Onstad, "Fort Hoskins," in D.A.R. *Oregon Historic Landmarks*, 34; Robbins, *Landscapes of Promise*, 73–109; Ruby and Brown, *The Cayuse Indians*, 216–20; Turnbull, *History of Oregon Newspapers*, 102–3, 225–26; Victor, *Early Indian Wars*, 585–87; Wojcik, *Brazen Overlanders*, 401, 510; WPA, *Inventory—Benton County*, A-40; Zucker, Hummel, and Hogfoss, *Oregon Indians*, 80–85, 112–13.

PERIODICALS: Nedry, "Willamette Valley in 1859," *OHQ* 46:252–53; Bromberg, "Frontier Humor," *OHQ* 61:296; Lansing, "The Tragedy of Charity Lamb," *OHQ* 101:40; Rockwood, "Diary of Reverend George H. Atkinson," *OHQ* 46:352; Young, "Financial History of Oregon: Part 2," *OHQ* 8:145–47.

NEWSPAPERS: *Milwaukie Review*, January 23, 1958; *Oregonian*, September 30, 1854, March 3, 1940; *Oregon Weekly Times*, May 20, September 23, 30, 1854; *Spectator*, September 9, 1851; *Statesman*, May 23, September 26, 1854, March 18, 1856; *Sunday Oregon Journal*, January 6, 1946.

LAWS: "Donation Land Claim Act" (1850), sections 2, 4, 6; "Hamilton Code" (1851), Crimes and Misdemeanors, section 38; "Oregon Code of 1854," County Prisons, section 9, p. 472.

DOCUMENTS: receipt of prisoner Nimrod O'Kelly, May 21, 1854, by penitentiary keeper Joseph Sloan, duplicate, January 8, 1855, #12038; T.J. Right, expense claim ($128) for transporting Nimrod O'Kelly to penitentiary (undated); Turnbull and Co., bill and receipt, January 10, 1855, to Joseph Sloan, penitentiary keeper, #11487; J.S. Dickinson, letter to Governor Curry, August 28, 1854, #10740; receipt, August 1, 1855, by Joseph Sloan, penitentiary keeper to territorial treasurer, #11480; bill and receipt, April 4, 1855, from A. Leland to penitentiary commissioners, #11495A; certification letter, election of Joseph Sloan on February 13, 1854, by Asa Fitch, penitentiary commissioner, #9777; Joseph(?) Wilson, letter to territorial auditor A.J. Thayer, August 5, 1855, #11495; deed, D.H. and Nancy Lownsdale to penitentiary commissioners, September 7, 1853, conveying lots 3, 4, 7, and 8 in block 107, Portland, #9730; receipt of prisoner Charity Lamb, September 18, 1854, by Joseph Sloan, penitentiary keeper, from Clackamas County deputy sheriff, March 18, 1855, duplicate, #6359, and undated original #7043; service and expense claims, Joseph Sloan, penitentiary keeper, to Oregon Territory, including prisoner rosters for period February 18, 1854, to November 1, 1855, #11471, #11473, #11474, #11485, and #11501; Court Clerk Slater's order to Sheriff Right, May 30, 1854, to levy execution upon Nimrod O'Kelly's property together with sheriff's "not found" return; "Benton County Circuit Court Fee Journal, 1851–1858," vol. 1, 13–14; "Benton County Judgment Docket 1852–1861," vol. 1, 5–6, June 1, 1854; "Benton County Property Assessment Rolls," 1854–56; Father James Croke, letter to Archbishop Blanchet, November 22, 1854; "DLC Notification

File No. 7606" (Montgomery Winkle); "Jackson County Assessment Roll for 1854," 45: Lane County Marriage Records, vol.1, 6; "Petition to Pardon," January 29, 1856; Proceedings of meeting at "Long Tom," March 15, 1854, Benton-Lane county citizens; survey field notes, T.13 S, R.5W (1854).

Chapter 28: Gone Withershins, 1856–59

BOOKS/MONOGRAPHS: Carey, *General History of Oregon*, vol. 2:504–6, 746–49; Douglas, *History of Southeast Missouri*, 798; Barker, *Financial Papers of Dr. John McLoughlin*, 12–15; Hendrickson, *Joe Lane of Oregon*, 151–52; Macon, *Four O'Kelley Sons*, 3–7; Munnick, *Catholic Church Records, [Portland]* 21; State Historical Society of Missouri, "Four Families," 187–95; Stover, *American Railroads*, 46, 48–49, 53.

PERIODICALS: Barker, "Estate of Dr. John McLoughlin," *OHQ* 50:162; McNary, "Oregon's First Reported Murder Case," *OHQ* 36:359, 363–64; "Missouri History Not Found in Textbooks," *Missouri Historical Review*, 44:426–27

NEWSPAPERS: *Greenville Democrat*, February 16, 1859; *Oregonian*, "Pioneer Days," August 1, 1886, "An Oregon Mystery," March 3, 1940 (p. 6 of Northwest magazine section).

LAWS: *Dred Scott v. Sanford*, 60 *U.S. Reports* 393 (1856); "Soldiers Bounty Land Act of 1855."

DOCUMENTS: Barry County, Missouri, marriage records, q.v. "Charles O'Kelly"; "Benton County Census Rolls," 1856–58; "Benton County Property Assessment Rolls," 1856–57; Nimrod O'Kelly, letters, to "Governor" Lane, December 5, 1851, and to Governor Davis, May 16, 1854; Nimrod O'Kelly, pension warrant file, Bounty Land Act of 1855; U.S. Seventh (1850) and Eighth (1860) Census, Shoal Creek Township, Barry County, Missouri, q.v. "Charles O'Kelly" family.

MAP: "Map of the Southern States Including Railroads, County Towns…," *Harper's*, 1863.

PERSONAL CONTACT: Linda Brown-Kubisch, (State Historical Society of Missouri), letter to author, August 1, 1995.

Chapter 29: Return to the Land, 1859–64

BOOKS/MONOGRAPHS: Bancroft, *History of Oregon*, vol. 2:268, 294, 295, 455–56, 482–84; Boag, *Environment and Experience*, 174 n.39; Carey, *History of Oregon,* 661 n.3; Clark, *Eden Seekers*, 284, 298; Corning, *Dictionary of Oregon History*, "W.W. Chapman" "Byron J. Pengra" "Knights of the Golden Circle" "Cyrus A. Reed" "Joseph Gervais" "Willamette Valley"; Corning, *Willamette Landings*, 44–48, 148–49, 153; Coe, *Stories My Mother Told Me*, 72; D.A.R., *Oregon Historic Landmarks*, 15, 17, 18; Davenport, *Best of the Old Northwest*, 37–38; Dobbs, *Men of Champoeg*, 154; Fagan, *History of Benton County*, 398–99, 514; Genealogical Forum, *Donation Land Claims, Abstracted*, "George Shultz" (3868) "Jeremiah Criss"(4059) "Asa Stark"(4060); Dorothy O. Johansen, "The [Role] of Land Laws in the Settlement of Oregon," Genealogical Forum, *Donation Land Claims, Abstracted*, vol. 1:intro.; Lockley, *Oregon Yesterdays*, 24–29; McArthur, *Oregon Geographic Names*, "Fort Hoskins"; McKay, *St. Paul, Oregon*, 44, 50; Munnick, *Catholic Church Records, [Oregon City]* 22, 25–26, 32, *[Jacksonville]* A-1, *[Roseburg]* 5–6; Nelson and Onstad, *A Webfoot Volunteer*, 6 et seq.; O'Hara, *Pioneer Catholic History*, 160–63; Preston E. Onstad, "Fort Hoskins," in D.A.R. *Oregon Historic Landmarks*, 34–35; Scofield, *Oregon's Historical Markers*, 75–76; Snyder, *We Claimed This Land*, ix; Turnbull, *History of Oregon Newspapers*, 226; Woodard, *Political Parties in Oregon*, 102–3, 128–43, 192–99, 262–63.

PERIODICALS: Dustin, "The Knights of the Golden Circle…Secessionists," *The Pacific Monthly* (November 1911):495; Edwards, "Six Oregon Leaders and…Civil War," *OHQ* 100:11–12, 18–21 passim; LaLande, "Dixie of the Pacific Northwest," *OHQ* 100:46, 75 n.26; Moore, "Cyrus Reed…Pioneer," *Oregon Magazine* (November 1924):22–23.

NEWSPAPER: *Oregonian*, August 1, 1886.

LAWS: "Deady-Lane Code of 1866," p. 64 n. 3; "Donation Land Claim Act" (1850), 4, 7, 13, 15, 21; *Keith v. Cheeny*, 1 *Oregon Reports* 285 (1860).

DOCUMENTS: Benton County Deed Records—Book F, 426, Nimrod O'Kelly to Archbishop Blanchet, Book F, 620, Nimrod and Sally O'Kelly to Jefelia O'Kelley, Book F, 621, Nimrod and Jefelia O'Kelly to Thomas and Phoebe Garrett, Book G, 203, Sally and Nimrod O'Kelly to Sarah Patterson; and Book G, 650, James and Sarah Patterson to Isaac Swearinger; V. June Collins research file, Linn County Museum, Brownsville, Oregon; Father James Croke, letter to Archbishop Blanchet, December 17, 1858; "DLC Notification File No. 2087" (Nimrod O'Kelly), containing *inter alia*, affidavits of claimant, and J.C. Alexander, J.C. Avery, and claimant's Oath of Allegiance; Lane County Marriage Records, vol. 1, 18; Nimrod O'Kelly, letter to Congress, August 30, 1851, and letter to Governor Davis, April 16, 1854; *Nimrod O'Kelly [Jr.] v. James Bruce*, Circuit Court, Benton County, November 1, 1869; U.S. Eighth Census (1860), Lane County, Oregon, Brice Precinct, q.v. "Benjamin O'Kelly."

MAPS/SURVEYS/FIELD NOTES: Jennyopolis Township Claims Map,1861; Jennyopolis Township Claims Map (corrected), 1919; private survey map in "DLC Notification File No. 3835" (John Thomas) (rejected); survey field notes [Jennyopolis], T. 13S, R 5W (1859).

PERSONAL CONTACTS: Diane Janes (Nimrod descendant), personal communication, August 1996; Carol Coe Ransom (Nimrod descendant), personal communication, July 1997; Ted W. Roller (Barry County Genealogical Society, Missouri), correspondence August 28, 1995, wherein cited Goodspeed, *History of Barry County* (1888) (a reprint).

Epilogue: The Claim

BOOKS/MONOGRAPHS: Applegate, *Recollections of My Boyhood*, 94; Barnhart and Metcalf, *America in So Many Words*, 159; Fagan, *History of Benton County*, 450; Helbock, *Oregon Post Offices*, "Rickard" "Bruce"; Inman, *Beautiful McKenzie*, 240; Munnick, *Catholic Records, [Portland]* 138, *[Roseburg]* 19; *Oregon Blue Book, 1993–94,* 388–89; Ruby and Brown, *Indians of the Pacific Northwest*, 208–10.

PERIODICAL: McNary, "Oregon's First Reported Murder Case," *OHQ* 36:359, 363–64.

NEWSPAPER: *Oregonian*, August 1, 1886.

LAW: "Donation Land Claim Act" (1850), section 26.

DOCUMENTS: Archbishop Blanchet, letters to Register Wade, May 14 and 17[?], 1871; Benton County Deed Records—Book G, 57, Sally O'Kelley to Caspar Rickard, Book G, 227, Sally O'Kelley to Francis N. Blanchet, Book G, 442, Francis N. Blanchet to "John" [James?] Kinney, Book H, 287, James Kinney to James Bruce, Book H, 81, James and Sarah Patterson to James Bruce, Book I, page 350, Sally and Benjamin O'Kelly to James Bruce, Book H, 451, Nimrod O'Kelly [Jr.] to James Bruce, and Book N, 439, U.S. patent to the O'Kellys; "DLC Patent," to Sally O'Kelly and heirs of Nimrod O'Kelly, February 4, 1867; "Last Will and Testament of Nimrod O'Kelly," June 28, 1852; *Nimrod O'Kelly [Jr.] v. James Bruce*, Benton County Circuit Court, November 1, 1869; Sally O'Kelly, letter to the Surveyor General, May 8, 1871; Sally O'Kelly, Certificate, May 19[?], 1871; U.S. Ninth Census (1870), Long Tom Township, Lane County, Oregon, q.v. "Benjamin O'Kelly."

MAPS/SURVEYS/FIELD NOTES: Jennyopolis Township Claims Map (corrected), 1919.

Appendices

BOOKS/MONOGRAPHS: *Atlas of Oregon*, 9, 20–21; Bancroft, *History of Oregon*, vol. 2:144 n.8, 169, 435–36, 455–46; Bowen, "Oregon Frontiersman," in Vaughan, *The Western Shore*, 186; U.S. Bureau of Census, *Historical Statistics*, 8, 10, 33; Carey, *General History of Oregon*, vol. 2:759, 764–65, 771–72, 780–81, 784, and *Oregon Constitution*, 35; Clark, *Eden Seekers*, 269; Corning, *Dictionary of Oregon History*, passim; Croke, "In Memoriam," 10–11; Dodds, *Oregon*, 154, 172; Fagan, *History of Benton County*, 514; Grauer, *Mount Hood*, 198–202; Hawthorne, *Story of Oregon*, 1:359–62; Hendrickson, *Joe Lane of*

Oregon, 230, 237–38, 249–52; *History of the Bench and Bar of Oregon*, various biographicals; *History of Crook County*, 199; Dorothy O. Johansen, "The [Role] of Land Laws in the Settlement of Oregon," Genealogical Forum, *Donation Land Claims, Abstracted*, vol. 1:intro.; Lang, *History of the Willamette Valley*, various biographicals; Larsell, *Doctors in Oregon*, 239, 294; McArthur, *Oregon Geographic Names*, "Greenberry" "Monroe"; Munnick, *Catholic Church Record, [Roseburg]* 12; Nash, *Oregon: There and Back*, 226; O'Callaghan, "Disposition of the Public Domain in Oregon," 2, 107, passim; *Portland City Directory*, 1885, 1887, 1903, 1912, 1914, "Nimrod O'Kelly" "Jefelia O'Kelly"; Ransom, "Stories My Mother Told Me," passim; *Report of the Adjutant General, 1865–66*, 180; Turnbull, *Governors of Oregon*, various biographicals, and *History of Oregon Newspapers*, 102–3, 134–35, 226; WPA, *Inventory—Benton County*, A-13–14; Zucker, Hummel, and Hogfoss, *Oregon Indians*, 93–112.

PERIODICALS: Gatke, "[Ketturah Belknap's] Bellfountain Settlement," *OHQ* 36:280–81; Himes, "History of the State Agricultural Society," *QOHS* 8:321; McNary, "Oregon's First Reported Murder Case" *OHQ* 36:359, 363–64; Menefree and Tiller, "Cutoff Fever," *OHQ* 78:142; Robbins, "Willamette Eden," *OHQ* 99:202; "Samuel A. Clarke," *Oregon Native Son*, 1:456–57; Teiser, "Cyrus Olney," *OHQ* 64:315, 319–21; Teiser, "O.C. Pratt," *OHQ* 49:188–90; West, "Famous Horses and Horsemen," *OHQ* 46:145–48, 154.

NEWSPAPERS: *Oregonian*, December 17, 20, 1919.

LAW: *Joachim Young v. Territory of Oregon*, 1 *Oregon Reports* 213 (1856).

DOCUMENTS: "Benton County Property Assessment Rolls," 1857; Lane County Marriage Records, 1852–1869," vol. 1, 18; William Nimrod O'Kelley, death certificate, 1942; *United States v. N. O'Kelly [Jr.]*, U.S. District Court, Oregon, October 16, 1877; U.S. Ninth Census (1870), Benton County, Oregon, q.v. "Thomas J. Right"; U.S. Tenth Census, (1880), Portland, Multnomah County, Oregon, q.v. "Nimrod O'Kelly."

Sources

Books and Monographs

Adams, William L. [alias "Breakspear"] *A Melodrame Entitled "Treason, Stratagems, and Spoils" in Five Acts.* George N. Belknap, ed. Hamden, CT: Shoe String Press, 1968.

Applegate, Jesse A. *Recollections of My Boyhood.* Roseburg, OR: Press of Review, 1914.

Atlas of Oregon. 2d ed. William Loy, ed.; Stuart Allan, et al., authors. Eugene, OR: University of Oregon Press, 2001.

Bancroft, Hubert Howe [albeit authored by Frances Fuller Victor]. *History of Oregon.* 2 vols. San Francisco, CA: History Company, 1880.

Banks, Louis Albert. *An Oregon Boyhood.* Boston, MA: 1898.

Barker, Burt Brown, ed. *The Financial Papers of Dr. John McLoughlin.* Portland, OR: Oregon Historical Quarterly reprint, 1949.

Barnhart, David K., and Allan A. Metcalf. *America in So Many Words: Words that Have Shaped America.* Boston, MA: Houghton Mifflin, 1997.

Beckham, Stephen Dow. *The Indians of Western Oregon: This Land Was Theirs.* Coos Bay, OR: Arago Books, 1977.

————. *Requiem for a People: The Rogue Indians and the Frontiersmen.* Norman, OK: University of Oklahoma Press, 1971.

Belknap, George N. *Oregon Imprints, 1845–1870.* Eugene, OR: University of Oregon Books, 1968.

Blanchet, Francis Norbert. *Historical Sketches of the Catholic Church in Oregon.* Edward J. Kowrach, ed. Fairfield, WA: Ye Galleon Press, 1983 [1878].

Boag, Peter. *Environment and Experience: Settlement Culture in Nineteenth-Century Oregon.* Berkeley, CA: University of California Press, 1992

Bourke, Paul, and Donald DeBats. *Washington County: Politics and Community in Antebellum America.* Baltimore, MD: Johns Hopkins University Press, 1995.

Buan, Carolyn M., ed. *The First Duty: A History of the U.S. District Court for Oregon.* Portland, OR: Oregon Historical Society Press, 1993.

Burnett, Peter H. *Recollections and Opinions of an Old Pioneer.* New York, NY: D. Appleton, 1880.

Carey, Charles Henry. *A General History of Oregon Prior to 1861.* 2 vols. Portland, OR: Metropolitan Press, 1935.

————. *History of Oregon.* 3 vols. Chicago, IL: Pioneer Historical Publishing, 1922.

————, ed. *The Oregon Constitution and Proceedings and Debates of the Constitutional Convention of 1857.* Salem, OR: State Printing Department, 1926.

Carstensen, Vernon. *The Public Lands: Studies in the History of the Public Domain.* Madison, WI: University of Wisconsin Press, 1962.

————, ed. *Pacific Northwest Letters of George Gibbs.* Portland, OR: Oregon Historical Quarterly reprint, 1954.

Clark, Keith, and Lowell Tiller. *Terrible Trail: The Meek Cutoff, 1845.* Caldwell, ID: Caxton, 1966.

Clark, Malcolm, Jr. *Eden Seekers: The Settlement of Oregon, 1818–1862.* Boston, MA: Houghton Mifflin, 1981.

————, ed. *Pharisee among Philistines: The Diary of Judge Matthew P. Deady, 1871–1892.* Portland, OR: Oregon Historical Society, 1971.

Clark, Robert Carlton. *History of the Willamette Valley, Oregon.* 3 vols. Chicago, IL: S.J. Clarke, 1927.

Clarke, Samuel A. *Pioneer Days of Oregon History.* 2 vols. Portland, OR: J.K. Gill, 1905.

Cole, George E. *Early Oregon: Jottings of Personal Recollections of a Pioneer of 1850.* Spokane, WA: Shaw and Borden, 1905.

Corning, Howard McKinley. *Dictionary of Oregon History.* Portland, OR: Binfords and Mort, 1956.

————. *Willamette Landings: Ghost Towns of the River.* 2d ed. Portland, OR: Oregon Historical Society, 1973.

Croke, James. "In Memoriam of the Very Reverend James Croke, D.D" [a memorial]. Westchester, NY: Boys New York Catholic Protectory Print, 1889.

Daughters of the American Revolution. *Oregon Historic Landmarks: Willamette Valley.* Portland, OR: 1963.

Davenport, Marge. *Best of the Old Northwest.* Tigard, OR: Paddlewheel Press, 1980.

Dicken, Samuel N. and Emily F. *The Making of Oregon: A Study in Historical Geography.* Portland, OR: Oregon Historical Society, 1979.

Dimon, Elizabeth F. *'Twas Many Years Since: 100 Years in the Waverley Area, 1847–1947.* Milwaukie, OR: E.F. Dimon, 1981.

Dobbs, Caroline. *Men of Champoeg: A Record of the Lives of the Pioneers Who Founded the Oregon Government.* Portland, OR: Metropolitan Press, 1932.

Dodds, Gordon B. *The American Northwest: A History of Oregon and Washington.* Arlington Heights, IL: Forum Press, 1986.

————. *Oregon: A Bicentennial History.* New York, NY: Norton, 1977.

Douglas, Robert Sidney. *History of Southeast Missouri: A Narrative Account of Its Historical Progress, Its People and Its Principal Interests.* Reprint. Cape Girardeau, MO.: Ramfree Press, 1961. [New York, NY: Lewis Publishing, 1912]

Evans, Elwood. *History of the Pacific Northwest.* 2 vols. Portland, OR: North Pacific History Company, 1889.

Fagan, David D. *History of Benton County, Oregon.* Portland, OR: A.G. Walling, 1885.

Fawkes, Ulla Staley, ed. *The Journal of Walter Griffith Pigman.* Mexico, MO: W.G. Staley, 1942.

Fisher, George. *Evidence.* New York, NY: Foundation Press, 2002.

Fogdall, Alberta Brooks. *Royal Family of the Columbia: Dr. John McLoughlin and His Family.* 2d ed. Portland, OR: Binford and Mort, 1982.

Friedman, Ralph. *Tracking Down Oregon.* Caldwell, ID: Caxton, 1990.

Gaston, Joseph. *The Centennial History of Oregon, 1811–1912.* 4 vols. Chicago, IL: S.J. Clarke, 1912.

Gates, Paul W. *History of Public Land Law Development.* Washington, DC: U.S. Government Printing Office, 1968.

Genealogical Material in Oregon Provisional Land Claims: Abstracted Volumes I–VIII, 1845–1849. Portland, OR: compiled and published by Genealogical Forum of Oregon, 1982.

Genealogical Material in Oregon Donation Land Claims: Abstracted. 5 vols. Portland, OR: compiled and published by Genealogical Forum of Oregon, 1957, 1959, 1962, 1967, 1975.

Grauer, Jack. *Mount Hood: A Complete History.* Self published, 1975.

Grun, Bernard. *The Timetables of History: A Horizontal Linkage of People and Events.* New York, NY: Simon and Schuster, 1982.

Harris, William Foster. *The Look of the Old West.* New York, NY: Bonanza, 1960.

Hawthorne, Julian. *The Story of Oregon: A History, with Portraits and Biographies.* 2 vols. New York, NY: American Historical Publishing, 1892.

Helbock, Richard W. *Oregon Post Offices, 1847–1982.* 2d ed. Lake Oswego, OR: Raven Press, 1985.

Hendrickson, James E. *Joe Lane of Oregon: Machine Politics and the Sectional Crisis, 1849–1861.* New Haven, CT: Yale University Press, 1967.

Hine, Robert V., and Edwin R. Bingham, eds. *The Frontier Experience: Readings in the Trans-Mississippi West.* Belmont, CA: Wadsworth Publishing, 1963.

Hine, Robert V., and Savoie Lottinville, ed. *Soldier in the West: Letters of Theodore Talbot during His Services in California, Mexico, and Oregon, 1845–1853.* Norman, OK: University of Oklahoma Press 1972.

The History of Crook County, Oregon. Prineville, OR: Crook County Historical Society, 1981.

History of the Bench and Bar of Oregon. Portland, OR: Historical Publishing, 1910.

Hodge, Frederick W. *Handbook of American Indians North of Mexico.* 2 vols. New York, NY: Rowan and Littlefield, 1959.

Hulbert, Archer Butler. *Frontiers: The Genius of American Nationality.* Boston, MA: Little, Brown, 1929.

Inman, Leroy B. *Beautiful McKenzie: A History of Central Lane County.* Bend, OR: South Fork Press, 1996.

Johansen, Dorothy O., and Charles M. Gates. *Empire of the Columbia: A History of the Pacific Northwest.* 2d. ed. New York, NY: Harper and Row, 1967.

Josephy, Alvin M., Jr. *The Indian Heritage of America.* New York, NY: Knopf, 1968.

Karolevitz, Robert F. *Newspapering in the Old West: A Pictorial History of Journalism and Printing on the Frontier.* Seattle, WA: Superior, 1965.

Land of the Multnomahs: Sketches and Stories of Early Oregon. Compiled by American Association of University Women, Creative Writing Group. Portland, OR: Binsford and Mort, 1973.

Lang, H.O. *History of the Willamette Valley.* Portland, OR: G.H. Himes, 1885.

Lansing, Jewel. *Portland: People, Politics, and Power, 1851–2001.* Corvallis, OR: Oregon State University Press, 2003.

Lansing, Ronald B. *Juggernaut: The Whitman Massacre Trial of 1850.* Pasadena, CA: 9th Judicial Circuit Historical Society, 1993.

Larsell, Olof. *The Doctor in Oregon: A Medical History.* Portland, OR: Oregon Historical Society, 1947.

Leeson, Fred. *Rose City Justice: A Legal History of Portland, Oregon.* Portland, OR: Oregon Historical Society Press, 1998.

Leroy, Bruce. *Lairds, Bards, and Mariners: The Scot in North America.* Tacoma, WA: Washington State Historical Society, 1978.

Lockley, Fred. *Conversations with Pioneer Women.* Eugene, OR: Rainy Day Press, 1981.

_____. *Oregon Yesterdays.* New York, NY: Knickerbocker Press, 1928.

MacColl, E. Kimbark, with Harry H. Stein. *Merchants, Money, and Power: The Portland Establishment, 1843–1913.* Portland, OR: Georgian Press, 1988.

Macon, Althea Jane. *Four O'Kelley Sons and Some of Their Descendants, Allied Families.* DC: 1970–71.

Maddux, Percy. *City on the Willamette: The Story of Portland, Oregon.* Portland, OR: Binfords and Mort, 1952.

Martin, George E., and Lawrence R. Fick. *A Road in the Wilderness.* Forest Grove, OR: Oregon Department of Forestry, 2002.

McArthur, Lewis A. *Oregon Geographic Names.* 6th ed. Portland, OR: Oregon Historical Society Press. 1992.

McKay, Harvey J. *St. Paul, Oregon, 1830–1890.* Portland, OR: Binford and Mort, 1980.

McMurtrie, Douglas C. *Oregon Imprints, 1847–1870.* Eugene, OR: University of Oregon Press, 1950.

Meeker, Ezra. *Personal Experiences on the Oregon Trail Sixty Years Ago.* St. Louis, MO: McAdoo, 1912.

Mills, Randall V. "Oregon Speechways." In *American Speech.* New York, NY: Columbia University Press, 1950 [reprint].

_____. *Stern-wheelers Up Columbia: A Century of Steamboating in the Oregon Country.* Palo Alto, CA: Pacific Books, 1947.

Mintonye, Edna A., *They Laughed Too.* San Antonio, TX: Naylor, 1968.

Moynihan, Ruth Barnes. *Rebel for Rights: Abigail Scott Duniway.* New Haven, CT: Yale University Press, 1983.

Munnick, Harriet Duncan, ed. *Catholic Church Records of the Pacific Northwest.* 6 vols. Portland, OR: Binford and Mort, 1972–86.

Nash, Wallis. *Oregon: There and Back in 1877.* Corvallis, OR: Oregon State University Press, 1976.

_____. *Two Years in Oregon.* New York, NY: D. Appleton, 1882.

Nelson, Herbert B., and Preston E. Onstad, eds. *A Webfoot Volunteer: The Diary of William M. Hilleary, 1804–1866.* Corvallis, OR: Oregon State University Press, 1965.

Newsom, E. Earl, intro. *David Newsom: The Western Observer, 1805–1882.* Portland, OR: Oregon Historical Society, 1972.

O'Callaghan, Jerry A. "Disposition of the Public Domain in Oregon," Ph.D. diss., Department of History, Stanford University. Washington, D.C.: Submitted to and printed by U.S. Senate, 1960.

O'Donnell, Terence. *An Arrow in the Earth: General Joel Palmer and the Indians of Oregon.* Portland, OR: Oregon Historical Society Press. 1991

_____, and Thomas Vaughan. *Portland: An Informal History and Guide.* 2d ed. Portland, OR: Western Imprint, 1984.

O'Hara, Edwin V. *Pioneer Catholic History of Oregon.* Portland, OR: Glass and Prudhomme, 1911.

The Oregon Blue Book: Official Directory for the State of Oregon. Salem, OR: Office of the Secretary of State, annual.

Oregon State Archives. *Echoes of Oregon, 1837–1859.* Salem, OR: 1987.

Parrish, Philip H. *Historic Oregon.* New York, NY: Macmillan, 1943.

Paxson, Frederic L. *History of the American Frontier, 1763–1893.* Boston, MA: Houghton Mifflin, 1924.

Peterson, Emil R., and Alfred Powers, *A Century of Coos and Curry: History of Southwest Oregon.* Portland, OR: Binfords and Mort, 1952.

Portland City Directory. Portland, OR: various publishers, 18851914 (annual).

Ramsey, Jarold, ed. *Coyote Was Going There: Indian Literature of the Oregon Country.* Seattle, WA: University of Washington Press, 1977.

Ransom, Carol Coe. "Stories My Mother Told Me (Family Stories of the Potter, Ebbert, and O'Kelley Families)." Self published genealogical study, April 1997 (photocopy).

Rau, Weldon Willis. *Surviving the Oregon Trail, 1852.* Pullman, WA: Washington State University Press, 2001.

Rawie, Velma Carter. "History of the Carter Family and the Town of Wells, Benton County, Oregon: 1845–1941." Oregon State University, Soap Creek Valley Project, Monograph #10, 1994.

Report of the Adjutant General of the State of Oregon National Guard, 1865–66. Salem, OR: State Printer, 1866.

Robbins, William G. *Landscapes of Promise: The Oregon Story, 1800–1940.* Seattle: University of Washington Press, 1997.

Ruby, Robert H., and John A. Brown, *The Cayuse Indians: Imperial Tribesmen of Old Oregon.* Norman, OK: University of Oklahoma Press, 1972.

_____. *Indians of the Pacific Northwest: A History.* Norman, OK: University of Oklahoma Press, 1981.

Russell, Carl P. *Firearms, Traps, and Tools of the Mountain Men.* New York: Alfred A. Knopf, 1967.

Sauter, John, and Bruce Johnson. *Tillamook Indians of the Oregon Coast.* Portland, OR: Binfords and Mort, 1974.

Scofield, W.M. *Oregon's Historical Markers.* Pleasant Hill, OR: Souvenir, 1966.

Scott, Harvey W. *History of the Oregon Country.* 6 vols. Compiled by Leslie M. Scott. Cambridge, MA: Riverside Press, 1924.

_____. *History of Portland, Oregon.* Syracuse, NY: D. Mason, 1890.

Shinn, Charles Howard. *Mining Camps: A Study in American Frontier Government.* New York, NY: A.A. Knopf, 1948.

Snyder, Eugene E. *Portland Names and Neighborhoods: Their Historic Origins.* Portland, OR: Binford and Mort, 1979.

_____. *We Claimed This Land: Portland's Pioneer Settlers.* Portland, OR: Binford and Mort, 1989.

Spencer, Lloyd, and Lancaster Pollard. *History of the State of Washington.* 4 vols. New York, NY: American Historical Society, 1937.

State Historical Society of Missouri. "Four Families through Georgia—Surname O'Kelly." Genealogical research of Revolutionary War Veterans' status, RFDS No. NC, sheet 6–11, pp. 187–95 [ca. 1976].

Stegner, Wallace. *Beyond the Hundredth Meridian: John Wesley Powell and the Second Opening of the West.* Boston, MA: Houghton, Mifflin, 1954.

Stover, John F. *American Railroads.* Chicago, IL: University of Chicago Press, 1961.

Thomas, Edward Harper. *Chinook: A History and Dictionary of the Northwest Coast Trade Jargon.* 2d ed. Portland, OR: Binfords and Mort, 1970.

Tobie, Harvey Elmer. *No Man Like Joe: The Life and Times of Joseph L. Meek.* Portland, OR: Binfords and Mort, 1949.

Turnbull, George S. *Governors of Oregon.* Portland, OR: Binfords and Mort, 1959.

_____. *History of Oregon Newspapers.* Portland, OR: Binfords and Mort, 1939.

U.S. Bureau of Census. *Historical Statistics of the United States, Colonial Times to 1970.* Washington, D.C.: Department of Commerce, 1975.

Vaughan, Thomas, ed. *The Western Shore: Oregon Country Essays Honoring the American Revolution.* Portland, OR: Oregon Historical Society, 1976.

Victor, Frances Fuller. *All Over Oregon and Washington.* San Francisco, CA: J.H. Carmany, 1872.

_____. *Atlantis Arisen: or, Talks of a Tourist about Oregon and Washington.* Philadelphia, PA: J.B. Lippincott, 1891.

_____. *The Early Indian Wars of Oregon.* Salem, OR: F.C. Baker, 1894.

Ward, Jean M., and Elaine A. Maveety, eds. *Pacific Northwest Women, 1815–1925: Lives, Memories, and Writings.* Corvallis, OR: Oregon State University Press, 1995.

Webber, Bert, ed. *The Oregon Trail Diary of Twin Sisters Cecelia Adams and Parthenia Blank in 1852: The Unabridged Diary.* Medford, OR: Webb Research Group, 1992.

Wiederhold, Kathleen M. *Exploring Oregon's Historic Courthouses.* Corvallis, OR: Oregon State University Press, 1998.

Winther, Oscar O., and Gayle Thornbrough, eds. "To Oregon in 1852: Letter of Dr. Thomas White." Indianapolis, IN: Indianapolis Historical Society, 1964.

Wojcik, Donna M. *The Brazen Overlanders of 1845.* Portland, OR: Wojcik, 1976.

Woodward, Walter Carleton. *The Rise and Early History of Political Parties in Oregon, 1843–1868*. Portland, OR: J.K. Gill, 1913.
Work Projects Administration. *Inventory of the County Archives of Oregon: No. 2, Benton County (Corvallis)*. Portland, OR: Oregon Historical Records Survey Project, 1942.
Zucker, Jeff, Kay Hummel, and Bob Hogfoss. *Oregon Indians: Culture, History and Current Affairs, An Atlas and Introduction*. Portland, OR: Oregon Historical Society Press, 1983.

Periodicals

Barker, Burt Brown, ed. "Estate of Dr. John McLoughlin: The Papers Discovered." *Oregon Historical Quarterly* 50 (1949).
Beardsley, Arthur S. "Code Making in Early Oregon." *Pacific Northwest Quarterly* 27 (1936). [A slightly revised reprint appears in *Oregon Law Review* 23 (1943).]
Berquist, James M. "The Oregon Donation Act and the National Land Policy." *Oregon Historical Quarterly* 58 (1957).
Boag, Peter. "The Valley of the Long Grasses." *Old Oregon* (Winter 1992).
Bromberg, Erik. "Frontier Humor: Plain and Fancy." *Oregon Historical Quarterly* 61 (1960).
Corning, Howard McKinley. "Ghost Towns on the Willamette of the Riverboat Period." *Oregon Historical Quarterly* 48 (1947).
Davenport, T.W. "Recollections of an Indian Agent-III." *Quarterly of Oregon Historical Society* 8 (1907).
Dustin, Charles Mial. "The Knights of the Golden Circle: The Story of the Pacific Coast Secessionists." *The Pacific Monthly* (November 1911).
Edwards, Thomas G. "Six Oregon Leaders and the Far-Reaching Impact of America's Civil War." *Oregon Historical Quarterly* 100 (1999).
Gatke, Robert Moulton, ed. "[Ketturah Belknap's] Chronicle of the Bellfountain Settlement." *Oregon Historical Quarterly* 36 (1937).
_____. "Letters of the Reverend William M. Roberts." *Oregon Historical Quarterly* 23 (1922).
Harris, Lawrence T. "History of the Oregon Code." *Oregon Law Review* 1 (1922).
Himes, George H. "A History of the Press of Oregon." *Quarterly of Oregon Historical Society* 3 (1902).
_____. "History of the State Agricultural Society. "*Quarterly of Oregon Historical Society* 8 (1907).
Horner, John B. "The Legend of Chintimini" *Oregon Magazine* (November 1924).
Howison, Neil M. "Report on Oregon, 1846." *Quarterly of the Oregon Historical Society* 14 (1913).
Hunt, Robert S. "Law and Land in a Stateless Society." *Wisconsin Law Review* (1980).
Ingersoll, E. "In the Wahlamet Valley of Oregon." *Harper's New Monthly Magazine* (October 1882).
Johnson, David A. "The Donation Land Act and the Making of Modern-Day Oregon." *Oregon Humanities* (Winter 1994).
Johnson, Donald C. "Politics, Personalities, and Policies of the Oregon Territorial Supreme Court, 1849–1859." *Environmental Law* 4 (1973).
Kelly, James K. "History of the Preparation of the First Code of Oregon." *Quarterly of Oregon Historical Society* 4 (1903).
Kirby, James E., ed. "[Simpson, (Bishop) Matthew] A Missionary Journey to Oregon, 1853–54." *Oregon Historical Quarterly* 102 (2001).
LaLande, Jeff. "'Dixie' of the Pacific Northwest: Southern Oregon's Civil War." *Oregon Historical Quarterly* 100 (1999).
Lansing, Ronald B. "The Tragedy of Charity Lamb: Oregon's First Convicted Murderess." *Oregon Historical Quarterly* 101 (2000).
McNary, Lawrence A. "Oregon's First Reported Murder Case." *Oregon Historical Quarterly* 36 (1935).
Menefree, Leah Collins, and Lowell Tiller. "Cutoff Fever." *Oregon Historical Quarterly* 78 (1977).
"Missouri History Not Found in Textbooks." *Missouri Historical Review* 44 (1950).
Moore, Chas B. "Cyrus Reed…Pioneer." *Oregon Magazine* (November 1924).
Nedry, H.S. "Willamette Valley in 1859: The Diary of a Tour." *Oregon Historical Quarterly* 46 (1945).
Perry, James R., et al., eds. "Spousal Letters of Samuel R. Thurston, Oregon's First Territorial Delegate to Congress: 1849–1851." *Oregon Historical Quarterly* 96 (1995).
Pisani, Donald J. "Squatter Law in California." *Western Historical Quarterly* 25 (1994).
Robbins, William G. "Willamette Eden: The Ambiguous Legacy." *Oregon Historical Quarterly* 99 (1998).

Rockwood, E. Ruth, ed. "Diary of Reverend George H. Atkinson." *Oregon Historical Quarterly* 46 (1945).

Pratt, Harry E., ed. "Twenty Two Letters of David Logan, Pioneer Oregon Lawyer." *Oregon Historical Quarterly* 44 (1943).

"Samuel A. Clarke." *Oregon Native Son* 1 (January 1900).

Sheldon, Charles H. "Then and Now: The Roots of the Legal Progression in the American West." *Oregon State Bar Bulletin* (November 1955).

Stoel, Caroline. "The McLoughlin Land Grab: The Case That Was Never Heard." *Oregon Benchmark*: 7 (Bulletin of the U.S. District Court of Oregon Historical Society) (1991), No. 2.

Strong, W.D. "Knickerbocker Views of the Oregon Country: Judge William Strong's Narrative." *Oregon Historical Quarterly* 62 (1961).

_____. "Reuben P. Boise, Last Associated Justice of the Oregon Territory Supreme Court." *Oregon Historical Quarterly* 66 (1965).

Teiser, Sidney. "Cyrus Olney, Associate Justice of the Territorial Courts." *Oregon Historical Quarterly* 64 (1963).

_____. "First Associate Justice of Oregon Territory: O.C. Pratt." *Oregon Historical Quarterly* 49 (1948).

_____. "The First Chief Justice of Oregon Territory: Justice William P. Bryant." *Oregon Historical Quarterly* 48 (1947).

_____. "Life of George H. Williams: Almost Chief-Justice." *Oregon Historical Quarterly* 47 (1946).

_____. "Obediah B. McFadden, Oregon and Washington Territorial Judge." *Oregon Historical Quarterly* 66 (1965).

_____. " A Pioneer Judge of Oregon: Matthew P. Deady." *Oregon Historical Quarterly* 61 (1943).

_____. "The Second Chief Justice of Oregon Territory: Thomas Nelson." *Oregon Historical Quarterly* 48 (1947).

_____. "William Strong, Associate Justice of the Territorial Courts." *Oregon Historical Quarterly* 64 (1963).

Vaughan, Thomas and Martin Winch. "Joseph Gervais: A Familiar Mystery Man." *Oregon Historical Quarterly* 66 (1965).

West, Oswald. "Famous Horses and Horsemen of the Pioneer Period." *Oregon Historical Quarterly* 46 (1945).

Woodward, Walter C. "The Rise and Early History of Political Parties in Oregon II." *Quarterly of Oregon Historical Society* 12 (1911).

Young, F.G. "Financial History of Oregon: Part Two." *Quarterly of Oregon Historical Society* 8 (1907).

Newspapers

Camp Adair Sentry, October 15, 1942.

Corvallis Gazette, December 31, 1880.

Corvallis Gazette-Times, June 7, 1935.

Greenville Democrat, February 16, 1859.

Milwaukie Review, January 23, 1958.

Oregon Weekly Times, July 10, August 28, September 4, 1852; May 20, September 23, 30, 1854.

Oregonian, December 6, 1851; June 3, July 17, August 7, 21, September 11, 18, 1852; June 4, July 7, 1853; April 15, September 30, 1854; August 1, 1886; December 17, 20, 1919; March 3, 1940; March 31, 1957.

Spectator, May 27, 1847; April 20, May 18, June 1, September 7, 1848; November 1, 1849; September 9, 1851; June 1, 1852; February 18, 1854.

Statesman, November 11, 1851; June 1, 12, July 10, August 14, 28, September 4, 11, 18, 25, October 9, 16, November 27, December 25, 1852; February 12, 19, March 26, December 27, 1853; January 10, March 21, May 16, 23, September 26, 1854; March 18, 1856.

Sunday Oregon Journal, January 6, 1946.

Maps/Surveys/Field Notes

"A Diagram of Oregon," showing the extent of surveyed townships as of 1859, by Oregon Surveyor General W.W. Chapman, Salem, August 31, 1859.

"A Diagram of Public Surveys of Oregon," showing the extent of surveyed townships as of 1863, by Oregon Surveyor General B.J. Pengra, Eugene City, August 24, 1863.

"Jennyopolis Township Claims Map, 1861 and 1919" [so identified herein, *Nimrod: Courts, Claims, and Killing on the Oregon Frontier*], Township No. 13 South, Range No. 5 West, Willamette Meridian Plat Maps (cadastral) showing Nimrod O'Kelly's claim and claims north thereof:

* Examined and approved by Surveyor General B.J. Pengra, Eugene City, October 26, 1861.

* Corrected copy, U.S. Surveyor Generals' Office, Portland, December 18, 1919, showing: Pengra's approval of O'Kelly claim, December 28, 1864; Surveyor General E.L. Applegate's approval of Grimsley Claim, April 14, 1870; Surveyor General W.H. Odell's approval of Stark and Criss claims (no date).

"Jennyopolis Township Topographical Map, 1853" [so identified herein, *Nimrod*], Township No. 13 South, Range No. 5 West, Willamette Meridian, field map showing surface land features in Nimrod's township, Surveyor General Jno. B. Preston, Oregon City, March 18, 1853.

"A Map of the City of Portland," C.B. Talbot, 1868.

"Map of the Southern States Including Railroads..." *Harper's Pictorial History of the Civil War*, December 1863.

"Marysville Township Topographical Map, 1853" [so identified herein, *Nimrod*], Township No. 12 South, Range No. 5 West, Willamette Meridian, field map showing surface land features in the township north of Nimrod O'Kelly's claim, by Surveyor General Jno. B. Preston, Oregon City, May 5, 1853.

"Oregon Country and Oregon Counties 1843–1941," showing the chronological growth of Oregon counties; from Ralph N. Preston, *Early Oregon Atlas* (Portland, OR: Binford and Mort, 1978).

"Portland-Milwaukie Topographical Map, 1852" [so identified herein, *Nimrod*], Township No. 1 South, Range No. 1 East, Willamette Meridian, by Surveyor General Jno. B. Preston, Oregon City, May 20, 1852.

"Sketch of the Wallamette Valley showing the purchases and reservations...to treat with the Indians of Oregon," by George Gibbs and Edward A. Stadling, April and May 1851.

Special Claims Map (cadastral) of T. 13S, R. 5W, sections 26, 27, 28, 33, 34, 35, showing conflicting claims of "N. O'Kelly" and "Mary Jane (Mahoney) Thomas." Located in John Thomas DLC Notification File No. 3835 (rejected claim), ca. Feb.–March 1854.

"Starrs Point Township Claims Map, 1861" [so identified herein, *Nimrod*], Township No. 14 South, Range No. 5 West of Willamette Meridian, plat map (cadastral) showing claims immediately south of Nimrod O'Kelly's claim, by Surveyor General, approved April 13, 1861.

"Starrs Point Township Topographical Map, 1853" [so identified herein, *Nimrod*], Township No. 14 South, Range No. 5 West, Willamette Meridian, field map showing surface land features in the township south of Nimrod O'Kelly's claim, by Surveyor Jno. B. Preston, Oregon City, May 5, 1853.

"Surveyed Portion of the Oregon Territory" (North Willamette Valley), by Oregon Surveyor General Jno. W. Preston, Oregon City, October 21, 1852.

Personal Contacts

Barclay, Janice (wife of James "Sib" Barclay descendant), telephone communication and correspondence, September 1994.

Brown-Kubisch, Linda (State Historical Society of Missouri), telephone communication and correspondence, August 1995.

Collins, V. June (Nimrod O'Kelly descendant), telephone communication, June 1998.

Ellis, James R. (Irwin Winkle descendant), telephone communication, June 1998.

Garrett, James (Nimrod O'Kelly descendant), telephone communication, July 1998.

Janes, Diane (Nimrod O'Kelly descendant), personal communication, August 1996.

Karavanich, Kipp (Nimrod O'Kelly descendant), telephone communication and correspondence, June 1997.

McArthur, Scott (lawyer for the estate of Charles Lee O'Kelly, a Nimrod O'Kelly descendant), personal communication, November 1997.

Ransom, Carol Coe (Nimrod O'Kelly descendant), telephone communication and correspondence, July 1997.

Roller, Ted W. (Barry County Genealogical Society, Missouri), correspondence, August 1995.

Sorber, Mary Jane (descendant of Robert Heron, Benton County pioneer at Irish Bend), personal communication, August 1994.

Wagner, Diane Masters (Irwin Winkle descendant), personal communication, June 1998.

Laws

"An Act for the Relief of Polk and Benton Counties." *Legislative Assembly of the Territory of Oregon: At the Fourth Regular Session Thereof, Begun and Held at Salem, December 6, 1852.* Asahel Bush, Public Printer, 1853: pp 18–19.

"Big Bluebook" [so identified herein, *Nimrod: Courts, Claims, and Killing on the Oregon Frontier*]. *Revised Statute Laws of Iowa, 1843.* Adopted by the Oregon Provisional government in 1849.

"Deady Code of 1866" [so identified herein, *Nimrod*]. *Organic and other General Laws of Oregon Together with the National Constitution and other Public Acts and Statutes of the United States, 1845–1864.* Compiled by M.P. Deady. Henry L. Pittock, State Printer, 1866.

"Deady-Lane Code of 1874" [so identified herein, *Nimrod*]. *Organic and other General Laws of Oregon: Together with the National Constitution, and other Public Acts and Statutes of the United States, 1843–1872.* Compiled by Matthew P. Deady and Lafayette Lane. Eugene Semple, State Printer, 1874. Containing *inter alia*, the following reprints of pertinent laws:

"Northwest Ordinance of 1787" [so identified herein, *Nimrod*]. U.S. Congressional *Articles of Compact Contained in the Ordinance of 1787, for the Government of the North-West Territory:* p. 59, n. 5.

The 1845 *Organic Law of the Provisional Government of Oregon:* p. 46.

The 1846 *Treaty with Great Britain* establishing the Pacific Northwest boundary between Canada and the United States: p. 43.

The 1848 U.S. Congressional *Act to Establish the Territorial Government of Oregon:* p. 52.

The 1850 *Act of Congress Relating to Public Lands in Oregon* [the "Donation Land Claim Act"]: p. 63. Together with amendments of 1853, p. 70, and 1854, p. 71.

Proposed *Constitution of the State of Oregon (1857):* p. 75.

The 1859 *Act of Congress Admitting the State of Oregon into the Union:* p. 101.

"Hamilton Code" [so identified herein, *Nimrod*]. *Statutes of a General Nature Passed by the Legislative Assembly of the Territory of Oregon.* Compiled by E. Hamilton, Secretary of Oregon Territory. Asahel Bush, Territorial Printer, 1851.

"Johnson v. McIntosh." Reports in the Supreme Court of the United States (1832), vol. 5, p.1.

"Little Bluebook" [so identified herein, *Nimrod*]. *Revised Statute Laws of Iowa, 1839.* Adopted by the Oregon Provisional government in 1843.

"Nimrod O'Kelly v. Territory of Oregon." Reports of Cases Decided in the Supreme Court of the Territory of Oregon and of the State of Oregon from 1853 to 1862, vol. 1, pp. 51–59. San Francisco, Bancroft-Whitney Company, 1911. The case is also reported in *Journal of the Council of the Legislative Assemdly* [sic] *of the Territory of Oregon: Fifth Annual Session,* containing under separate title page and pagination, *"Oregon Territory v. Nimrod O'Kelly," Reprints of the Decisions in the Supreme Court of the Territory of Oregon–December term–1853* (published 1854).

"Oregon Code of 1854" [so identified herein, *Nimrod*]. *Statutes of Oregon, Enacted and Continued in Force by the Legislative Assembly at the Session Commencing 5th December 1853.* Compiled by James K. Kelly and Reuben P. Boise. Asahel Bush, Public Printer, 1854.

"Oregon Code of 1855" [so identified herein, *Nimrod*]. *Statutes of Oregon Enacted and Continued in Force by the Legislative Assembly at the Fifth and Sixth Regular Sessions thereof.* Asahel Bush, Public Printer, 1855.

"Oregon Location of Seat of Government." House Documents 32d Congress. Executive Document No. 104. Washington, D.C., 1852.

Short v. Ermitinger ("Location Quarrel Case"). Opinion decision of Justices Nelson and Strong, as printed in the *Oregonian,* December 6, 1851.

"Soldiers Bounty Land Act of 1855," as so-called. *An Act…Granting Bounty Land to Certain Officers and Soldiers Who Have Engaged in the Military Service of the United States,* 10 stat. 90, enacted March 3, 1855. Found in *Statutes at Large and Treaties of the United States of America,* vol. X, p. 701 (Boston 1855).

"Twenty Acts Code" [so identified herein, *Nimrod*]. *Acts of the Legislative Assembly of the Territory of Oregon—Passed at their session…in July 1849 and May 1850.* Compiled by W.W. Buck and Geo. L. Curry. Robert Moore, Printer.

Documents

Benton County Courthouse Records, Corvallis, Oregon—
"Benton County Commissioners' Journal, 1850–1854." Transcribed by Mark Phinney, Oregon Historical Records Survey, May 1940. Containing payment of coroner, coroner jury, and Mahoney burial costs, pp. 24–29, 35–38, 42–44, 54, 58, 71–72, 80.
"Benton County Deed Records." Books F through L, containing various transfers of the O'Kelly claim; and Book N containing the patent filed June 10, 1881.
"Coroner Inquest Held over the Body of Jeremiah Mahoney." Containing the minutes of proceedings, arrest warrant, and Isaac Winkle's return of service, filed May 24, 1852. [Copy also located in Oregon Archives.]
"Last Will and Testament of Nimrod O'Kelly." Benton County Will Book, vol. 1, p. 1, dated June 28, 1852, and filed August 15, 1852.
Nimrod O'Kelly [Jr.] v. James Bruce, Case File No. 23. Containing civil complaint; copy of Nimrod O'Kelly's [senior] 1852 last will and testament; summons; motion to strike; and demurrer, filed November 1–12, 1869.
"Proceeding before Justice Newton, Territory of Oregon v. Nimrod O'Kelly." Containing affidavit of Lewis Dennis; arrest warrant and Sheriff Starr's return of service; witness summons; and Nimrod O'Kelly's original "declaration," filed June 3, 1852.
Territory of Oregon v. Nimrod O'Kelly (trial papers). Containing subpoenas with returns of service for 47 prosecution and defense witnesses, June 19–30, 1852; original indictment for murder with true bill (final page missing), filed June 29, 1852; original jury verdict with jurymen's alleged signatures, filed June 30, 1852; motions of counsel; territorial supreme court mandate to Benton County court to proceed with execution of Nimrod O'Kelly, dated February 9, 1854, and filed March 6, 1854.

Oregon Historical Society, Portland, Oregon—
Bush, Asahel, letter to Matthew Deady. September 17, 1852. OHS Ms. 48.
Deady, Matthew, letter to Asahel Bush, September 20, 1852. OHS Ms. 581.
Earl, Robert, "Reminiscences." OHS Ms. 793.
Irwin, Richard, letter to John B. Preston, September 27, 1853. OHS Ms. 914.
O'Kelly, Benjamin, letter to Surveyor General, August 15, 1853. OHS Ms. 914.
O'Kelly, Nimrod, letter to U.S. Congress, August 30, 1851. OHS Ms. 624.
_____, letter to John B. Preston, April 14, 1853. OHS Ms. 914.

Oregon Provisional and Territorial Government Records, Microfilm Reels (catalogued in most regional historical libraries)—
Reel #1. "Benton County Property Assessment Rolls," 1850–57, 1865.
Reel #19. "Penitentiary Commission, Convict Register," pp. 2–4.
Reel #29. "Executive Actions Journal, 1849–1859." [Daily record, Oregon territorial governors.]
Reel #52. Sheriff Samuel F. Starr, "Lists of Benton County taxpayers south and north of Marysville [Corvallis]," ca. August 1852, docs. #4776 and #4777.
Reel #53. "Marion County Assessment Roll for 1853."
Reel #54.
　　Alexander, J.C., "Survey Report," July 30, 1852, doc. #5490.
　　"Commutation Petitions" on behalf of Nimrod O'Kelly, 1852, docs. #5491–92, #5497, #5509.
　　Ellis, Miletus W., affidavit re: trial evidence, August 23, 1852, doc. #5507.
　　Fitzgerald, Ambrose and Mary Ann, letter to Nimrod O'Kelly, March 7, 1852, doc. #5499.
　　Irwin, Richard, and Isaac W. Winkle, letter to Governor Gaines protesting pardon or commutation, August 17, 1850 [sic 1852], doc. #5508.
　　Mahoney, Mary S., certificate, August 13, 1852, doc. #5505.
　　O'Kelly, Charles L. and Rebecca, March 28, 1852, doc. #5502.
　　O'Kelly, Nimrod, declaration (undated), filed June 3, 1852, doc. #5506.
　　_____, letter to Oregon Territorial Legislature, July 1852, doc. #5495.
　　Starr, S.F., affidavit, August 23, 1852, doc. #5501.
　　Statements, letters, certificates, and affidavits on behalf of Nimrod O'Kelly, by L.G. Hoge, J.P. Welsh, J.C. Alexander, Thomas Norris and A. Whitley, William F. Dixon, James P. Mulkey, and John Thorp, to Governor Gaines, summer 1852, docs. #5493–94, #5496, #5498, #5500, #5503–4.

Reel #55.

Brooks, Charles B., et al., letter to Governor Davis, May 15, 1854, doc. #5537.

Communication Petition on behalf of Nimrod O'Kelly, summer 1852, doc. #5534

Cornelius, Benjamin, Sr., and Paton Wilkes, affidavits, February 25, 1854, doc. #5527.

Dixon, William F., affidavit, August 16, 1852, doc. #5520.

Fortson, John T., letter to Governor Gaines, August 12, 1852, doc. #5510.

Hinton, R.B., letter to Nimrod O'Kelly, July 16, 1852, doc. #5532.

Holbrook, Amory, letter to Governor Davis, January 24, 1854, doc. #5523.

_____, et al., Pardon Petition "A," summer 1852, doc. #5518.

Kelly, James K., letter to Governor Davis, February 11, 1854, doc. #5526.

O'Kelly, Nimrod, letter to Governor Davis, April 16, 1854, doc. #5530.

_____, letter to Governor Davis, May 16, 1854, doc. #5529.

Martin, Jacob, Miletus W. Ellis, and Henry Powell (jurors), affidavit, August 16, 1852, doc. #5519.

Pardon Petitions on behalf of Nimrod O'Kelly, summer 1852, docs. #5515–17, #5521–22.

Pardon Petitions on behalf of Nimrod O'Kelly, February 1854, docs. #5524–25.

Patterson, James C., letter to Governor Davis, May 15, 1854, doc. #5536.

Powell, Henry, affidavit, August 23, 1852, doc. #5528.

Pratt, O.C., letter to Governor Davis, February 22, 1854, doc. #5535.

Proceedings of meeting at "Long Tom," March 15, 1854, doc. #5531.

Remonstrance Petitions against Pardon or Commutation, summer 1852, docs. #5511–14.

(Trial) "Transcript of Oregon Territory v. Nimrod O'Kelly, District Court, Benton Co.," including minutes, verdict, and sentence. True copies of originals, June 29–30, July 1, 1852, doc. #5533. [Originals archived at Benton County Courthouse.]

Reel #57. Right, Sheriff T.J., expense claim to Benton County Commissioners, filed June 8[?], 1854, doc. #6451.

Reel #70. Building of the penitentiary (1850s), docs. #9675–10089.

Reel #74. Penitentiary operations, including lists of inmates.

Reel #78. "Jackson County Assessment Roll for 1854," doc. #12281A.

Call No. C-141, Roll #165. U.S. Federal Census, Seventh through Tenth 1850–1880, for Benton, Lane, Jackson, Marion, and various Oregon counties, precincts, and townships.

Oregon State Archives, Salem, Oregon—

"Benton County Circuit Court Fee Journal, 1851–1858." Loc. #1/7/9/3, vol. 1.

"Benton County Circuit Court Files, 1852–1859." Containing various pertinent case files, vol. 12: "Isaac Moore v. John and Mary Jane Thomas, mortgagors, and J.C. Avery and Joseph Prescott, mortgagees," case no. 43 (1854); "Melinda Winkle v. Montgomery Winkle," case no. 44 (1854); "Oregon Territory v. Gird," case no. [unknown] (1854).

"Benton County Judgment Docket, 1852–1861." Loc. #1/15/08/07, container 2 (leather bound), vol. 1, pp. 5–6.

"Benton County Circuit Court Journals, 1849–1858." Loc. #1/7/9/5, containing Governor Joe Lane's proclamation establishing O.C. Pratt as judge and J.C. Avery's house as place of court, May 23, 1849, p. 1; minutes of regular term of court, April 5–9, 1852, p. 6; minutes of special term of court, trial of Nimrod O'Kelly, in the judge's original handscript, June 29–July 1, 1852, pp. 21–26.

"Oregon Provisional Government Land Claim Records," 8 vols. (microfilm).

"Petition for the Pardon of Nimrod O'Kelly," to Governor George Curry, January 29, 1856, doc. #10757.

"Preliminary Judgment of Justice of Peace Abiather Newton, Territory of Oregon v. Nimrod O'Kelly," filed June 3, 1852. [Also located in the "Preston Omstead" file at Benton County Historical Society Museum, Philomath, Oregon.]

Supreme court file re: *Nimrod O'Kelly, Appel. v. Territory of Oregon, Res.*, microfilm no. 50 B.3, p. 26. Containing *inter alia*: Judge William Strong's grant of Writ of Error, September 17, 1852; Order to stay execution, September 18, 1852; grand jury indictment, June 29, 1852; Clerk Hovey's orders to sheriff to summon grand jurors and petit jurors, June 18, 1852; Motions for Judgment and Arrested of Judgment, June 30, 1852; the Verdict (undated); Court minutes, June 29–July 1, 1852; and Clerk Hovey's certification that all of the above are his "true copies," October 8, 1852. [Also, see originals of some of the above in the Benton County Courthouse files.]

U.S. National Archives, Pacific Northwest Region, Seattle, Washington—
"Donation Land Claim Certificate No. 2822," May 31, 1866; "Land Patent to Sally O'Kelly and Heirs of
    Nimrod O'Kelly"; and correspondence, May 1871. Microcopy M815, Roll 32.
"Donation Land Claim Notification File No. 2087," re: Nimrod O'Kelly. Containing oath of allegiance,
    affidavits, letter of Joseph O'Kelly to Surveyor General, May 20, 1854. Microcopy M815, Roll 59.
"Donation Land Claim Notification File No. 2151," re: Mary Jane (Mahoney) Thomas, April 22, 1853;
    "No. 3835," re: John Thomas, February 20, 1854. Microcopy M815, roll 59.
"Executive Actions Journal, 1849–1859." Microcopy C-145, Roll No. 1. [Oregon territorial governors'
    actions.]
"United States v. N.O. Kelly [Jr.], File No. 641, District Court of the U.S. for District of Oregon," filed
    October 16, 1877. Judge Roll 601, Reg. No. 641.

Miscellany Locations—
Application of and Warrant Issued to Nimrod O'Kelly under Bounty Land Act of 1855. Containing cover
    jacket, military muster roll, company pay rolls, affidavit of claim, affidavit for re-issuance of duplicate
    warrant, affidavit of newspaper announcement of lost warrant, notice of caveat on issuance of patent,
    November 5, 1857, to May 6, 1859. Department of the Interior, Veterans Land Bounties 1855; gar-
    nered from documentation compiled by Connie James. U.S. Archives, Washington, D.C.,
Collins, V. June (Blivens), research file (two folders). Containing *inter alia,* copies of Nimrod O'Kelly letter
    to "Gov. Lane," December 5, 1851, and June 4, 1852, Linn County Museum, Brownsville, Oregon.
Croke, Father James, letters to Archbishop François Norbert Blanchet. August 9 and October 26, 1853,
    November 22, 1854, and December 17, 1854. Catholic Archdiocese Archives, Portland, Oregon.
"Lane County Marriage Records, 1852–1869" (abstracts), vol. 1. Cottage Grove, Genealogical Society,
    Cottage Grove, Oregon.
"Marriage Records, Barry County; Missouri, 1854–1867." State Historical Society of Missouri, Columbia,
    Missouri.
(Survey field notes) "Surveyor's Walk and Description of Countryside." Township 13 South, Range 5 West,
    of Sections 26, 27, 34, 35 concerning the O'Kelly, Grimsley, Stark, and Criss land claim borders in
    1853, 1854, 1859, 1870, 1873 (microfiche). U.S. Bureau of Land management, Portland, Oregon.

Index

The Author

Ronald B. Lansing is a Professor of Law at the Northwestern School of Law of Lewis and Clark College in Portland, Oregon. A graduate of Valparaiso University (B.A., 1954) and the Willamette University College of Law (J.D., *cum laude*, 1960), he has taught at Lewis and Clark College for nearly four decades. He was the founding editor-in-chief of the *Willamette Law Review*, and currently is a member of the Oregon State Bar.

Lansing's hobbies include poker playing and sketching, and his office is decorated with antique puzzles and memorabilia of the Old West. Although having never taken an art class, he is known around campus for his caricatures of tenured and tenure-track professors. In 1991, a collection of his sketches won a Gold Award from the Council for the Advancement and Support of Education, District VIII. Lansing's caricatures grace the hallways of the college's Legal Research Center. The maps and try-square sketches in *Nimrod: Courts, Claims, and Killing on the Oregon Frontier* are his creations.

Lansing also is the author of the highly acclaimed *Juggernaut: The Whitman Massacre Trial of 1850* (1993), and a novel about law school, *Skylarks and Lecterns: A Law School Charter* (1983). His wife Jewel has long served in government and likewise is a writer of the Oregon scene; her book, *Portland: People, Politics, and Power, 1851–2001*, was released in 2003.

In narrative form, Lansing looks at events of history from the "bottom up," instead of the "top down," in order to give a special feeling for the setting and times about which he writes.